1980

Readings in
Organizational Behavior
and Performance

Readings in Organizational Behavior and Performance

Second Edition

Edited by

Andrew D. Szilagyi, Jr.
Associate Professor of Organizational
    Behavior and Management
University of Houston

Marc J. Wallace, Jr.
Associate Professor of Business
    Administration
University of Kentucky

Goodyear Publishing Company, Inc.
Santa Monica, California

Current Printing (last number):

10 9 8 7 6 5 4 3 2 1

Printed in the United States of America

Library of Congress Cataloging in Publication Data

Main entry under title:

Readings in organizational behavior and performance.

   Includes bibliographies.
   1. Organizational behavior—Case studies.
2. Management—Case studies. I. Szilagyi, Andrew D.
II. Wallace, Marc J., 1944–
HD58.7.R4 1980   301.18′32′08   79-19726
ISBN 0-8302-6505-8

Contents G 301.1832 8998

90924

Preface

Organizational behavior, a new and emerging area of scientific study, deals with the way individuals and groups, as well as the total organization, act to create outputs such as goods, services, and jobs for the betterment of society as a whole. As a field of study, organizational behavior is currently in a state of theoretical, empirical, and applied growth. Scholars and practicing managers have begun to synthesize principles, concepts, models, and theories to better understand the behavior of people in organizations.

As a field of study, organizational behavior uses the scientific method; is interdisciplinary; studies individuals, groups, organizations, and the environment; is contingency oriented; and stresses the importance of applying knowledge and concepts to actual organizational problems. These key characteristics of the growing field suggest that a wealth of information is available for those interested in improving organizational performance.

This book, *Readings in Organizational Behavior and Performance*, brings together a selection of articles that bear directly on the field of organizational behavior and its emphasis on understanding performance. The contributors of these articles are representatives of a variety of behavioral sciences, including psychology, sociology, and social psychology. Though diverse in background and training, the contributors share a common interest in integrating theory and research and applying them to the problems that face managers.

The modern manager must be applications oriented. Thus, we have chosen articles that are applicable in different and numerous settings. In selecting this book's thirty articles, we have obviously omitted some outstanding presentations. However, the articles included in this reader will provide the reader with a "feel" for organizational behavior. They are up to date, of high professional quality, readable, relevant, and realistic.

This second edition is almost totally new—only seven of the original articles remain. Two criteria were used to select the new readings. First, we updated concepts with the most current articles that have been published. Second, we were more "applications" oriented than in the first edition in our selections; we particularly sought articles that view the behavior of people from the stance of the practitioner of management. Consequently, articles from such publications as *Business Week*, *Fortune*, *Management Review*, *Personnel*, and *Newsweek* make up a major portion of the selections.

The book is divided into five parts. The first part presents an introduction to the field of organizational behavior. Articles in this section are designed to provide an overview of the field. Part II focuses on the individual dimensions of the field. Such topics as perception, reinforcement theory, and the modified work week are discussed. In Part III, six articles discuss groups, leadership, and conflict. Part IV investigates organizational structure and processes. Articles focusing on the environment, organizational design, decision making, communications, and career development are presented. Finally, in

Part V, organizational change is discussed. Included are articles on managerial stress, goal setting, team building, and the management of change.

A major use of this book is as a supplement for textbooks or other instructional materials being used in the organizational behavior course. We have included a cross-reference table of the newest and most widely cited books in the field of organizational behavior. Practicing managers or executives in training or development programs could also use this book to update their organizational behavior knowledge base or supplement the training experience.

We wish to especially thank the authors and publishers of the individual readings. Of course, without their cooperation this type of integrative reader could not be compiled.

Andrew D. Szilagyi, Jr.
Marc J. Wallace, Jr.

Contributors

Alexander, T.
Burck, C. G.
Costello, Timothy W.
Cummings, L. L.
Cunningham, J. B.
Davis, S. M.
Dowling, W. F.
Galbraith, Jay R.
Greene, Charles N.
Hall, D. T.
Hamner, W. C.
Holland, W. E.
Ivancevich, J. M.
Janis, I. L.
Johnson, Alton C.
Kahn, Robert L.
Lawler, Edward E., III
Lawrence, P. R.
Lorsch, J. W.
Lubin, J. S.
Matteson, M. T.
Mayer, A. J.
McMahon, J. T.
Meyer, H. E.
Miles, Raymond E.
Mintzberg, H.
Morgan, M. A.
Oliver, C.
Patten, T. H.
Pfeffer, Jeffrey
Ransom, J. H.
Ruby, M.
Schulz, Rockwell
Snow, Charles C.
Streidl, J. W.
Szilagyi, A. D.
Tubbs, S. L.
Vroom, Victor H.
Wellbank, H. L.
Widgery, R. N.
Zalkind, Sheldon S.

Cross-Reference Table For relating the articles in this reader to the authors' Organizational Behavior and Performance (Santa Monica, Calif.: Goodyear Publishing Co., 1980) and other similar textbooks.

Selected Organizational Behavior Oriented Textbooks	Parts in Readings in Organizational Behavior and Performance				
	PART I. An Overview of Organizational Behavior and Performance	PART II. Individual Dimensions of Organizational Behavior	PART III. Groups and Interpersonal Influence	PART IV. Organizational Structure and Process	PART V. Organizational Change and Development
Coffey, Robert E.; Athos, Anthony G.; and Raynolds, Peter A., *Behavior in Organizations* (Englewood Cliffs, N.J.: Prentice-Hall, 1975)	Chaps. 1, 14	Chaps. 2, 9, 13	Chaps. 3, 4, 5, 6, 7, 8, 10	Chap. 11	Chap. 12
Davis, Keith, *Human Behavior at Work* (New York: McGraw-Hill, 1978)	Chaps. 1, 26	Chaps. 2, 4, 5, 13, 16	Chaps. 3, 6, 7, 8, 14, 15, 18, 19, 22, 23	Chaps. 11, 12, 17, 20, 21, 24, 25	Chaps. 9, 10
Dubin, Andrew J., *Fundamentals of Organizational Behavior* (New York: Pergamon Press, 1974)	Chap. 1	Chaps. 2, 4	Chaps. 5, 6, 7, 10	Chaps. 3, 8, 9, 11	Chaps. 12, 13, 14
Gibson, James L.; Ivancevich, John M.; and Donnelly, James H., Jr., *Organizations: Behavior, Structure, Processes*, 3d ed. (Dallas: Business Publications, 1979)	Chaps. 1, 2, 3	Chaps. 4, 5, 6, 7, 8, 9	Chaps. 10, 11, 12	Chaps. 13, 14, 15	Chaps. 17, 18, 19
Filley, Alan C.; House, Robert J.; and Kerr, Steven, *Managerial Process and Organizational Behavior* (Glenview, Ill.: Scott, Foresman and Co., 1976)	Chaps. 1, 2, 3, 4	Chaps. 4, 5, 6, 8, 9, 10, 11, 12	Chaps. 13, 15, 16, 17, 18	Chaps. 7, 19	Chaps. 20, 21, 22
Hamner, W. Clay, and Organ, Dennis W., *Organizational Behavior* (Dallas: Business Publications, 1978)	Chaps. 1, 2	Chaps. 3, 4, 5, 6, 7, 8, 9, 10, 11, 12, 13, 14, 15, 16, 17			Chap. 18
Hampton, David; Summer, Charles E.; and Webber, Ross A., *Organizational Behavior and the Practice of Management* (Glenview, Ill.: Scott, Foresman and Co., 1978)		Chaps. 1, 2, 4, 8, 10, 11	Chaps. 6, 7	Chaps. 3, 5, 9	Chap. 12

Reference					
Hellriegel, Don, and Slocum, John W., Jr., *Organizational Behavior: Contingency Views* (St. Paul: West Publishing Co., 1979)	Chaps. 1, 2	Chaps. 5, 6, 7, 8, 11, 12	Chaps. 9, 10, 13, 14	Chaps. 3, 4	Chaps. 15, 16, 17
Huse, Edgar F., and Bowditch, James L., *Behavior in Organizations* (Reading, Mass: Addison-Wesley Publishing Co., 1973)	Chaps. 1, 2	Chaps. 3, 4, 5, 6	Chaps. 7, 8, 9, 10	Chaps. 11, 12, 13, 14, 15	Chaps. 16, 17, 18
Korman, Abraham K. *Organizational Behavior* (Englewood Cliffs, N.J.: Prentice-Hall, 1977)	Chaps. 1, 2, 6, 14, 15	Chaps. 3, 4, 5, 7, 8, 9		Chap. 10	Chaps. 11, 12, 13
Luthans, Fred, *Organizational Behavior* (New York: McGraw-Hill, 1977)	Chaps. 1, 2, 3, 4, 5	Chaps. 11, 12, 13, 14, 15, 16, 17, 18	Chaps. 6, 7, 19	Chaps. 8, 9, 10	Chaps. 20, 21, 22
Porter, Lyman W.; Lawler, Edward E., III; and Hackman, J. Richard, *Behavior In Organizations* (New York: McGraw-Hill, 1975)	Chap. 1	Chaps. 2, 4, 5, 6, 13, 14	Chaps. 3, 8, 9, 10	Chaps. 11, 12	Chaps. 7, 15, 16, 17
Reitz, H. Joseph, *Behavior In Organizations* (Homewood, Ill.: Richard D. Irwin, 1977)	Chaps. 1, 2	Chaps. 3, 4, 5, 6, 9, 10, 11, 12, 13, 16, 17, 18, 19		Chaps. 7, 8, 14, 15	Chap. 21
Szilagyi, Andrew D., Jr., and Wallace, Marc J., Jr., *Organizational Behavior and Performance*, 2nd ed. (Santa Monica, Calif.: Goodyear Publishing Co., 1980)	Chaps. 1, 2	Chaps. 3, 4, 5, 6	Chaps. 7, 8, 9	Chaps. 10, 11, 12, 13, 14	Chaps. 15, 16
Tosi, Henry L., and Carroll, Stephen J., *Organizational Behavior* (Chicago: St. Clair Press, 1977)	Chaps. 1, 2	Chaps. 3, 4, 5, 8	Chaps. 6, 7	Chaps. 9, 10, 11, 12	Chaps. 13, 14, 15, 16, 17, 18
Robbins, Stephen, *Organizational Behavior* (Englewood Cliffs, N.J.: Prentice-Hall, 1979)	Chaps. 1, 2	Chaps. 3, 4, 5, 6	Chaps. 6, 7	Chaps. 9, 10, 11, 12	Chaps. 13, 14, 15, 16, 17, 18
Bobbitt, H. Randolph, Jr.; Breinholt, Robert H.; Doktor, Robert H.; and McNaul, James P., eds., *Organizational Behavior* (Englewood Cliffs, N.J.: Prentice-Hall, 1978)	Chaps. 1, 2	Chaps. 3, 4, 5, 6	Chaps. 6, 7	Chaps. 9, 10, 11, 12	Chaps. 13, 14, 15, 16, 17, 18

*Readings in
Organizational Behavior
and Performance*

An Overview of Organizational Behavior and Performance

Editors' Summary Comments

*T*oday's practitioner is continually seeking ways to improve individual, group, and overall organizational performance. Without satisfactory performance at these three levels, an organization cannot survive. Therefore, performance is a prominent, if not the foremost, goal of organizations. The articles in this reader present helpful information for the achievement of improved performance.

The subject area that emphasizes the analysis of performance within work settings is organizational behavior. Practitioners in this relatively new area of inquiry have attempted to apply many behavioral theories, models, and concepts to actual organizational problems, such as motivating employees, leading workers, designing jobs and the organization, and developing managers and nonmanagers. The applicability of organizational behavior research has resulted in increased interest among managers who must deal with people-related problems.

This introductory section of the reader contains three articles. In the first, "Toward Organizational Behavior," Larry Cummings provides an analysis of organizational behavior as a field of inquiry that is distinct from other related fields. He identifies three basic themes of organizational behavior: (1) a way of thinking; (2) a system of technology; and (3) a body of constructs, models, and factors. Suggested are not only some directions for future work, but also a proposal for more integration and less segmentation of activities.

In "Making Behavioral Science More Useful," Jay Lorsch points out that universal theories of behavior do not always fit the situations in which they are used, and management practice is no exception. He suggests that situational theories of behavior are harder to apply than universal ones but they more often work; more theories and models should be developed to fit different situations, and managers and their staffs should be educated in their use.

In the final selection in this first part, J. Barton Cunningham provides seven alternative strategies for assessing organizational effectiveness in different situations: routine goal, systems, managerial process, organizational development, bargaining, structural functional, and functional. Each has advantages in the evaluation of specific organizational situations and problems.

1

Toward Organizational Behavior

L. L. Cummings

*A*ttempting to describe a field as dynamic and as multifaceted, or even as confusing, as Organizational Behavior (OB) is not a task for the timid. It may be a task that only the foolish, yet concerned, would even tackle.

What motivates one toward accepting such an undertaking? Two forces are operating. First, there is a clear need to parcel out knowledge into more understandable and convenient packages. Students, managers, and colleagues in other departments request that we respond to straightforward, honest questions like: What is OB? How is OB different from management? How is it different from human relations? It is difficult for students to understand the philosophy or the systematic nature of a program or curriculum if they cannot define the parts. Our credibility with the managerial world is damaged when OB comes out in executive programs as "a little of everything," as "a combination of behavioral jargon and common sense," or as "touchy-feely" without content. The field's lack of confidence in articulating its structure is occasionally reflected in ambiguous and fuzzy suggestions for improvement in the world that managers face.

Second, identification or assertion of the themes and constructs underlying OB, or any other discipline, represents an important platform for expanding knowledge. Without assumptions about what is included, excluded, and on the boundary, duplication among disciplines results. The efficiency of knowledge generation and transmission is hampered. Until a field is defined in relation to its

SOURCE: L. L. Cummings, "Toward Organizational Behavior," *Academy of Management Review*, January 1978, pp. 90–98. Reprinted with permission. This article was first developed as a paper for the 1976 National Academy of Management Convention. The author gratefully acknowledges the comments and critiques of: Michael Aiken, Alan Filley, Barbara Karmel, Johannes Pennings, Jeffrey Pfeffer, Donald Schwab, George Strauss, and Karl Weick.

intellectual cousins, it may develop in redundant directions. This leads to the usual awakening that parallel, and perhaps even superior, developments already have occurred in adjacent fields about which we are ignorant. Repetition of such occurrences in a field lessens its intellectual credibility among scholars. All of this is not to deny the benefits to be gained from cross-fertilization and exchange across subfields once these are delineated and common concerns and interests are discovered.

These are the forces underlying the concern. What is said here represents an unfinished product—a thought in process—not a finished, static, intellectually frozen definition. In fact, the argument is made that stimulating, dynamic fields are defined *in process* and that the processes of emergence and evolution should never end.

Perspectives on Organizational Behavior

Several partitions have been used in attempting to distinguish OB from related disciplines. Tracing some of these provides perspective on our task and builds a critical platform for appraising where the field is today.

Probably the most common segmentation of subfields relating behavior and organization is based on *units of analysis* where the units are differentiated by level of aggregation. Typically, using this framework, OB is defined as the study of individuals and groups within organizations. The units of analysis are individual and micro (e.g., dyadic) interactions among individuals. Organizational characteristics (e.g., structure, process, climate) are seen either as "givens" which assume a constant state or as independent variables whose variations are assumed to covary with or cause variations in the relevant dependent variables. These relevant dependent variables are measures of individual or micro unit affective and/or behavioral reactions.

Organizational Theory (OT) is typically defined by its focus upon the *organization as the unit of analysis*. Organizational structure, process, goals, technology, and, more recently, climate are the relevant dependent variables, assumed to vary systematically with variations in environmental characteristics but not with characteristics embedded within systematically clustered individuals. A comparative, cross-organizational framework is essential for development of knowledge in OT. Studies of single organizations add little to understanding of organizations when the unit of analysis and variation is assumed to be the organization itself. This realization is increasingly reflected in the empirical literature of OT.[1]

Some have distinguished the field of inquiry based upon an attribution of *typical or modal methodologies* to the respective subfields. OB is defined as studies utilizing laboratory and, occasionally, field experimentation. OT is identified with the predominant use of survey and, occasionally, case designs. While the simplicity of this methodological distinction is attractive, it does not reflect the current diversity of designs underlying current research on people in organizations and on organizations per se.

The adjective pairs "normative-descriptive" and "empirical-theoretical" are attractive labels for describing *epistemological differences*. Certainly, the two predominant versions of classical OT have been characterized, and criticized, as excessively normative and not descriptive of behavioral and organizational realities. Both Taylor and Fayol on the one hand, and Weber on the other, have provided much of the focus for the normative critics. Some OB scholars view their field's mission as adding descriptive, empirically-based facts to what they see as the essentially normative and theoretical biases of classical OT. With the advent of data among OT scholars and the infusion of organizational development (OD) into the OB tent, these distinctions are no longer descriptive of our domain. Descriptive, empirical, theoretical, and normative can each be used to characterize some work in both OB and OT. Complexity now overshadows the simple straw man of yesterday.

As OD began to emerge a few years ago, the theme of several corridor conversations was that OB *was becoming the applied cousin of OT.* After all, some claimed, OT deals with the theory of organizations by definition. For a moment the distinctions between OB and OD became blurred, and that opaqueness was attractive for some. Reading between the lines, OT was to become the reservoir of accepted and evolving constructs, and OB would emerge as the behavioral engineering function. For managers and consultants we would have OB; for scholars, OT. The largest obstacle to enacting such a distinction is that scholars and appliers do not generally read or listen to one another. The OB people must have their own constructs and theories. The OT people need their own applications, their own means of establishing credibility within the world of action. From this insulation, two OD camps have emerged with their own strategies for change. One focuses on change via the individual and micro unit within the organization and the other on change through structural and environmental manipulation. Alas, another simple, definitional distinction melts!

My preference among these alternative taxonomic bases is the first. The unit of analysis perspective seems cleanest. The most severe problem with this view is finding intellectual bridges to link the subfields. This linkage is crucial for understanding the way organizations function, the impacts they exert, and the opportunities they provide. Some bridges begin to emerge which are at least suggestive. For example, an organization's structure (i.e., number of levels, average span of supervision, degree of horizontal differentiation) can be viewed as a construct linking OT and OB. In OT, structure is typically positioned in a nomological network as a dependent variable. In OB, structure is typically positioned as an independent variable. This differential positioning of the same construct suggests a possible general role that several constructs might take in linking OT and OB. Structure, climate, task design, reward systems, and leader behavior can each be conceived of as intervening between causal forces in the environment of organizations and the behavior and attitudes of persons within organizations. Each is beginning to be modeled as a dependent variable in one context and an independent variable in another.

This differentiation of subfields by unit of analysis and their integration by intervening constructs is subject to limitations. The boundaries of aggregation between levels of analysis are arbitrary, with no fundamental laws underlying the distinctions. That is a limitation shared with the biological and physical sciences, where subfields have arisen as linking mechanisms (e.g., biophysics, biochemistry, psychopharmacology). The conception also lacks feedback loops with reversible intervening constructs. It is likely that such reciprocal causation reflects reality and that models that omit these loops will not provide a full understanding.

If we were to assume his posture of differentiation, what would be the result? Remembering that the distinctions are based primarily on levels of analysis with a slight nod toward the other distinctions, we can propose the definitions in Figure 1.

A Dimensional Characterization of Organizational Behavior

I believe that OB is evolving toward the model presented in Figure 2. The field is being enacted, not defined in some a priori sense, by scholars and teachers in ways that imply the dimensional, thematic conception suggested in that figure.

Figure 1   *Distinctions Among Organizational Behavior, Organizational Psychology, Organizational Theory and Personnel and Human Resources*

Organizational Behavior-Organizational Psychology (OP)	Both fields focus upon explaining human behavior within organizations. Their difference centers on the fact the OP restricts its explanatory constructs to those at the psychological level. OB draws constructs from multiple disciplines. As the domain of OP continues to expand, the difference between OB and OP is diminishing, perhaps to the point of identity between the fields.
Organizational Behavior-Organizational Theory (OT)	The distinction is based on two differences: unit of analysis and focus of dependent variables. OB is defined as the study of individual and group behavior within organizations and the application of such knowledge. OT is the study of structure, processes, and outcomes of the organization per se. The distinction is neither that OB is atheoretical and concerned only with behavior nor that OT is unique or exclusive in its attention to theory. Alternatively, the distinction can be conceived as between micro and macro perspectives on OB. This removes the awkward differentiation of behavior and theory.
Organizational Behavior-Personnel and Human Resources (P&HR)	This distinction usually depicts OB as the more basic of the two and P&HR as more applied in emphasis. OB is seen as more concept oriented while P&HR is viewed as emphasizing techniques or technologies. The dependent variables, behavior and affective reactions within organizations, are frequently presented as similar. P&HR can be seen as standing at the interface between the organization and the individual, focusing on developing and implementing the system for attracting, maintaining, and motivating the individual within the organization.

Figure 2   Dimensions and Themes of Organizational Behavior

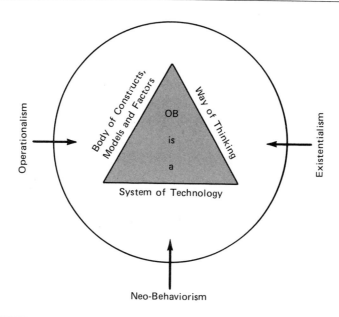

Three dimensions define the conceptual domain of OB. Most disciplines and emerging fields of inquiry that stand at the interface between science and professional practice are describable in terms of these dimensions. The specific articulation of the dimensions depends significantly upon the underlying epistemological themes adopted by the discipline.

A Way of Thinking

OB is a *way of thinking*, a manner of conceiving problems and articulating research and action solutions which can be characterized by five postures. First, problems and questions are typically formulated within an independent variable(s)-dependent variable(s) framework. Recently, OB has begun to incorporate personal and situational moderators into this framework. OB's assertion that behavior within organizations is subject to systematic study is based on conceptualization of the object of study as non-random, systematic, and generally purposive. This way of thinking is significantly influencing our methodologies. The field is engaged in a sometimes painful search for cause and effect within our models.

A second component of OB as a way of thinking is its orientation toward change as a desirable outcome for organizations and persons within organizations. Static phenomena possess diminishing prestige as topics of study. Conditions for stimulating change and models for evaluating change are an increasingly important part of the field.

Third, there is a distinctly humanistic tone within OB, reflected in concern for self development, personal growth, and self actualization.

Although its influence on research and teaching seems to ebb and flow, and its reflection in scholarship and pedagogy varies by school, it is there, and its presence is causing both strain (given its positioning adjacent to scientism) and excitement, even relevance, within OB. The striving is toward humanism without softness. OB shares this dilemma with most of the person-oriented disciplines that attempt to combine basic, good science with a change orientation. Yet this tone of humanism is only one side of the current, slightly schizophrenic posture of OB. The other side is reflected in a heavy emphasis on operant learning models and behavioral modification techniques, an orientation toward environmental determinism rather than self actualization.

Fourth, OB is becoming increasingly performance oriented, with more studies including a performance-oriented dependent variable. The field is beginning to capture an important distinction between two types of dependent variables. One perspective focuses on description of a behavior, activity, or outcome, that is, the proper focus for scientific analysis and thinking. The other aims at application of a preference function to these behaviors, activities, or outcomes, resulting in a scaling of effectiveness or success. This is the proper focus for an engineering analysis—a managerial mind set.[2] We are beginning to hear the demands for relevance in our research and teaching. Unless OB can increase its performance payoffs, the field may be in danger of losing some of its hard battles for a niche in the curriculum or a moment in the board room.

Finally, OB uses the discipline imposed by the scientific method. The field is substantially influenced by norms of skepticism, caution, replication, and public exposure of knowledge based on facts. In many ways, this posture of "scientism" confuses some students and clients. It can be seen as the antithesis of several other postures that characterize OB thinking. Yet it is generally accepted as a crucial posture. It helps to keep the field straight, and it is the key ingredient in whatever longevity the field may possess. Scientific method, applied to OB, provides the mechanism for feed-back and self-renewal.

A Body of Constructs, Models, and Facts

Even though OB is characterized by some definitional confusion, an implicit agreement is emerging about some of its components. Differences exist concerning the relative weighting of components and the emphasis given to basic science versus application in transmitting the field to others. But most treatments of the field now include coverage of constructs, models, and facts on: motivation, learning or socialization, group structure and process, leader behavior, task design, interpersonal communication, organizational structure, interpersonal change and conflict, and material on relevant dependent variables (e.g. satisfaction, other attitudes, participation measures, performance dimensions, and other behaviors).

This emergence of an identity for the field is evidenced by the second generation of OB textbooks, which are more similar in topical coverage than their ancestors. Some models sell and are thus influential in structuring the introductory level curricula underlying our field. Others stretch the field at its boundaries but do not become a part of the core. That core is gradually developing toward an identifiable body of components.

A System of Technology

OB is also a system or a collection of technologies. These have evolved out of the primary areas of study identified as the independent variables of OB. Techniques now exist for: training leaders, designing tasks, designing organizations, evaluating performances, rewarding behaviors, and modeling behaviors.

The uncritical eye might be pleased with OB's tool kit. Superficially, it appears that the field is ready to move into the world of action with vigor and confidence. But our posture of scientism keeps the field honest. These technologies are largely exploratory, unvalidated and, in a few cases, under evaluation. The field has even spawned an occasional technology that has been adopted and later found damaging to an organization and its participants. In most cases, even when the technologies work, the field's theoretical models are not sufficiently developed to explain why they were effective. So, a system or collection of technologies? Yes. A behavioral engineering discipline? No.

Themes Influencing Organizational Behavior

As depicted in Figure 2, three themes span the dimensions defining OB and influence the way each dimension is articulated. The relative emphasis given to each theme over time, by the various schools of thought within OB, determines our ways of thinking, constructs and facts, and development of technologies.

Existentialism

The emphasis here is upon the uncertain, contingent environment of people within organizations (and organizations). Existentialism emphasizes that in the face of this type of environment, persons must exercise self control in pursuit of their own objectives. The ultimate responsibility for designing productive and satisfying organizational environments rests with human beings. It is their responsibility to fashion themselves—to implement self control. This philosophical posture leaves a legacy of concepts within OB—goal, purpose, expectation, expectancy, instrumental, path, and contingency.

This theme is forcing OB to become a more complex discipline. It asserts that no meaning exists in absolutes. All meaning derives from comparison; meaning is always relative. Activities and outcomes within organizations are meaningful only within a context including implicit or explicit statements of purpose. This is at the core of one important, current development in conceptualizing the influence of most of the independent variables treated in OB—the concept of contingency.

With the realization that an independent variable's effects depend, the next logical question becomes: Depend on what? When? etc. *Why* did *who* do *what* with *whom* with what *outcomes?* This seemingly simple question can be applied to most independent-dependent variable linkages currently of concern in OB. The *why* focuses on the causes, the reasons, the antecedents of variance in the dependent variable. The *who* focuses on the initiating party (individual, group, or organization). The *what* requires description of the behavior in question. The *whom* provides the interaction component, adding dimensionality to the search for meaningfulness. It provides a vertical, horizontal, or diagonal vector to the reality that OB attempts to understand. The *outcomes* provide the ultimate meaning to the field. Existentialism implies that the meaning in any act exists in its consequences, and OB seems to be moving toward this realization.

Operationalism

Operationalism is reflected in three ways. First, the field is searching for theories of the middle range in most of its subareas. The grand, general, abstract models of motivation, leadership, environment-structure interaction, and change are not yielding satisfying, systematic, cumulative data. Some models posit relations between environmental and organizational characteristics and individual attitudes and behaviors. Models are needed to describe the processes through which environment impacts structure and structure impacts attitudes and behavior.

Second, emphasis is being given to the operations or behaviors through which people within organizations function. Whether describing what managers do or analyzing the impact of leaders, the importance of formulating the issue in operational terms is being realized. The literature is beginning to be characterized by questions like:

1. Through what operations is structure actually designed?
2. Through what operations does a leader impact a subordinate?
3. Through what operations do rewards and punishments effect change?
4. Through what operations do groups actually make decisions?

In each case, the field is beginning to examine the physiology of behavior within organizations. The anatomy of OB is important, but its study has not led to understanding the processes through which persons and organizations interact.

Third, measurement issues are impacting the field. Questions of reliability and validity must be faced, and questions of scaling and measurement confronted. We are increasingly anxious about our inability to explain large amounts of variance in dependent variables. Three rather lengthy streams of research have reached the point where lack of early attention to how we operationalized constructs and validated measures has caused major problems for continued, meaningful work. Cases in point are research on: the two-factor model of motivation (with faulty measurement procedures); expectancy formulations of motivation (with testing of inappropriate models); and the impact of organizational design on attitudes and behaviors (with designs that confound independent variables). While not completely pessimistic, I believe that the field has been extremely inefficient and myopic in the research strategies applied in some areas.

Neo-behavioralism

Finally, many causal assumptions and models in OB are moving toward a behavioristic orientation with a cognitive overtone. Motivation theory, under the influence of expectancy models, has moved in this direction. Leadership studies reflect the notion of instrumental, goal-oriented behavior with a significant emphasis on leader behavior being partially a function of the consequences which it produces. The concept of contingency plays a major role in several fields within OB, its general intellectual structure deriving directly from the behavioristic notion of structure and process evolving toward forms that are reinforcing to the organism. The behavioristic perspective also has surfaced in literature dealing with organizational design and organizational control and power. Distributions of influence and power are partially explained by environmental consequences of attempts at influence. The exercise of power generates consequences which, in turn, affect structural configurations of the organization.

Radical behaviorism is not the dominant theme, but rather a combination of general behavioral constructs *and* cognitions. It is not clear what functions are provided by the incorporation of cognitions within OB models. Little research has been addressed to the question of the variance explained in most OB models by cognitions beyond that explained by environmental determinants. Perhaps cognitive concepts do explain added variance, or perhaps they constitute a residual reservoir of unexplained variance to which we inappropriately attribute meaning.

Conclusions and Implications

What are the implications of this perspective on the field? First, ultimately the definitions of the domains of OB, OT, OP, and OD are arbitrary. Definitions should be tested by their usefulness in specifying constructs and functional relations. Definitions are needed to guide the field toward middle range and operational theory. Movement toward definition by induction is needed. It may prove fruitful to aim toward definition through describing what is happening in the main streams of research within OB. Definitions established by assertion lead to debate without fruitful results.

Second, realities in organizations change so rapidly that our descriptions (ways of thinking, constructs and technologies) do not keep pace with the rate of change in the objects of our study.[3] I see two implications of this for OB. First, incredibly long periods of time are needed to assess organizations and to identify the fundamental, underlying nature of the field. Second, increasing energy will be devoted to collapsing the time intervals needed to develop relevant constructs and models and to testing these models. This implies that management, as a general field, will accelerate adoption of both simulation and experimental designs. These designs permit the modeling of time lags. Contrary to the usual evaluation of such designs, they will allow us to become more realistic in our modeling and measurement of OB.

Third, what might this line of reasoning mean for the Academy of Management and its members? The Academy is presently the only camp which attempts to house OB, OT, OD, and P&HR. For the moment, these fields have separate tents within the camp, but I believe that the traditional distinctions are beginning to melt. Several examples illustrate this permeability. The 1976 doctoral consortium conducted at the National Academy Convention included topics from both OT and OB. I suspect it is impossible to talk at an advanced level about one domain without the other. The P&HR division's program at the 1976 National Academy Convention consists of about 40 percent OB material. This reflects a healthy trend for both P&HR and OB. It is naive to deal with many of the important issues in P&HR without incorporating OB models and research. The *Academy of Management Journal,* the *Academy of Management Review, Organizational Behavior and Human Performance,* and *Administrative Science Quarterly* exhibit trends in submissions that reflect an increasing emphasis on *multiple* levels of analysis in both the independent and dependent variable domains.

I believe we are moving toward an enacted field, perhaps best labeled organizational analysis or organizational science (if we wish to emphasize the scientific lineage of our interests and our aspirations). Basically, we now have five divisions within the Academy, composing organizational analysis or science. These are Organizational Behavior, Organization and Management Theory, Personnel and Human Resources, Organization Development, and Organizational Communication. Such segmentation continues to provide important functions for the Academy and its members, but it remains an open question whether segmentation is the most efficient strategy to advance our common interest in behavior *in* and *of* organizations.

As Thurston said:

> It is the faith of all science that an unlimited number of phenomena can be comprehended in terms of a limited number of concepts or ideal constructs. Without this faith no science could ever have any motivation. To deny this faith is to affirm the primary chaos of nature and the consequent futility of scientific effort. The constructs in terms of which natural phenomena are comprehended are man-made inventions. To discover a scientific law is merely to discover that a man-made scheme serves to unify, and thereby to simplify, comprehension of a certain class of natural phenomena. A scientific law is not to be thought of as having an independent existence which some scientist is fortunate to stumble upon. A scientific law is not a part of nature. It is only a way of comprehending nature.

Notes

1. Hannan and Freeman have argued quite convincingly that comparative analyses of organizational effectiveness are inappropriate for scientific purposes.

2. My thinking here has been significantly influenced by Robert Kahn of the University of Michigan. His comments at the 1976 Carnegie-Mellon Workshop on Organizational Effectiveness have been particularly helpful.
3. I am indebted to Professor Lou Pondy for stimulating this notion.

References

Hannan, M. T. and J. Freeman. "Obstacles for Comparative Studies," in P. S. Goodman and J. M. Pennings (Eds.), *New Perspectives in Organizational Effectiveness* (San Francisco: Jossey-Bass, 1977), pp. 106–131.

Thurston, L. S. *Multiple-Factor Analysis* (Chicago: University of Chicago Press, 1947).

2

Making Behavioral Science More Useful

Jay W. Lorsch

Since World War II management thought and practice have undergone great change. The computer has revolutionized information processing and, along with operations research and other quantitative techniques, has improved management decision making. New methods of market and consumer research also provide better information on which to base decisions. All these developments mean better tools for obtaining and analyzing information for more effective management.

During the same period the behavioral sciences—anthropology, psychology, social psychology, and sociology—have also contributed many potential ideas and theories to management. Unlike the first set of management tools, these ideas have focused not only on how decisions are made, but also on how employees from top management levels to the factory floor implement them. Thus these ideas should be of use to every manager: how to communicate effectively; how to give performance evaluations to employees; how to resolve conflicts between individuals or between one department and another; how to design organization structures, measurement systems, and compensation packages; how to introduce changes in organization, procedures, and strategy.

In spite of their potential for wide application, however, these ideas have been only sparingly used. Surely, General Foods, Volvo, and Procter & Gamble have introduced innovations in some factory organizations, and some management organizations have done so as well, but how many other company managements have failed to use the available knowledge? Further, why have the companies that have

SOURCE: Jay W. Lorsch, "Making Behavioral Science More Useful," *Harvard Business Review,* March–April 1979, pp. 171–81. Reprinted with permission. Copyright © 1979 by the President and Fellows of Harvard College; all rights reserved.

claimed success in one location or division been so reluctant to apply the ideas in other appropriate places?

One obvious reason seems to be the confusion, skepticism, and controversy about the relevance of these ideas in the minds of many managers. For example: Is participative management a suitable style for all managers? Can job enrichment be applied in a unionized factory? Will managers set realistic goals with a management by objectives program? Has laboratory training improved managerial effectiveness? And, ultimately, some hard-headed manager always asks, "What does all this psychological mumbo-jumbo contribute to the bottom line?" The list of such questions may seem endless, but, equally discouraging, the answers the experts provide often seem unpersuasive and even contradictory.

Another facet of the situation, however, concerns me even more. The behavioral sciences occasionally burst with enthusiasm about certain ideas. Job enlargement, T-Groups, creative thinking, participative leadership, and management by objectives are cases in point. Each set of ideas or each technique becomes almost a fad with strong advocates who tout its early successes. Then, as a growing number of companies try the ideas or techniques and as reports of failure and disappointment mount, the fad quickly dies. This often repeated pattern has caused many managers to lose interest in trying other behavioral science ideas which could help them.

In this article, I explore why so much heat and confusion have arisen around these behavioral science ideas and why, consequently, they have had such a limited impact on management practice. Because this is a matter of applying knowledge developed in the academic world to the problems of practicing managers, I am addressing both managers and academics. What can managers do themselves to make better use of the behavioral sciences? What can they demand from academics to get more practical knowledge? What can the academics working in this field do to provide more knowledge practitioners can use?

Lure of the Universal Theory

One major reason for the difficulties in applying behavioral science knowledge has been the interpretation that such ideas are applicable to all situations. From their earliest attempts to apply these ideas, both behavioral scientists developing the knowledge and managers applying it have at one time or another maintained the universality of the ideas. For example, Rensis Likert's participative-management ("Systems 4" Management) model was a call by a behavioral scientist for a universal application of ideas regardless of industry, company size, or geographic location.[1]

Over the past few years, Likert's voice has been joined by many other behavioral scientists who assume that their theories are also universally appropriate. Many of these theories were derived from studies carried out during and after World War II. The data from these studies were interpreted as supporting, for example, the notion that all employees have strong needs for group membership at work and, consequently, the universal superiority of participative management. Researchers were not concerned whether these ideas were more appropriate in one setting than in another, with different groups of employees, with different jobs, and so forth.

Along with this search for the universal went a tendency to invent specific techniques for applying the theories, which it was argued would lead to improved results in all situations. Examples are management by objectives, autonomous work groups, laboratory training, job enrichment, and participative leadership.

By now many managers have tried these techniques, and their attempts have led to numerous difficulties stemming from the variable conditions existing in different companies. For example, a basic premise underlying management by objectives is that if people set their own goals, they will be committed to them. Because of the nature of the business or of the technology, however, in some situations employees can have little or no real voice in setting goals.

To illustrate, consider the case of the back office of a large bank, where managers down to first-line supervisors were directed to become involved in an MBO program. The quantity, schedule, and quality of their work, however, were imposed on them by the work flow from other groups in the bank and by their customers' requests, rather than being set by the managers themselves. Moreover, upper managers trying to meet strategic goals set their cost targets. These lower-level managers had little or no leeway in which to choose their own goals. As a result, they soon saw the management by objectives program as a sham.

Another example of a situation not fitting a theory occurs when a manager's personality is not consistent with what is demanded of a participative leader. As Harry Levinson and Abraham Zaleznik, among others, have indicated, although personality development is a life-long process, a 35-year-old's character is generally stable and is unlikely to change in radically new directions.[2] Since one's style of dealing with others is closely linked to one's personality makeup, it is not surprising that some managers are comfortable with one way of managing subordinates and some with another.

To illustrate my point: Companies have faced a major difficulty in introducing autonomous work groups and similar techniques. These techniques require supervisors to involve their subordinates more heavily in decision making, and many of these managers find it difficult to adjust to this new "participative" style. Not only have they spent many years managing in a different way, but also they consciously or unconsciously chose to be foremen because their personalities were suited to the traditional, more directive role.

Such situational problems are a primary reason that so many of these techniques are flashes in the pan. They are applied successfully in a few companies where conditions are right and receive attention and publicity. Without considering the differences, managers, consultants, and academics alike decide the technique can be applied to other situations. Because conditions are not right, the second-generation attempts are often failures, and the enthusiasm dies.

Each Situation Is Unique

Neither universal theories nor the resulting techniques have been the only behavioral science ideas available to managers. Another set of ideas is built on the premise that the organization can be viewed as a social system. This approach developed out of the Hawthorne studies by Elton Mayo, F. J. Roethlisberger, and William Dickson.[3]

In this well-known study, it was learned that worker behavior is the result of a complex system of forces including the personalities of the workers, the nature of their jobs, and the formal measurement and reward practices of the organization. Workers behave in ways that management does not intend, not because they are irresponsible or lazy but because they need to cope with their work situation in a way that is satisfying and meaningful to them. From this perspective, what is effective management behavior and action depends on the specifics in each situation.

Although many scholars, including Roethlisberger and Mayo themselves, elaborated on these ideas and taught them at many business schools, managers never gave them the attention they gave to the universal ideas. Interestingly enough, many saw the central significance of the Hawthorne studies as being either the *universal* importance of effective interpersonal communication between supervisors and workers or the so-called "Hawthorne Effect." The latter is the notion that any change in practice will *always* lead to positive results in the short run simply because of the novelty of the new practice.

In essence, this world-renowned study, which its authors saw as proving that human issues need to be viewed from a "social system," or situational perspective, was interpreted by others as a call for universal techniques of "good human relations." (For Roethlisberger's comments on this, see *The Elusive Phenomena*.)[4]

Of course, stating that one should *always* take a situational perspective could be seen as a universal prescription itself. My concern is not with universal ideas, such as this and others which I shall mention shortly, which seem to hold generally true. Rather, it is with techniques invented under a specific set of conditions, which have not been more widely tried but which their advocates argue have universal application.

Why these social-system concepts did not catch on is a matter of conjecture, but one reasonable explanation is that managers naturally prefer the simplest apparent approach to a problem. When faced with the choice between the complex and time-consuming analysis required to apply such situational ideas and the simpler, quicker prescriptions of universal theories and techniques, most managers seem to prefer the simpler universal approach. The human tendency to follow the fads and fashions also adds to the appeal of these techniques. If competitors are trying T-groups for management development, shouldn't we? If the company across the industrial park is using MBO, shouldn't we as well?

In spite of the rush to simple popular solutions in the last decade, some behavioral scientists have become aware that the universal theories and the techniques they spawned have failed in many situations where they were inappropriate. These scholars are trying to understand situational complexity and to provide managers with tools to analyze the complex issues in each specific situation and to decide on appropriate action. Examples of these efforts are listed in *Exhibit I*.

These behavioral scientists do not all agree on what variables are important to understand. At this stage, people conceptualize the issues and define the variables and the important relationships among them in many different ways. Also, the "theories" they have developed often throw light on a limited set of applications.

All these behavioral scientists focusing on situational theories, however, share two fundamental assumptions. First, the proper target of behavioral science knowledge is the complex interrelationships that shape the behavior with which all managers must deal. Harold J. Leavitt, in his well-known text *Managerial Psychology*, presents a diagram (see *Exhibit II*) that illustrates clearly the basic set of relationships.[5] Behavior in an organization results, he writes, from the interaction of people's needs, their task requirements, and the organization's characteristics. He uses two-headed arrows to both suggest this complex interdependence and indicate that behavior itself can influence the other forces over time.

Although Leavitt's was an early and, from today's perspective, a simplified view of the relationships involved, it captures the essential issues in situational theories and is very close to the Roethlisberger and Dickson conception.

The second assumption that behavioral scientists focusing on situational theories seem to share is that, at this juncture, they cannot hope to provide a grand and general theory of human behavior in organizations. Rather, what the behavioral sciences can, and should, provide are what L. J. Henderson called "walking sticks" to guide the managers along complex decision-making paths about human affairs.[6] In this case, by walking sticks I mean conceptual models for understanding the complexity of the human issues a manager faces.

Such models represent the product these scholars have to offer managers. Universal prescriptions or techniques are like a mirage. Each situation is unique and the manager must use these conceptual models to diagnose it. With an understanding of the complex and interrelated causes of behavior in the organization, the manager can use his or her intellect and creative ability to invent a new solution or to judge what existing solutions might fit the situation.

An Applied Example

The case of a major insurance company illustrates how a situational walking stick can help managers. Like many of its competitors, the top management of this company was concerned about the high rate of turnover among its younger professional staff. The managers felt that they did not understand the causes of this turnover and were unwilling to accept the conclusion that their competitors reached—namely, that the basic cause was low pay. Instead, they used an in-house consultant to help them diagnose the causes of their problem.

Exhibit I   Examples of Situational Frameworks

Author	Publication	Major Focus
Fred E. Fiedler	*A Theory of Leadership Effectiveness* (New York: McGraw-Hill, 1967).	Leadership of a work unit
John P. Kotter	*Organizational Dynamics* (Reading, Mass.: Addison-Wesley, 1978).	Organizational change
Edward E. Lawler	*Pay and Organizational Effectiveness: A Psychological View* (New York: McGraw-Hill, 1971).	Employee motivation
Paul R. Lawrence and Jay W. Lorsch	*Organization and Environment* (Division of Research, Harvard Business School, Harvard University, 1967).	Organizational arrangements to fit environmental requirements
Harry Levinson	*Men, Management and Mental Health* (Harvard University Press, 1962).	Employee motivation
Jay W. Lorsch and John Morse	*Organizations and Their Members* (New York: Harper and Row, 1975)	Organizational arrangements and leadership in functional units
Edgar H. Schein	*Career Dynamics: Matching Individual and Organizational Needs* (Reading, Mass.: Addison-Wesley, 1978).	Life stage careers, and organizational requirements
Robert Tannenbaum and Warren H. Schmidt	*"How To Choose A Leadership Pattern"* (HBR May-June 1973).	Leadership
Victor H. Vroom and Philip W. Yetton	*Leadership and Decision-Making* (University of Pittsburgh Press, 1973).	Leadership behavior for different types of decisions
Joan Woodward	*Industrial Organization: Theory and Practice* (Oxford University Press, 1965).	Organizational design

This consultant used a relatively simple situational model—the concept of the psychological contract as a framework for diagnosing the causes of the problem.[7] From this perspective, the relationship between a group of employees and the company is seen as an implicit, as well as explicit, contract.

While this contract is not binding in the legal sense, it is of psychological importance. Employees have certain expectations about what they are to get from their work in the company—both

Exhibit II   Basic Forces Shaping Behavior

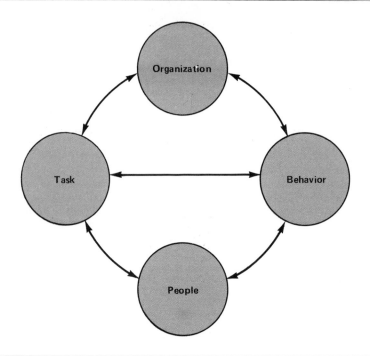

economically and psychologically. If these expectations are not met, the employees become dissatisfied, and ultimately can express themselves by walking out the door.

With these ideas in mind, the consultant, through a series of interviews in offices that had varying levels of turnover, sought the answers to two basic questions: What did the employees expect from the company? And how well were these expectations being met?

He learned that these young employees considered their current salary level relatively unimportant. More important to them were future career opportunities, the chance to do their jobs with minimum interference from above, and immediate supervisors who cared about their progress and tried to facilitate their learning. Furthermore, the consultant found that staff turnover was much lower in offices where managers were meeting expectations than where they were not.

From this diagnosis, top management developed an approach to improve the skills of its middle managers in meeting the expectations of its younger staff. By discovering the basic causes of its turnover problem, the company avoided the trap its competitors with identical problems fell in of mistakenly relying on salary increases as a way of trying to buy the loyalty of its younger staff.

Potential of Situational Theories

The insurance company case illustrates the greatest potential the behavioral sciences have for managers at present. They can provide situational theories to analyze, order, understand, and deal with the complex social and human issues managers face. By their nature the universal theories make simplified assumptions about the human and business factors involved in a situation.

For example, many universal theories do not recognize that not all employees have the same career expectations. Yet we now know that while older managers may be more interested in jobs that enable them to develop subordinates and build the organization for the future, younger persons, such as the professionals just mentioned, are at a stage of life where advancement is usually critical.[8]

Similarly, different business tasks do not all lend themselves to similar leadership styles or reward schemes; running a production shop may require directive leadership, but managing a group of professional underwriters for an insurance company may require employee involvement in decisions.

Even though they neither provide ready-made solutions nor solve all classes of human problems, the situational theories are tools to understand the variety and complexity of these problems. The manager has to select the theory that seems most relevant to his or her specific problem, analyze the situation according to it, develop his or her own action alternatives, and choose among them.

A hospital laboratory provides a useful analogy. It is full of diagnostic tools, but the doctor has to make the choice of the appropriate ones. Then, he makes a diagnosis and decides on the appropriate treatment. So it will be for managers. The behavioral sciences can provide conceptual frameworks for analyzing problems. They will indicate what data are required, on some cases how best to collect them, how the problem areas are related to each other, and the outcomes with which the managers will be concerned. With this analysis the managers can then use their experience, intuition, and intellect to decide which actions make sense.

From this description, the analytical process may seem difficult and time-consuming. How true this is will depend to some extent on the complexity of the problem and the experience that a manager has in applying these tools. A manager with experience can apply them with the same ease and skill a physician displays in using his diagnostic tools. Applying these tools to complex and infrequently encountered issues, however, may require some expertise beyond the scope of a typical line manager—a problem I shall deal with shortly.

The trend toward more situational theories signifies only a decline in emphasis on universal theories and the techniques they have spawned, not that these theories and techniques should or will disappear. Undoubtedly, on a limited number of issues, such generalizations are useful guides to actions. The problem for a manager is to identify those issues where a universal theory is helpful, and not confuse them with issues where the solution depends on the situation.

For example, certain maxims about interpersonal communication seem to be generally useful in conducting performance appraisal interviews. And it seems clear that it is absolutely necessary for the top management of a unit undergoing a change to be committed to the process for it to be successful. Use of such valid generalizations from the behavioral sciences should continue and expand.

But the application of techniques and universal principles that are inappropriate in a variety of situations must decline. Because of the tendency toward fads in both managers and academics, I am not naive enough to think that the misapplications of universal theories will suddenly end. My hope is that the increasing availability and use of situational theories will gradually make universal ideas less attractive. As managers become more sophisticated diagnosticians, they will be less likely to try an idea or a technique simply because it is a fad.

Managers need also to recognize a number of current difficulties in using situational theories and must, with the help of those who are developing these ideas, seek solutions to them. In essence, in the behavioral science market they must act as consumers who influence the end product, and in their companies they must, among other things, act as teachers so that they and their associates are prepared to use these tools.

The Manager as a Consumer

If a manager, acting as a consumer, begins to explore the relevant literature, what is he likely to find? To what extent are the situational theories in a useful, usable form? Unfortunately, much needs to be done to make many of these tools more widely applicable. As managers become informed and demanding consumers, I hope they can influence behavioral scientists to take steps to overcome the current problems.

The Tower of Babel

One difficulty with today's situational tools is that each scholar (or group of scholars) has developed his or her own language and methods and makes interpretations based on his or her values, assumptions, and research about individual behavior. Also, in the same way physical scientists and engineers have done, each set of scholars, not surprisingly, prefers its own ideas and rejects those "not invented here." Understandably, communication among behavioral scientists and their communication with managers is confused. Different scholars use different labels to mean the same thing. Because no one relates his ideas to those of others, an academic Tower of Babel develops.

Managers and scholars alike find it difficult to understand what one label means in one model as compared to another or how the ideas developed by one group relate to those developed elsewhere. Clearly, what managers and academics can and must do is judge future studies more carefully and explicitly to determine whether they are related to each other. In this way, we will be able to see the parallels and differences in various theories and will be able to make more informed decisions about their relevance to particular problems. Similarly, such action should gradually reduce much of the variation in language and terminology that characterizes the behavioral sciences.

Lack of Parsimony

Many of these concepts are so complex that managers need to learn how to define the concepts and their relationships before they can apply them. All this takes time and, naturally, makes these ideas less appealing to the busy line executive. By their preference for complex and elegant theories that greatly exceed the needs of most managers, academics have compounded the problem. Rather than worrying about how to help managers, many academics seem preoccupied with impressing their colleagues. In my own experience, moreover, it is the relatively simple concepts that managers find most useful.

As consumers of knowledge, managers can and should reject those theories that are too complex and seek those simple enough to be understood and implemented by intelligent managers. But academics must strive to develop such theories, what Sheldon has called "friendly" models.[9] By this, he means theories that are not so complex as to intimidate potential users, yet are complete enough to enable them to deal with the real human complexities they face.

One way to ensure such a balance is for managers to encourage and for academics to conduct more research focusing on managerial issues. Experience in medicine and space technology, for example, has demonstrated anew the axiom that research leading to a productive and practical payout will also likely lead to important theoretical results. Certainly, encouraging the design of research programs that tie real managerial concerns to theoretical behavioral science issues should also lead to gains in knowledge complete enough to be useful and simple enough to use.

Managers should also look for research that clarifies the conditions where findings are relevant and where they are not. In this manner, the distinction between situationally relevant ideas and universally applicable ones should be clearer. This, in turn, should reduce some of the misuses of behavioral science and also discourage academics from developing techniques in a vacuum.

An Aside to Academics

Although HBR readers are primarily practitioners, much of my preceding argument has particular relevance to my academic colleagues. Managers can only influence us indirectly by their reactions as consumers. The responsibility for the changes in the development of knowledge for which I am calling lies directly with academics. Yet, in many centers of behavioral science research, researchers are more concerned with proving a minor but neat conceptual point or resolving a measurement issue than with tackling issues that have clear practical application. Disciplinary traditions, the promotion criteria in most universities, and the acceptance standard for most relevant publications place more emphasis on theoretical elegance and methodological perfection than on practical use of knowledge.
It will, therefore, require more than just pressure from consumers to make the necessary changes in our approach to knowledge-building. It is going to require dedication and courage from the behavioral scientists who believe, as I do, that our tools are still too little used.

The Manager as Manager

If academics can be encouraged to move in such directions, the manager's job will be easier. He or she will gradually acquire simpler conceptual tools that are relevant to real problems, specific about the range of situations to which they apply, and related to each other.

Even today, however, a few such conceptual tools exist. The issue for managers is how to select the specific set of tools relevant to a particular type of problem. To help in this regard, in *Exhibit III* I compare the conceptual tools from *Exhibit I* as to their major focus, the type of management or organizational issues for which they are most relevant, and some of the key questions managers must be able to answer to use these tools.

In examining *Exhibit III,* bear in mind some caveats. First, the list represents my personal choices. It is not exhaustive. It is based on my own and some of my colleagues' experiences in helping managers deal with these problems. Second, many of these tools are relatively new and still somewhat crude. Although, in some cases, fairly sophisticated and validated techniques have been developed for answering the key questions, in others the manager will have to rely on his or her own knowledge and judgment of the situation. Third, in such a compact article, it is obviously not possible to define the variables in each conceptual framework or state the relationships among them. For this the reader will have to refer to the original works listed in *Exhibit I.*

By using tools such as these, managers will be forced to be more diagnostic. They will have to approach human problems with the same analytical rigor they devote to marketing or financial issues. This approach means less acceptance of the latest fad in management practice, whether it be management by objective, job enrichment, office of the president, sensitivity training, or whatever. Instead, managers can use these tools to identify problems and diagnose their causes. Then they can invent their own solutions or even examine what other companies are doing to see what might be relevant to their situation. In this process, managers should not ignore their intuitive hunches and past experience. Accordingly, this more rigorous analysis should be compared with such insights to arrive at the best possible judgments.

Need for Education

Because these situational tools require more skill, knowledge, and time, line managers may need help and support in the longer run to realize their full potential. Education and training, in both university courses and company management-development programs, can and should aim at giving managers knowledge about these tools and the skills necessary to apply them. Such programs will have to provide not only content, but also, and equally important, practice in using these tools for analysis and problem solving.

In calling for management education, I am not suggesting that line managers can or should develop knowledge of or skill in applying a broad range of these ideas. Rather, as *Exhibit I* shows, they should gain understanding about those concepts which are relevant to the problems they regularly encounter. For example, concepts that focus on understanding leadership issues with a small group of workers (e.g., Fiedler's) would be of value to first-level supervisors.

At the general manager level, concepts that enhance understanding of multiple-unit organizations would be more relevant (e.g., Lawrence and Lorsch). This is not to say that some of these tools will not have utility at many organizational levels. For example, managers concerned with compensation issues might find Lawler's ideas useful whether their subordinates are salesmen, blue collar workers, or general managers.

Role of Staff

In the long run, along with educational programs, corporations will need to develop staff specialists with a broader range of knowledge about the behavioral sciences. These specialists, whatever their titles—organization development agent, human resources expert, organization designer, behavioral scientist—should be able to apply their wider and deeper behavioral science knowledge to a broader range of issues.

Their role would be analogous to what market research analysts, cost analysts, and so on, perform. Their job should be first to help managers decide what concepts will be most useful in understanding the problems they face, to design studies to gather data, to analyze them, and to work with their line colleagues to develop solutions. Again, academics have an important contribution to make. They can develop courses and programs to educate the professionals to staff these functions.

Awareness of One's Values and Style

To use these tools effectively, both line and staff managers will need to be aware of their own values and their own preferred management styles. Without such awareness, one can easily and unwittingly confuse one's own sense of what is right or appropriate with what the situation seems to require and objective analysis seems to suggest. With self-knowledge about one's values and preferences, one can at least be explicit when making choices between what a situation requires and one's own preferences.

Achieving such self-awareness is not easy. It requires a willingness to be introspective and cognizant of one's limits as well as one's strengths, one's preferences as well as one's dislikes. Such probing is difficult for many managers; yet it is something that a number of seasoned, mature, and successful managers achieve. With this self-understanding, they are better able to comprehend their relationships with others around them. These same qualities must also be put to work to apply behavioral science knowledge effectively.

Tools Are Available Now

Based on what you have read here, you may conclude that it is better to defer trying these situational tools until they have been improved, expanded, and refined. No doubt such improvements are needed. But if managers use the best of the existing situational tools now, in spite of their shortcomings, they will no doubt achieve improved effectiveness in dealing with the complex human problems of management.

The need for solving these human problems has never been more pressing. The increased size of organizations makes this so, as do the inflationary pressures on personnel costs and the rate of change in the

Exhibit III Situational Frameworks and Their Applications

Framework	Major Focus	Issues: Leadership	Management Selection	Career Planning	Measurement and Performance Feedback	Compensation	Job Design	Division and Coordination of Activities	Organizational Change	Diagnostic Questions
Fiedler	Leadership of a work unit	●	●				●			What is the preferred leadership style of the relevant manager(s) on a continuum from permissive, passive, considerate, to controlling, active, and structuring? What is the quality of leader relations with the members of the subordinate group(s)? How well-defined and structured are the activities being performed by subordinates? How much positional authority does the leader(s) have?
Kotter	Organizational change				●			●	●	Is management concerned with short-term, moderate-term, or long-term change? If *short-term*, what is the current state of the organization's human and financial resources, its organization process and structure, its technology, and its external environment? If *moderate-term*, how well are the organization's resources, structure, and process aligned with each other and the external environment and the goals of management? If these are not well aligned, what changes have caused this? If *long-term*, are major changes likely in top management, in the organization's human and financial resources, its structure and processes, or its technology and external environment, which would make one or two of these elements out of line with the other? How malleable are the other elements so that a new alignment can be created? Is the organization inventing resources to achieve sufficient flexibility to adapt to such major changes?
Lawler	Employee motivation				●	●	●			What do the relevant individuals expect to get as rewards for their behavior on the job? How valuable are these rewards to these individuals? How hard do these individuals believe it will be to achieve the results expected of them?

Theorist	Model / Concept	Diagnostic questions
Lawrence and Lorsch	Organizational arrangements to fit environmental requirements	How different are the organizational practices, traditions, and the goals and time horizons of members of various organization units? To what extent are these differences consistent with the different activities each unit is performing (e.g., selling products versus manufacturing them, versus designing them)? To what extent is it necessary for these units to work collaboratively and to what extent can they perform activities independent of each other? Do the existing mechanisms for dividing and coordinating work (e.g., authority structure, coordinating rules, cross-unit committees, rewards, and measurement) facilitate the necessary division of work and coordination?
Levinson et al	Employee motivation	What is the psychological contract between the relevant individuals and the company? What does each party expect to receive from the other? How well is each party living up to its part of the contract?
Lorsch and Morse	Organizational arrangements and leadership in functional units	What is the nature of the unit's tasks? How certain are they? What goals do members have to work toward? How quickly is feedback about results available? What are members' shared psychological predispositions in terms of working together versus alone, preference for close supervision or not, preference for clear and predictable activities or for ambiguous ones? How well does existing leadership style, unit structure, measurement, and job design fit the unit task and members' predisposition?
Schein	Life stage, careers, and organizational requirements	At what stage of life is (are) the relevant individual(s)? Where are these people in their careers? What are their underlying career interests? What are the key dimensions of jobs available now and in the future? What are future personnel requirements for these jobs?
Vroom and Yetton	Leadership behavior for different types of decisions	Who among the boss and his subordinates have information to make a high-quality decision? Is the problem well-defined or not? Is acceptance of decisions by subordinates critical to implementation? Do subordinates share the organizational goals to be attained in making these decisions? Is conflict among subordinates likely in seeking solutions?

environment of many companies. Additionally, demands from many employees for a more rewarding organizational life are growing. These situational tools offer a virtually untapped resource to provide more effective management of the human assets of most companies.

To use these tools will not be easy, and managers will have to make efforts at many levels: to be more critical consumers of behavioral science knowledge; to become more analytic and diagnostic, to gradually build educational programs and staff resources for developing skill and knowledge in using these tools; and, finally, to become more self-aware, so they can discriminate between their own preferences, current fads, and what will be most effective in their particular situations.

These efforts will be difficult, but to defer doing these things is to neglect these new and valuable tools that the behavioral sciences are making available, and this would be a tragic waste.

Notes

1. Rensis Likert, *New Patterns of Management* (New York: McGraw-Hill, 1961).
2. Harry Levinson, *The Exceptional Executive* (Cambridge, Mass.: Harvard University Press, 1968); Abraham Zaleznik, *Human Dilemmas of Leadership* (New York: Harper and Row, 1966).
3. Elton Mayo, *The Human Problems of an Industrial Civilization* (New York: Viking Press, 1960); F. J. Roethlisberger and William Dickson, *Management and the Worker* (Cambridge, Mass.: Harvard University Press, 1939).
4. F. J. Roethlisberger, *The Elusive Phenomena*, ed. George F. F. Lombard (Boston: Division of Research, Harvard Business School, 1977).
5. Harold J. Leavitt, *Managerial Psychology* (Chicago, Ill.: University of Chicago Press, 1958), p. 286.
6. L. J. Henderson, *On The Social System: Selected Writings* (Chicago, Ill.: University of Chicago Press, 1970).
7. The concept of the psychological contract was first developed by Harry Levinson et al. in *Men, Management and Mental Health* (Cambridge, Mass.: Harvard University Press, 1966).
8. See Daniel Levinson et al., *The Seasons of A Man's Life* (New York: Alfred Knopf, 1978); or Edgar H. Schein, *Career Dynamics* (Reading, Mass.: Addison-Wesley, 1978).
9. Alan Sheldon, "Friendly Models," *Science, Medicine, and Man,* Vol. 1, 1973, p. 49.

3

Approaches to the Evaluation of Organizational Effectiveness

J. Barton Cunningham

Selection of the appropriate basis for assessing organizational effectiveness presents a challenging problem for managers and researchers. There are no generally accepted conceptualizations prescribing the best criteria. The literature abounds with criteria ranging from productivity and efficiency considerations to behavioral factors such as morale, organizational flexibility, and job satisfaction (26, 27, 34, 44, 45, 52). Criteria are selected on the basis of an author's particular interest or specialty (52).

This article first reviews the underlying conceptual frameworks of the range of criteria associated with the concept of organizational effectiveness. It then discusses the appropriateness of each framework for particular organizational situations.

Approaches to Organizational Effectiveness

Different organizational situations—pertaining to the performance of the organization's structure, the performance of the organization's human resources, and the impact of the organization's activities—require different criteria. Examples are listed in Table 1.

Organizational effectiveness encompasses a range of evaluation possibilities. Specific evaluation situations require appropriate criteria such as: accomplishments and achievements, efficiency and stress,

SOURCE: J. Barton Cunningham, "Approaches to the Evaluation of Organizational Effectiveness," *Academy of Management Review,* July 1977, pp. 463–74. Reprinted with permission.

Table 1 Criteria Appropriate to Specific Applications of Evaluation Approaches

ORGANIZATIONAL EFFECTIVENESS APPROACH

Evaluating the Performance of the Organizational Structure		Evaluating the Performance of the Organization's Human Resources		Evaluating the Impact of Organizational Functions or Activities		
Rational Goal	Systems Resource	Managerial Process	Organizational Devel.	Bargaining	Structural Functional	Functional
Accomplishments: Goals of the Esso Standard Oil Company for Preparing Employees for Retirement: 1. Increasing industrial efficiency, prestige, worker satisfaction; reducing costs; increasing public good will. 2. Aiding the nation and community to solve problems of the aged. 3. Helping the worker be well-adjusted in retirement. (3)	Efficiency and Satisfaction Criteria for the Systems Need of Adapting to a Changing and Turbulent Environment: 1. Adaptability—the ability to solve problems and to react with flexibility to changing internal and external circumstances. 2. Identity—knowledge and insight on the part of the organization of what it is and what it is to do. This involves (a) determining to what extent the organizational goals are understood and accepted by the personnel and (b) ascertaining to what extent the organization is perceived vertically	Productivity and Capability Criteria (Managerial Principles): 1. Planning—shaping the future direction of the organization. 2. Organizing—recognition of the organization's personnel needs, obtaining people to meet these needs, and attempting to place people so that individual and organizational needs are in harmony. 3. Staffing—recognition of the organization's personnel needs, obtaining the people to meet these needs, and attempting to place people so that individual and organizational needs are in harmony.	Interpersonal Competence and Job Satisfaction Criteria: 1. Improvement in interpersonal competence. 2. Development of the norm that human factors and feelings are legitimate. 3. Increased understanding between and within working groups in order to reduce tensions. 4. Development of more effective team management. 5. Development of more rational and "open" methods of conflict resolution rather than suppression, compromise and unprincipled power. 6. Development of organic rather than mechanical systems. (5)	Resource Utilization Criteria (Dimensions of Exchange): 1. The parties to the exchange—their affiliation, function, prestige, size, personal characteristics, and numbers and types of clients served. 2. The kinds of quantities exchanged—the actual elements exchanged (consumer, labor services and resources other than labor services), and information on the availability of these organizational elements and on rights and obligations regarding them. 3. The agreement underlying the exchange—terms explicitly defined by	Structural Viability—Performance (Functional) Elements: 1. Satisfying the interests of members and clientele groups. 2. Producing a quantity, quality and mixture of outputs. 3. Investing in the system through hard goods, people, subsystems, and external relations. 4. Using inputs efficiently to achieve potential and profitability. 5. Acquiring resources such as money, people, goods. 6. Observing codes of laws and organizational rules. 7. Using relevant technical knowledge and administrative methods to behave rationally.	Functional Criteria: 1. Goal attainment—planning, programming, scheduling, rule making. 2. Adaptation—procurement, property management, office services, budgeting, personnel. 3. Integration—work flow procedures, internal rule making process, informal organizational status system, wage determination system. 4. Pattern maintenance—consideration given to agency's legal mandate, clientele needs, public interest, professional and mission oriented

CRITERIA

by the personnel.
3. Capacity to test reality—the ability to search out, accurately perceive, and correctly interpret the real properties of the environment. (4)

4. Leading—motivation of people to reach goals without deterioration of morale both of themselves and the organization.
5. Controlling—activity that checks actual progress against planned progress and suggests ways of modifying activities falling below expected levels of performance (17).

The principles are John G. Hutchison's suggested redefinition of Henri Fayol's ideas using more modern terminology.

one party or mutually defined by a number of parties.
4. The direction of the exchange—the direction of the flow of organizational elements (unilateral, reciprocal, or joint). (19)

Structural Elements:
1. Number and character of people.
2. Physical and monetary assets of nonhuman resources.
3. Type, location, form and differentiation of subsystem.
4. Conflict, conflict resolution, superior/subordinate relations, bargaining procedures, formal and informal communications defining the organization's internal relations.
5. External organizations, agencies, roles, and environment characterizing the organization's external relations.
6. Values describing the organization's orientation; i.e., competitive, active.
7. The internal structure support base defining the guidance system. (16)

(These criteria, although defined in Bertram Gross' social systems model, are appropriate within Philip Selznick's definition of structural-functionalism.)

values of the organization, employee satisfaction and morale, social norms of informal groups within the organization. (12)

interpersonal competence and job satisfaction, productivity and capability, resource utilization, structural viability, and functionality. Each type, as suited to given evaluation approaches, is described in the following paragraphs.

The Rational Goal Model

The rational goal approach focuses on the organization's ability to achieve its goals. Evaluation criteria are derived from a definition of goals the organization is expected to achieve (9, 10, 15, 40, 41, 42, 49, 50, 51). These criteria are determined by various factors (44, 50). One common practice is to use the formal statements of goals found in charters, manuals, and other documents. Informal but operative goals constitute other useful criteria. Still others may be derived from conceptualizations of societal missions or functions of the organization.

The basis of the rational goal approach is the Weberian concept of functional rationality (53). According to Weber, modern organizations are characterized by networks of roles; divisions of labor; and hierarchies defining the relationship of each activity, project, program, and function to the overall goals of the organization. In this scheme, an organization is rational if the above elements are organized for the achievement of its goals. When a series of actions is effectively organized to achieve a goal, every element has a defined role or function that is related (35).

An organization's goals are identified by establishing the general goal, discovering means or objectives for its accomplishment, and defining a set of activities for each objective. The organization is evaluated by comparing the activities accomplished with those planned for. The process is valuable in defining the organization's accomplishments or achievements relative to specific activities, objectives and goals.

The Systems Resource Model

The systems resource model defines the organization as a network of interrelated subsystems. The outputs of one subsystem may become the inputs of another subsystem; the organizational system functions effectively to the degree that its subsystems are in harmony and are coordinated to work together (9, 14, 15, 46, 54). The central question in the use of this model is: Under given conditions, how close does the organization's allocation of resources approach an optimal distribution among the various subsystems? Optimality is the key word: what counts is a balanced distribution of resources among the various subsystems' needs, not maximal satisfaction of these needs. The value of resources to the decision-maker is derived from their utility as (more or less) generalized means for subsystems needs rather than from their attachment to some organizational goal (15, 54).

The organization, according to proponents of this approach, strives to survive and satisfy the needs of its components. In this context, needs refer to the requirements subsystems must meet in order to survive. These subsystems' needs may be classified as:

1. Bargaining position—ability of the organization to exploit

its environment in acquisition of scarce and valued resources (54);

2. Ability of the system's decision-makers to perceive, and correctly interpret, the real properties of the external environment;
3. Ability of the system to produce a certain specified output;
4. Maintenance of internal day-to-day activities;
5. Ability of the organization to coordinate relationships among the various subsystems;
6. Ability of the organization to respond to feedback regarding its effectiveness in the environment;
7. Ability of the organization to evaluate the effect of its decisions;
8. Ability of the organization's system to accomplish its goals.

The effectiveness of the organization in satisfying these systems' needs hinges on a combination of two measures:

1. *Efficiency:* an indication of the organization's ability to use its resources in responding to the most important subsystems' needs; and
2. *Stress:* the tension produced by the system in fulfilling or not fulfilling its needs (20).

Thus, each of the subsystem's needs should be evaluated from two focal points—efficiency and stress.

The Managerial Process Model

The managerial process model evaluates an organization's effectiveness by its ability to perform effectively certain managerial functions—decision-making, planning, budgeting, and the like. The model assumes that goals are set and met as a result of the effectiveness of the various management processes (8, 11, 43). The evaluation of the organization is determined by the capability of its processes to realize envisioned goals. Changes in management processes affect and are affected by planned changes in organizational goals. It is important to specify the processes related to achieving these goals and to adapt them to any planned changes. Thus, the model provides a measure of the capability or productivity of the managerial processes for attaining goals. Productivity becomes a yardstick of the organization's accomplishments within specified managerial processes.

The managerial process model is based on the intuitive concept of substantial rationality, which interrelates the drives, impulses, wishes, feelings, needs, and values of the individuals to the functional goals of the organization (28). An organization can be considered rational when its various processes and patterns enhance the individual's productivity and capability to respond to the goals of the organization.

The Organizational Development Model

The organizational development (OD) model sees effectiveness in terms of the organization's problem-solving and renewal capabilities (1, 23,

24, 25). The model focuses on developing management practices to foster:

1. Supervisory behavior manifesting interest and concern for workers;
2. Team spirit, group loyalty, and teamwork among workers and between workers and management;
3. Confidence, trust and communication between workers and management;
4. More freedom to set their own objectives (23).

Using knowledge and techniques from the behavioral sciences, this model attempts to integrate organizational goals with individual needs for growth. The purpose is to design a more effective and functioning organization in which the potential of each member is fully realized. In short, it fosters a "development" approach.

The model's procedures attempt to answer four main questions about the organization's capacity to understand and manage its own growth:

1. Where are we?
2. Where do we want to go?
3. How will we get there?
4. How will we know when we do get there?

These questions can be divided into four areas. Question one is concerned with diagnosis, question two with the setting of goals and plans, question three with the implementation of goals, and question four with evaluation.

This model is concerned with changing beliefs, attitudes, values, and organizational structures so that individuals can better adapt to new technologies and challenges. While the ultimate goal is to make the organization more effective, this cannot be accomplished until the constraints that operate within it are resolved.

The OD model assumes that:

> *Pressure-oriented, threatening, punitive management yields lower productivity, higher costs, increased absenteeism, and less employee satisfaction than supportive, employee-centered management which uses group methods of supervision coupled with high performance expectations (23, p. 45).*

Basic foundations underlying this approach are:

1. The negative attitudes toward work held by most members of organizations, and their resultant work habits, are usually reactions to their work environment and how they are treated by the organization, rather than intrinsic personality characteristics;
2. Work which is organized to meet people's needs as well as organizational requirements tends to result in the highest productivity.

The essential task of management is to arrange conditions and operations so that people can adjust their own goals accordingly. This means creating opportunities, releasing potential, removing obstacles, encouraging growth, and providing guidance. It is a process of management by objectives in contrast to management by control (25).

The Bargaining Model

The bargaining model conceives of an organization in terms of exchanges and transactions of individuals and groups pursuing a diversity of goals (2, 13, 22, 31, 54). The capacity to make decisions is firmly rooted in exchanges between the organization's components. Decisions, problems and goals are more useful when shared by a greater number of people. Larger programs require sharing because no one organization can command the resources to carry them out. Organizational accomplishments are the outcome of a complex process of accommodation and adjustment between elements. This does not mean that all the exchanges made throughout the organization must be analyzed to arrive at a decision. Only exchanges important to the particular problem being studied need to be considered.

The bargaining model presumes that an organization is a cooperative, sometimes competitive, resource distributing system. Each individual and group, having a defined value of resources (time, money, human resources), is in a specific systematic relationship for the accomplishment of definite goals. In contributing and exchanging resources, groups can achieve objectives important to them (30). An organization is effective only if its goals elicit sufficient contributions from participants (2). The goals most likely to be accomplished are those in which numerous groups share a common interest.

The bargaining model's emphasis is on how various decision-makers, with different resources and capabilities, utilize their resources. Each decision-maker bargains with other groups for scarce resources which are vital in solving problems and meeting goals. Organizations resemble games such as chess, poker, and bridge, in that each decision-maker is required to choose one strategy or combination of strategies to achieve an objective. The overall outcome is a function of the particular strategies selected by various decision-makers in their bargaining relationships.

The procedure for measurement involves identifying decision-makers' allocation of resources towards their objectives. A high degree of cooperation occurs if they pool their resources, through bargaining, to respond to established priorities. A city manager's bargaining capability, for instance, may be seen in the ability to obtain the resources of other policy makers (i.e. mayor, city council) in the pursuit of the city's objectives.

Each organizational problem requires a specific allocation of resources. The decision to allocate resources is usually made on the basis of the possible payoff for solving the problem. The payoff is the return (lives or material worth) obtained for the use of certain resources. A decision-maker should, logically, use his or her resources to respond to problems of the highest payoff first. During periods of over-demand for resources, decision-makers would wish to secure the resources of others and to transfer them to problems having the highest value or payoff.

Decision-makers will enter into negotiations to gain payoffs which might not result without an agreement. This is based on the assumption that a subsystem should be able to obtain a higher payoff by cooperating than by acting alone. The organization's bargaining capability is a ratio of its actual results through cooperation to its optimal results if each player acted alone. This method of computation can be used as a measure of each subsystem's bargaining capability and the organization's total bargaining position.

The Structural Functional Model

The structural functional approach attempts to understand the structural patterns developed by the organization to maintain itself and grow (17, 47, 48). An organization's effectiveness is enhanced by its ability to develop structures—alliances, traditions, doctrines, contracts, commitments, and mechanisms of participation. Without this ability, it will deteriorate.

According to this model, all systems need maintenance and continuity. The following aspects define this:

1. Security of the organization as a whole in relation to the social forces in its environment. This relates to the system's ability to forestall threatened aggressions or deleterious consequences from the actions of others.
2. Stability of lines of authority and communication. This refers to the continued capacity of leadership to control and have access to individuals in the system.
3. Stability of informal relations within the organization. This develops effective mechanisms for individuals and subgroups to adjust to each other.
4. Continuity of policy-making. This pertains to the ability to re-examine policy on a continuing basis.
5. Homogeneity of outlook. This refers to the ability to effectively orient members to organization norms and beliefs (47).

The system, in responding to these needs, develops mechanisms for protecting and securing itself. Such structural formulations as "concern for people" and "community input" may emerge as defense mechanisms, but remain as doctrine when specified in administrative procedure.

The structural functional model is implemented by defining the organizational structures which evolve as the system maintains itself and stabilizes its relationships with its environment. Ideologies, cooptation[1], and commitments are viewed as a result of the lack of elements for effective maintenance of the organization's needs. Effective organizations are able to survive by developing structures that do not restrict their freedom of action.

The Functional Model

In the functional approach an organization's effectiveness is determined by the social consequences of its activities (12, 31, 32, 33, 36, 37, 38, 39). The frame of reference for this assessment is not the organization structure itself, but how its activities benefit society. The crucial question to be answered is: how well do the organization's activities serve the needs of its client groups?

With this approach, every system must define its purpose for being (goal attainment), determine resources to achieve its goals (adaptation), establish a means for coordinating its efforts (integration), and reduce the strains and tensions in its environment (pattern maintenance). Goal attainment centers on definition of goals and evaluation of accomplishments. Adaptation treats the functional area of procurement of resources, budgeting, management, and personnel. Integration is accomplished through division of tasks and responsibilities as well as their coordination. In pattern maintenance, tensions are reduced by answering clientele needs, considering the public interest, and promoting employee satisfaction and morale. Two of these functional variables, goal attainment and integration, are regarded as ends in themselves; the other two, adaptation and pattern maintenance, are facilitative or instrumental in accomplishing these ends (12, 32).

The appraisal of an organization's effectiveness should consider whether these activities are functions or dysfunctions in fulfilling the organization's goals. Functional consequences are observed behaviors that change existing conditions in the direction of desired objectives. Dysfunctions are observed consequences that change existing conditions in the direction contrary to those valued, or that interfere with the achievement of desired objectives. Functions meet existing needs, whereas dysfunctions generate new needs in the system. Hence functions and dysfunctions modify organizational conditions, but in varying ways. Both are experienced in terms of prevailing values, as necessitating some improvements.

Selecting an Appropriate Evaluation Approach

These seven models have their strengths and shortcomings depending upon the organizational situation being evaluated.

The choice of evaluation approach usually hinges on the organizational situation that needs to be addressed. Specific situations pertain to the performance of the organization's structure, the performance of individuals in certain administrative and organizational positions, and the impact of the organization on the surrounding environment.

Evaluating the Performance of Organizational Structures

The rational goal and the systems resource models provide information on the overall effectiveness of the organization's structure. This includes information on its progress in reaching its goals as well as on the decision-maker's efficiency in allocating and utilizing resources to fulfill systems needs.

Each model has characteristic strengths and weaknesses. On the positive side, the rational goal model gives feedback about the organization's effectiveness in achieving its goals. It focuses attention on the systematic relationship of each activity, role, and function to the overall goals and objectives of the organization. The systems resource model is also useful in evaluating effectiveness. But effectiveness in goal attainment is only one of the requirements or needs the organization seeks to accomplish; other activities relate to survival—maintenance, evaluation, feedback, etc.

Each model has shortcomings. The rational goal model's results frequently show that organizations do not reach their goals effectively, a fact which may be deduced from the way studies are conducted. Goals represent targets of given people at a given time, while organizations tend to be less consistent and perfect than their cultural anticipations (9, 10). This is similar to comparing objects on different levels of analysis as, for example, when the present state of an organization (a real state) is compared with a goal (an ideal state) as if the goal were also a real state. For this reason, the rational goal model should not be used to test the absolute effectiveness or ineffectiveness of a general program or organization.

Another problem lies with the difficulty in identifying the ultimate goals of the organization. Goals are defined from the formal documents and policy decisions rather than from the directions of individuals in the organization. An adequate conceptualization of an organization's goals cannot be formulated unless all the salient factors of the total organization and its purposes are incorporated into the framework.

The main difficulty with the systems resource model is in establishing unambiguous and acceptable criteria for measuring efficiency. The emphasis on efficiency may produce stress (16, 19, 20). Individuals are likely to feel anxious when they cannot achieve the efficiency they demand of themselves or that is demanded of them by their occupational roles (16). Over- or under-emphasis on efficiency may create feelings of frustration, resentment, and anxiety (16).

Evaluating the Performance of the Organization's Human Resources

The managerial process and OD models assess the behaviors of individuals in the organizaton. They provide information on administrative capabilities, productivity, values, beliefs, organizational norms and habits, mannerisms, job satisfaction and motivation. This information creates the focal point for developing people's competence to perform administrative processes, and to be more responsive to the needs of other individuals and the organization as a whole.

Both models are directed toward the informal organization and assume that its improvement will result in a more effective organization. The managerial process model provides information on how individuals in the organization judge the usefulness of the various managerial processes in achieving goals and objectives. The OD model—in generating information about feelings, interpersonal communication, trust and openness—attempts to construct an organization in line with the interests and desires of the individuals in it. Its major strength is in developing a self-renewing, self-correcting quality in people who learn to organize themselves in a variety of ways to do the work they have to do.

One problem of the OD model is that it emphasizes the informal rather than the formal organization. Clearly, the informal culture of any organization is a strong determinant of how individuals behave; therefore, it must be addressed in organization change efforts. But the model fails to deliver a statement on the organization's ability to achieve results.

A problem of both models is that, however well-intentioned people are, they may be reluctant to accept the interpersonal feedback supplied by the models. Administrative improvement and OD thrive on developing skills in communication, leadership, problem-solving, openness, expression of what one feels and thinks, and acceptance and understanding of all organizational members. If the program is undertaken in an organization not ready for it, then it might have the serious consequence of polarizing organizational members.

Evaluating the Impact of Organizational Activities

The functional, structural functional, and bargaining models rely on information to analyze the relationship of the organization with its surrounding environment. The models analyze distribution of resources among key decision-makers, impact of the organization's activities on key client groups, power alliances in the execution of key decisions, and type of emerging administrative structures as the organization buffers itself from the environment.

The common basis for all three models is the assumption that an organization is effective if it appropriately serves its defined needs. In this context, needs refer to requirements the organization has to meet in order to relate effectively to other parts of the organizational system. The functional approach sheds light on the organization's ability to meet the needs of key client groups in its environment. It pinpoints the functions it should carry out to facilitate realization of its goals. The structural functional approach is useful in detecting how organizational structures develop in response to the needs for their survival. Attention is focused on the structural conditions—bureaucratic and administrative requirements—influencing organizational behavior and functioning. The bargaining model, in assessing the capacity of existing resources to achieve organizational goals through alliances or coalitions, should indicate the cooperation or antagonism taking place between them. The model's strength lies in its use as a policy device for identifying individuals and groups who should be using their resources to achieve goals.

The major limitation of these three models is their emphasis on very specific aspects of the organization's effectiveness. The functional approach analyzes the impact of the organization's goal activities on key audiences; the structural functional approach views how organization structure develops in responding to the environment; the bargaining model detects how decision-makers use the organization's scarce resources. While each analysis points to a relevant aspect of the organization's functioning, there is nothing to suggest that improvements in these transactions will result in correspondingly greater productivity. Nonetheless, the models yield valuable insight into an organization's interaction with its environment.

Each model's conceptual framework is based on certain unfounded assumptions of organizational effectiveness. Functional theory states that an organization's effectiveness is based on four related activities—goal attainment, integration, adaptation, and pattern maintenance. Structural functionalism is equally limited in attributing a system's survival to its ability to satisfy five needs: security of the organization in relation to the environment, stability of lines of authority and communication, stability of informal relations in the organization, continuity of policy-making and homogeneity of outlook. The bargaining model defines effectiveness by the decision-maker's ability to utilize resources for specific goals.

Conclusion

The selection of an approach for evaluating organizational effectiveness depends on the information the decision-maker requires. Table 2 provides a summary of each approach. Each model provides unique information about the organization:

1. The *rational goal* approach evaluates the organization's ability to achieve its goals.
2. The *systems resource* model analyzes the decision-maker's capability to efficiently distribute resources among various subsystems' needs.
3. The *managerial process* model assesses the capability and productivity of various managerial processes— decision-making, planning, and the like—for performing goal-related tasks.
4. The *organizational development* model appraises the organization's ability to work as a team and to fit the needs of its members.
5. The *bargaining* model measures the ability of decision-makers to obtain and use resources for responding to problems important to them.
6. The *structural functional* approach tests the durability and flexibility of the organization's structure for responding to a diversity of situations and events.
7. The *functional* approach relates the usefulness of the organization's activities to its client groups.

This article's definition of organizational effectiveness avoids the debate over which models and criteria are paramount. The judgment on each model's criterion will not be seen as an assessment of its universal meaning for organizational effectiveness. The different approaches are strategies for evaluating organizational effectiveness dictated by the type of information needed by the decision-maker.

The applicability and relevance of each approach depend on the particular organizational problem that has to be resolved. The manager or researcher must determine whether the problem concerns the performance of the organization's structure or human resources or both, or its impact on the environment. The various strategies allow a wide latitude in evaluating an organization's effectiveness.

Note

1. Cooptation: ". . . the process of absorbing elements into the leadership or policy-determining structure of an organization as a means of averting threats to its stability or existence . . ." (48, p. 13).

References

1. Addison-Wesley Series on Organizational Development, including books authored by: Richard Beckhard, Warren Bennis, Robert Blake and Jane Mouton, Jay Galbraith, Paul Lawrence and Jay Lorsch, Richard Roeber, Edgar Schein, Fred Steele, and Richard Walton.
2. Barnard, Chester I. *The Functions of the Executive* (Cambridge, Mass.: Harvard University Press, 1938).
3. Bass, Bernard M. "Ultimate Criteria of Organizational Worth," in Jaisingh Ghorpade, *Assessment of Organizational Effectiveness* (Pacific Palisades, Calif.: Goodyear, 1971).
4. Bennis, Warren, "Toward a Truly Scientific Management: The Concept of Organizational Health," in *Changing Organizations* (New York: McGraw-Hill, 1966), 32–63.
5. Bennis, Warren. *Organizational Development: Its Nature, Origins and Prospects* (Reading, Mass.: Addison-Wesley, 1969), p. 15.
6. Blau, Peter. "Functional Theory," in *The Dynamics of Bureaucracy* (Chicago: University of Chicago Press, 1955), pp. 6–13.
7. Cunningham, Barton. *Evaluation Methodologies for Organizational Effectiveness: Applications of Decision Theory and Game Theory* (Ph.D. dissertation, University of Southern California, 1975).
8. Cyert, Richard M., and James G. March. *A Behavioral Theory of the Firm* (Englewood Cliffs, N.J.: Prentice-Hall, 1963).
9. Etzioni, Amitai. "Two Approaches to Organizational Analysis: A Critique and a Suggestion," *Administrative Science Quarterly,* Vol. 5 (1960), 257–278.
10. Etzioni, Amitai. *Modern Organizations* (Englewood Cliffs, N.J.: Prentice-Hall, 1964).
11. Filley, Alan C., and Robert J. House. *Managerial Process and Organizational Analysis* (Glenview, Ill.: Scott, Foresman, 1969).
12. Fremont, James Lyden. "Using Parsons' Functional Analysis in the Study of Public Organizations," *Administrative Science Quarterly,* Vol. 20 (1975), 59–70.
13. Georgiou, Petro. "The Goal Paradigm and Notes Towards a Counter Paradigm," *Administrative Science Quarterly,* Vol. 18, No. 3 (September 1973), 291–310.
14. Georgopoulos, Basil S., and Arnold S. Tannenbaum. "A Study of Organizational Effectiveness," *American Sociological Review,* Vol. 22 (1957), 534–540.
15. Ghorpade, Jaisingh. *Assessment of Organizational Effectiveness: Issues, Analysis and Readings* (Pacific Palisades, Calif.: Goodyear, 1971).
16. Gowler, Dan, and Karen Legge. "Stress, Success, and Legitimacy," in Dan Gowler and Karen Legge, *Managerial Stress* (1975), pp. 34–51.
17. Gross, Bertram H. *The State of the Nation: Social Systems Accounting* (London: Tavistock, 1966).
18. Hutchinson, John G. *Organizations: Theory and Classical Concepts* (New York: Holt, Rinehart, and Winston, 1967).

Table 2 *Summary of Organizational Effectiveness Approaches*

Organizational Effectiveness Model	Organizational Situation	Central Focus or Purpose	Assumption	Limitations
Rational Goal	Evaluation of performance of organizational structures.	Determine degree to which organizations are able to achieve their goals.	An organization is rational if its activities are organized to achieve its goals.	The model frequently shows that organizations do not reach their goals. There is also a difficulty in identifying and defining organizational goals.
Systems Resource	Evaluation of performance of organizational structures.	Determine decision-maker's efficiency in allocating and utilizing resources for fulfilling various systems needs.	An organization, in order to survive, must satisfy some basic needs: 1. Acquiring resources, 2. Interpreting the real properties of the external environment, 3. Production of outputs, 4. Maintenance of day-to-day internal activities, 5. Coordinating relationships among the various subsystems, 6. Responding to feedback, 7. Evaluating the effect of its decisions, 8. Accomplishing goals.	Measures of all systems needs are difficult to develop.
Managerial Process	Evaluation of performance of organization's human resources.	Determine capability or productivity of managers or managerial processes.	An organization can be considered rational when its various managerial processes and patterns enhance the individual's productivity or capability to obtain objectives.	Measures of productivity and capabilities pinpoint personal problems and limitations.

Model	Evaluation	Determine / Purpose	Description	Limitations
Organizational Development	Evaluation of performance of organization's human resources.	Determine organization's ability to work as a team and fit the needs of its individual members.	Work which is organized to meet people's needs as well as organizational requirements tends to produce the highest productivity.	Emphasis on the informal organization takes precedence over the formal. Individuals may be reluctant to accept interpersonal feedback supplied by the model.
Bargaining	Evaluation of impact of decisions.	Determine use or uses which decision-makers make of their resources in achieving organizational goals.	An organization is a cooperative, sometimes competitive, resource distributing system.	The model deals with a very specific part of the organization's activities.
Structural Functional	Evaluation of impact of organization's structure on performance.	Determine organization's ability to develop structures to maintain and strengthen performance.	A system's survival is equated to satisfying five basic needs: 1. Security of organization in relation to environment, 2. Stability of lines of authority and communication, 3. Stability of informal relations in organization, 4. Continuity of policy-making, 5. Homogeneity of outlook.	The model deals with a very specific part of the organization's activities.
Functional	Evaluation of impact of organizational activities.	Provide information on social consequences of organizational activities and on organization's ability to meet needs of key client groups in its environment.	Every system must define its purpose for being (goal attainment), determine resources to achieve its goals (adaptation), establish means for coordinating its efforts (integration), and reduce strains and tensions in its environment (pattern maintenance).	The model deals with a very specific part of the organization's activities.

19. Jaques, Elliot. *Equitable Payment* (Heinemann Educational Books, 1961).
20. Kahn, R. L., D. L. Wolfe, R. P. Quinn, J. D. Snoek, and R. A. Rosenthal. *Organizational Stress: Studies in Role Conflict and Ambiguity* (New York, John Wiley and Sons, 1964).
21. Katz, Daniel, and Robert L. Kahn. *The Social Psychology of Organizations* (New York: John Wiley and Sons, 1966).
22. Levine, Sol, and Paul E. White. "Exchange as a Conceptual Framework for the Study of Interorganizational Relationships," *Administrative Science Quarterly,* Vol. 5 (1960), 583–601.
23. Likert, Rensis. "Measuring Organizational Performance," *Harvard Business Review,* Vol. 36, No. 2 (March–April 1958), 41–51.
24. Likert, Rensis. "Human Resource Accounting: Building and Assessing Productive Organizations," *Personnel,* Vol. 50, No. 3 (May–June 1973), 8–24.
25. MacGregor, Douglas. *The Human Side of Enterprise* (New York: McGraw-Hill, 1960).
26. Mahoney, Thomas A. "Managerial Perceptions of Organizational Effectiveness," *Management Science,* Vol. 14 (1967), B76–B91.
27. Mahoney, Thomas A., and William Weitzel, "Managerial Models of Organizational Effectiveness," *Administrative Science Quarterly,* Vol. 14 (1969), 357–365.
28. Mannheim, Karl. *Man and Society in an Age of Reconstruction,* translated by Edward Shils (New York: Harcourt, Brace, and World, 1947), p. 53.
29. March, James G., and Herbert A. Simon. *Organizations* (New York: John Wiley and Sons, 1958).
30. March, James G., and Herbert A. Simon. "The Theory of Organizational Equilibrium," in Amitai Etzioni (Ed.), *A Sociological Reader on Complex Organizations* (New York: Holt, Rinehart, and Winston, 1969).
31. Merton, Robert K. *Social Theory and Social Structure* (New York: Free Press, 1956), pp. 195–206.
32. Mitchell, William. "The Polity and Society: A Structural-Functional Analysis," *Midwest Journal of Political Science,* Vol. 2 (1958), 403–420.
33. Mitchell, William. *Sociological Analysis and Politics: The Theories of Talcott Parsons* (New York: Prentice-Hall, 1967).
34. Mott, Paul E. *The Characteristics of Effective Organizations* (New York: Harper and Row, 1972).
35. Mouzelis, Nicos P. *Organization and Bureaucracy* (Chicago: Aldine Publishing Co., 1968).
36. Parsons, Talcott. "Suggestions for a Sociological Approach to the Theory of Organizations," *Administrative Science Quarterly,* Vol. 1 (1956), 63–85.
37. Parsons, Talcott. "General Theory in Sociology," in Robert Merton and Leonard S. Cottrell Jr. (Eds.), *Sociology Today* (New York: Basic Books, 1959), pp. 3–38.
38. Parsons, Talcott. *Structure and Process in Modern Society* (Glencoe, Ill.: Free Press, 1960).
39. Parsons, Talcott. *Politics and Social Structure* (New York: Free Press, 1969).
40. Perrow, Charles. "Goals in Complex Organizations," *American Sociological Review,* Vol. 26 (1961), 859–866.
41. Perrow, Charles. "A Framework for the Analysis of Complex Organizations," *American Sociological Review,* Vol. 32 (1967), 194–208.
42. Perrow, Charles. "Organization Goals," in *International Encylopaedia of the Social Sciences,* Vol. 11 (1968), pp. 305–316.
43. Pfiffner, John M., and Frank P. Sherwood. *Administrative Organization* (Englewood Cliffs, N.J.: Prentice-Hall, 1960).
44. Price, James L. *Organizational Effectiveness: An Inventory of Propositions* (Homewood, Ill.: Irwin, 1968).

45. Price, James L. "The Study of Organizational Effectiveness," *Sociological Quarterly*, Vol. 13 (1972), 3–15.
46. Rice, Charles E. "A Model for the Empirical Study of a Large Social Organization," *General Systems Yearbook*, Yearbook of the Society for General Systems Research, Vol. 6, pp. 101–106.
47. Selznick, Philip. "Foundations of the Theory of Organizations," *American Sociological Review*, Vol. 13 (1948), 25–35.
48. Selznick, Philip. *TVA and the Grass Roots* (Berkeley, Calif.: University of California Press, 1953).
49. Simon, Herbert A. "On the Concept of Organizational Goals," *Administrative Science Quarterly*, Vol. 9 (1964), 1–22.
50. Thompson, James D., and William J. McEwen. "Organizational Goals and Environment," *American Sociological Review*, Vol. 23 (1958), 21–33.
51. Warner, W. Keith, and A. Eugene Havens. "Goal Displacement and the Intangibility of Organizational Goals," *Administrative Science Quarterly*, Vol. 12 (1968), 539–555.
52. Webb, Ronald J. "Organizational Effectiveness and the Voluntary Organization," *Academy of Management Journal*, Vol. 17 (1974), 663–677.
53. Weber, Max. *The Theory of Social Economic Organizations*, edited with an introduction by Talcott Parsons (New York: Free Press, 1964), pp. 330–332.
54. Yuchtman, Ephraim, and Stanley E. Seashore. "A Systems Resource Approach to Organizational Effectiveness," *American Sociological Review*, Vol. 32 (December 1967), 891–903.

PART II

Individual Dimensions of Organizational Behavior

Editors' Summary Comments

*M*ost current behavioral scholars view the field of organizational behavior as consisting of a threefold framework: (1) individual behavior; (2) group behavior and interpersonal influence; and (3) the impact of organizational structure and design on performance. Each of these three framework components will be discussed in the next sections of this book, beginning with individual behavior.

Individuals in organizations differ in many respects. First, individuals differ in what attributes they bring with them to organizational life. Motives, needs, perceptions, personality, attitudes, and learning capacity are some of the crucial attributes affecting performance within organizations.

Second, individuals differ in terms of the determinants of their state of motivation. Motivation has been described differently in various theories, some of which emphasize needs, expectancies, equity, or reward contingencies. Although there is no all-encompassing model of motivation, it is known that the leader, the group, the reward system, the degree of or emphasis on change and development, and, of course, the individual's attitudes, skills, and effort expended all influence motivation.

Finally, individuals differ with respect to their reactions to the work they perform. The design of the work—relating to job content, functions, and relationships—may influence individuals quite differently depending on their needs, skills, and attitudes.

In the first article, Sheldon Zalkind and Timothy Costello discuss the importance of understanding the nature of the perceptual process in organizations. They describe how certain process components, such as stereotyping, halo effect, and projection, exist in individuals and how they influence the way we judge other workers. They point out the necessity for managers to be aware of perceptual inaccuracies and their impact on organizational performance.

A continuing topic of discussion among behavioral scientists and managers concerns the causal relationship between individual job satisfaction and performance. Does job satisfaction lead to job performance, or is the reverse true? In "The Satisfaction-Performance Controversy," Charles Greene reviews the research on this topic and argues that rewards, far more than performance, are the major factors that influence job satisfaction. Greene suggests that more attention should be given to reward systems and, particularly, establishment of appropriate performance-reward contingencies as methods to improve individual performance.

Our first *Business Week* selection, "How to Earn 'Well Pay'," discusses the ways one organization has found success in the application of reinforcement theory principles. Described are the various techniques—well pay, retro pay, safety pay, and profit sharing—associated with a reward system that can be effective in improving employee performance. The key feature of the new system is that each reward technique is tied to the employee's level of performance—the performance-contingent foundation of reinforcement theory.

Joann Lublin presents an interesting discussion of the effects on employee behavior—both within and outside the organization—of the four-day work week. While leisure time has increased—a positive feature of the new schedule—so have the tensions and strain associated with working 10-hour days.

In the last selection in this part, Edward E. Lawler III, in the article "The Individualized Organization: Problems and Promise," discusses the notion of individual differences and how organizations respond to them. Individual differences are examined in terms of pay systems, leadership, training, selection, and structuring jobs. Lawler concludes by suggesting that the shaping of organizations to people should be further developed and tested.

4

Perception:
Some Recent Research
and Implications for Administration

Sheldon S. Zalkind and Timothy W. Costello

Management practice is being increasingly influenced by behavior science research in the areas of group dynamics, problem solving and decision making, and motivation.[1] One aspect of behavior which has not been fully or consistently emphasized is the process of perception, particularly the recent work on person perception.

In this paper we shall summarize some of the findings on perception as developed through both laboratory and organizational research and point out some of the administrative and managerial implications. We discuss first some basic factors in the nature of the perceptual process including need and set; second, some research on forming impressions; third, the characteristics of the perceiver and the perceived; fourth, situational and organizational influences on perception; and finally, perceptual influences on interpersonal adjustment.

Nature of the
Perceptual Process

What are some of the factors influencing perception? In answering the question it is well to begin by putting aside the attitude of naive realism, which suggests that our perceptions simply register accurately what is "out there." It is necessary rather to consider what influences distort one's perceptions and judgments of the outside world. Some of the considerations identified in the literature up to the time of Johnson's

SOURCE: Sheldon S. Zalkind and Timothy W. Costello, "Perception: Some Recent Research and Implications for Administration," *Administrative Science Quarterly* 7, no. 2 (September 1962); 218–32. Reprinted by permission.

1944 review of the research on object perception (where distortion may be even less extreme than in person perception) led him to suggest the following about the perceiver[2]:

1. He may be influenced by considerations that he may not be able to identify, responding to cues that are below the threshold of his awareness. For example, a judgment as to the size of an object may be influenced by its color even though the perceiver may not be attending to color.
2. When required to form difficult perceptual judgments, he may respond to irrelevant cues to arrive at a judgment. For example, in trying to assess honesty, it has been shown that the other person's smiling or not smiling is used as a cue to judge his honesty.
3. In making abstract or intellectual judgments, he may be influenced by emotional factors—what is liked is perceived as correct.
4. He will weigh perceptual evidence coming from respect (or favored) sources more heavily than that coming from other sources.
5. He may not be able to identify all the factors on which his judgments are based. Even if he is aware of these factors he is not likely to realize how much weight he gives to them.

These considerations do not imply that we respond only to the subtle or irrelevant cues or to emotional factors. We often perceive on the basis of the obvious, but we are quite likely to be responding as well to the less obvious or less objective.

In 1958, Bruner, citing a series of researches, described what he called the "New Look" in perception as one in which personal determinants of the perceptual process were being stressed.[3] Bruner summarized earlier work and showed the importance of such subjective influences as needs, values, cultural background, and interests on the perceptual process. In his concept of "perceptual readiness" he described the importance of the framework or category system that the perceiver himself brings to the perceiving process.

Tapping a different vein of research, Cantril described perceiving as a "transaction" between the perceiver and the perceived, a process of negotiation in which the perceptual end product is a result both of influences within the perceiver and of characteristics of the perceived.[4]

One of the most important of the subjective factors that influence the way we perceive, identified by Bruner and others, is *set*. A study by Kelley illustrated the point.[5] He found that those who were previously led to expect to meet a "warm" person not only made different judgments about him but also behaved differently toward him, than those who were expecting a "cold" one. The fact was that they simultaneously were observing the same person in the same situation. Similarly, Strickland indicated the influence of set in determining how closely supervisors feel they must supervise their subordinates.[6] Because of prior expectation one person was trusted more than another and was thought to require less supervision than another, even though performance records were identical.

Forming Impressions of Others

The data on forming impressions is of particular importance in administration. An administrator is confronted many times with the task of forming an impression of another person—a new employee at his desk, a visiting member from the home office, a staff member he has not personally met before. His own values, needs, and expectations will play a part in the impression he forms. Are there other factors that typically operate in this area of administrative life? One of the more obvious influences is the physical appearance of the person being perceived. In a study of this point Mason was able to demonstrate that people agree on what a leader should look like and that there is no relationship between the facial characteristics agreed upon and those possessed by actual leaders.[7] In effect, we have ideas about what leaders look like and we can give examples, but we ignore the many exceptions that statistically cancel out the examples.

In the sometimes casual, always transitory situations in which one must form impressions of others it is a most natural tendency to jump to conclusions and form impressions without adequate evidence. Unfortunately, as Dailey showed, unless such impressions are based on important and relevant data, they are not likely to be accurate.[8] Too often in forming impressions the perceiver does not know what is relevant, important, or predictive of later behavior. Dailey's research furthermore supports the cliche that, accurate or not, first impressions are lasting.

Generalizing from other research in the field, Soskin described four limitations on the ability to form accurate impressions of others.[9] First, the impression is likely to be disproportionately affected by the type of situation or surroundings in which the impression is made and influenced too little by the person perceived. Thus the plush luncheon club in which one first meets a man will dominate the impression of the man himself. Secondly, although impressions are frequently based on a limited sample of the perceived person's behavior, the generalization that the perceiver makes will be sweeping. A third limitation is that the situation may not provide an opportunity for the person perceived to show behavior relevant to the traits about which impressions are formed. Casual conversation or questions, for example, provide few opportunities to demonstrate intelligence or work characteristics, yet the perceiver often draws conclusions about these from an interview. Finally, Soskin agrees with Bruner and Cantril that the impression of the person perceived may be distorted by some highly individualized reaction of the perceiver.

But the pitfalls are not yet all spelled out; it is possible to identify some other distorting influences on the process of forming impressions. Research has brought into sharp focus some typical errors, the more important being stereotyping, halo effect, projection, and perceptual defense.

Stereotyping

The word *stereotyping* was first used by Walter Lippmann in 1922 to describe bias in perceiving peoples. He wrote of "pictures in people's heads," called stereotypes, which guided (distorted) their perceptions of others. The term has long been used to describe judgments made about people on the basis of their ethnic group membership. For example, some say "Herman Schmidt [being German] is industrious." Stereotyping also predisposes judgments in many other areas of interpersonal relations. Stereotypes have developed about many types of groups, and they help to prejudice many of our perceptions about their members. Examples of stereotypes of groups other than those based on ethnic identification are bankers, supervisors, union members, poor people, rich people, and administrators. Many unverified qualities are assigned to people principally because of such group memberships.

In a research demonstration of stereotyping, Haire found that labeling a photograph as that of a management representative caused an impression to be formed of the person, different from that formed when it was labeled as that of a union leader.[10] Management and labor formed different impressions, each seeing his opposite as less dependable than his own group. In addition each side saw his own group as being better able than the opposite group to understand a point of view different from its own. For example, managers felt that other managers were better able to appreciate labor's point of view, than labor was able to appreciate management's point of view. Each had similar stereotypes of his opposite and considered the thinking, emotional characteristics, and interpersonal relations of his opposite as inferior to his own. As Stagner points out, "It is plain that unionists perceiving company officials in a stereotyped way are less efficient than would be desirable.[11] Similarly, company executives who see all labor unions as identical are not showing good judgment or discrimination."

One of the troublesome aspects of stereotypes is that they are so widespread. Finding the same stereotypes to be widely held should not tempt one to accept their accuracy. It may only mean that many people are making the same mistake. Allport has demonstrated that there need not be a "kernel of truth" in a widely held stereotype.[12] He has shown that while a prevalent stereotype of Armenians labeled them as dishonest, a credit reporting association gave them credit ratings as good as those given other ethnic groups.

Bruner and Perlmutter found that there is an international stereotype for "businessmen" and "teachers."[13] They indicated that the more widespread one's experience with diverse members of a group, the less their group membership will affect the impression formed.

An additional illustration of stereotyping is provided by Luft.[14] His research suggests that perception of personality adjustment may be influenced by stereotypes, associating adjustment with high income and maladjustment with low income.

Halo Effect

The term *halo effect* was first used in 1920 to describe a process in which a general impression which is favorable or unfavorable is used by judges to evaluate several specific traits. The "halo" in such case serves as a screen keeping the perceiver from actually seeing the trait he is judging. It has received the most attention because of its effect on rating employee performance. In the rating situation, a supervisor may single out one trait, either good or bad, and use this as the basis for his judgment of all other traits. For example, an excellent attendance record causes judgments of productivity, high quality of work, and so forth. One study in the U.S. Army showed that officers who were liked were judged more intelligent than those who were disliked, even though they had the same scores on intelligence tests.

We examine halo effect here because of its general effect on forming impressions. Bruner and Taguiri suggest that it is likely to be most extreme when we are forming impressions of traits that provide minimal cues in the individual's behavior, when the traits have moral overtones, or when the perceiver must judge traits with which he has had little experience.[15] A rather disturbing conclusion is suggested by Symonds that halo effect is more marked the more we know the acquaintance.[16]

A somewhat different aspect of the halo effect is suggested by the research of Grove and Kerr.[17] They found that knowledge that the company was in receivership caused employees to devalue the higher pay and otherwise superior working conditions of their company as compared to those in a financially secure firm.

Psychologists have noted a tendency in perceivers to link certain traits. They assume, for example, that when a person is aggressive he will also have high energy or that when a person is "warm" he will also be generous and have a good sense of humor. The logical error, as it has been called, is a special form of the halo effect and is best illustrated in the research of Asch.[18] In his study the addition of one trait to a list of traits produced a major change in the impression formed. Knowing that a person was intelligent, skillful, industrious, determined, practical, cautious, and warm led a group to judge him to be also wise, humorous, popular, and imaginative. When warm was replaced by cold, a radically different impression (beyond the difference between warm and cold) was formed. Kelley's research illustrated the same type of error.[19] This tendency is not indiscriminate; with the pair "polite—blunt," less change was found than with the more central traits of "warm—cold."

In evaluating the effect of halo on perceptual distortion we may take comfort from the work of Wishner, which showed that those traits that correlate more highly with each other are more likely to lead to a halo effect than those that are unrelated.[20]

Projection

A defense mechanism available to everyone is projection, in which one relieves one's feelings of guilt or failure by projecting blame onto someone else. Over the years the projection mechanism has been assigned various meanings. The original use of the term was concerned with the mechanism to defend oneself from unacceptable feelings. There has since been a tendency for the term to be used more broadly, meaning to ascribe or attribute any of one's own characteristics to other people. The projection mechanism concerns us here because it influences the perceptual process. An early study by Murray illustrates its effect.[21] After playing a dramatic game, "Murder," his subjects attributed much more maliciousness to people whose photographs were judged than did a control group which had not played the game. The current emotional state of the perceiver tended to influence his perceptions of others; i.e., frightened perceivers judged people to be frightening. More recently, Feshback and Singer revealed further dynamics of the process.[22] In their study subjects who had been made fearful judged a stimulus person (presented in a moving picture) as both more fearful and more aggressive than did nonfearful perceivers. These authors were able to demonstrate further that the projection mechanism at work here was reduced when their subjects were encouraged to admit and talk about their fears.

Sears provides an illustration of a somewhat different type of projection and its effect on perception.[23] In his study projection is seeing our own undesirable personality characteristics in other people. He demonstrated that people high in such traits as stinginess, obstinacy, and disorderliness, tended to rate others much higher on these traits than did those who were low in these undesirable characteristics. The tendency to project was particularly marked among subjects who had the least insight into their own personalities.

Research thus suggests that our perceptions may characteristically be distorted by emotions we are experiencing or traits that we possess. Placed in the administrative setting the research would suggest, for example, that a manager frightened by rumored organizational changes might not only judge others to be more frightened than they were, but also assess various policy decisions as more frightening than they were. Or a general foreman lacking insight into his own incapacity to delegate might be oversensitive to this trait in his superiors.

Perceptual Defense

Another distorting influence, which has been called perceptual defense, has also been demonstrated by Haire and Grunes to be a source of error.[24] In their research they ask, in effect, "Do we put blinders on to defend ourselves from seeing those events which might disturb us?" The concept of perceptual defense offers an excellent description of perceptual distortion at work and demonstrates that when confronted with a fact inconsistent with a stereotype already held by a person, the perceiver is able to distort the data in such a way as to eliminate the inconsistency. Thus, by perceiving inaccurately, he defends himself from having to change his stereotypes.

Characteristics of Perceiver and Perceived

We have thus far been talking largely about influences on the perceptual process without specific regard to the perceiver and his characteristics. Much recent research has tried to identify some characteristics of the perceiver and their influence on the perception of other people.

The Perceiver

A thread that would seem to tie together many current findings is the tendency to use oneself as the norm or standard by which one perceives or judges others. If we examine current research, certain conclusions are suggested:

1. *Knowing oneself makes it easier to see others accurately.* Norman showed that when one is aware of what his own personal characteristics are he makes fewer errors in perceiving

others.[25] Weingarten has shown that people with insight are less likely to view the world in black-and-white terms and to give extreme judgments about others.[26]

2. *One's own characteristics affect the characteristics he is likely to see in others.* Secure people (compared with insecure) tend to see others as warm rather than cold, as was shown by Bossom and Maslow.[27] The extent of one's own sociability influences the degree of importance one gives to the sociability of other people when one forms impressions of them.[28] The person with "authoritarian" tendencies is more likely to view others in terms of power and is less sensitive to the psychological or personality characteristics of other people than is a nonauthoritarian.[29] The relatively few categories one uses in describing other people tend to be those one uses in describing oneself.[30] Thus traits which are important to the perceiver will be used more when he forms impressions of others. He has certain constant tendencies, both with regard to using certain categories in judging others and to the amount of weight given to these categories.[31]

3. *The person who accepts himself is more likely to be able to see favorable aspects of other people.*[32] This relates in part to the accuracy of his perceptions. If the perceiver accepts himself as he is, he widens his range of vision in seeing others; he can look at them and be less likely to be very negative or critical. In those areas in which he is more insecure, he sees more problems in other people.[33] We are more likely to like others who have traits we accept in ourselves and reject those who have the traits which we do not like in ourselves.[34]

4. *Accuracy in perceiving others is not a single skill.* While there have been some variations in the findings, as Gage has shown, some consistent results do occur.[35] The perceiver tends to interpret the feelings others have about him in terms of his feelings towards them.[36] One's ability to perceive others accurately may depend on how sensitive one is to differences between people and also to the norms (outside of oneself) for judging them.[37] Thus, as Taft has shown, the ability to judge others does not seem to be a single skill.[38]

Possibly the results in these four aspects of person perception can be viewed most constructively in connection with earlier points on the process of perception. The administrator (or any other individual) who wishes to perceive someone else accurately must look at the other person, not at himself. The things that he looks at in someone else are influenced by his own traits. But if he knows his own traits, he can be aware that they provide a frame of reference for him. His own traits help to furnish the categories that he will use in perceiving others. His characteristics, needs, and values can partly limit his vision and his awareness of the differences between others. The question one could ask when viewing another is:

"Am I looking at him, and forming my impression of his behavior in the situation, or am I just comparing him with myself?"

There is the added problem of being set to observe the personality traits in another which the perceiver does not accept in himself, e.g., being somewhat autocratic. At the same time he may make undue allowances in others for those of his own deficiencies which do not disturb him but might concern some people, e.g., not following prescribed procedures.

The Perceived

Lest we leave the impression that it is only the characteristics of the perceiver that stand between him and others in his efforts to know them, we turn now to some characteristics of the person being perceived which raise problems in perception. It is possible to demonstrate, for example, that the status of the person perceived is a variable influencing judgments about his behavior. Thibaut and Riecken have shown that even though two people behave in identical fashion, status differences between them cause a perceiver to assign different motivations for the behavior.[39] Concerning cooperativeness, they found that high status persons are judged as wanting to cooperate and low status persons as having to cooperate. In turn, more liking is shown for the person of high status than for the person of low status. Presumably, more credit is given when the boss says, "Good morning," to us than when a subordinate says the same thing.

Bruner indicated that we use categories to simplify our perceptual activities. In the administrative situation, status is one type of category, and role provides another. Thus the remarks of Mr. Jones in the sales department are perceived differently from those of Smith in the purchasing department, although both may say the same thing. Also, one who knows Jones's role in the organization will perceive his behavior differently from one who does not know Jones's role. The process of categorizing on the basis of roles is similar to, if not identical with, the stereotyping process described earlier.

Visibility of the traits judged is also an important variable influencing the accuracy of perception.[40] Visibility will depend, for example, on how free the other person feels to express the trait. It has been demonstrated that we are more accurate in judging people who like us than people who dislike us. The explanation suggested is that most people in our society feel constraint in showing their dislike, and therefore the cues are less visible.

Some traits are not visible simply because they provide few external cues for their presence. Loyalty, for example, as opposed to level of energy, provides few early signs for observation. Even honesty cannot be seen in the situations in which most impressions are formed. As obvious as these comments might be, in forming impressions many of us nevertheless continue to judge the presence of traits which are not really visible. Frequently the practical situation demands judgments, but we should recognize the frail reeds upon which we are leaning and be prepared to observe further and revise our judgments with time and closer acquaintance.

Situational Influences on Perception

Some recent research clearly points to the conclusion that the whole process of interpersonal perception is, at least in part, a function of the *group* (or interpersonal) context in which the perception occurs. Much of the research has important theoretical implications for a psychology of interpersonal relations. In addition, there are some suggestions of value for administrators. It is possible to identify several characteristics of the interpersonal climate which have direct effect on perceptual accuracy. As will be noted, these are characteristics which can be known, and in some cases controlled, in administrative settings.

Bieri provides data for the suggestion that when people are given an opportunity to interact in a friendly situation, they tend to see others as similar to themselves.[41] Applying his suggestion to the administrative situation, we can rationalize as follows: Some difficulties of administrative practice grow out of beliefs that different interest groups in the organization are made up of different types of people. Obviously once we believe that people in other groups are different, we will be predisposed to see the differences. We can thus find, from Bieri's and from Rosenbaum's work, an administrative approach for attacking the problem.[42] If we can produce an interacting situation which is cooperative rather than competitive, the likelihood of seeing other people as similar to ourselves is increased.

Exline's study adds some other characteristics of the social context which may influence perception.[43] Paraphrasing his conclusions to adapt them to the administrative scene, we can suggest that when a committee group is made up of congenial members who are willing to continue work in the same group, their perceptions of the goal-directed behavior of fellow committee members will be more accurate, although observations of purely personal behavior (as distinguished from goal-directed behavior) may be less accurate.[44] The implications for setting up committees and presumably other interacting work groups seem clear: Do not place together those with a past history of major personal clashes. If they must be on the same committee, each must be helped to see that the other is working toward the same goal.

An interesting variation in this area of research is the suggestion from Ex's work that perceptions will be more influenced or swayed by relatively unfamiliar people in the group than by those who are intimates.[45] The concept needs further research, but it provides the interesting suggestion that we may give more credit to strangers for having knowledge, since we do not know, than we do to our intimates whose backgrounds and limitations we feel we do know.

The *organization*, and one's place in it, may also be viewed as the context in which perceptions take place. A study by Dearborn and Simon illustrates this point.[46] Their data support the hypothesis that the administrator's perceptions will often be limited to those aspects of a situation which relate specifically to his own department, despite an attempt to influence him away from such selectivity.

Perception of self among populations at different levels in the hierarchy also offers an opportunity to judge the influence of organizational context on perceptual activity. Porter's study of the self-descriptions of managers and line workers indicated that both groups saw themselves in different terms, which corresponded to their positions in the organization's hierarchy.[47] He stated that managers used leadership-type traits (e.g., inventive) to describe themselves, while line workers used follower-type terms (e.g., cooperative). The question of which comes first must be asked: Does the manager see himself this way because of his current position in the organization? Or is this self-picture an expression of a more enduring personal characteristic that helped bring the manager to his present position? This study does not answer that question, but it does suggest to an administrator the need to be aware of the possibly critical relationship between one's hierarchical role and self-perception.

Perceptual Influences on Interpersonal Adjustment

Throughout this paper, we have examined a variety of influences on the perceptual process. There has been at least the inference that the operations of such influences on perception would in turn affect behavior that would follow. Common-sense judgment suggests that being able to judge other people accurately facilitates smooth and effective interpersonal adjustments. Nevertheless, the relationship between perception and consequent behavior is itself in need of direct analysis. Two aspects may be identified: (1) the effect of accuracy of perception on subsequent behavior; and (2) the effect of the duration of the relationship and the opportunity for experiencing additional cues.

First then, from the applied point of view, we can ask a crucial question: Is there a relationship between accuracy of social perception and adjustment to others? While the question might suggest a quick affirmative answer, research findings are inconsistent. Steiner attempted to resolve some of these inconsistencies by stating that accuracy may have an effect on interaction under the following conditions: when the interacting persons are cooperatively motivated, when the behavior which is accurately perceived is relevant to the activities of these persons, and when members are free to alter their behavior on the basis of their perceptions.[48]

Where the relationship provides opportunity only to form an impression, a large number of subjective factors, i.e., set, stereotypes, projections, etc., operate to create an early impression, which is frequently erroneous. In more enduring relationships a more balanced appraisal may result as increased interaction provides additional cues for judgment. In his study of the acquaintance process, Newcomb showed that while early perception of favorable traits caused attraction to the perceived person, over a four-month period the early cues for judging favorable traits became less influential.[49] With time, a much broader basis was used which included comparisons with others with whom one had established relationships. Such findings suggest that the warnings about perceptual inaccuracies implicit in the earlier sections of this paper apply with more force to the short-term process of impression forming than to relatively extended acquaintance-building relationships. One could thus hope that rating an employee after a year of service would be a more objective performance than appraising him in a selection interview—a hope that would be fulfilled only when the rater had provided himself with opportunities for broadening the cues heeded in forming his first impressions.

Summary

Two principal suggestions which increase the probability of more effective administrative action emerge from the research data. One suggestion is that the administrator be continuously aware of the intricacies of the perceptual process and thus be warned to avoid arbitrary and categorical judgments and to seek reliable evidence before judgments are made. A second suggestion grows out of the first: increased accuracy in one's self-perception can make possible the flexibility to seek evidence and to shift position as time provides additional evidence.

Nevertheless, not every effort designed to improve perceptual accuracy will bring about such accuracy. The dangers of too complete reliance on formal training for perceptual accuracy are suggested in a study by Crow.[50] He found that a group of senior medical students were somewhat less accurate in their perceptions of others after a period of training in physician-patient relationships than were an untrained control group. The danger is that a little learning encourages the perceiver to respond with increased sensitivity to individual differences without making it possible for him to gauge the real meaning of the differences he has seen.

Without vigilance to perceive accurately and to minimize as far as possible the subjective approach in perceiving others, effective administration is handicapped. On the other hand, research would not support the conclusion that perceptual distortions will not occur simply because the administrator says he will try to be objective. The administrator or manager will have to work hard to avoid seeing only what he wants to see and to guard against fitting everything into what he is set to see.

We are not yet sure of the ways in which training for perceptual accuracy can best be accomplished, but such training cannot be ignored. In fact, one can say that one of the important tasks of administrative science is to design research to test various training procedures for increasing perceptual accuracy.

Notes

1. Portions of this article were originally presented at the Eighth Annual International Meeting of The Institute of Management Sciences in Brussels, August, 1961.
2. D. M. Johnson, "A Systematic Treatment of Judgment," *Psychological Bulletin* 42 (1945); 193–224.
3. J. S. Bruner, "Social Psychology and Perception," in E. Maccoby, T. Newcomb, and E. Hartley, eds., *Readings in Social Psychology,* 3d ed, (New York, 1958), pp. 85–94.
4. H. Cantril, "Perception and Interpersonal Relations," *American Journal of Psychiatry* 114 (1957); 119–26.
5. H. H. Kelley, "The warm-cold variable in first impressions of persons, *Journal of Personality* 18 (1950); 431–39.

6. L. H. Strickland, "Surveillance and Trust," *Journal of Personality* 26 (1958); 200–215.
7. D. J. Mason, "Judgments of Leadership Based upon Physiognomic Cues," *Journal of Abnormal and Social Psychology* 54 (1957); 273–74.
8. C. A. Dailey, "The Effects of Premature Conclusion upon the Acquisition of Understanding of a Person," *Journal of Psychology* 33 (1952): 133–52.
9. W. E. Soskin, "Influence of Information on Bias in Social Perception," *Journal of Personality* 22 (1953): 118–27.
10. M. Haire, "Role Perceptions in Labor-Management Relations: An Experimental Approach," *Industrial and Labor Relations Review* 8 (1955): 204–16.
11. R. Stagner, *Psychology of Industrial Conflict* (New York, 1956), p. 35.
12. G. Allport, *Nature of Prejudice* (Cambridge, Mass., 1954).
13. J. S. Bruner and H. V. Perlmutter, "Compatriot and Foreigner: A Study of Impression Formation in Three Countries," *Journal of Abnormal and Social Psychology* 55 (1957): 253–60.
14. J. Luft, "Monetary Value and the Perception of Persons," *Journal of Social Psychology* 46 (1957): 245–51.
15. J. S. Bruner and A. Taguiri, "The Perception of People," ch. xvii in G. Lindzey, ed., *Handbook of Social Psychology* (Cambridge, Mass., 1954).
16. P. M. Symonds, "Notes on Rating," *Journal of Applied Psychology* 7 (1925): 188–95.
17. B. A. Grove and W. A. Kerr, "Specific Evidence on Origin of Halo Effect in Measurement of Morale," *Journal of Social Psychology* 34 (1951): 165–70.
18. S. Asch, "Forming Impressions of Persons," *Journal of Abnormal and Social Psychology* 60 (1946): 258–90.
19. Kelley, "The Warm-Cold Variable in First Impressions of Persons."
20. J. Wishner, "Reanalysis of 'Impressions of Personality,'" *Psychology Review* 67 (1960): 96–112.
21. H. A. Murray, "The Effect of Fear upon Estimates of the Maliciousness of Other Personalities." *Journal of Social Psychology* 4 (1933): 310–29.
22. S. Feshback and R. D. Singer, "The Effects of Fear Arousal upon Social Perception," *Journal of Abnormal and Social Psychology* 55 (1957): 283–88.
23. R. R. Sears, "Experimental Studies of Perception, 1. Attribution of Traits," *Journal of Social Psychology* 7 (1936): 151–63.
24. M. Haire and W. F. Grunes, "Perceptual Defenses: Processes Protecting an Original Perception of Another Personality," *Human Relations* 3 (1958): 403–12.
25. R. D. Norman, "The Interrelationships among Acceptance-Rejection, Self-Other Identity, Insight into Self, and Realistic Perception of Others," *Journal of Social Psychology* 37 (1953): 205–35.
26. E. Weingarten, "A Study of Selective Perception in Clinical Judgment," *Journal of Personality* 17 (1949): 369–400.
27. J. Bossom and A. H. Maslow, "Security of Judges as a Factor in Impressions of Warmth in Others," *Journal of Abnormal and Social Psychology* 55 (1957): 147–48.
28. D. T. Benedetti and J. G. Hill, "A Determiner of the Centrality of a Trait in Impression Formation," *Journal of Abnormal and Social Psychology* 60 (1960): 278–79.
29. E. E. Jones, "Authoritarianism as a Determinant of First-Impressions Formation," *Journal of Personality* 23 (1954): 107–27.
30. A. H. Hastorf, S. A. Richardson, and S. M. Dornbusch, "The Problem of Relevance in the Study of Person Perception," in R. Taguiri and L. Petrullo, *Person Perception and Interpersonal Behavior* (Stanford, Calif., 1958).
31. L. J. Cronbach, "Processes Affecting Scores on 'Understanding of Others' and 'Assumed Similarity,'" *Psychological Bulletin* 52 (1955): 177–93.

32. K. T. Omwake, "The Relation Between Acceptance of Self and Acceptance of Others Shown by Three Personality Inventories," *Journal of Consulting Psychology* 18 (1954): 443–46.
33. Weingarten, "A Study of Selective Perception in Clinical Judgment."
34. R. M. Lundy, W. Katovsky, R. L. Cromwell, and D. J. Shoemaker, "Self Acceptability and Descriptions of Sociometric Choices," *Journal of Abnormal and Social Psychology* 51 (1955): 260–62.
35. N. L. Gage, "Accuracy of Social Perception and Effectiveness in Interpersonal Relationships," *Journal of Personality* 22 (1953): 128–41.
36. R. Taguiri, J. S. Bruner, and R. Blake, "On the Relation between Feelings and Perceptions of Feelings among Members of Small Groups," in Maccoby *et al, Readings in Social Psychology.*
37. U. Bronfenbrenner, J. Harding, and M. Gallway, "The Measurement of Skill in Social Perception," in H. L. McClelland, D. C. Baldwin, U. Bronfenbrenner, and F. L. Strodtbeck, eds., *Talent and Society* (Princeton, N.J., 1958), pp. 29–111.
38. R. Taft, "The Ability to Judge People," *Psychological Bulletin* 52 (1955): 1–21.
39. J. W. Thibaut and H. W. Riecken, "Some Determinants and Consequences of the Perception of Social Causality," *Journal of Personality* 24 (1955): 113–33.
40. Bruner and Taguiri, "The Perception of People."
41. J. Bieri, "Change in Interpersonal Perception Following Interaction," *Journal of Abnormal and Social Psychology* 48 (1953): 61–66.
42. M. E. Rosenbaum, "Social Perception and the Motivational Structure of Interpersonal Relations," *Journal of Abnormal and Social Psychology* 59 (1959): 130–33.
43. R. V. Exline, "Interrelations among Two Dimensions of Sociometric Status, Group Congeniality and Accuracy of Social Perception," *Sociometry* 23 (1960): 85–101.
44. R. V. Exline, "Group Climate as a Factor in the Relevance and Accuracy of Social Perception," *Journal of Abnormal and Social Psychology,* 55 (1957): 382–88.
45. J. Ex, "The Nature of the Relation Between Two Persons and the Degree of Their Influence on Each Other," *Acta Psychologica* 17 (1960): 39–54.
46. D. C. Dearborn and H. A. Simon, "Selective Perception: A Note on the Departmental Identifications of Executives," *Sociometry* 21 (1958): 140–44.
47. L. W. Porter, "Differential Self-Perceptions of Management Personnel and Line Workers," *Journal of Applied Psychology* 42 (1958): 105–9.
48. I. Steiner, "Interpersonal Behavior as Influenced by Accuracy of Social Perception," *Psychological Review* 52 (1955): 268–75.
49. T. M. Newcomb, "The Perception of Interpersonal Attraction," *American Psychologist* II (1956): 575–86, and *The Acquaintance Process* (New York, 1961).
50. W. J. Crow, "Effect of Training on Interpersonal Perception," *Journal of Abnormal and Social Psychology* 55 (1957): 355–59.

Satisfaction-Performance Controversy

Charles N. Greene

*A*s Ben walked by smiling on the way to his office Ben's boss remarked to a friend: "Ben really enjoys his job and that's why he's the best damn worker I ever had. And that's reason enough for me to keep Ben happy." The friend replied: "No, you're wrong! Ben likes his job because he does it so well. If you want to make Ben happy, you ought to do whatever you can to help him further improve his performance."

Four decades after the initial published investigation on the satisfaction-performance relationship, these two opposing views are still the subject of controversy on the part of both practitioners and researchers. Several researchers have concluded, in fact, that "there is no present technique for determining the cause-and-effect of satisfaction and performance." Current speculations, reviewed by Schwab and Cummings, however, still imply at least in theory that satisfaction and performance are causally related although, in some cases, the assumed cause has become the effect, and, in others, the relationship between these two variables is considered to be a function of a third or even additional variables.[1]

Theory and Evidence

'Satisfaction Causes Performance'

At least three fundamental theoretical propositions underlie the research and writing in this area. The first and most pervasive stems from the human relations movement with its emphasis on the well-being of the individual at work. In the years following the investigations at Western

SOURCE: Charles N. Greene, "The Satisfaction-Performance Controversy," *Business Horizons* 15 (1972): 31–41. Copyright 1972 by the Foundation for the School of Business at Indiana University. Reprinted by permission.

Electric, a number of studies were conducted to identify correlates of high and low job satisfaction. The interest in satisfaction, however, came about not so much as a result of concern for the individual as concern with the presumed linkage of satisfaction with performance.

According to this proposition (simply stated and still frequently accepted), the degree of job satisfaction felt by an employee determines his performance, that is, satisfaction causes performance. This proposition has theoretical roots, but it also reflects the popular belief that "a happy worker is a productive worker" and the notion that "all good things go together." It is far more pleasant to increase an employee's happiness than to deal directly with his performance whenever a performance problem exists. Therefore, acceptance of the satisfaction-causes-performance proposition as a solution makes good sense, particularly for the manager because it represents the path of least resistance. Furthermore, high job satisfaction and high performance are both good, and, therefore, they ought to be related to one another.

At the theoretical level, Vroom's valence-force model is a prime example of theory-based support of the satisfaction-causes-performance case.[2] In Vroom's model, job satisfaction reflects the valence (attractiveness) of the job. It follows from his theory that the force exerted on an employee to remain on the job is an increasing function of the valence of the job. Thus, satisfaction should be negatively related to absenteeism and turnover, and, at the empirical level, it is.

Whether or not this valence also leads to higher performance, however, is open to considerable doubt. Vroom's review of twenty-three field studies, which investigated the relationship between satisfaction and performance, revealed an insignificant median static correlation of 0.14, that is, satisfaction explained less than 2 percent of the variance in performance. Thus, the insignificant results and absence of tests of the causality question fail to provide support for this proposition.

'Performance Causes Satisfaction'

More recently, a second theoretical proposition has been advanced. According to this view, best represented by the work of Porter and Lawler, satisfaction is considered not as a cause but as an effect of performance, that is, performance causes satisfaction.[3] Differential performance determines rewards which, in turn, produce variance in satisfaction. In other words, rewards constitute a necessary intervening variable and, thus, satisfaction is considered to be a function of performance-related rewards.

At the empirical level, two recent studies, each utilizing time-lag correlations, lend considerable support to elements of this proposition. Bowen and Siegel, and Greene reported finding relatively strong correlations between performance and satisfaction expressed later (the performance-causes-satisfaction condition), which were significantly higher than the low correlations between satisfaction and performance which occurred during the subsequent period (the "satisfaction-causes-performance" condition).[4]

In the Greene study, significant correlations were obtained between performance and rewards granted subsequently and between rewards and subsequent satisfaction. Thus, Porter and Lawler's predictions that differential performance determines rewards and that rewards produce variance in satisfaction were upheld.

'Rewards' as a Causal Factor

Closely related to Porter and Lawler's predictions is a still more recent theoretical position, which considers both satisfaction and performance to be functions of rewards. In this view, rewards cause satisfaction, and rewards that are based on current performance cause affect subsequent performance.

According to this proposition, formulated by Cherrington, Reitz, and Scott from the contributions of reinforcement theorists, there is no inherent relationship between satisfaction and performance.[5] The results of their experimental investigation strongly support their predictions. The rewarded subjects reported significantly greater satisfaction than did the unrewarded subjects. Furthermore, when rewards (monetary bonuses, in this case) were granted on the basis of performance, the subjects' performance was significantly higher than that of subjects whose rewards were unrelated to their performance. For example, they found that when a low performer was not rewarded, he expressed dissatisfaction but that his later performance improved. On the other hand, when a low performer was in fact rewarded for his low performance, he expressed high satisfaction but continued to perform at a low level.

The same pattern of findings was revealed in the case of the high performing subjects with one exception: the high performer who was not rewarded expressed dissatisfaction, as expected, and his performance on the next trial declined significantly. The correlation between satisfaction and subsequent performance, excluding the effects of rewards, was 0.000, that is, satisfaction does *not* cause improved performance.

A recent field study, which investigated the source and direction of causal influence in satisfaction-performance relationships, supports the Cherrington-Reitz-Scott findings.[6] Merit pay was identified as a cause of satisfaction and, contrary to some current beliefs, was found to be a significantly more frequent source of satisfaction than dissatisfaction. The results of this study further revealed equally significant relationships between (1) merit pay and subsequent performance and (2) current performance and subsequent merit pay. Given the Cherrington-Reitz-Scott findings that rewards based on current performance cause improved subsequent performance, these results do suggest the possibility of reciprocal causation.

In other words, merit pay based on current performance probably caused variations in subsequent performance, and the company in this field study evidently was relatively successful in implementing its policy of granting salary increases to an employee on the basis of his performance (as evidenced by the significant relationship found between current performance and subsequent merit pay). The company's use of a fixed (annual) merit increase schedule probably obscured some of the stronger reinforcing effects of merit pay on performance.

Unlike the Cherrington-Reitz-Scott controlled experiment, the fixed merit increase schedule precluded (as it does in most organizations) giving an employee a monetary reward immediately after he successfully performed a major task. This constraint undoubtedly reduced the magnitude of the relationship between merit pay and subsequent performance.

Implications for Management

These findings have several apparent but nonetheless important implications. For the manager who desires to enhance the satisfaction of his subordinates (perhaps for the purpose of reducing turnover), the implication of the finding that "rewards cause satisfaction" is self-evident. If, on the other hand, the manager's interest in his subordinates' satisfaction arises from his desire to increase their performance, the consistent rejection of the satisfaction-causes-performance proposition has an equally clear implication: increasing subordinates' satisfaction will have no effect on their performance.

The finding that rewards based on current performance affect subsequent performance does, however, offer a strategy for increasing subordinates' performance. Unfortunately, it is not the path of least resistance for the manager. Granting differential rewards on the basis of differences in his subordinates' performance will cause his subordinates to express varying degrees of satisfaction or dissatisfaction. The manager, as a result, will soon find himself in the uncomfortable position of having to successfully defend his basis for evaluation or having to put up with dissatisfied subordinates until their performance improves or they leave the organization.

The benefits of this strategy, however, far outweigh its liabilities. In addition to its positive effects on performance, this strategy provides equity since the most satisfied employees are the rewarded high performers and, for the same reason, it also facilitates the organization's efforts to retain its most productive employees.

If these implications are to be considered as prescriptions for managerial behavior, one is tempted at this point to conclude that all a manager need do in order to increase his subordinates' performance is to accurately appraise their work and then reward them accordingly. However, given limited resources for rewards and knowledge of appraisal techniques, it is all too apparent that the manager's task here is not easy.

Moreover, the relationship between rewards and performance is often not as simple or direct as one would think, for at least two reasons. First, there are other causes of performance that may have a more direct bearing on a particular problem. Second is the question of the appropriateness of the reward itself, that is, what is rewarding for one person may not be for another. In short, a manager also needs to consider other potential causes of performance and range of rewards in coping with any given performance problem.

Nonmotivational Factors

The element of performance that relates most directly to the discussion thus far is effort, that element which links rewards to performance. The employee who works hard usually does so because of the rewards or avoidance of punishment that he associates with good work. He believes that the magnitude of the reward he will receive is contingent on his performance and, further, that his performance is a function of how hard he works. Thus, effort reflects the motivational aspect of performance. There are, however, other nonmotivational considerations that can best be considered prior to examining ways by which a manager can deal with the motivational problem.

Direction Suppose, for example, that an employee works hard at his job, yet his performance is inadequate. What can his manager do to alleviate the problem? The manager's first action should be to identify the cause. One likely possibility is what can be referred to as a "direction problem."

Several years ago, the Minnesota Vikings' defensive end, Jim Marshall, very alertly gathered up the opponent's fumble and then, with obvious effort and delight, proceeded to carry the ball some fifty yards into the wrong end zone. This is a direction problem in its purest sense. For the employee working under more usual circumstances, a direction problem generally stems from his lack of understanding of what is expected of him or what a job well done looks like. The action indicated to alleviate this problem is to clarify or define in detail for the employee the requirements of his job. The manager's own leadership style may also be a factor. In dealing with an employee with a direction problem, the manager needs to exercise closer supervision and to initiate structure or focus on the task, as opposed to emphasizing consideration or his relations with the employee.[7]

In cases where this style of behavior is repugnant or inconsistent with the manager's own leadership inclinations, an alternative approach is to engage in mutual goal setting or management-by-objectives techniques with the employee. Here, the necessary structure can be established, but at the subordinate's own initiative, thus creating a more participative atmosphere. This approach, however, is not free of potential problems. The employee is more likely to make additional undetected errors before his performance improves, and the approach is more time consuming than the more direct route.

Ability What can the manager do if the actions he has taken to resolve the direction problem fail to result in significant improvements in performance? His subordinate still exerts a high level of effort and understands what is expected of him—yet he continues to perform poorly. At this point, the manager may begin, justifiably so, to doubt his subordinate's ability to perform the job. When this doubt does arise, there are three useful questions, suggested by Mager and Pipe, to which the manager should find answers before he treats the problem as an ability deficiency: Could the subordinate do it if he really had to? Could he do it if his life depended on it? Are his present abilities adequate for the desired performance?[8]

If the answers to the first two questions are negative, then the answer to the last question also will be negative, and the obvious conclusion is that an ability deficiency does, in fact, exist. Most managers, upon reaching this conclusion, begin to develop some type of formal training experience for the subordinate. This is unfortunate and frequently wasteful. There is probably a simpler, less expensive solution. Formal training is usually required only when the individual has never done the particular job in question or when there is no way in which the ability requirement in question can be eliminated from his job.

If the individual formerly used the skill but now uses it only rarely, systematic practice will usually overcome the deficiency without formal training. Alternatively, the job can be changed or simplified so that the impaired ability is no longer crucial to successful performance. If, on the other hand, the individual once had the skill and still rather frequently is able to practice it, the manager should consider providing him greater feedback concerning the outcome of his efforts. The subordinate may not be aware of the deficiency and its effect on his performance, or he may no longer know how to perform the job. For example, elements of his job or the relationship between his job and other jobs may have changed, and he simply is not aware of the change.

Where formal training efforts are indicated, systematic analysis of the job is useful for identifying the specific behaviors and skills that are closely related with successful task performance and that, therefore, need to be learned. Alternatively, if the time and expense associated with job analysis are considered excessive, the critical incidents approach can be employed toward the same end.[9] Once training needs have been identified and the appropriate training technique employed, the manager can profit by asking himself one last question: "Why did the ability deficiency develop in the first place?"

Ultimately, the answer rests with the selection and placement process. Had a congruent man-job match been attained at the outset, the ability deficiency would have never presented itself as a performance problem.[10]

Performance Obstacles When inadequate performance is not the result of a lack of effort, direction, or ability, there is still another potential cause that needs attention. There may be obstacles beyond the subordinate's control that interfere with his performance. "I can't do it" is not always an alibi; it may be a real description of the problem. Performance obstacles can take many forms to the extent that their number, independent of a given situation, is almost unlimited.

However, the manager might look initially for some of the more common potential obstacles, such as a lack of time or conflicting demands on the subordinate's time, inadequate work facilities, restrictive policies or "right ways of doing it" that inhibit performance, lack of authority, insufficient information about other activities that affect the job, and lack of cooperation from others with whom he must work.

An additional obstacle, often not apparent to the manager from his face-to-face interaction with a subordinate, is the operation of group goals and norms that run counter to organizational objectives. Where the work group adheres to norms of restricting productivity, for example, the subordinate will similarly restrict his own performance to the extent that he identifies more closely with the group than with management.

Most performance obstacles can be overcome either by removing the obstacle or by changing the subordinate's job so that the obstacle no longer impinges on his performance. When the obstacle stems from group norms, however, a very different set of actions is required. Here, the actions that should be taken are the same as those that will be

Figure 1   Rewards and Effort

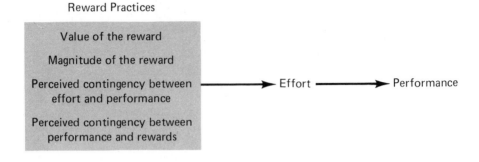

considered shortly in coping with lack of effort on the part of the individual. In other words, the potential causes of the group's lack of effort are identical to those that apply to the individual.

The Motivational Problem

Thus far, performance problems have been considered in which effort was not the source of the performance discrepancy. While reward practices constitute the most frequent and direct cause of effort, there are, however, other less direct causes. Direction, ability, and performance obstacles may indirectly affect effort through their direct effects on performance. For example, an individual may perform poorly because of an ability deficiency and, as a result, exert little effort on the job. Here, the ability deficiency produced low performance, and the lack of effort on the individual's part resulted from his expectations of failure. Thus, actions taken to alleviate the ability deficiency should result in improved performance and, subsequently, in higher effort.

Effort is that element of performance which links rewards to performance. The relationship between rewards and effort is, unfortunately, not a simple one. As indicated in the figure, effort is considered not only as a function of the (1) value and (2) magnitude of reward, but also as a function of the (3) individual's perceptions of the extent to which greater effort on his part will lead to higher performance, and (4) that his high performance, in turn, will lead to rewards. Therefore, a manager who is confronted with a subordinate who exerts little effort must consider these four attributes of reward practices in addition to the more indirect, potential causes of the lack of effort. The key issues in coping with a subordinate's lack of effort—the motivation problem—or in preventing such a problem from arising involve all four of the attributes of rewards just identified.[11]

Appropriateness of the Reward   Regardless of the extent to which the individual believes that hard work determines his performance and subsequent rewards, he will obviously put forth little effort unless he *values* those rewards—that is, the rewards must have value in terms of his own need state. An accountant, for example, may value recognition from his boss, an opportunity to increase the scope of his job, or a salary increase; however, it is unlikely that he will place the same value on a ten-year supply of budget forms.

In other words, there must be consistency between the reward and what the individual needs or wants and recognition that there are often significant differences among individuals in what they consider rewarding. Similarly, individuals differ in terms of the *magnitude* of that valued reward they consider to be positively reinforcing. A 7 or 8 percent salary increase may motivate one person but have little or no positive effect on another person at the same salary level. Furthermore, a sizable reward in one situation might be considered small by the same individual in a different set of circumstances.

These individual differences, particularly those concerning what rewards are valued, raise considerable question about the adequacy of current organization reward systems, virtually none of which make any formal recognition of individual differences. Lawler, for example, has suggested that organizations could profit greatly by introducing "cafeteria-style" wage plans.[12] These plans allow an employee to select any combination of cash and fringe benefits he desires. An employee would be assigned "X" amount in compensation, which he may then divide up among a number of fringe benefits and cash. This practice would ensure that employees receive only those fringe benefits they value; from the organization's point of view, it would reduce the waste in funds allocated by the organization to fringe benefits not valued by its members. As a personal strategy, however, the manager could profit even more by extending Lawler's plan to include the entire range of nonmonetary rewards.

Rewards can be classified into two broad categories, extrinsic and intrinsic. Extrinsic rewards are those external to the job or in the context of the job, such as job security, improved working facilities, praise from one's boss, status symbols, and, of course, pay, including fringe benefits. Intrinsic rewards, on the other hand, are rewards that can be associated directly with the "doing of the job," such as a sense of accomplishment after successful performance, opportunities for advancement, increased responsibility, and work itself.

Thus, intrinsic rewards flow immediately and directly from the individual's performance of the job and, as such, may be considered as a form of self-reward. For example, one essentially must decide for himself whether his level of performance is worthy of a feeling of personal achievement. Extrinsic rewards, to the contrary, are administered by the organization; the organization first must identify good performance and then provide the appropriate reward.

Generally speaking, extrinsic rewards have their greatest value when the individual is most strongly motivated to satisfy what Maslow has referred to as lower level needs, basic physiological needs and needs for safety or security, and those higher level ego needs that can be linked directly to status. Pay, for example, may be valued by an individual because he believes it is a determinant of his social position within the community or because it constitutes a means for acquiring status symbols.

Intrinsic rewards are likely to be valued more by the individual after his lower level needs have been largely satisfied. In other words, there must be an adequate level of satisfaction with the extrinsic rewards before intrinsic rewards can be utilized effectively. In order to make the subordinate's job more intrinsically rewarding, the manager may want to consider several actions.

Perhaps most important, the manager needs to provide meaningful work assignments, that is, work with which the subordinate can identify and become personally involved. He should establish challenging yet attainable goals or, in some cases, it may be more advantageous for him to create conditions that greatly enhance the likelihood that his subordinate will succeed, thus increasing the potential for attaining feelings of achievement, advancement, and recognition. The manager may also consider such means as increased delegation and job enlargement for extending the scope and depth of the subordinate's job and thereby increasing the subordinate's opportunity to make the job into something more compatible with his own interests.

In short, the manager should as best he can match the rewards at his disposal, both extrinsic and intrinsic rewards, with what the subordinate indicates he needs or wants. Second, he should, by varying the magnitude and timing of the rewards granted, establish clearly in the subordinate's mind the desired effort-performance-reward contingencies.

Establishing the Contingencies   The contingency between effort and performance (that is, the extent to which the individual believes that by working harder, he will improve his performance) is largely a function of his confidence in his own abilities and his perceptions of the difficulty of the task and absence of obstacles standing in the way of successful task performance. When the effort-performance contingency is not clear for these reasons, the manager should consider several actions. He can reassign work or modify the task to be more consistent with the individual's perceptions of his own abilities; treat the problem as a "real" ability deficiency; remove the apparent performance obstacles; or simply reassure the individual.

The second contingency, the individual's belief that the rewards he receives reflect his accomplishments, is usually more difficult to establish. Here, two rather vexing predicaments are frequently encountered, both of which stem primarily from administration of extrinsic rewards. First, the instrument (usually a merit evaluation or performance appraisal device) may inaccurately measure the individual's contribution and thus his performance is rewarded in error. Reward schedules constitute the source of the second problem. Given fixed reward schedules (that is, the ubiquitous annual salary increase) adopted by the great majority of organizations, there is more frequently than not a considerable delay between task accomplishment and bestowal of the reward. As a result, the individual may not only fail to perceive the intended contingency but may incorrectly associate the reward with his behavior just prior to being rewarded. In other words, he may perceive a nonexistent contingency, and his subsequent behavior will reflect that contingency and, this time, go unrewarded.

Reward Schedules   The manner in which a given reward, or reinforcer, is scheduled is as strong a determinant of the effectiveness of that reward as is the value of the reward itself, or, for that matter, any other attribute of the reward. In organizations, the only plausible forms of reward schedules are intermittent as opposed to the continuous reward schedule in which the reward or punishment is administered after every behavioral sequence to be conditioned. In the case of the intermittent schedules, the behavior to be conditioned is reinforced only occasionally. There are four schedules of interest to the manager, each with varying effects on performance as a number of investigations in the field of experimental psychology have revealed.

1. *Fixed-interval schedule.* Rewards are bestowed after a fixed period, usually since the last reward was granted. This schedule is equivalent to the annual salary increase schedule in organizations, and its effects on performance are well-known. Typically, the individual "saves up," that is, he exerts a high level of effort just prior to the time of the reinforcement, usually his annual performance review. His performance more than likely will then taper off until the time just prior to his next annual review.

2. *Variable-interval schedule.* Rewards are administered at designated time periods, but the intervals between the periods vary. For example, a reward may be given one day after the last rewarded behavior sequence, then three days later, then one week later, and so on, but only if the behavior to be conditioned actually occurs. This schedule results in fairly consistent rates of performance over long periods of time. Praise or other forms of social reinforcement from one's peers and superior, as an example, usually occur according to a variable-interval schedule, not by intention but simply because they are too involved with their own affairs to provide systematic reinforcement.

3. *Fixed-ratio schedule.* Reinforcement is provided after a fixed number of responses or performances by the individual. Incentive wage plans so frequently utilized in organizations constitute the prime example of this type of schedule. It is characterized by higher rates of effort than the interval schedules unless the ratio is large. When significant delays do occur between rewards, performance, much like in the fixed schedule, declines immediately after the reward is bestowed and improves again as the time for the next reward approaches.

4. *Variable-ratio schedule.* The reward is administered after a series of responses or performances, the number of which varies from the granting of one reward to the next.
   For example, an individual on a 15:1 variable-interval schedule might be reinforced after ten responses, then fifteen responses, then twenty responses, then ten responses, and so on, an average of one reinforcement for every fifteen responses. This schedule tends to result in performance that is higher than that of a comparable fixed ratio schedule, and the variation in performance both before and after the

occurrence of the reward or reinforcement is considerably less.

Virtually all managers must function within the constraints imposed by a fixed-interval schedule (annual salary schedule) or fixed ratio schedule (wage incentives). However, this fact should not preclude consideration of the variable schedules, even within the framework of fixed schedules. Given their more positive effects on performance, such consideration is indeed highly desirable. It is conceivable, at least in a sales organization, for example, that monetary rewards (bonuses in this case) could be administered according to a variable-ratio schedule. From a more practical point of view, the entire range of nonmonetary rewards could be more profitably scheduled on a variable-interval basis, assuming that such scheduling was done in a systematic fashion.

Conclusions

This article has reviewed recent research concerning the relationship between satisfaction and performance and discussed the implications of the results of this research for the practicing manager. As noted at the outset, current speculation on the part of most practitioners and researchers continue to imply that satisfaction and performance are causally related, although confusion exists concerning the exact nature of the relationship. While the performance-causes-satisfaction proposition is a more recent development, the contention that satisfaction causes performance, nonetheless, remains the more widely held of the two beliefs, particularly among practitioners.

The recent research findings, however, offer only moderate support of the former view and conclusively reject the latter. Instead, the evidence provides rather strong indications that the relationship is more complex: (1) rewards constitute a more direct cause of satisfaction than does performance and (2) rewards based on current performance (and not satisfaction) cause subsequent performance.

For the manager who is concerned about the well-being of his subordinates, the implication of the finding that rewards cause satisfaction is self-evident. In order to achieve this end, the manager must provide rewards that have value or utility in terms of the subordinate's own need state and provide them in sufficient magnitude to be perceived as positively reinforcing. The manager whose goal is to increase a subordinate's performance, on the other hand, is faced with a more difficult task for two reasons. First, the relationship between rewards and performance is not a simple one. Second, there are other causes of performance—direction, the subordinate's ability, and existence of performance obstacles standing in the way of successful task performance—which the manager must also deal with.

The relationship between rewards and performance is complex because in reality there is at least one intervening variable and more than one contingency that needs to be established. An employee exerts high level effort usually because of the valued rewards he associates with high performance. Effort, the intervening variable, may be considered a function of the value and magnitude of the reward and the extent to which the individual believes that high effort on his part will lead to high performance and that his high performance, in turn, will lead to rewards.

Therefore, the manager, in addition to providing appropriate rewards, must establish contingencies between effort and performance and between performance and rewards. The first contingency, the extent to which the individual believes that "how hard he works" determines his performance, is perhaps the more readily established. This contingency is a function, at least in part, of the individual's confidence in his own abilities, his perceptions of the difficulty of the task, and the presence of performance obstacles. When a problem does arise here, the manager can take those actions indicated earlier in this article to overcome an apparent ability deficiency or performance obstacle. The performance-reward contingency requires the manager, by means of accurate performance appraisals and appropriate reward practices, to clearly establish in the subordinate's mind the belief that his own performance determines the magnitude of the rewards he will receive.

The establishment of this particular contingency, unfortunately, is becoming increasingly difficult as organizations continue to rely more heavily on fixed salary schedules and nonperformance-related factors (for example, seniority) as determinants of salary progression. However, the manager can, as a supplement to organizationally determined rewards, place more emphasis on nonmonetary rewards and both the cafeteria-style reward plans and variable-interval schedules for their administration.

It is apparent that the manager whose objective is to significantly improve his subordinates' performance has a difficult but by no means impossible task. The path of least resistance—that is, increasing subordinates' satisfaction—simply will not work.

However, the actions suggested concerning reward practices and, particularly, establishment of appropriate performance-reward contingencies will result in improved performance, assuming that such improvement is not restricted by ability or direction problems or by performance obstacles. The use of differential rewards may require courage on the part of the manager, but failure to use them will have far more negative consequences. A subordinate will repeat that behavior which was rewarded, regardless of whether it resulted in high or low performance. A rewarded low performer, for example, will continue to perform poorly. With knowledge of this inequity, the high performer, in turn, will eventually reduce his own level of performance or seek employment elsewhere.

Notes

1. Initial investigation by A. A. Kornhauser and A. W. Sharp, "Employee Attitudes: Suggestions from a Study in a Factory," *Personnel Journal* X (May 1932): 393–401.

   First quotation from Robert A. Sutermeister, "Employee Performance and Employee Need Satisfaction—Which Comes First?" *California Management Review*, XIII (Summer 1971): 3.

   Second quotation from Donald P. Schwab and Larry L. Cummings, "Theories of Performance and Satisfaction: a Review," *Industrial Relations* IX (October 1970): 408–30.

2. Victor H. Vroom, *Work and Motivation* (New York: John Wiley & Sons, Inc., 1964).
3. Lyman W. Porter and Edward E. Lawler III, *Managerial Attitudes and Performance* (Homewood, Ill.: Richard D. Irwin, Inc., 1968).
4. Donald Bowen and Jacob P. Siegel, "The Relationship between Satisfaction and Performance: The Question of Causality," paper presented at the annual meeting of the American Psychological Association, Miami Beach, September 1970. Charles N. Greene, "A Causal Interpretation of Relationship Among Pay, Performance, and Satisfaction," paper presented at the annual meeting of the Midwest Psychological Association, Cleveland, Ohio, May 1972.
5. David J. Cherrington, H. Joseph Reitz, and William E. Scott, Jr., "Effects of Contingent and Non-contingent Reward on the Relationship Between Satisfaction and Task Performance," *Journal of Applied Psychology* LV (December 1971): 531–36.
6. Charles N. Greene, "Source and Direction of Causal Influence in Satisfaction-Performance Relationships," paper presented at the annual meetings of the Eastern Academy of Management, Boston, May 1972. Also reported in Greene, "Causal Connections Among Managers' Merit Pay, Satisfaction, and Performance," *Journal of Applied Psychology,* 1972 (in press).
7. For example, a recent study reported finding that relationships between the leader's initiating structure and both subordinate satisfaction and performance were moderated by such variables as role ambiguity, job scope, and task autonomy perceived by the subordinate. See Robert J. House, "A Path Goal Theory of Leader Effectiveness," *Administrative Science Quarterly* XVI (September 1971): 321–39.
8. Robert F. Mager and Peter Pipe, *Analyzing Performance Problems* (Belmont, Calif.: Lear Siegler, Inc., 1970), p. 21.
9. See, for example, J. D. Folley, Jr., "Determining Training Needs of Department Store Personnel," *Training Development Journal* XXIII (January, 1969: 24–27, for a discussion of how the critical incidents approach can be employed to identify job skills to be learned in a formal training situation.
10. For a useful discussion of how ability levels can be upgraded by means of training and selection procedures, the reader can refer to Larry I. Cummings and Donald P. Schwab, *Performance in Organizations: Determinants and Appraisal* (Glenview, Ill.: Scott, Foresman & Co., 1972).
11. The discussion in this section is based in part on Cummings and Schwab, *Performance in Organizations,* and Lyman W. Porter and Edward E. Lawler III, "What Job Attitudes Tell About Motivation," *Harvard Business Review* LXVI (January-February 1968): 118–26.
12. Edward E. Lawler III, *Pay and Organizational Effectiveness: a Psychological View* (New York: McGraw-Hill Book Company, 1971).

6

How to Earn 'Well Pay'

*T*he woman in blue jeans and a logger's shirt looks up from the production line and says grimly: "I can't miss work today. It's almost the end of the month, and I'm going to earn that 'well pay' if it kills me."

At Parsons Pine Products Inc. in Ashland, Ore., "well pay" is the opposite of sick pay. It is an extra eight hours' wages that the company gives workers who are neither absent nor late for a full month. It is also one of four incentives that owner James W. Parsons has built into a "positive reinforcement plan" for workers: well pay, retro pay, safety pay, and profit-sharing pay.

Beating the Tax Man

The formula, Parsons says, enables him and his wife to beat the combination of federal and state income taxes that leaves them only 14% of any increase in earnings; it allows them to pass along much of the potential tax money to the workers. Under the Parsons system, an employee earning $10,000 a year can add as much as $3,500 to his income by helping the plant operate economically.

Parsons Pine employs some 100 workers to cut lumber into specialty items—primarily louver slats for shutters, bifold doors, and blinds, and wooden bases for rat traps. It is reportedly the U.S.'s biggest producer of these items, with sales last year of $2.5 million.

The company began handing out "well pay" in January, 1977. "We had a problem with lateness," Parsons explains. "Just before the 7 a.m. starting time, the foreman in a department would take a head count and assign three people to this machine and six over there. Then a few minutes later someone else comes in and he has to recalculate and reshuffle. Or he may be so short as to leave a machine idle."

"Well pay" brought lateness down to almost zero and cut absenteeism more than Parsons wanted it reduced, because some workers came to work even when they were sick. He dealt with this awkwardness by reminding them of "retro pay." Says Parsons: "I'd say, 'By being here while not feeling well, you may have a costly accident, and that will not only cause you pain and suffering, but it will also affect the retro plan, which could cost you a lot more than one day's well pay.'"

Reducing Accidents

The retro plan offers a bonus based on any reductions in premiums received from the state's industrial accident insurance fund. Before the retro plan went into effect in 1976, Parsons Pine had a high accident rate, 86% above the statewide base, and paid the fund accordingly. Parsons told his workers that if the plant cut its accident rate, the retroactive refund would be distributed to them. The upshot was a 1977 accident bill of $2,500 compared to a 1976 bill of $28,500. After deducting administrative expenses, the state will return $89,000 of a $100,000 premium, some $900 per employee.

The retro plan did not improve the accident rate unaided, Parsons concedes. "We showed films and introduced every safety program the state has," he says. "But no matter what you do, it doesn't really make a dent until the people themselves see that they are going to lose a dollar by not being safe. When management puts on the pressure, they say, 'He's just trying to make a buck for himself,' but when fellow workers say, 'Let's work safe,' that means a lot."

The 'Little Hurts'

Employees can also earn safety pay—two hours' wages—by remaining accident-free for a month. "Six hours a quarter isn't such a great incentive," says Parsons, "but it helps. When it didn't cost them anything, workers would go to the doctor for every little thing. Now they take care of the little hurts themselves."

As its most substantial incentive, the company offers a profit-sharing bonus—everything the business earns over 4% after taxes, which is Parsons' idea of a fair profit. Each supervisor rates his employees in four categories of excellence, with a worker's bonus figured as a percentage of his wages multiplied by his category. Top-ranked employees generally receive bonuses of 8% to 10%. One year they got 16½%. Two-thirds of the bonus is paid in cash and the rest goes into the retirement fund.

To illustrate how workers can contribute to profits, and profit-sharing bonuses, Parsons presents a dramatic display that has a modest fame in Ashland. Inviting the work force to lunch, he sets up a pyramid of 250 rat trap bases, each representing $10,000 in sales. Then he knocks 100 onto the floor, saying. "That's for raw materials. See why it is important not to waste?" Then he pushes over 100 more, adding: "That's for wages." And pointing to the 50 left, he says: "Out of this little pile we have to do all the other things—maintenance, repairs, supplies, taxes. With so many blocks gone, that doesn't leave much for either you or me."

A Vote for Work

The lunch guests apparently find the display persuasive. Says one nine-year veteran: "We get the most we can out of every piece of wood after seeing that. When new employees come, we work with them to cut down waste."

The message also lingered at the last Christmas luncheon, when, after distribution of checks, someone said: "Hey, how about the afternoon off?" Parsons replied: "O.K., our production is on schedule and the customers won't be hurt. But you know where the cost comes from." Parsons recalls that someone asked him, "How much?" and he replied that the loss would be about $3,000.

"There was a bit of chatter and we took a vote," he says. "Only two hands were raised for the afternoon off. That was because they knew it was not just my money. It was their money, too."

7

The 4-Day Week:

Employe Lives Change as More Firms Adopt New Work Schedules

Joann S. Lublin

South Padre Island, a Texas resort area, was nearly deserted when Terry and Vicki Shea and their two sons arrived for a winter weekend late last year. They had driven 300 miles to the national seashore from their San Antonio home on a Thursday night. They had the whole place to themselves the next day, but by noon Saturday hordes of sunseekers were swarming over the beach. "I enjoyed Friday much more than Saturday," says Mr. Shea, who is director of research for United Services Automobile Association, an insurance company.

Ralph and Cindee Hurlburt also have their Fridays off, but instead of relaxing like the Sheas, they "moonlight" in an effort to build their hobby, raising quarter horses, into a business. It's a tough grind, but they figure it will be worth it if it allows them to escape their tedious and tiring regular jobs on the assembly line of a frozen-food plant in Fairmont, Minn.

What Mr. Shea and the Hurlburts have in common is that their Fridays are free regularly, and so are their Saturdays and Sundays. They are among an estimated 1.2 million Americans for whom the four-day workweek, with all of its attendant problems and pleasures, has become a reality. This represents about 2% of the full-time work force, and the number seems sure to mount steadily in the near future.

Last fall, the United Auto Workers Union's settlements with the auto and farm-implement industries gave 852,000 workers 12 extra paid days off over the next two years; the union says it sees this provision as the opening wedge in its drive to make the four-day, 32-hour week

SOURCE: Joann S. Lublin, "The 4-Day Week: Employe Lives Change as More Firms Adopt New Work Schedules," *Wall Street Journal* (Vol. LIX, No. 33), p. 1. Reprinted with permission.

standard in those industries. The United Steelworkers Union says it will follow the UAW's lead and give a shorter workweek high priority in talks with the steel industry that began on Monday.

President Carter recently suggested that government agencies and private industry temporarily make the switch to a four-day week to cut consumption of dwindling natural-gas supplies. But federal law requires payment of overtime for more than an eight-hour day to U.S. government workers and companies with federal contracts of more than $10,000. And Mr. Carter stopped short of requesting Congress to suspend overtime provisions of these laws.

Even before the current energy crisis, a bill was introduced in Congress that would allow several hundred thousand federal workers to try out both the four-day week and flexible daily starting and quitting times over a three-year period. If the experiment works, the scheduling options could be offered to all of the government's 2.8 million employes. The bill's chances for passage are considered good.

'An Idea Here to Stay'

A sizable number of firms—perhaps 10,000 in all—have adopted the four-day week hoping that it would reduce absenteeism, boost productivity and improve employe morale. Interest in the short week was high in the early 1970s, but lagged during the 1974-75 recession. Now it is reviving again.

"I pretty well think the idea is here to stay," says Kenneth E. Wheeler, a Lowell, Mass., management consultant who advises companies on rearranged workweeks. Mr. Wheeler says his firm has been contacted by "a lot of companies," including several Fortune 500 concerns.

He and other experts foresee many social consequences as the four-day week or similar reshufflings in the standard work time come into vogue. Everything from consumer spending habits to school hours and family relationships could be affected.

For example, people may decide to live in barracks-like dwellings in the city during the week, commuting on weekends to their distant "real" homes near, say, a favorite fishing hole. "You might get some very interesting (housing) patterns," says John D. Owen, professor of economics at Wayne State University in Detroit. "The second-home movement would get a tremendous boost from the four-day workweek," he says.

Exodus from the Cities

Getting away for the weekend—and going farther away—will become more common. Longer weekends will "produce an even greater exodus from urban places into outdoor settings," taxing the resources of already overburdened national parks and forests, says Tony A. Mobley, dean of Indiana University's school of health, public education and recreation. He also thinks that such recreational facilities as private campgrounds and amusement parks will burgeon.

With fewer or rearranged working hours, men will be at home more. Their presence may strengthen solid marriages and weaken troubled ones, authorities say. Men with working wives may assume more parenting and household-maintenance chores.

Economists think that moonlighting will increase to perhaps double its current rate. Government figures place the incidence of moonlighting at 5% now, but some experts say the real figure probably is much higher. Many wage earners will need a second job to pay for expensive recreational pursuits, such as owning a boat or traveling abroad. "How do you afford the leisure time? I think that is a matter of concern to all jobholders," says Frank H. Cassell, professor of industrial relations at Northwestern University's graduate school of management.

The demand for extra income is likely to be especially acute among young blue-collar workers who, like the Hurlburts, are in their late twenties. Younger employes, lacking seniority and purchasing power, are "still trying to make it," observes Brian E. Moore, associate professor of management at the University of Texas's school of business.

The dual pattern of more blue-collar moonlighting and more leisure for executives and professionals comes across strongly in closer examinations of how the four-day week has changed the lives of the Sheas and the Hurlburts.

Terry Shea didn't know that USAA was on an unusual schedule when he applied. But he soon felt the effects of working a four-day, 40-hour week (with a half-hour off for lunch), an arrangement most companies on short weeks use.

The 10-hour day was two hours longer than he was used to, so he found himself worn out by the end of the day. He began drinking lots of water to stay awake until quitting time (he dislikes coffee), gave up serving on church committees that met weekday evenings and started going to bed at 10 o'clock.

Another disadvantage is that like many managers on a four-day week, Mr. Shea doesn't get to take full advantage of long weekends. One or two Fridays a month, the 35-year-old executive is at his desk for a half-day. "You don't work by the clock if you're in management," explains Mr. Shea, a large, square-jawed man who earns more than $30,000 a year. Freed of jangling phones, demanding subordinates and long meetings, he uses these Friday mornings to write reports.

On the plus side, Fridays off have given the Sheas their first opportunity to be alone since their children were born. One recent Friday, Mr. Shea left his modern, sprawling office building around 1 p.m. and met his wife for a leisurely lunch and an afternoon of shopping at a suburban mall. (Seven-year-old Tim was in school, and Mrs. Shea dropped off four-year-old Kevin at a daycare center.)

While these excursions mean spending more money, they're also helping to strengthen the Sheas' marriage. "I probably know her a little better as a person," Mr. Shea says. "It's easy to regard your wife only as a mother and housekeeper."

Time for the Family

Mr. Shea's sons reap the benefits of his extra time off as well. Frequently, Mr. Shea spends Fridays mowing the lawn, running errands and fixing up his house. (He built a sidewalk recently and is considering constructing a waterfall in his backyard.) This frees him on Saturday to coach Tim's football team or to draw posters with Kevin. "I get to play with my Dad more," Tim says with a grin.

The Shea family has taken five weekend trips in the year and a half they have been in Texas, driving to Mexico, Dallas and the Gulf Coast. They never took any short trips when they lived in Bloomington, Ill., where Mr. Shea worked for State Farm Mutual Automobile Insurance Co. A weekend in the mountains near El Paso is planned for later this winter. "That's something you really couldn't do if you just had Saturday and Sunday," Mr. Shea observes. El Paso is 600 miles from San Antonio.

Terry Shea finds that the longer weekend means he's more rested and relaxed on Monday mornings. He hasn't missed a day of work since joining USAA, although this may be attributable as much to the mild Texas climate as to the four-day week.

Fewer Absences

Still, Mr. Shea remembers that at State Farm, he used to stay home several days a year because he was feeling lethargic or depressed about his job. When such feelings occur now, he can hold out "because I know that Friday is coming," he says. "Before, I couldn't hold out until Saturday."

Exhaustion and lethargy are bigger problems for blue-collar employes on four-day-week routines. Compared to management or clerical types, they often hold more physically taxing jobs, and their work environment is not as pleasant. Certainly this is true for Armour & Co. workers Cindee and Ralph Hurlburt.

Nearly every work day, Ralph Hurlburt shovels five tons of ground beef from a grinding machine to a metal hopper. He earns $4.06 an hour, tossing meat from 6:30 a.m. to 5 p.m., with a 30-minute lunch break. Even though Mr. Hurlburt used to work a seven-day week as a farm manager, he says that at Armour, he's "ready to drop by the end of the day." He also has developed an arm injury from the strain.

Cindee Hurlburt's $3.73-an-hour job is less strenuous but equally boring. The easy-going, soft-spoken woman usually stands for an entire 10-hour shift, fingering pieces of cooked chicken to see if the bones have been entirely removed.

Her tasks vary on some days. On a recent afternoon in the noisy, chilly plant (where the temperature hovers around 50 degrees), Mrs. Hurlburt carries 15-pound trays laden with wrapped ham sandwiches over to shipping cartons and then loads them. Closing time approaches; she pauses to flex her shoulder and complain, "Oooh, my whole side aches."

Some of her co-workers, mostly middle-aged women, grumble that if their union asked them, they would vote to abolish the four-day week. The 140 members of the Teamsters local originally approved the shorter week in 1971. But Mrs. Hurlburt doesn't mind the long hours. "If I have to work, I want to get it all done in four days," she says. (She took a three-month maternity leave beginning in late January; her second child is due later this month.)

More important, the compressed workweek permits the couple to raise and train quarter horses on their five-acre farm. It's an expensive hobby that they hope to turn into a full-time occupation someday. Feeding, grooming and exercising their six horses take up nearly all their spare time and cash.

On weekday evenings, Mr. Hurlburt does chores in the two barns while his wife prepares dinner and helps their seven-year-old son, Robbi, with his homework. Robbi is in bed by 7 o'clock, and his parents usually fall asleep an hour later. "We don't have enough time to argue with each other," Mr. Hurlburt says.

Weekend Work

In the winter, Fridays are "barn day." They clean horse stalls, buy hay or get the animals shod. They also go grocery shopping and to the bank, which is closed Saturdays.

They arrange conferences with Robbi's teacher on Fridays, too. The first time they both showed up, Mr. Hurlburt recalls, "the teacher just about fell over" because he was the only father of a first-grader to attend a conference this year.

Between January and October, the Hurlburts spend numerous weekends displaying their animals at shows in Minnesota, Iowa and Wisconsin. They went away seven times for the entire three-day weekend last summer, but usually limit their trips to two days during the school year. Their regular attendance at such shows, where they compete against full-time trainers, is helping to build their stable's reputation.

Armour laid them off for 18 months between the fall of 1974 and the spring of 1976. (Mr. Hurlburt had previously worked there for one month and Mrs. Hurlburt for four years.) When they were called back, she was employed as a store clerk and he as a truck driver. At the time, they considered giving up the food-plant jobs—not only because of the fatigue, but also because they feared future layoffs.

Then they realized that the four-day schedule would help them move closer to their dream of a horse-training business. The rearranged hours represent something else that's just as important to them: personal independence, or "more of your own time," as Mr. Hurlburt puts it. His wife adds: "You feel freer when you don't have to go out and work at a job on Fridays."

Management's Side

At Norgren Corporation, a Colorado machine-tool manufacturer, the management side of the 4-day work week is revealed. The new scheduling was the idea of Mr. R. C. Norgren, company president. "A lot of preliminary work was conducted before the plan was implemented," he recalls. The key goal, he says, was to maintain productivity levels and, "with luck," improve them. "We worried about employe fatigue, made models of all kinds of scheduling and wondered how customers would react. We also worried about the social impact on workers with families."

In August 1970, five months after the study began and after consultations with employes, a six-month trial of the plan began. Paid holidays were reduced to five a year from eight, the number of breaks and their length were cut, and the new schedule went into effect.

That schedule, concedes John Karpan, vice president for industrial relations, is "incredibly complex." Most office employes and about half of the factory workers were put on the standard day shift, which runs from 7 a.m. to 5 p.m. Monday through Thursday, with a half-hour off for lunch. The standard night shift, also Monday through Thursday, goes from 5 p.m. to 3 a.m., with a half-hour for lunch. On Thursday, the work day is reduced by an hour for day-shifters and by two hours for night workers.

Because part of the reason for the changeover was to reduce production during the 1970 recession, the factory remained closed Friday through Sunday except to fill emergency orders. But when orders picked up, additional day and night shifts were added on Wednesday through Saturday. And the hundred or so employes in the capital-intensive casting and plastic molding operations went on three-day-a-week, 12-hour shifts that enabled them to operate equipment around the clock six days a week.

Despite the upheaval, workers responded favorably. "It's noisy, boring work," says a factory worker over the din in Norgren's 139,000-square-foot plant. "Once you're here, you may as well keep going an extra couple of hours and get a three-day weekend." A company study found that the only employes who didn't like the new schedule were working mothers who couldn't see their children off to school because of the early starting hours.

Some companies whose workers are on a four-day week have foremen and supervisors work five-day shifts, to help insure continuity in the production process. At Norgren, however, everyone works four days. With different shifts, managers would resent the workers' long weekends, Mr. Karpan explains.

The changeover at Norgren resulted in some initial loss of productivity. "It was pretty disorganized with people not used to the schedule," says George Loury, vice president for production. But in about two months, when the schedule became routine, productivity per hour returned to normal. Eventually, it even improved because of operating efficiencies such as shorter breaks and fewer cleanup and start-up periods.

There were some snafus, of course. Customer service suffered at first because order takers who were on duty Fridays weren't around on Mondays to follow through on orders. "We were dropping the ball too many times," says Phillip Thompson, vice president for marketing. The solution: Order takers were scheduled Tuesday through Friday one week and Monday through Thursday the next. This assured continuity, and gave the workers alternating two-day and four-day weekends.

A Flood of Applicants

Also, with the shipping department closed on Fridays, some customers complained about delays in their shipments. "We corrected that quickly," Mr. Thompson says, by reassigning people on Fridays. He notes that Norgren's air filters, regulators, lubricators and valves are crucial equipment in many factories where air-powered tools are used. (Norgren's products also go into air-powered wrenches used at gas stations, and into dentists' high-speed drills.)

But for the most part, the new schedule had its desired effect. Costly employe turnover dropped to 16% annually—"about a third of the normal rate in our business," Mr. Karpan says. In addition, he says the company has found recruiting, especially for skilled craftsmen, a lot easier. Indeed, Norgren received over 2,100 unsolicited job applications the first week after the changeover. And absenteeism fell to 4.1% last year from about 7% before the change. "There's less malingering in general," Mr. Karpan concludes.

The fear that workers would be unduly tired from the long hours proved unfounded. "Oh, there was some complaining at first," Mr. Loury says. "But we've measured their efficiency and it holds up pretty well over the course of the shift." He adds that Norgren hasn't seen an increase in its accident rate, "and that's the first place fatigue would have shown up."

Unions Lose Out

Finally, the four-day week served the company well in its fight against unionization. The International Association of Machinists "has been trying to organize us since 1946," says Mr. Norgren, whose father was known locally as an ardent right-to-work advocate. Since 1970, the United Rubber Workers and the UAW have also tried to organize the plant. All include the popularity of the four-day week among reasons for their failure.

"I helped handbill the gates of the plant there," says Richard Beasley, a UAW organizer. "The guys were worried that if they got a union in, they'd lose the four-day week."

The four-day week may not be for everyone, but consultant Riva Poor says many companies can benefit by juggling schedules. Specifically, she cites manufacturers in tight labor markets and those that can't afford to expand downtown production facilities because real-estate values are so high. The latter, she says, can enhance production simply by rearranging scheduling. Other potential beneficiaries include employers in service fields that have peaks and valleys in demand during the workday, such as police and fire departments and hospitals.

And Mr. Norgren, pointing to the Rocky Mountain view from his office, thinks a pleasant locale is necessary, so that employes can take advantage of the added day of leisure. "People who move to Colorado want to enjoy it here," he says. "That makes the extra day off so much more important."

8

The Individualized Organization:
Problems and Promise

Edward E. Lawler III

Two easily identified and distinctly different approaches to the study of behavior in organizations have dominated the organizational behavior literature for the past half century. One emphasizes the differences among people, the other the similarities.

The first and least dominant approach has its foundation in differential psychology and is concerned with the study of individual differences. The basic assumptions underlying this approach are that people differ in their needs, skills, and abilities; that these differences can be measured; that valid data about people's competence and motivation can be obtained by organizations; and that these data can be used to make organizations more effective.

When behavioral scientists who take this approach look at organizations, they tend to see selection and placement. Their concern is with selecting those people who are right for a given job by measuring the characteristics of both the people and jobs and then trying to achieve the best fit. Their paradigm of the ideal organization would seem to be one where everyone has the ability and motivation to do the job to which he is assigned. Rarely do behavioral scientists with this orientation try to change the design of jobs or of organizations. Jobs are taken as a given, and the focus is on finding the right people for them. Where efforts at job redesign have been made, they typically are instituted in the tradition of human engineering. That is, jobs have been made simpler so that more people can do them.

What is needed if this approach is to work?

SOURCE: Edward E. Lawler III, "The Individualized Organization: Problems and Promise," *California Management Review* 17 (Winter 1974): 31–39. © 1974 by the Regents of the University of California. Reprinted from California Management Review, volume XVII, number 2, pp. 31 to 39, by permission of the Regents.

1. People must differ in meaningful ways.
2. Valid data about the characteristics of people must exist.
3. People who are suited for the jobs must apply.
4. A favorable selection ratio must exist (a large number of qualified applicants must apply for the job).

The second approach has generally assumed that all employees in an organization are similar in many ways and that certain general rules or principles can and should be developed for the design of organizations. It is universalistic, propounding that there is a right way to deal with all people in organizations. This type of thinking is present in the work of such traditional organization theorists as Urwick and Taylor. It is also present in the writings of the human relations theorists such as Mayo and in the work of the human resource theorists such as McGregor and Likert. As John Morse notes, all these approaches contain either implicitly or explicitly the assumption that there is a right way to manage people.[1]

Douglas McGregor's discussion of Theory X and Theory Y points out that, although scientific management and the more modern theories make different assumptions about the nature of man, both emphasize the similarities among people rather than differences.[2] Based upon the Theory Y view of the nature of people, McGregor develops a normative organization theory that, like Theory X, stresses universal principles of management. For any of the universality theories to be generally valid, a certain type of person must populate society: one that fits its assumptions about the nature of people. In the case of the human resource theorists, this universal person will respond favorably to such things as enriched jobs, participative leadership, and interpersonal relationships characterized by openness, trust, and leveling. For the scientific management theorists, the universal type responds well to the use of financial rewards and the simplification of work. Thus, the validity of all these theories rests upon the correctness of the assumptions about the nature of people.

The work of those behavioral scientists who are concerned with individual differences suggests that the assumptions of all the universal theorists are dangerous over-simplifications for one very important reason: they fail to acknowledge the significant differences (in needs, personalities, and abilities) that cause individuals to react differently to organization practices concerned with job design, pay systems, leadership, training, and selection. Although many studies of individual behavior in organizations have not looked for individual differences, there are some that have found significant diversities. They are worth reviewing briefly since they clearly illustrate what is wrong with all organization theories which make universal assumptions about the nature of people.

Job Design

Job enrichment is one of the key ideas in most of the recent human resource theories of organization. According to the argument presented by Frederick Herzberg and others, job enrichment can lead to appreciable increases in employee motivation, performance, and satisfaction.[3] In fact, there is a fairly large body of evidence to support this view.[4]

There is, however, also a considerable amount of evidence that all individuals do not respond to job enrichment with higher satisfaction, productivity, and quality. In many studies, the researchers have not been concerned with explaining these individual differences and have treated them as error variance. In others, however, attempts have been made to find out what distinguishes those people who respond positively to job enrichment. It has been pointed out that the type of background a person comes from may be related to how he or she responds to an enriched job.[5] According to some analyses, employees from rural backgrounds are more likely to respond positively to enrichment than are workers from urban environments.

More recent findings have shown that individual differences in need strength determine how people respond to jobs; the reason previous researchers have found urban-rural differences to be important lies in the kind of needs that people from these backgrounds have.[6] Rural background people have stronger higher-order needs (self-actualization, competence, self-esteem), and people with these needs respond positively to job enrichment, while those who don't fail to respond. It is argued that job enrichment creates conditions under which people can experience growth and self-esteem, motivating them to perform well. Clearly, for those employees who do not want to experience competence and growth, the opportunity to experience them will not be motivating, and not everyone should be expected to respond well to enriched jobs.[7]

Pay Systems

The scientific management philosophy strongly emphasizes the potential usefulness of pay as a motivator as in many piece-rate, bonus, profit sharing, and other pay incentive plans. There is abundant evidence to support the point that, when pay is tied to performance, motivation and performance are increased.[8] However, there is also evidence to indicate that not everyone responds to pay incentive plans by performing better. In one study, certain types of employees responded to a piece-rate incentive system while others did not.[9] Who responded? Workers from rural backgrounds who owned their homes, were Protestants, and social isolates—workers who, in short, saw money as a way of getting what they wanted and for whom social relations were not highly important.

There are many different kinds of pay incentive systems; and the kind of pay system that will motivate one person often does not motivate others. For example, group plans apparently work best with people who have strong social needs.[10] This suggests that not only do the members of an organization have to be treated differently according to whether they will or will not respond to a pay incentive, but that those who will respond to pay systems may have to be subdivided according to the type of system to which they will respond.

There is abundant evidence that individuals differ in their responses to the fringe benefits they receive. Large differences, determined by such things as age, marital status, education, and so on, exist among individuals in the kind of benefits they want and need.[11] Most organizations ignore this and give everyone the same benefits, thereby often giving high-cost benefits to people who do not want them. Maximizing individual satisfaction with fringe benefits would require a unique plan for each employee.

Leadership

Research on leadership style during the past two decades has stressed the advantages that can be gained from the use of the various forms of power equalization. Participation, flat organizations, decentralization, and group decision making are all power-equalization approaches to motivating and satisfying employees. There is a considerable body of evidence to suggest that power equalization can lead to higher subordinate satisfaction, greater subordinate motivation, and better decision making.[12] Unfortunately, much of this literature has only given brief mention to the fact that not all subordinates respond in the same way to power equalization and the fact that not all superiors can practice power equalization.

Victor Vroom was one of the first to point out that at least one type of subordinate does not respond positively to participative management.[13] His data show that subordinates who are high on the F-scale (a measure of authoritarianism) do not respond well when they are subordinates to a boss who is oriented toward participative management. Later studies have shown that at times the majority of the membership of a work group may not respond positively to power-equalization efforts on the part of superiors.[14]

Many superiors cannot manage in a democratic manner.[15] This, combined with the poor responses of many employees to democratic management styles, raises the question of whether it is advisable even to think of encouraging most managers to lead in a democratic manner. Many superiors probably *cannot* adopt a democratic leadership style, and because of the likely responses of some of their subordinates they *shouldn't*—regardless of task and situational considerations.

Training

To most modern organization theorists, training is an important element of organization design. It is particularly helpful in resolving individual differences. T-groups, managerial grid seminars, and leadership courses are some examples of the kinds of human relations training that organizations use. These training approaches help assure that most people in the organization have certain basic skills and abilities and that some valid assumptions about the capacity of the people in the organization can be made.

Once again, the problem is that the very individual employee differences greatly affect the ability to learn from things such as T-groups and managerial grid seminars; this type of training is simply wasted on many people.[16] In fact, the training may end up increasing the range of individual differences in an organization rather than reducing it. It is also likely that while one type of human relations training may not affect a person, another type could have a significant impact. The same point can be made with respect to training people in the area of occupational skills. One person may learn best from a teaching machine while another learns the same material best from a lecture format.

Selection

In the work on selection, the assumption has typically been made that people are sufficiently similar so that the same selection instruments can be used for everyone. Thus, all applicants for a job are often given the same battery of selection criteria—overlooking the fact that different instruments might work better as predictors for some groups than for others. This would not be a serious problem if individual difference factors were not related to the ability of the selection instruments to predict performance; but recent evidence suggests that they are. Certain kinds of tests work better for some segments of the population than for others.[17] However, this uniformity in selection testing is not the only reason for poor job performance prediction.

Differential psychologists have developed numerous valid tests of people's ability to perform jobs, but they have failed to develop tests that measure how employees will fit into particular organizational climates and how motivated they will be in particular organizations. All too often, they have tried to predict individual behavior in organizations without measuring the characteristics of the organization. Trying to predict behavior by looking only at personal characteristics must inevitably lead to predictions whose validity is questionable.

All this is beginning to change, but it is doubtful if highly accurate predictions will ever be obtained. The measurement problems are too great and both organizations and people change too much. The research evidence also shows that people sometimes don't give valid data in selection situations and that some important determinants of individual behavior in organizations are difficult to measure.[18]

Individual Differences

One clear implication of the research on individual differences is that for any of the universalistic theories to operate effectively in a given organization or situation, one of two things must occur: either the organization must deal with the individuals it hires so that they will change to meet the assumptions of the theory, or it must hire only those individuals who fit the kind of system that the organization employs. Unfortunately, there is no solid evidence that individuals can be trained or dealt with in ways that will increase the degree to which they respond to such things as enriched jobs and democratic supervision. Proponents of job enrichment often stress that people will come to like it once they have tried it, but this point remains to be proven.

The validity of most selection instruments is so low that organizations should not count on finding instruments that will allow them to select only those who fit whatever system they use. There is always the prospect that the differential psychologist can develop appropriate measures and that this will lead to organizations being able to select more homogenous work forces. This, in turn, would allow approaches such as the human resources approach to be effectively utilized in some situations. However, it seems unlikely that they could ever be used in large complex organizations. Even if measures are developed, it may not be possible for large homogenous populations of workers to be selected by organizations. Effective selection depends on favorable selection ratios, which are rare, and on the legal ability of organizations to run selection programs. It is also obvious that there has been and will continue to be a large influx into the labor market and into organizations of people from different socioeconomic backgrounds. This has and will continue to create more diversity rather than homogeneity in the work forces of most organizations, decreasing the likelihood that large organizations can ever be completely staffed by people who fit the assumptions of scientific management, Theory X, Theory Y, or any other organization theory that is based upon the view that people are similar in important ways.

Further, it soon may not be legally possible for organizations to conduct the kind of selection programs that will by themselves produce good individual-organization fits. The federal government restrictions on testing for selection purposes soon could create conditions under which testing will no longer be practical. Organizations may find themselves in a situation where they must randomly select from among the "qualified applicants" for a job. Thus, even if valid tests were developed, work forces probably could not be selected that would contain only people that fit either the human resources or the scientific management assumptions about people.

There is evidence in the literature that some organization theorists are moving away from the view that one style of management or one organization design is right for most organizations.[19] However, the focus so far has been on environmental variables such as degree of uncertainty and stability, and production variables such as whether the task is predictable and whether the product can be mass, process, or unit produced. The researchers point out that different structures and different management styles are appropriate under different conditions. Some of the evidence they present is persuasive: products and environmental factors need to be considered when organizations are being designed. However, they often fail to point out that the nature of the work force also needs to be considered and they fail to suggest organization structures that allow for the fact that the people in any organization will vary in their response to such things as tight controls, job enrichment, and so on.

What seems to be needed is an organization theory based upon assumptions like the following, which recognize the existence of differences among individuals:

1. Most individuals are goal-oriented in their behavior but there are large differences in the goals people pursue.
2. Individuals differ both in what they enjoy doing and in what they can do.
3. Some individuals need to be closely supervised while others can exercise high levels of self-control.

In order to design an organization based on these assumptions, it is necessary to utilize various normative theories as guides to how different members of the same organization should be treated. In addition, measures of individual needs and abilities, like those developed by differential psychologists, are needed. As will become apparent, it probably also is necessary to depend on the ability of individuals to help make decisions about where and how they will work. In short, it requires a synthesis of the individual differences approach and the work of the organization theorists into a new paradigm of how organizations should be designed—a new paradigm that emphasizes structuring organizations so that they can better adapt themselves to the needs, desires, and abilities of their members.

Structuring the Individualized Organization

The research on job design, training, reward systems, and leadership provides a number of suggestions about what an organization designed on the basis of individual differences assumptions would look like. A brief review will help to illustrate how an individualized organization might operate and identify some of the practical problems of the approach.

The research on job design shows that jobs can be fit to people if organizations can tolerate having a wide range of jobs and tasks. One plant in Florida has done this by having an assembly line operating next to a bench assembly of the same product. Employees are given a choice of which kind of job they want. The fact that some want to work on each kind is impressive evidence of the existence of individual differences. Robert Kahn has suggested that the fit process can be facilitated by allowing individuals to choose among different groups of tasks or modules that would be several hours long.[20] In his system, workers would bid for those tasks which they would like to do. For this system to work, all individuals would, of course, have to know a considerable amount about the nature of the different modules, and the approach would probably have to take place in conjunction with some job enrichment activities. Otherwise, the employee might be faced with choosing among modules made up of simple, repetitive tasks, thus giving them no real choice. As Kahn notes, the work module concept is also intriguing because it should make it easier for individuals to choose not to work a standard forty-hour workweek. This is important because of the difference in people's preferences with respect to hours of work. The whole module approach rests on the ability of individuals to make valid choices about when and where they should work.

The leadership research shows that people respond to different types of leadership. This could be handled by fitting the superior's style to the personality of subordinates—the superior who can only behave in an authoritarian manner will be given subordinates who perform well under that type of supervision; the superior who can only behave participatively could be given only people who respond to that style; and the superior who is capable of varying his style could be given either people who respond to different styles in different conditions or a mix of people with which he or she would be encouraged to behave differently.

The research shows that training needs to be individualized so that it will fit the needs and abilities of the employee. Implementation requires careful assessment of the individual's abilities and motivation, and good career counseling. Once it has been accepted that not everyone in the organization can profit from a given kind of training, then training becomes a matter of trying to develop people as much as possible with the kind of training to which they will respond. It requires accepting the fact that people may develop quite different leadership styles or ways of behaving in general and trying to capitalize on these by fitting the job the person holds and the groups he supervises to his style.

The research shows that pay systems need to be fit to the person. Fringe benefit packages are a good example of this; several companies have already developed cafeteria-style fringe benefit packages that allow employees to select the benefits they want. The research also suggests that those individuals whose desire for money is strong should be placed on jobs that lend themselves to pay incentive plans.

In summary, an organization based on individual differences assumptions would have a job environment for each person which fits his or her unique skills and abilities. It would accomplish this by a combination of good selection and self-placement choices in the areas of fringe benefits, job design, hours of work, style of supervision, and training programs. But creating truly individualized job situations presents many practical problems in organization design—it is difficult to create gratifying jobs for both the person who responds to an enriched job and the person who responds to a routinized job. One way of accomplishing this could be by creating relatively autonomous subunits that vary widely in climate, job design, leadership style, and so on. For example, within the same organization the same product might be produced by mass production in one unit and by unit production using enriched jobs in another. One subunit might have a warm, supportive climate while another might have a cold, demanding one. The size of the subunit would also vary depending upon the type of climate that is desired and the type of production it uses. This variation is desirable as long as the placement process is able to help people find the modules that fit them.

An organization would have to have an immense number of subunits if it were to try to have one to represent each of the possible combinations of climate, leadership style, incentive systems, and job design. Since such a large number is not practical, a selection should be made based on a study of the labor market, attention to the principles of motivation and satisfaction, and the nature of the product and market. A study of the labor market to see what type of people the organization is likely to attract should help determine what combinations will be needed to fit the characteristics of most of the workers. In most homogeneous labor markets, this may be only a few of the many possible combinations. Traditional selection instruments can help the organization decide who will fit into the subunits; and, if individuals are given information about the nature of the subunits, they can often make valid decisions themselves.

Motivation theory argues that when important rewards are tied to performance, it is possible to have both high satisfaction and high performance.[21] This suggests that all new work modules must meet one crucial condition: some rewards that are valued by members of that part of the organization must be tied to performance. This rules out many situations. For example, a situation in which no extrinsic rewards such as pay and promotion are tied to performance and which has authoritarian management and repetitive jobs should not exist. Finally, the research on job design and organization structure shows that the type of product and type of market limit the kind of subunit which can be successful. For example, authoritarian management, routine jobs, and tall organization structures are not effective when the product is technically sophisticated and must be marketed in a rapidly changing environment.

Creating subunits with distinctly different climates and practices is one way, but not the only way, to create an individualized organization. In small organizations, this probably is not possible; thus, it is important to encourage differences within the same unit. This may mean training supervisors to deal differently with subordinates who have distinctly different personal characteristics. It may also mean designing jobs that can be done in various ways. For example, in one group a product might be built by a team and passed from one member to another while in another group everyone might build the entire product without help. Obviously, this approach generally will not allow for as much variation as does the approach of building distinctive subunits, but it permits some degree of individualization.

It is not yet entirely clear how such divergent organization practices as work modules, cafeteria-style pay plans, and job enrichment that is guided by individual difference measures can be integrated in practice. Research on how organizations can be individualized and on how individual differences affect behavior in organizations is sorely needed.

Research on Individual Differences

The work on measuring individual differences that has been done so far has focused largely on measuring the "can do" aspects of behavior for the purpose of selection. The effective individualization of organizations depends on the development of measures which tap the "will do" aspects of behavior, such as measures of motivation and reactions to different organizational climates, and measures that can be used for placing people in positions that best fit their needs.

This is not to say that selection should be ignored; the kinds of individual differences that exist in an organization should be kept at a manageable number and those who clearly cannot do the job should be excluded. But it is important that, in selection, measures of such things as motivation, reactions to different leadership styles, and preferred organization climate be collected and evaluated in relationship to the climate of the organization, the psychological characteristics of the jobs in the organizations, and the leadership style of various managers. The same measures are obviously relevant when consideration is given to placing new employees in different parts of the organization or in different jobs. The difficulty in doing this kind of selection and placement is that there are few measures of the relevant individual differences, of the organization climate, and of the psychological characteristics of jobs. In many cases, it is not even known what the relevant individual difference variables are when consideration is being given to predicting how people will react to different administrative practices, policies, and to different organization climates. This is where the differential psychologist can make a major contribution.

Also needed is research on selection that is responsive to the new demands that society is placing on organizations and which recognizes that individuals can contribute to better selection decisions. Since organizations are rapidly losing the ability to select who their members will be, research is needed on how the selection situation can be turned into more of a counseling situation so that enlightened self-selection will operate. There is evidence that when job applicants are given valid information about the job, they will make better choices. Joseph Weitz showed this long ago with insurance agents, and more recently it has been illustrated with West Point cadets and telephone operators.[22] In the future, the most effective selection programs will have to emphasize providing individuals with valid data about themselves and about the nature of the organization. After this information is presented to the applicants, they will make the decision of whether to join the organization. Before this kind of "selection" system can be put into effect, however, much research is needed to determine how this process can be handled. We need to know, for example, what kind of information should be presented to individuals and how it should be presented. However, the problems involved in the approach are solvable and, given the current trends in society, this approach represents the most viable selection approach in many situations.

Conclusions

The research on reward systems, job design, leadership, selection, and training shows that significant individual differences exist in how individuals respond to organizational policies and practices. Because of this, an effective normative organization theory has to suggest an organization design that will treat individuals differently. Existing normative theories usually fail to emphasize this point. There are, however, a number of things that organizations can do now to deal with individual differences. These include cafeteria-style pay plans and selective job enrichment. Unfortunately, a fully developed practical organization theory based upon an individual difference approach cannot be yet stated. Still, it is important to note that approaches to shaping organizations to individuals are developing. It seems logical, therefore, to identify these and other similar efforts as attempts to individualize organizations. It is hoped that the identification of these efforts and the establishment of the concept of individualization will lead to two very important developments: the generation of more practices that will individualize organizations and work on how these different practices can simultaneously be made operational in organizations. Only if these developments take place will individualized organizations ever be created.

Notes

1. John J. Morse, "A Contingency Look at Job Design," *California Management Review,* Fall 1973, pp. 67–75.

2. Douglas McGregor, *The Human Side of Enterprise* (New York: McGraw-Hill, 1960).
3. Frederick Herzberg, *Work and the Nature of Man* (Cleveland: World, 1966).
4. Robert Blauner, *Alienation and Freedom* (Chicago: University of Chicago, 1964); and Edward E. Lawler, "Job Design and Employee Motivation," *Personnel Psychology* 22 (1969): 426–35.
5. Arthur Turner and Paul R. Lawrence, *Industrial Jobs and the Worker* (Boston: Harvard University School of Business Administration, 1965); and Charles L. Hulin and Milton R. Blood, "Job Enlargement, Individual Differences, and Worker Responses," *Psychological Bulletin* 69 (1968) 41–55.
6. J. Richard Hackman and Edward E. Lawler, "Employee Reactions to Job Characteristics," *Journal of Applied Psychology* 55 (1971): 259–86.
7. John J. Morse, "A Contingency Look at Job Design."
8. Edward E. Lawler, *Pay and Organizational Effectiveness: A Psychological View* (New York: McGraw-Hill, 1971).
9. William F. Whyte, *Money and Motivation* (New York: Harper, 1955).
10. Edward E. Lawler, *Pay and Organizational Effectiveness: A Psychological View.*
11. Stanley Nealy, "Pay and Benefit Preferences," *Industrial Relations* 3 (1963): 17–28.
12. Chris Argyris, "Personality and Organization Revisited," *Administrative Science Quarterly* 18 (1973): 141–167.
13. Victor H. Vroon, *Some Personality Determinants of the Effects of Participation* (Englewood Cliffs, N.J.: Prentice-Hall, 1960).
14. John R. P. French, J. Israel, and Dagfin As, "An Experiment on Participation in a Norwegian Factory," *Human Relations* 13 (1960): 3–19; and George Strauss, "Some Notes on Power-Equalization," in H. J. Leavitt, ed., *The Social Science of Organizations* (Englewood Cliffs, N.J.: Prentice-Hall, 1963).
15. Frederick E. Fiedler, "Predicting the Effects of Leadership Training and Experience from the Contingency Model," *Journal of Applied Psychology* 56 (1972): 114–19.
16. John P. Campbell and Marvin D. Dunnette, "Effectiveness of T-Group Experiences in Managerial Training and Development," *Psychological Bulletin* 70 (1968): 73–104.
17. Edwin E. Ghiselli, "Moderating Effects and Differential Reliability and Validity," *Journal of Applied Psychology* 47 (1963): 81–86.
18. Robert M. Guion, *Personnel Testing* (New York: McGraw-Hill, 1965).
19. Joan Woodward, *Industrial Organization: Theory and Practice* (London: Oxford University Press, 1965); Paul R. Lawrence and Jay W. Lorsch, *Organization and Environment* (Boston: Division of Research, Graduate School of Business Administration, Harvard University, 1967); Chris Argyris, *Integrating the Individual and the Organization* (New York: John Wiley, 1964); and Tom Burns and G. M. Stalker, *The Management of Innovation* (London: Tavistock Publications Limited, 1961).
20. Robert Kahn, "The Work Module—A Tonic for Lunchpail Lassitude," *Psychology Today* 6 (1973): 94–95.
21. Victor Vroom, *Work and Motivation* (New York: Wiley, 1964).
22. Joseph Weitz, "Job Expectancy and Survival," *Journal of Applied Psychology* 40 (1956): 245–47; and John P. Wanous, "Effect of a Realistic Job Preview on Job Acceptance, Job Survival and Job Attitudes," *Journal of Applied Psychology,* in press.

PART III

Groups and Interpersonal Influence

Editors' Summary Comments

*T*he behavior of groups in organizations poses an interesting yet perplexing problem for managers. On one hand, the manager must deal with a collection of individuals with varying characteristics; on the other hand, the group is itself an important entity with very definite characteristics of its own. Managers must, therefore, face the everyday occurrence of understanding the behavior of individuals, the behavior of individuals composing a group, and the behavior of one group in relationship with other groups.

Attempts at influencing behavior must be made from knowledge and understanding of the characteristics of both individuals and groups. First, individuals bring to the group various needs, dispositions, attitudes, and personality traits that serve to create the composition of the group. Second, over time this collection of individuals called a group develops behavioral norms, status systems, role prescriptions, emergent leaders, and cohesive characteristics. In the following articles, we will examine how managers must develop the necessary diagnostic skills that will lead to improved effectiveness.

In the first of six selections in this part, Irving Janis discusses a common problem of highly cohesive groups—that is, the tendency toward "groupthink." He describes situations in which cohesive groups composed of talented individuals sometimes plan and implement programs that are quite inappropriate and ineffective. Janis illustrates the groupthink phenomena with case examples from high-level governmental fiascos, and then suggests some guidelines for preventing groupthink.

A somehwat different approach to the study of groups is provided by James Ransom in "The Group Executive's Job: Mission Impossible?" The article illustrates a trend in organizations to replace strict functional divisions of responsibility with the group executive, or profit-center manager, position. The article provides the reader with a view of how a change to a pseudo-group activity can benefit the organization, but be somewhat troubling to the individual manager.

An often overlooked factor in the study of groups and interpersonal influence in organizations is the effect—sometimes significant effect—of the office environment. In "Keys to Success with Open Planned Offices," the authors discuss and summarize a number of studies of organizations that have changed to the open office plan. They point out that the state of employee morale *before* the move, key interdependencies and communications patterns, and the nature of the work can have a significant impact on how well a new office plan will be accepted and function.

The existence of conflict in hospital environments is examined by Rockwell Schulz and Alton Johnson in their article, "Conflict in Hospitals." The authors discuss institutional conflict, individual conflict, interpersonal conflict, administration-medical staff conflict, and nursing conflict. They conclude their selection by proposing an action program that involves procedures for diagnosing and resolving conflict.

To provide a more applied approach to the study of leadership, we have selected "Conversation with Fletcher Byrom." Byrom, chairman of Koppers, is a unique man and an exceptional executive. His "commandments" for managers—such as "hang loose," "listen to the winds of change," "keep your intuition well lubricated," and "use growth as a means of getting and keeping good people, and use those people as a means of achieving continued growth"—tell the reader how a successful manager interprets and uses situational leadership approaches in the world of the practitioner.

In the final selection in this part, "Managerial Work: Analysis From Observation," Henry Mintzberg presents some of the major features and characteristics of the manager's job. He believes that the manager's job can be best described by an analysis of the different roles that must be performed. The three main role categories—interpersonal, informational, and decisional—suggest that the manager must be able to perform in multiple roles in order to be effective.

9

Groupthink

Irving L. Janis

*H*ow could we have been so stupid?" President John F. Kennedy asked after he and a close group of advisers had blundered into the Bay of Pigs invasion. For the last two years I have been studying that question, as it applies not only to the Bay of Pigs decision-makers but also to those who led the United States into such other major fiascos as the failure to be prepared for the attack on Pearl Harbor, the Korean War stalemate and the escalation of the Vietnam War.

Stupidity certainly is not the explanation. The men who participated in making the Bay of Pigs decision, for instance, comprised one of the greatest arrays of intellectual talent in the history of American Government—Dean Rusk, Robert McNamara, Douglas Dillon, Robert Kennedy, McGeorge Bundy, Arthur Schlesinger Jr., Allen Dulles and others.

It also seemed to me that explanations were incomplete if they concentrated only on disturbances in the behavior of each individual within a decision-making body: temporary emotional states of elation, fear, or anger that reduce a man's mental efficiency, for example, or chronic blind spots arising from a man's social prejudices or idiosyncratic biases.

I preferred to broaden the picture by looking at the fiascos from the standpoint of group dynamics as it has been explored over the past three decades, first by the great social psychologist Kurt Lewin and later in many experimental situations by myself and other behavioral scientists. My conclusion after poring over hundreds of relevant documents—historical reports about formal group meetings and informal conversations among the members—is that the groups that committed the fiascos were victims of what I call "groupthink."

"Groupy"

In each case study, I was surprised to discover the extent to which each group displayed the typical phenomena of social conformity that are regularly encountered in studies of group dynamics among ordinary citizens. For example, some of the phenomena appear to be completely in line with findings from social-psychological experiments showing that powerful social pressures are brought to bear by the members of a cohesive group whenever a dissident begins to voice his objections to a group consensus. Other phenomena are reminiscent of the shared illusions observed in encounter groups and friendship cliques when the members simultaneously reach a peak of "groupy" feelings.

Above all, there are numerous indications pointing to the development of group norms that bolster morale at the expense of critical thinking. One of the most common norms appears to be that of remaining loyal to the group by sticking with the policies to which the group has already committed itself, even when those policies are obviously working out badly and have unintended consequences that disturb the conscience of each member. This is one of the key characteristics of groupthink.

1984

I use the term groupthink as a quick and easy way to refer to the mode of thinking that persons engage in when *concurrence-seeking* becomes so dominant in a cohesive ingroup that it tends to override realistic appraisal of alternative courses of action. Groupthink is a term of the same order as the words in the newspeak vocabulary George Orwell used in his dismaying world of *1984*. In that context, groupthink takes on an invidious connotation. Exactly such a connotation is intended, since the term refers to a deterioration in mental efficiency, reality testing and moral judgments as a result of group pressures.

The symptoms of groupthink arise when the members of decision-making groups become motivated to avoid being too harsh in their judgments of their leaders' or their colleagues' ideas. They adopt a soft line of criticism, even in their own thinking. At their meetings, all the members are amiable and seek complete concurrence on every important issue, with no bickering or conflict to spoil the cozy, "we-feeling" atmosphere.

Kill

Paradoxically, soft-headed groups are often hard-hearted when it comes to dealing with outgroups or enemies. They find it relatively easy to resort to dehumanizing solutions—they will readily authorize bombing attacks that kill large numbers of civilians in the name of the noble cause of persuading an unfriendly government to negotiate at the peace table. They are unlikely to pursue the more difficult and controversial issues that arise when alternatives to a harsh military solution come up for discussion. Nor are they inclined to raise ethical issues that carry the implication that *this fine group of ours, with its humanitarianism and its high-minded principles, might be capable of adopting a course of action that is inhumane and immoral.*

Norms

There is evidence from a number of social-psychological studies that as the members of a group feel more accepted by the others, which is a central feature of increased group cohesiveness, they display less overt conformity to group norms. Thus we would expect that the more cohesive a group becomes, the less the members will feel constrained to censor what they say out of fear of being socially punished for antagonizing the leader or any of their fellow members.

In contrast, the groupthink type of conformity tends to increase as group cohesiveness increases. Groupthink involves nondeliberate suppression of critical thoughts as a result of internalization of the group's norms, which is quite different from deliberate suppression on the basis of external threats of social punishment. The more cohesive the group, the greater the inner compulsion on the part of each member to avoid creating disunity, which inclines him to believe in the soundness of whatever proposals are promoted by the leader or by a majority of the group's members.

In a cohesive group, the danger is not so much that each individual will fail to reveal his objections to what the others propose but that he will think the proposal is a good one, without attempting to carry out a careful, critical scrutiny of the pros and cons of the alternatives. When groupthink becomes dominant, there also is considerable suppression of deviant thoughts, but it takes the form of each person's deciding that his misgivings are not relevant and should be set aside, that the benefit of the doubt regarding any lingering uncertainties should be given to the group consensus.

Stress

I do not mean to imply that all cohesive groups necessarily suffer from groupthink. All ingroups may have a mild tendency toward groupthink, displaying one or another of the symptoms from time to time, but it need not be so dominant as to influence the quality of the group's final decision. Neither do I mean to imply that there is anything necessarily inefficient or harmful about group decisions in general. On the contrary, a group whose members have properly defined roles, with traditions concerning the procedures to follow in pursuing a critical inquiry, probably is capable of making better decisions than any individual group member working alone.

The problem is that the advantages of having decisions made by groups are often lost because of powerful psychological pressures that arise when the members work closely together, share the same set of values and, above all, face a crisis situation that puts everyone under intense stress.

The main principle of groupthink, which I offer in the spirit of Parkinson's Law, is this: *The more amiability and esprit de corps there is among the members of a policy-making ingroup, the greater the danger that independent critical thinking will be replaced by groupthink, which is likely to result in irrational and dehumanizing actions directed against outgroups.*

Symptoms

In my studies of high-level governmental decision-makers, both civilian and military, I have found eight main symptoms of groupthink.

1 Invulnerability   Most or all of the members of the ingroup share an *illusion* of invulnerability that provides for them some degree of reassurance about obvious dangers and leads them to become over-optimistic and willing to take extraordinary risks. It also causes them to fail to respond to clear warnings of danger.

The Kennedy ingroup, which uncritically accepted the Central Intelligence Agency's disastrous Bay of Pigs plan, operated on the false assumption that they could keep secret the fact that the United States was responsible for the invasion of Cuba. Even after news of the plan began to leak out, their belief remained unshaken. They failed even to consider the danger that awaited them: a worldwide revulsion against the U.S.

A similar attitude appeared among the members of President Lyndon B. Johnson's ingroup, the "Tuesday Cabinet," which kept escalating the Vietnam War despite repeated setbacks and failures. "There was a belief," Bill Moyers commented after he resigned, "that if we indicated a willingness to use our power, they [the North Vietnamese] would get the message and back away from an all-out confrontation. . . . There was a confidence—it was never bragged about, it was just there—that when the chips were really down, the other people would fold."

A most poignant example of an illusion of invulnerability involves the ingroup around Admiral H. E. Kimmel, which failed to prepare for the possibility of a Japanese attack on Pearl Harbor despite repeated warnings. Informed by his intelligence chief that radio contact with Japanese aircraft carriers had been lost, Kimmel joked about it: "What, you don't know where the carriers are? Do you mean to say that they could be rounding Diamond Head (at Honolulu) and you wouldn't know it?" The carriers were in fact moving full-steam toward Kimmel's command post at the time. Laughing together about a danger signal, which labels it as a purely laughing matter, is a characteristic manifestation of groupthink.

2 Rationale   As we see, victims of groupthink ignore warnings; they also collectively construct rationalizations in order to discount warnings and other forms of negative feedback that, taken seriously, might lead the group members to reconsider their assumptions each time they recommit themselves to past decisions. Why did the Johnson ingroup avoid reconsidering its escalation policy when time and again the expectations on which they based their decisions turned out to be wrong? James C.

Thompson Jr., a Harvard historian who spent five years as an observing participant in both the State Department and the White House, tells us that the policymakers avoided critical discussion of their prior decisions and continually invented new rationalizations so that they could sincerely recommit themselves to defeating the North Vietnamese.

In the fall of 1964, before the bombing of North Vietnam began, some of the policy-makers predicted that six weeks of air strikes would induce the North Vietnamese to seek peace talks. When someone asked, "What if they don't?" the answer was that another four weeks certainly would do the trick.

Later, after each setback, the ingroup agreed that by investing just a bit more effort (by stepping up the bomb tonnage a bit, for instance), their course of action would prove to be right. *The Pentagon Papers* bear out these observations.

In *The Limits of Intervention,* Townsend Hoopes, who was acting Secretary of the Air Force under Johnson, says that Walt W. Rostow in particular showed a remarkable capacity for what has been called "instant rationalization." According to Hoopes, Rostow buttressed the group's optimism about being on the road to victory by culling selected scraps of evidence from news reports or, if necessary, by inventing "plausible" forecasts that had no basis in evidence at all.

Admiral Kimmel's group rationalized away their warnings, too. Right up to December 7, 1941, they convinced themselves that the Japanese would never dare attempt a full-scale surprise assault against Hawaii because Japan's leaders would realize that it would precipitate an all-out war which the United States would surely win. They made no attempt to look at the situation through the eyes of the Japanese leaders—another manifestation of groupthink.

3 Morality   Victims of groupthink believe unquestioningly in the inherent morality of their ingroup; this belief inclines the members to ignore the ethical or moral consequences of their decisions.

Evidence that this symptom is at work usually is of a negative kind—the things that are left unsaid in group meetings. At least two influential persons had doubts about the morality of the Bay of Pigs adventure. One of them, Arthur Schlesinger Jr., presented his strong objections in a memorandum to President Kennedy and Secretary of State Rusk but suppressed them when he attended meetings of the Kennedy team. The other, Senator J. William Fulbright, was not a member of the group, but the President invited him to express his misgivings in a speech to the policymakers. However, when Fulbright finished speaking the President moved on to other agenda items without asking for reactions of the group.

David Kraslow and Stuart H. Loory, in *The Secret Search for Peace in Vietnam,* report that during 1966 President Johnson's ingroup was concerned primarily with selecting bomb targets in North Vietnam. They based their selections on four factors—the military advantage, the risk to American aircraft and pilots, the danger of forcing other countries into the fighting, and the danger of heavy civilian casualties. At their regular Tuesday luncheons, they weighed these factors the way school teachers grade examination papers, averaging them out. Though evidence on this point is scant, I suspect that the group's ritualistic adherence to a standardized procedure induced the members to feel morally justified in their destructive way of dealing with the Vietnamese people—after all, the danger of heavy civilian casualties from U.S. air strikes was taken into account on their checklists.

4 Stereotypes Victims of groupthink hold stereotyped views of the leaders of enemy groups: they are so evil that genuine attempts at negotiating differences with them are unwarranted, or they are too weak or too stupid to deal effectively with whatever attempts the ingroup makes to defeat their purposes, no matter how risky the attempts are.

Kennedy's groupthinkers believed that Premier Fidel Castro's air force was so ineffectual that obsolete B-26s could knock it out completely in a surprise attack before the invasion began. They also believed that Castro's army was so weak that a small Cuban-exile brigade could establish a well-protected beachhead at the Bay of Pigs. In addition, they believed that Castro was not smart enough to put down any possible internal uprisings in support of the exiles. They were wrong on all three assumptions. Though much of the blame was attributable to faulty intelligence, the point is that none of Kennedy's advisers even questioned the CIA planners about these assumptions.

The Johnson advisers' sloganistic thinking about "the Communist apparatus" that was "working all around the world" (as Dean Rusk put it) led them to overlook the powerful nationalistic strivings of the North Vietnamese government and its efforts to ward off Chinese domination. The crudest of all stereotypes used by Johnson's inner circle to justify their policies was the domino theory ("If we don't stop the Reds in South Vietnam, tomorrow they will be in Hawaii and next week they will be in San Francisco," Johnson once said). The group so firmly accepted this stereotype that it became almost impossible for any adviser to introduce a more sophisticated viewpoint.

In the documents on Pearl Harbor, it is clear to see that the Navy commanders stationed in Hawaii had a naive image of Japan as a midget that would not dare to strike a blow against a powerful giant.

5 Pressure Victims of groupthink apply direct pressure to any individual who momentarily expresses doubts about any of the group's shared illusions or who questions the validity of the arguments supporting a policy alternative favored by the majority. This gambit reinforces the concurrence-seeking norm that loyal members are expected to maintain.

President Kennedy probably was more active than anyone else in raising skeptical questions during the Bay of Pigs meetings, and yet he seems to have encouraged the group's docile, uncritical acceptance of defective arguments in favor of the CIA's plan. At every meeting, he allowed the CIA representatives to dominate the discussion. He permitted them to give their immediate refutations in response to each tentative doubt that one of the others expressed, instead of asking whether anyone shared the doubt or wanted to pursue the implications of the new worrisome issue that had just been raised. And at the most crucial meeting, when he was calling on each member to give his vote for or against the plan, he did not call on Arthur Schlesinger, the one man there who was known by the President to have serious misgivings.

Historian Thompson informs us that whenever a member of Johnson's ingroup began to express doubts, the group used subtle social pressures to "domesticate" him. To start with, the dissenter was made to feel at home, provided that he lived up to two restrictions: 1) that he did not voice his doubts to outsiders, which would play into the hands of the opposition; and 2) that he kept his criticisms within the bounds of acceptable deviation, which meant not challenging any of the fundamental assumptions that went into the group's prior commitments. One such "domesticated dissenter" was Bill Moyers. When Moyers arrived at a meeting, Thompson tells us, the President greeted him with, "Well, here comes Mr. Stop-the-Bombing."

6 Self-censorship Victims of groupthink avoid deviating from what appears to be group consensus; they keep silent about their misgivings and even minimize to themselves the importance of their doubts.

As we have seen, Schlesinger was not at all hesitant about presenting his strong objections to the Bay of Pigs plan in a memorandum to the President and the Secretary of State. But he became keenly aware of his tendency to suppress objections at the White House meetings. "In the months after the Bay of Pigs I bitterly reproached myself for having kept so silent during those crucial discussions in the cabinet room," Schlesinger writes in *A Thousand Days*. "I can only explain my failure to do more than raise a few timid questions by reporting that one's impulse to blow the whistle on this nonsense was simply undone by the circumstances of the discussion."

7 Unanimity Victims of groupthink share an *illusion* of unanimity within the group concerning almost all judgments expressed by members who speak in favor of the majority view. This symptom results partly from the preceding one, whose effects are augmented by the false assumption that any individual who remains silent during any part of the discussion is in full accord with what the others are saying.

When a group of persons who respect each other's opinions arrives at a unanimous view, each member is likely to feel that the belief must be true. This reliance on consensual validation within the group tends to replace individual critical thinking and reality testing, unless there are clear-cut disagreements among the members. In contemplating a course of action such as the invasion of Cuba, it is painful for the members to confront disagreements within their group, particularly if it becomes apparent that there are widely divergent views about whether the preferred course of action is too risky to undertake at all. Such disagreements are likely to arouse anxieties about making a serious error. Once the sense of unanimity is shattered, the members no longer can feel complacently confident about the decision they are inclined to make. Each man must then face the annoying realization that there are troublesome uncertainties and he must diligently seek out the best information he can get in order to decide for himself exactly how serious the risks might be. This is one of the unpleasant consequences of being in a group of hardheaded, critical thinkers.

To avoid such an unpleasant state, the members often become inclined, without quite realizing it, to prevent latent disagreements from surfacing when they are about to initiate a risky course of action. The group leader and the members support each other in playing up the areas of convergence in their thinking, at the expense of fully exploring divergencies that might reveal unsettled issues.

"Our meetings took place in a curious atmosphere of assumed consensus," Schlesinger writes. His additional comments clearly show that, curiously, the consensus was an illusion—an illusion that could be maintained only because the major participants did not reveal their own reasoning or discuss their idiosyncratic assumptions and vague reservations. Evidence from several sources makes it clear that even the three principals—President Kennedy, Rusk and McNamara—had widely differing assumptions about the invasion plan.

8 Mindguards Victims of groupthink sometimes appoint themselves as mindguards to protect the leader and fellow members from adverse information that might break the complacency they shared about the effectiveness and morality of past decisions. At a large birthday party for his wife, Attorney General Robert F. Kennedy, who had been constantly informed about the Cuban invasion plan, took Schlesinger aside and asked him why he was opposed. Kennedy listened coldly and said, "You may be right or you may be wrong, but the President has made his mind up. Don't push it any further. Now is the time for everyone to help him all they can."

Rusk also functioned as a highly effective mindguard by failing to transmit to the group the strong objections of three "outsiders" who had learned of the invasion plan—Undersecretary of State Chester Bowles, USIA Director Edward R. Murrow, and Rusk's intelligence chief, Roger Hilsman. Had Rusk done so, their warnings might have reinforced Schlesinger's memorandum and jolted some of Kennedy's ingroup, if not the President himself, into reconsidering the decision.

Products

When a group of executives frequently displays most or all of these interrelated symptoms, a detailed study of their deliberations is likely to reveal a number of immediate consequences. These consequences are, in effect, products of poor decision-making practices because they lead to inadequate solutions to the problems being dealt with.

First, the group limits its discussions to a few alternative courses of action (often only two) without an initial survey of all the alternatives that might be worthy of consideration.

Second, the group fails to reexamine the course of action initially preferred by the majority after they learn of risks and drawbacks they had not considered originally.

Third, the members spend little or no time discussing whether there are nonobvious gains they may have overlooked or ways of reducing the seemingly prohibitive costs that made rejected alternatives appear undesirable to them.

Fourth, members make little or no attempt to obtain information from experts within their own organizations who might be able to supply more precise estimates of potential losses and gains.

Fifth, members show positive interest in facts and opinions that support their preferred policy; they tend to ignore facts and opinions that do not.

Sixth, members spend little time deliberating about how the chosen policy might be hindered by bureaucratic inertia, sabotaged by political opponents, or temporarily derailed by common accidents. Consequently, they fail to work out contingency plans to cope with foreseeable setbacks that could endanger the overall success of their chosen course.

Support

The search for an explanation of why groupthink occurs has led me through a quagmire of complicated theoretical issues in the murky area of human motivation. My belief, based on recent social psychological research, is that we can best understand the various symptoms of groupthink as a mutual effort among the group members to maintain self-esteem and emotional equanimity by providing social support to each other, especially at times when they share responsibility for making vital decisions.

Even when no important decision is pending, the typical administrator will begin to doubt the wisdom and morality of his past decisions each time he receives information about setbacks, particularly if the information is accompanied by negative feedback from prominent men who originally had been his supporters. It should not be surprising, therefore, to find that individual members strive to develop unanimity and esprit de corps that will help bolster each other's morale, to create an optimistic outlook about the success of pending decisions, and to reaffirm the positive value of past policies to which all of them are committed.

Pride

Shared illusions of invulnerability, for example, can reduce anxiety about taking risks. Rationalizations help members believe that the risks are really not so bad after all. The assumption of inherent morality helps the members to avoid feelings of shame or guilt. Negative stereotypes function as stress-reducing devices to enhance a sense of moral righteousness as well as pride in a lofty mission.

The mutual enhancement of self-esteem and morale may have functional value in enabling the members to maintain their capacity to take action, but it has maladaptive consequences insofar as concurrence-seeking tendencies interfere with critical, rational capacities and lead to serious errors of judgment.

While I have limited my study to decision-making bodies in Government, groupthink symptoms appear in business, industry and any other field where small, cohesive groups make the decisions. It is vital, then, for all sorts of people—and especially group leaders—to know what steps they can take to prevent groupthink.

Remedies

To counterpoint my case studies of the major fiascos, I have also investigated two highly successful group enterprises, the formulation of the Marshall Plan in the Truman Administration and the handling of the Cuban missile crisis by President Kennedy and his advisers. I have found it instructive to examine the steps Kennedy took to change his group's decision-making processes. These changes ensured that the mistakes made by his Bay of Pigs ingroup were not repeated by the missile-crisis ingroup, even though the membership of both groups was essentially the same.

The following recommendations for preventing groupthink incorporate many of the good practices I discovered to be characteristic of the Marshall Plan and missile-crisis groups:

1. The leader of a policy-forming group should assign the role of critical evaluator to each member, encouraging the group to give high priority to open airing of objections and doubts. This practice needs to be reinforced by the leader's acceptance of criticism of his own judgments in order to discourage members from soft-pedaling their disagreements and from allowing their striving for concurrence to inhibit criticism.
2. When the key members of a hierarchy assign a policy-planning mission to any group within their organization, they should adopt an impartial stance instead of stating preferences and expectations at the beginning. This will encourage open inquiry and impartial probing of a wide range of policy alternatives.
3. The organization routinely should set up several outside policy-planning and evaluation groups to work on the same policy question, each deliberating under a different leader. This can prevent the insulation of an ingroup.
4. At intervals before the group reaches a final consensus, the leader should require each member to discuss the group's deliberations with associates in his own unit of the organization—assuming that those associates can be trusted to adhere to the same security regulations that govern the policy-makers—and then to report back their reactions to the group.
5. The group should invite one or more outside experts to each meeting on a staggered basis and encourage the experts to challenge the views of the core members.
6. At every general meeting of the group, whenever the agenda calls for an evaluation of policy alternatives, at least one member should play devil's advocate, functioning as a good lawyer in challenging the testimony of those who advocate the majority position.
7. Whenever the policy issue involves relations with a rival nation or organization, the group should devote a sizable block of time, perhaps an entire session, to a survey of all

warning signals from the rivals and should write alternative scenarios on the rivals' intentions.

8. When the group is surveying policy alternatives for feasibility and effectiveness, it should from time to time divide into two or more subgroups to meet separately, under different chairmen, and then come back together to hammer out differences.

9. After reaching a preliminary consensus about what seems to be the best policy, the group should hold a "second-chance" meeting at which every member expresses as vividly as he can all his residual doubts, and rethinks the entire issue before making a definitive choice.

How

These recommendations have their disadvantages. To encourage the open airing of objections, for instance, might lead to prolonged and costly debates when a rapidly growing crisis requires immediate solution. It also could cause rejection, depression and anger. A leader's failure to set a norm might create cleavage between leader and members that could develop into a disruptive power struggle if the leader looks on the emerging consensus as anathema. Setting up outside evaluation groups might increase the risk of security leakage. Still, inventive executives who know their way around the organizational maze probably can figure out how to apply one or another of the prescriptions successfully, without harmful side effects.

They also could benefit from the advice of outside experts in the administrative and behavioral sciences. Though these experts have much to offer, they have had few chances to work on policy-making machinery within large organizations. As matters now stand, executives innovate only when they need new procedures to avoid repeating serious errors that have deflated their self-images.

In this era of atomic warheads, urban disorganization and ecocatastrophes, it seems to me that policymakers should collaborate with behavioral scientists and give top priority to preventing groupthink and its attendant fiascos.

10

The Group Executive's Job:
Mission Impossible?

James H. Ransom

John Doughtery is 48 years old, prosperous, and by most measures a clear success. John, his wife of 20 years, Mary, and their three children live in a large home in an affluent suburban community, where they enjoy many of the pleasures of the good life, brought about through John's $150,000-plus income. To their friends and acquaintances, the Doughterys represent much of the best that American life has to offer.

Yet, over the past two years, Mary has seen John become increasingly discontented, frustrated, and irritable. He complains about a lack of any sense of accomplishment, a growing sense of isolation from both his peers and his subordinates, and nagging doubts about his own self-worth.

John is a group vice-president.

John came to his present position as group vice-president of industrial products at AFT Industries three years ago from Arnold Products, Inc., where he had been vice-president and general manager of the Cole Division, manufacturers of specialty molding machinery. In his seven years as general manager, with full control over Cole's key business functions, John had rebuilt his division's management team and refocused its division's strategy. He prided himself on his track record at Cole, and with reason. In his last five years there sales had more than doubled, reaching $130 million, and profits had tripled. John's personal touch in picking key personnel, in shaping the management controls, and in refocusing Cole's strategic direction had built a strong base for the parent company's continued profitable participation in this business.

Nevertheless, when Bill Hartwell of Hartwell, Calder & Associates, approached John about a possible jump from Arnold to a group executive's post at AFT Industries, he listened with real interest. After

SOURCE: James H. Ransom, "The Group Executive's Job: Mission Impossible. Reprinted, by permission of the publisher, from *Management Review,* March 1979, pp. 9–14, © 1979 by AMACOM, a division of American Management Associations. All rights reserved.

all, Cole was in good shape, and he saw no early opportunities for advancement at Arnold. The position at AFT seemed to promise much broader responsibilities and more of a top-management role—and it offered an immediate salary increase of over 30 percent, plus a potentially more attractive bonus. So John took the bait and made his move.

Three years later, John finds himself not only frustrated and unhappy, but also worried about his own capabilities, his contribution at AFT, and his longer-term future. In the course of a long talk, several basic causes of John's frustration emerge:

> John's decision latitude has not grown; in some ways, it has actually narrowed. Although John is nominally responsible for five divisions with total sales of more than $500 million, the degree of commonality between the divisions' products, technology, and markets is very limited. Thus, the key strategic business unit is the division, not the group. Key decisions relative to product or market are made at the division level. At the group level, John's strategic options are narrow—the whole is not greater than the sum of its parts.

> John's role as profit center executive is unclear. His responsibility and authority appear to be completely out of balance. On paper he appears to have direct line authority over his devisions, but his ability to exercise that authority is compromised by the need to build entrepreneurial responsibility and authority at the division level. Thus, as group executive, John feels himself responsible for divisional performance (he is in fact, largely paid on this basis), yet he cannot often intervene directly with specific corrective action. He finds himself in the role of thinker, planner, and director yet confronted with the responsibilities of a doer.

> John's supposed top-management role and expected contribution are equally vague. Although the opportunity to play "a key role" in AFT's top management had been a major factor in his decision to take the job, few signs of any such opportunity have been evident in the past three years. John is expected to concentrate on "providing leadership" to his own group; his chances to contribute to other groups or to overall corporate direction are minimal. He feels he is little more than a conduit between the chief executive and the divisional general managers. In fact, the CEO has more than once bypassed him and gone directly to his division managers, thus undercutting John's authority and undermining his capacity to "be responsible."

What Is the Problem?

Unfortunately—as any executive search firm can corroborate—John's experience is far from unique. Discussions with numerous group executives confirm a high degree of dissatisfaction with this position.

And, most CEOs will admit that the position is not without its problems. They recognize that many group executives find these positions neither attractive nor personally rewarding. Often few seem to feel that their contribution to corporate management amounts to much more than administrative simplification.

Why is the group executive's role such a problematic one? There are three principal reasons.

First, the group executive is generally considered a general manager—either a super division manager or a CEO with something less than the total pie. Yet neither of these concepts meets the test of reality. As in John's case, the position rarely carries either the operational decision latitude of a division manager or the strategic options of a CEO. Thus, the group executive is neither fish nor fowl. If he made his mark as a hard-driving functional and division general manager and aspires to "run the whole show," he is inevitably frustrated in such a situation. One central problem, then, is that of role definition.

Second, the group executive's position often lacks the mechanisms or resources to contribute much to the performance of his divisions or to the overall direction of the corporate entity. He has few if any staff resources of his own and too little corporate staff support to help him participate effectively in either division or corporate affairs. Hence, the corporation has a group of energetic, talented and highly-paid executives who find themselves little more than "administrators, consolidators of the numbers and information conduits." A second issue, then, relates to the group executive's ability to contribute.

Finally, there is the problem of motivation and reward. John, like most group executives, is well paid by any standard, yet finds little satisfaction in his compensation. He is essentially a long-term director and strategist with little direct impact on his divisions' year-to-year performance, yet his annual income is directly tied to their collective short-term financial results. Moreover, his nonfinancial rewards—his prestige, if you will—again is based not on strategic contribution but on operational performance. Thus, it is his divisional managers who get the lion's share of the credit. He is viewed by the CEO as the general manager of the group and little more, and thus John finds little tendency on the part of his CEO to share credit or even recognize John's contribution to AFT's overall strategic performance. The final issue, therefore, is individual recognition.

Given John's experience and that of many others like him, one might argue that the group executive concept is a failure and ought to be scrapped. Regrettably, however, no fundamentally different structured alternative has been put forth. Most organizational practitioners defend the concept in principle, and most CEOs of highly diversified corporations seem to agree that some sort of management layer is needed between themselves and their numerous operating divisions. Somehow these diverse business activities must be grouped into a manageable number of units. Enter the group executive.

Despite its apparent shortcomings, then, the group executive organizational structure is likely to persist as a fact of corporate life. How well it works will depend less on its inherent structural wisdom than on the manner of its execution.

Making the Broad Concept Workable

If the CEO of a highly diversified company must adopt some sort of group concept, if only for the sake of administrative simplicity, how can he maximize the position's contribution to the company's total management capability? Or, to put it more simply, how can the group executive's job be made meaningful? Initiatives under way in a number of companies seem to suggest that the full answer requires some modification of management style as well as concept.

1 Shifting the CEO's Attitude Though they would deny it, many CEOs act as if the group executive were there to remedy shortcomings in division management performance rather than to enhance their own capacity to manage a diverse and complex corporate enterprise. A recent discussion with the CEO of a problem-ridden diversified industrial goods company pointed up this problem. Two of the three groups had been performing well below the CEO's expectations for several years. To remedy the problem, the CEO had hired no less than four different group executives within the past seven years. Had he urged any of them to replace any division managers? Not at all; in fact, he had acted to prevent any such changes. Many of these managers had long careers with the corporation. Perhaps they weren't all "fully qualified general managers," but all they needed was the sort of "guidance and support" that "a good group vice-president" should be able to provide.

Where the real issue, as in this case, is divisional rather than corporate management capabilities, it is surely better to take corrective action at the division level, either by replacing the general manager or by augmenting his functional or staff resources. Merely installing a "super division manager" above the senior division executive is no remedy for substandard divisional performance.

The CEO must recognize that the adoption of a group executive structure reflects not a shortcoming in divisional management capability, but rather a limitation of top-management capacity. The decision to move to a group executive structure logically implies a sharing and extension of top-management (CEO) responsibilities to a broader group of executives. It does not imply the creation of a new "super division," called the group, which the CEO can now manage in his traditional style.

In most cases, key functional resources and decisions remain at the division level. Often, as in the case of John Doughtery's company, AFT, the groups simply represent areas of business interests or emphasis—that is, industrial products—with limited strategic commonality. Thus, the group as a new business unit is, in general, more a theoretical concept than practical reality. Division and corporate must remain the primary areas of management emphasis.

If corporate top-management capacity is to be augmented by the addition of several group executives to the top-management structure, then some of the CEO's responsibilities and authority must neccesarily flow to the group executives. In plain language, the CEO must share some of his power rather than continuing to "manage through" the group executives.

If the CEO is to share his responsibilities, he must be prepared to adopt a style more akin to that of a chairman of a management council. And, indeed, the more effective group structures reflect such a participative style on the part of the CEO. In such companies, the group executive's role is one of advising, counseling, and sharing decisions.

2 Adjusting the Structural Concept   If the primary purpose of the group level is to augment and enhance top-management capacity of the CEO, this notion should be reflected in the top-management structure. Typically, however, the organization chart reinforces the concept of the "super division" managed by the CEO "through" the group executive. Little, if any, flavor of shared top-management responsibility is evident.

A standard corporate group structure is illustrated in Figure 1. Heavy emphasis is placed on line authority flowing through the group executives to division management. Group executive responsibility and authority are clearly narrow in scope directed downward to specific divisions. The organization chart suggests no interaction among group executives; it places primary emphasis on individual rather than collective performance. It is a picture of top and group management—not of top and divisional management.

Figure 2 suggests a very different sort of group executive concept. The adoption of an Executive Council as the key top-management structural element, comprising the CEO, group executives, and the senior corporate staff officers, identifies the group executive as an integral part of top management and reinforces the need for a participative top management style. Line authority flows from the Council to the divisions; group executives continue to have divisional interests, but they focus more heavily on corporate-wide priorities and requirements.

Figure 1   Standard Corporate Group Structure

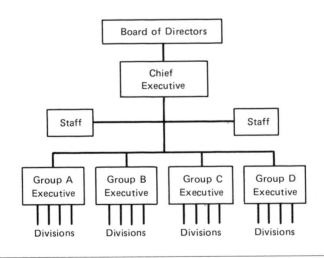

Figure 2   Executive Council Concept of Group Structure

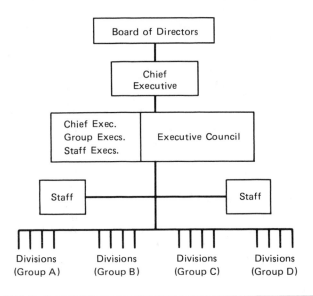

Figures 1 and 2 also suggest a substantially different working relationship between the group executive and CEO. Figure 1 emphasizes one-on-one interaction between the CEO and group executive—interaction that might on occasion be extended downward to include a particular division manager. The focus of communication tends to be narrow, from the CEO down through the group executive to the division. Figure 2, in contrast, implies participative discussion among group executives, the CEO, and corporate staff. It suggests an open executive forum for consideration, debate, and decision.

Under the Executive Council concept, the group executive is no longer merely a conduit for the CEO's decisions; he becomes the primary communicator of decisions reached by the Council. At the same time, his role of thinker, planner, and director is reinforced. Week to week, he will continue to work with, support, and advise the division and general managers within his group. But he will do so in the context of the total corporate strategy, with the authority and judgment of the council and perspective of the CEO. He will be able to effectively *direct* the efforts of the divisions, without attempting to manage their day-to-day operations and performance.

3 Emphasizing Division Performance   A third key element in the successful implementation of a group structure is maintaining performance emphasis at the divisional and corporate levels rather than at group. Demanding and measuring performance at the group level is usually an unrealistic overextension of the profit concept, since significant managerial leverage is usually very restricted at this level. Only at divisional level are enough managerial and staff resources concentrated to materially effect profit performance. Hence, responsibility for profit and loss should continue to center on the division general manager.

The fictional nature of the "group performance" concept was brought home in a recent conversation with a veteran group vice-president of a divisional food manufacturing concern. Over the past year, there had been much internal debate over the assignment of divisions to specific groups, as certain divisions did not seem to fit logically into any broader strategic or business category. Eventually, however, some reassignments were agreed to. Persistent questioning finally revealed the rationale for the reassignments: its was to balance profit performance among groups—that is, to ensure in advance that all groups, *as* groups, would turn in an acceptable performance.

Although consolidated group numbers may be interesting, they are rarely actionable—and it should never be forgotten that they may mask outstanding or disastrous performance by individual divisions. Moreover, their value as an index of the group executive's contribution is almost always severely limited. Adding the numbers up by group is typically a rather academic exercise that tends to distract the chief executive's attention from the much more meaningful issue of divisional performance.

4 Altering the Rewards System   A final step in reinforcing the concept of the group executive as an integral part of top management is reshaping the rewards system. Outstanding division performance should be rewarded at the division level; outstanding corporate performance at the corporate level. Group performance, per se, whether outstanding or marginal, should seldom be an important factor, or indeed a factor at all.

If a group executive is expected to pull his weight as a member of top management, his rewards must largely be predicated on his contribution to total corporate success or failure. Clearly in the case of an effective group structure, this contribution should not be confined to the economic contribution of the group of divisions that happen to have been assigned to him. Rather, it should be measured mainly in terms of his judgment and contribution to top-management decisions.

This refocusing of the rewards system has three implications:

> The CEO must be willing to share the limelight with his group executives—his Executive Council—both publicly and privately. He must be willing for the good of the group to suppress his personal need for ego reinforcement. He must find ways for each group executive to represent the total corporate entity both internally and externally. And he must reinforce the top-management role of the group executives in their interactions with division general managers.
>
> Perhaps one of the most effective ways of ensuring a viable external role for the group executive is to help him win a position of importance in the local or national community. One CEO I know has developed an individual external-relations program for each of his senior executives. This group of talented senior executives has been able by

active service on local and national nonprofit boards to provide substantial corporate and personal contributions to the community. At the same time, their involvement has reduced the external demands on the CEO's own time.

Second, the financial reward system must also reinforce the group executive's top-management role. His compensation should be tied, not to the size of his group and its economic contribution to the corporation, but to his personal contribution to top management. By the same token, group incentives or bonuses should be tied much more closely to overall corporate performance than to short-term group profit contribution.

Third, rewards of both credit or money should be tied to the long-term performance of the corporation. Emphasis should be placed on an individual group executive's contribution to carrying out the *total* corporate strategic plan and aiding the achievement of longer-term strategic goals. Group compensation plans tied to overall corporate performance over the longer term tend to be most effective in building an integrated top-management team.

5 Picking the right managers   No ingredient is more important at the top, of course, than individual capability, and this holds true as well at the group level. Group executives should not be picked merely for their demonstrated ability to "run a business" or for their knowledge of a particular industry. These may be useful in predicting performance, but they do not suffice to ensure outstanding contribution at this level. At least three additional criteria are probably essential:

The group executive must be an effective team player. At the group level, the ability to work effectively with peers and with staff units over which one has no direct authority is more important than the ability to build a management team. Often, this capability can only be assessed by evaluating an individual's performance before he becomes a general manager at the business unit level.

The group executive must be able to take a broad-gauge, top-management perspective. A parochial viewpoint centering on a particular industry or function will severely limit his contribution to the top-management team and undercut his credibility with his peers.

Executives with wide industry and functional experience often make the best group executives, just as they tend to make the best chief executive officers.

The group executive must also be an effective representative of the corporation to its external public—stockholders, security analysts, government agencies, and so on. He must communicate the corporate viewpoint effectively without grandstanding or focusing attention on himself at the expense of his top-management colleagues.

The task of picking top management talent is arduous at best, for there is no reliable winning formula. Nevertheless, these three additional criteria suggest that the outstanding division general manager and outstanding group executive are not always one and the same person.

Looking Ahead

Despite its faults and frustrations, the group executive structure will probably be an integral part of the corporate world for some time to come. Observation of successful group organizations suggests that the effectiveness of the group structure can be enhanced and the contribution of the individual group executives magnified if the roles of the CEO and the group executive are appropriately modified. If these role changes are reinforced by a sound structural concept, the right performance focus, a balanced rewards system, and sound selection criteria, the group executive should be able to contribute far more effectively to sound corporate performance.

11

Keys to Success with Open Planned Offices

Andrew D. Szilagyi,
Winford E. Holland
and Christie Oliver

*A*s dwellers in the modern phenomenon known as the office building, we make decisions, supervise, communicate, and interact with other employees within the confines of the office environment. An important but frequently overlooked factor is that the *effectiveness* of our decisions, supervision, communications, and interactions can be significantly influenced by the degree to which the design of the office meets the needs and work requirements of the organization. In other words, a properly designed office can have a positive effect on employee productivity and job satisfaction.

This statement gains in importance when we are confronted with the significant evolution that is occurring today in the office design industry. Many of the new office buildings—and some remodeled older structures—have been designed around what has been variously termed the "open planned office" concept, or the "office landscaping" principle. Even the most casual observer of these new open planned offices, however, will recognize that two distinctly different sets of attitudes prevail among the office workers. Some employees love the new office layout, and some thoroughly hate it! Organizations need to know more about the process of changing offices before they spend hundreds of thousands of dollars that may lock them into a design that doesn't work for them.

The authors believe that a major reason for these mixed reactions, and a primary cause of the differing sets of employee attitudes, is that

SOURCE: Andrew D. Szilagyi, Winford E. Holland, and Christie Oliver, "Keys to Success with Open Planned Offices," *Management Review* (in press).

the changing of office configurations is more than an artistic exercise. In reality, a change in office configuration is a significant *organizational change intervention* that can influence the attitudes and performance of involved employees.

Stated differently, the architect and space designer are working, on one hand, to create a new office image which is appealing to the client—a physical layout that is more colorful, more elaborate, or more flexible and conservative in space. The client organization, on the other hand, may be openly asking for this new image, but underneath there remains the implicit requirement that the organization be equally or more effective after the move to the new space. The effectiveness of any new office design is dependent on the manner in which the "visual change" orientation of the architect and designer is integrated with the "behavioral change" perspective of the client's managers, so that the result is an improvement in employee satisfaction and productivity. This integration of visual and behavioral change is the subject of this paper.

The authors have recently conducted a series of studies in a number of organizations that have changed to the new open planned office. We will attempt to summarize and share our findings in order to point out the benefits and problems associated with this significant trend in office design. The open planned office is not for everyone, and it may have been overpromoted. With proper diagnosis and a knowledge of the keys to success, however, this new office design concept can prove to be quite beneficial to many organizations.

The Open Planned Office Design

The open design, while only of fairly recent vintage in offices, has been implemented in other structures for nearly two decades. Early applications were in elementary schools, later in secondary schools, and finally in higher education. In commercial establishments, open planned offices today account for slightly more than 15 percent of all existing office space in the U. S., with the trend continuing rapidly upward. Most architects, interior designers, and office furniture manufacturers point to statistics that show that new buildings—and major remodeling efforts in older structures—utilizing open office designs are increasing twice as fast as units incorporating traditional plans.

The open planned design is founded on two principles: flexibility and cost savings. First, the traditional office tends to be low in flexibility, with solid doors and floor-to-ceiling walls that often hinder the process of work, and it tends to locate employees on the basis of rank and status in the organization. Such an arrangement not only can discourage interaction and communications between employees, but it could act as a major obstacle when making office rearrangements dictated by an organizational structural change. The open planned office may be a viable alternative to the traditional office because of its flexible use of movable partitions, its emphasis on freedom of employee interaction, and its use of modularized furniture. An extensive use of plants, special lighting, and masking sound systems frequently accompanies the open planned design and provides additional flexibility.

Second, from a cost perspective, the open planned office offers a significant savings in office costs, especially during new construction and physical rearrangements. With today's increasing lease costs, such savings on the cost of space are great. Some architects indicate that there may be as much as 40 percent savings in construction costs when the open plan is used. The built-in flexibility and cost saving associated with the open design are positive factors, particularly when such changes as new projects or a needed redesign in responsibility and authority relationships occur. Both Eastman Kodak and Pizza Hut Incorporated have successfully used the open planned concept to facilitate flexible and cost saving rearrangements of their headquarters.

Besides space flexibility and cost savings, the hoped-for outcome of a move could be a more effective organization. Unfortunately, few studies have been conducted or reported that have shown solid improvements in productivity or job satisfaction in organizations that have adopted the open planned design. In fact, using observational methods, the results of open planned office changes have been anything but consistently positive. The most frequently mentioned problems concern issues related to increased noise levels, crowding, and lack of privacy, status, and security. These results can possibly be attributed to the fact that the important factors influencing office design effectiveness have not been properly diagnosed or considered.

Factors Related to Office Design Effectiveness

As pointed out above, if office design changes are considered as an organizational change intervention, the process can be looked at from a totally different viewpoint. From this perspective, the universal, or "one office design fits all" strategy is strongly rejected. Instead, the emphasis is placed on diagnosis and understanding of the key characteristics of the organization *before* any design change is planned or implemented. On the basis of the authors' recent studies on open office designs, three categories or factors, shown in Exhibit 1, were found to significantly influence design effectiveness. These are: (1) the state of employee morale; (2) work flow requirements; and (3) individual job characteristics.

State of Employee Morale

The state of employee morale, possibly the most important factor impacting office design success, concerns the general attitudes held by employees *before the space change* toward the practices, policies, and relationships in the organization. In essence, the state of morale will probably dictate the employees' *reaction* to the new office design and their level of receptivity.

Architects speak in design terms such as visual status, physical freedom, security, privacy, and adaptability. Our studies have shown that employee satisfaction with the reward system (e.g., pay and promotion), the work itself, and supervision will directly affect the employees' reaction to these design characteristics.

Exhibit 1 Factors in Office Design Effectiveness

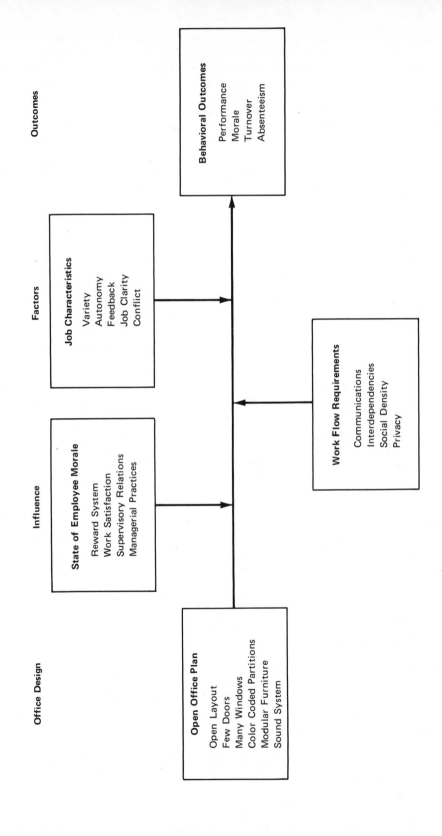

Office Design

Influence

Factors

Outcomes

Open Office Plan

Open Layout
Few Doors
Many Windows
Color Coded Partitions
Modular Furniture
Sound System

State of Employee Morale

Reward System
Work Satisfaction
Supervisory Relations
Managerial Practices

Job Characteristics

Variety
Autonomy
Feedback
Job Clarity
Conflict

Behavioral Outcomes

Performance
Morale
Turnover
Absenteeism

Work Flow Requirements

Communications
Interdependencies
Social Density
Privacy

For example, in all of our studies we found that the employees' pay satisfaction and promotion satisfaction were related to their attitudes about the office's visual status and security components. When significant levels of pay dissatisfaction existed—either from an inadequate performance evaluation system or because pay raises didn't equal inflation rates—the open office was perceived as an additional threat to the employees' security. Or consider the recently promoted manager who had been struggling for years for the "big" office. He or she moves to the open office and the hard-fought-for walls, solid doors, big desk, and thick rug disappear. Needless to say, the visual status component of the new office may not be highly valued by that employee.

Attitudes about the degree of physical freedom and adaptability in the office are influenced by the employees' level of work satisfaction. Employees in potentially boring, mundane, and dissatisfying jobs such as secretarial and clerical positions generally viewed office design changes as an ineffective mechanism to reduce their dissatisfaction. On the other hand, employees who hold challenging, complex jobs (engineers, computer specialists, and other professionals) were found in our studies to view the office's freedom and adaptability features in a positive manner.

Finally, our results revealed that the state of supervisor-subordinate relations influenced attitudes towards privacy and physical freedom of the office. In particular, when poor supervisory relations existed, subordinates viewed the open concept as just another managerial ploy to reduce their freedom of interaction and to allow supervisors to better "keep an eye" on workers.

A key managerial factor to remember is this: the state of employee morale establishes the *foundation* for the reaction to the new open office. High employee morale will enhance employee design receptivity; low morale will hinder receptivity. The latter describes the case where organizational factors are so inadequate that nothing looks good to employees, not even a sparkling new office!

Work Flow Requirements

Another important success factor for managers to investigate is the important work flow requirements needed for high productivity levels. Three basic considerations should be evaluated.

First, where are the key interdependencies among employees; or, in other words, what are the visual and verbal communications requirements between employees? Our study in a claims and adjustment department of a large insurance firm can illustrate these critical employee relationships. Initially, the 150-employee department was arranged in a large bull-pen type design with no visual barriers other than file cabinets and structural pillars. The department manager occupying a corner office had an unobstructed view of all employees and their interactions. During a slack season, the office floor on which the department was located was re-designed along an open planned design (i.e., eight-foot high color-coded partitions with built-in furniture and files). The immediate result was chaos—employee conflict increased and productivity dropped dramatically. What the architects, designers, and department manager failed to consider was that the process of settling an insurance claim required visual and verbal communications between employees, particularly when a policy holder was held on the phone. Partitions prohibited the needed communications and interfered with employee dependency relationships.

During the four months the open plan was in use (the "old" office plan was later readopted), some interesting employee coping behaviors were found. Initially, extra chairs were added by employees to stand on in order to look over the partitions. Later, many partitions were found with holes unceremoniously cut in them so that employees could talk to one another.

The *second* work flow requirement concerns the concept of social density. *Social density* for each worker is defined as a map of the possible physical accessibility of the worker to colleagues. The important measurement difference between physical density and social density should be carefully considered. Physical density concerns the architectural concept of the number of workers within a particular straight-line radius, while social density relates to the number of workers within a particular *walking distance*. Walking distance (e.g., 50 feet), as opposed to straight-line radius, was considered by the authors as a much better measure of the effort needed for face-to-face employee interactions. For example, some employees could share a floor-to-ceiling wall and be physically only 8 feet apart; if face-to-face communications were required, one employee would need to walk 30 feet to the other office. As shown in Exhibit 2, two office designs equal in terms of physical density can be quite different when looked at from a social density perspective.

The studies we have conducted to date have shown that the effect of social density changes is strongly related to the type of work being done by employees. For example, a product planning and new business development department of a large petroleum company physically moved from a traditional office layout to a more open office just two city blocks away. Those employees who experienced a significant social density increase experienced less conflict, greater job clarity, and increased job satisfaction when compared with the old, traditional office. Professional interactions and information flow—key factors for successful job performance—were apparently improved, resulting in the reported positive effects.

On the other hand, social density decreases experienced by long-distance and information-assistance telephone operators resulted in a dramatic drop in worker morale and a rise in customer complaints. Further investigation revealed that the new office arrangement—a change from the long operating board to a modular, open planned design—eliminated the valued employee factor of *social* interaction. The routine, mundane nature of the telephone operator's job created both tension and boredom. In the old office arrangement these negative features were partially countered by the ability to talk to one's closest colleagues. By placing operators in work modules separated by partitions, the operators' ability to release tension and boredom was reduced, resulting in decreased morale and work performance.

Exhibit 2   Physical Space and Social Density Space

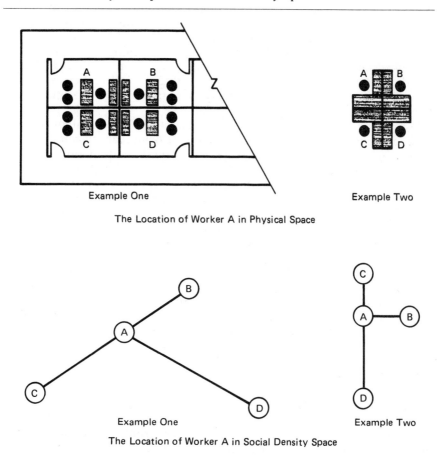

Example One   Example Two

The Location of Worker A in Physical Space

Example One   Example Two

The Location of Worker A in Social Density Space

The third important work flow requirement is to maintain the level of privacy needed by the employees to perform day-to-day activities. The openness associated with 6-foot high partitions can have a negative effect when delicate and secret discussions are conducted in individual offices. International Harvester Company, after converting several sections of its Chicago headquarters to an open plan, had to revert back to the floor-to-ceiling design in the personnel and corporate planning departments. Managers in these departments apparently felt that the open planned concept could not guard the confidentiality of certain conversations. This resulted in a *lessening* of communications, which is just the opposite of what the open plan had been designed to do!

Job Characteristics
For nearly two decades, behavioral scientists have stressed the importance of the nature of the job as an important factor in employee motivation. Such approaches as job enlargement, Herzberg's job enrichment, and the

more current job redesign approach continue to be studied and discussed in both research and practitioner literature. The salient proposal made by these approaches is that making the employee's job more challenging, complex, and meaningful will result in improved motivation, morale, and productivity. In office planning, a frequently overlooked factor is that changes in physical layout can possibly change individual jobs and the way employees view these jobs. In other words, motivation, morale, and/or productivity may unknowingly be enhanced or retarded by changing the office design.

Most job design specialists define the characteristics or content of jobs in a number of terms, the most frequent being variety, autonomy, performance feedback, and challenge. The overall assumption is that improvements in any one characteristic (or some combination) will commensurately improve motivation. In the previously discussed study in the petroleum company, we found that changes in some job characteristics occurred when social density increased as a result of the move to the new office. For those professionals experiencing a social density *increase,* performance feedback increased but autonomy decreased when the new design was compared to the old traditional office. In essence, being brought physically closer by the new design enabled these professionals to receive more information and feedback on their activities from their colleagues. The "closeness," however, removed some of the autonomy and freedom of action they previously enjoyed. The decrease in autonomy appeared not to have a significant negative effect on morale or motivation; the positive effects of the increase in feedback overshadowed any negative effects from the decreases in autonomy.

Keys to Success

A number of keys to success can be developed from the experience of managers and from the studies reported here on the open planned office design. While these keys to success are not intended to be all-inclusive, they are presented to assist managers to both understand and interpret actual and anticipated employee reactions to a change in office design.

1. *Set definite goals for the office change.* Explicit goals for the move should be set whether they be a simple need for more space or a need for increased coordination between office personnel. One goal for the move should always be to improve or at least hold the present level of organizational morale, motivation, and performance. An office move can do some things but not others. For example, an office move will rarely diminish problems of morale that stem from poor supervisory relations or the reward system. On the other hand, an office move can impact employee satisfaction with co-workers. In no case should a move be made with the expectation that new walls, colors, and appointments will "turn the organization around" or "give us a new breath of fresh air."

2. *Put the right people in charge of the office change.* Two people play critical roles in the planning and implementation of the office change: the interior architect and the company's "move coordinator." The interior architect should know his or her business and know how his or

her business affects *your* business. He must be able to design to the goals you have set for the move. If your architect goes cross-eyed when you ask how his design will impact the organizational pattern of information flow, you need to start looking for a different space designer. The company's move coordinator will be responsible for pulling off a major organization change and not just a rearrangement of furniture. The coordinator needs the management skills and the organizational credibility to handle a complex and potentially powerful organizational maneuver. Criteria for selection of the coordinator should *not* be the ones we have used for years: (1) he's got nothing else to do right now; (2) he can't do anything else; and/or (3) we need to get him out of our hair for a while. The ability to arrange the prompt arrival of furniture (or even to select it from a catalog) is not the needed prerequisite for the move coordinator. These two key people must work as a team to insure that the goals of the move are met with the greatest efficiency and the least disruption of organizational life.

3. *Conduct an organizational diagnosis prior to the design of the new office space.* For the designer to meet the goals of the move, he or she needs information about the state of the organization. He needs to know the overall morale level so that employee reactions can be anticipated. He needs to know the organizational climate characteristics so that his design can retain positive features and work toward eliminating negative ones. The move coordinator also needs diagnostic information that will help him or her locate and cope with the inevitable pockets of resistance to the office change. In addition, the move coordinator may use diagnostic information to work with management to re-frame some (or all) of the recently formed goals for the office change. For example, if the diagnosis points toward significant horizontal communications problems, a "communication improvement" goal may need to be included in the goals set for the move.

4. *Evaluate the level of importance that status symbols are given by employees.* The open planned office, with its emphasis on freedom of interaction and communications, rarely can match the traditional office plan in terms of the impact of status symbols. The desire for a spacious office with a solid wood door, a large desk, windows with a desirable view, and the security associated with the important feeling of solitude, is a powerful ego drive and, hence, a powerful motivational factor for many managers. The move to an open planned office, at least initially, may be viewed by some employees as a blow to their egos, particularly when status symbols are valued highly. Our studies indicate that this issue is more of a problem when it concerns hierarchical or *level* status (e.g., manager versus supervisor) rather than *professional* status (e.g., planner versus computer programer). Professional status differences tend to decrease with time as employees adapt to the new office. Level status differences, however, can remain for a considerable length of time, resulting in conflict, an increase in dissatisfaction, and/or turnover. The organizations in our study that successfully overcame this problem allowed employees with the title "manager" or "director" to have private offices for confidential conversation activities (e.g., employee performance reviews). In accordance with open planned designs, these private offices, however, did not differ greatly from the other open

offices in terms of decor elements (e.g., furniture). In addition, managers in these private offices were required to be located as close to their subordinates as possible in order to maintain the freedom of interaction and communication principles.

5. *Examine the work flow requirements, communications patterns, and worker interdependencies in the old and new office designs for their impact on performance.* Any physical movement of personnel and facilities can alter well established communications patterns and worker interactions. An office design should strengthen or at least not disrupt such interactions, particularly if they are needed for effective performance. It would also behoove the manager to think of office designs not only in terms of physical density, but also in terms of social density. The impact of social density changes on employees will vary significantly, depending on the work being performed. Employees such as product planners or management information system specialists, whose jobs require a high level of information flow and interaction to be effective, probably would react favorably to the social density increases common to open designed offices. On the other hand, where jobs require a great deal of independence and privacy (e.g., personnel specialists or corporate officers) a social density increase with an open planned office might be viewed as a disadvantage.

6. *Carefully evaluate the impact of the office design change on the individual worker's job so that the motivating potential of the job is not seriously damaged.* If we internalize the view that an office design rearrangement is really an organizational change intervention, then managers should be concerned about the side effects of the change. One such side effect—changes in job characteristics—can have a direct and significant impact on how motivated employees are to perform their jobs. The autonomy and performance feedback characteristics can be dramatically altered in an open designed office. A visually appealing office is of secondary importance when the motivation levels of employees decrease.

7. *Forecast your future manpower and office equipment needs/trends so that the right amount of flexibility can be part of the office design.* Recent surveys and statements by knowledgeable authorities suggest that the office of the future will be characterized by an increased emphasis on accessibility to computer terminals, electronic typing, sophisticated telecommunications, and filing, printing, and copying equipment. In addition, organizational design specialists have suggested that the trend toward the use of the matrix organizational structure will continue at a rapid pace in all types of institutions. Each of these factors is clearly more feasible in an open planned office than in more traditional office designs. In other words, the long-term benefits of the open planned office may far overshadow some of the short-term problems.

8. *Encourage participation of functional managers and subordinates in both the design and implementation stages of the new office change.* Participation by potentially affected employees in the change process is a logical but infrequently used mechanism in office design changes. Such participation can benefit the organization in two ways. First, since these managers and subordinates must live in this new work environment, knowledge of the key factors for high productivity could create a better

design. For example, process engineers and geologists require extensive wall space for displaying and examining drawings and diagrams. Building this component into the new office design *before* the change, as opposed to alterations *after* the change, could save the organization significant costs associated with work-flow disruptions and lost time. Second, successful participation in a change process increases the probability of employee *commitment* to the design change. By acquiring a feeling that they have had some say in the change, employees can develop a sense of "ownership" that can reduce resistance to change and help smooth the transition and acceptance of the new office plan.

Summary

In summary, the open planned office concept is now, and will probably continue to be, a significant factor in the work environment of many employees. With the rising costs of leasing and operating expenses, the space savings and flexibility benefits of the open office will become increasingly important to many organizations. We have attempted in this article to stress that not only are open offices not for everyone, but where actually adopted, certain key factors in the organization—the state of employee morale, work flow requirements, and job characteristics—must be carefully considered. It is only through the use of thorough diagnostic activities, careful design, and careful implementation that managers can reap the potential benefits of an office design change.

12

Conflict in Hospitals

Rockwell Schulz and
Alton C. Johnson

*E*vidence of conflict in hospitals is readily apparent. Nurse and nonprofessional hospital employee strikes receive wide publicity. Periodically, administrator-medical staff conflicts break into public view. Furthermore, hospital-client conflicts seem to be increasing as consumers of hospital service level charges of inefficiency and inattention to consumer expectations. Internally, the administrator is continually faced with eruptions of personal or departmental conflicts.

The first step in resolving conflict is to identify the underlying forces fostering it. This paper reviews empirical research reported in management, sociological and hospital literature for insight into some of these underlying forces. The scope of this review includes a brief consideration of hospital-client, interpersonal and individual conflicts. Conflicts related to administrators, medical staff and nursing groups are discussed in somewhat greater depth. Finally, some mitigators of conflict are suggested.

Modern management literature describes benefits that are derived from a reasonable amount of organizational and individual conflict.[1] Indeed, confrontation is sometimes necessary in order to achieve overdue reforms. Just how serious, then, is conflict in hospitals?

One might expect conflict to affect quality of patient care adversely. This tends to be confirmed by studies of Georgopoulos and Mann, who found higher quality care in hospitals where physicians and nurses had a greater understanding of each other's work, problems and needs.[2] Studies in mental hospitals report patients are affected adversely by staff conflict.[3] While conflict might foster institutional innovation and progress, the

SOURCE: R. Schulz and A. C. Johnson, "Conflict in Hospitals," *Hospital and Health Services Administration.* Reprinted with permission from the quarterly journal of the American College of Hospital Administrators, Hospital Administration (Now retitled, *Hospital & Health Services Administration*) 16, no. 3 (Summer 1971): 36–50.

welfare of the individual patient is served more effectively with institutional stability and harmony. Moreover, conflict can be debilitating for participants, rigidify the social system in which it occurs, and lead to gross distortions of reality.[4] Thus, this paper assumes that minimizing conflict is an important goal and it suggests sources and mitigators of conflict.

Institutional Conflict

Evidence of client-hospital conflict is increasing; however, few empirical studies have been conducted to examine this problem. Patients have very little voice in hospital matters, nor, until quite recently, have they seemed to desire one; largely we suspect, because they've assumed that professionals know what's best for them. Etzioni notes that only in public monopolies (e.g., the post office) do clients have less influence than in hospitals.[5] Apparently, he does not see current constituencies of hospital governing boards as an effective voice for the client. The recent report by the Urban Coalition tends to support the view that patients, especially the poor, do not have a proper voice in decision making.[6]

A lack of clearly defined community service goals could be an underlying factor in hospital-client hospital conflict. Etzioni suggests that "sometimes an organizational goal becomes the servant of the organization rather than its master. . . . Goals can be distorted by frequent measuring of organizational efforts, because as a rule, some aspects of its output are more measurable than others."[7] Certainly, hospitals are susceptible to this inversion of ends and means. The hospital financial statement, for example, is one of the few easily understood measurements available to trustees and administrators, and it usually stresses institutional goals as opposed to patient goals.

Conflict or competition between hospitals is evident from the major programs, such as comprehensive health planning, designed to reduce it. However, there appears to be little empirical research on the seriousness, underlying sources, or measurable effects of such conflict. It can be assumed that displacement of community service goals by institutional goals would be an important factor in such conflicts. What is best for an individual hospital is not always best for the society it serves.

Conflict Within Institutions

Certain internal characteristics inherent in the hospital organization foster conflict. For example, interdependence, specialization and heterogeneity of personnel and levels of authority, all appear to be related positively to conflict.[8] In fact, few organizations are composed of as many diverse skills as the hospital, which generally has nearly three employees for each patient and a heterogeneous health team influenced by over 300 different professional societies and associations.

Individual Conflict

An individual's role in the hospital can have a major effect on conflict to which he is subjected. His personal characteristics and past environment will determine the impact and his coping mechanisms to role conflict. Role theory, including role conflict, has received considerable study, although not in a hospital setting. It is easy to imagine role conflict faced by physicians, nurses, and administrators. The physician, for example, functions as an agent for an individual patient, his specialty, his profession, his staff, his institution, his community, and his own welfare as an individual practitioner. The welfare of these individuals and groups and obligations of the physician to them and to himself are periodically in conflict. The nurse is frequently caught between multiple lines of authority. The administrator usually functions in a boundary role; that is, he is frequently in a position between the nurse and physician, two physicians, patient and employee, etc.

Role ambiguity is related to role conflict. Role ambiguity can be defined as uncertainty about the way one's work is evaluated by superiors, uncertainty about scope of responsibility, opportunities for advancement, and expectations of others for job performance. A variety of studies have demonstrated that there is frequently a wide disparity between what a superior expects of his subordinate and what the subordinate thinks the superior expects of him. In an industrial setting Kahn found the individual consequences of role ambiguity generally comparable to individual effects of role conflict. They include, "low job satisfaction, low self-confidence, a high sense of futility, and a high score on the tension index."[9]

A Coping Mechanism: Retreat

Surveys in industrial enterprises found that tension and strain increase directly with occupational status. Individuals in professional and technical occupations experienced the most tension followed by managerial, then clerical and sales.[10] However, Kahn found the medical administrator in the industrial plant who works under conditions of high role conflict scored low on tension.[11] In a case study he found the administrator kept potential conflicts in a delicate balance by retreating into his own section of expertise, i.e., statistical and financial management. The obvious implication is that the administrator can minimize conflict and tension by restricting his role. While this represents one case study in a nonhospital setting, one can logically assume a relationship between the scope of an administrator's role and his effort to effect changes and administrative conflict. Such a coping mechanism may aid the equanimity of the administrator but will not help him fulfill his broader obligations and responsibilities. Kahn's studies also relate personality variables to experiences of strain from conflict.[12] He found tension more pronounced for introverts, for emotionally sensitive people, and individuals who are strongly achievement-oriented. Personality characteristics also affected exposure to role conflict and tension. Individuals who are relatively flexible and those who are achievement-oriented are more subjected to conflict pressures.

Interpersonal Conflict

Interpersonal conflict is defined broadly to include both (a) interpersonal disagreements over substantive issues, such as policies and practices; and (b) interpersonal antagonisms, that is, the more personal and emotional differences which arise between interdependent human beings.[13] Both forms are broadly evident in the hospital setting. Interpersonal antagonisms would seem to be more prevalent in hospital operations because by nature they deal with emotions. However, no studies were found related to relative frequency, severity, or source of interpersonal conflict in hospitals.

Administration-Medical Staff Conflict

Whereas in industry top executives usually enjoy both formal and informal power and status, power and status do not appear to be centered in the same individuals in the hospital organization. This characteristic, rather unique to hospital organization, is a basic source of administration-medical staff conflict.

Power has been defined as the maximum ability of a person or group to influence individuals or groups. Influence is understood as the degree of change that may be effected in individuals or groups. Authority has been defined as legitimate power.[14] In reviewing a variety of authors, Filley and House have summarized the basis of power being derived from (1) legitimacy; (2) control of rewards and sanctions, including money; (3) expertise; (4) personal liking; and (5) coercion.[15] Observation tells us that the hospital administrator usually has (1) legitimacy from delegated authority for hospital affairs from the governing board; (2) effective control of funds, beds, and other resources; (3) increasing expertise, particularly as management information systems improve; (4) personal liking; and (5) ability to coerce through demands of such sources as the Joint Commission on the Accreditation of Hospitals. Studies by Perrow and Georgopoulos and Mann tend to confirm the increasing dominance of the administrator.[16] Recent demands by the American Medical Association and medical staff in many hospitals for medical staff representation on hospital boards tend to confirm their protestations of declining influence.

The Factors of Status

Other studies are somewhat conflicting; however, they appear to relate more to factors of status. For example, Georgopoulos and Mann, after describing the administrator as most influential, describe his source of influence as delegated authority from trustees, while sources of physicians' influence include their expertise, prestige, status, and power among patients and the community.[17] A recent survey reported that "trustees and medical staffs do not view the administrator as a leader, but as a generally passive influence caught between the board and doctors."[18]

Goss suggests that physicians tend to view administration as a less prestigious kind of work.[19]

The hospital administrator's drive for professionalism and his desire for more prestigious titles such as president or executive vice president tend to suggest that he believes he needs to improve his status. As physicians attempt to maintain or increase their power, and administrators improve their status, presumably, both tend to feel threatened. Under such circumstances conflict increases.

Physicians and nurses, like professionals in other fields, have primary allegiance to professional status rather than to organizational status.[20] Hence, the potential for professional-institutional goal conflict is present.

The hospital organization is sometimes referred to as a duopoly with essentially autonomous administrative and medical staff organizations. Croog suggests that each system is oriented to a different set of values, one emphasizing provision of service, one emphasizing maintenance of operation of organization.[21] The Barr report related hospital inefficiencies to this dual management authority.[22] Other studies tend to confirm the presence of a conflict between bureaucractic routine and individualized patient care.[23] Perhaps a more flexible organizational structure with emphasis upon project teams would reduce this type of conflict.

Nursing Conflict

Considerable basic conflict in nursing is evident from many studies. Most of these inquiries indicate that nurses are satisfied with their vocation, but dissatisfied with specific conditions of salary, work load, working hours, etc.[24] However, Argyris suggests more basic problems, such as frustration of the dominant predispositions of nurses.[25] He reports nurses in the hospital he studied were not able to fulfill effectively important predispositions, such as being self-controlled, indispensable, compatible, and expert. Findings of Corwin, Taves and Scott, reported later in this paper, seem to support these conclusions.

Status may be a source of basic conflict among nurses. In years past, nursing was one of the few careers a woman could enter and attain some degree of professional prestige. Today, more vocational opportunities are opening to women as sex discrimination continues to decline. Women can, or at least sometimes believe they can, gain greater recognition in such fields as business, government, medicine and teaching.[26] Whereas nurses had been virtually the only professionals in the hospital outside of the physicians, they are now receiving increasing competition for status from a proliferation of allied health professionals, many of whom have higher standards of education, pay, and autonomy. In his survey of student nurses and personnel in three major hospitals, Taves found that "compared to student nurses who have a relatively high image of nursing on the average, the image that the general duty nurse holds seems to be especially low. . . . Head nurses have a somewhat better image of nursing than general duty nurses." He also found that other hospital personnel had an even lower image of nursing.[27]

Struggle for Professionalism

Frustrations are evident in nursing's struggle for professionalism. Corwin and Taves suggest that "the drive to gain professional status and achieve a unique place of importance within the hospital's division of labor, inevitably brings the group into conflict with the lay administration and physicians who are jealous of their prima donna status within the hospital scheme."[28] Scott states that the nurses' drive for professionalism may be based on carving out a special niche for themselves in which they can operate relatively independently from control by other groups and which allows them some claim to superior status.[29]

Organizational factors present conflicts for nurses. Nurses' career advancement has shifted from an individual to an organizational context wherein a nurse must move through the bureaucratic hierarchy to gain recognition. Rewards in this hierarchy, however, do not reflect professional patient care, but administrative duties. Argyris suggests that nurses believe that an administrator is a second-class citizen. He also suggests that the only area where a nurse is free to "blow her top" is in the administrative area, and this adds another factor which keeps administration in a low status function.[30] On the other hand, Taves found that nursing personnel who have higher ranking official positions in the organization are more satisfied with their jobs than lower ranking personnel.[31]

The Need to Mitigate and Control Conflict

Others suggest sources of nursing conflict can be a lack of role and job consensus,[32] type of care,[33] and dislike of working with nonprofessionals.[34]

Regardless of the source, it is evident that a considerable degree of conflict exists in hospitals. The problem then, is one of developing ways and means of mitigating or at least controlling conflict. The next section suggests some approaches to the resolution of this problem.

Action Program

Figure 1 presents a decision model related to diagnosing and mitigating conflict. It lists conflict participants and some of the underlying sources of conflicts presented in this paper. A brief description of the mitigators listed in the exhibit follows.

Comprehensive Institutional Goal Setting

Comprehensive institutional goal setting is a formalized program to define goals and objectives *explicitly*. Too often goals are defined implicitly, such as "high quality care at low cost." Explicit goals state measures affecting quality and costs. Often goals can be stated in terms of specially attainable objectives.

Goal definition should begin with a study of the needs of the society the institution intends to serve in order to obviate displacement of goals. Medical staff members and employees, in addition to administrators and trustees, should participate in setting goals. Sociologists, political scientists and economists, as well as planners and citizens of the publics served, can provide appropriate resource personnel to deliberations. Explicit institutional goals aid community understanding, assist internal and external evaluation of outputs reducing overemphasis on inputs such as costs and facilities, help to sublimate personal differences by focusing efforts on end results, and help to marshall required resources for attaining goals.

Organizational Changes, Public Relations Programs

Communications can be improved by broadening official lines of communication with citizens served by the institution. Policies for governing board membership might be revised to represent more

Figure 1*   *Decision Model for Diagnosing and Mitigating Hospital Conflict*

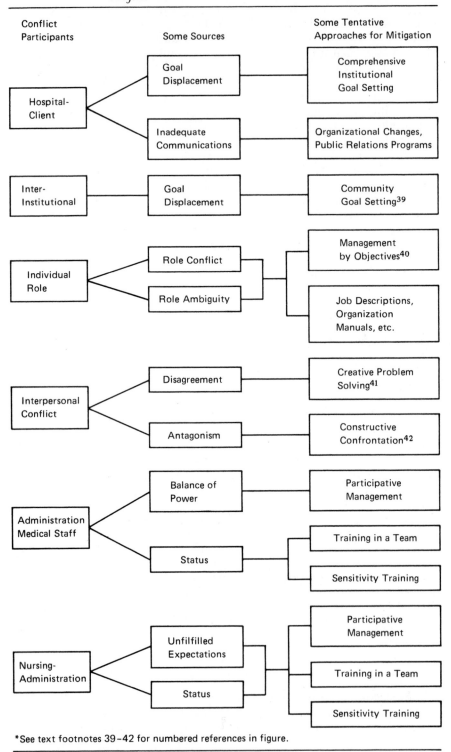

appropriately the constituencies served. Or, an advisory board might be established to review expressed needs of constituencies and hospital programs to meet needs. A public relations program based on appropriate client attitude surveys can be beneficial.

Community Goal Setting

While many communities are preparing plans for community health services, few have effectively articulated explicit goals and objectives that plans should serve. The City of Dallas is a notable exception.[35] There, community goals for health services provide a framework for institutions to coordinate individual goals and plans.

Management by Objectives and Role Definition

Management by objectives is the participation between the subordinate and his superior in setting the subordinate's goal.[36] Through interaction and discussion, a subordinate can determine precisely what is expected of him, thus reducing anxiety resulting from ambiguity, while at the same time improving worker independence in task performance and at the same time increasing accountability.

Role definition through job descriptions and administrative manuals can also help to reduce role conflict and ambiguity. These tools are familiar to most administrators.

Creative Problem-Solving

Creative problem-solving utilizes techniques that sublimate antagonistic conflict and fosters creativity in participative problem-solving. Maier notes the distinction between "choice behavior" which is an examination and a selection from the alternatives, and "problem-solving," which is a searching or idea-getting process.[37] By turning choice situations into problem-solving situations, participants are more apt to focus on end results rather than on who is presenting or standing for what. It maximizes creativity and sublimates hostility, self-pity, and rigidity. Creative problem solving promotes end results wherein everyone wins, rather than a choice situation in which there is a winner and loser or a compromise wherein everyone loses.

Constructive Confrontation

Issues of conflict tend to proliferate when there are interpersonal antagonisms between individuals. A manager can take steps to avoid issues that may result in open interpersonal conflict between individuals. However, indirect effects of interpersonal antagonism will frequently persist and in the long run may be more damaging than an open confrontation. Walton suggests using constructive confrontation with third-party intervention, particularly by consultants from outside the institution.[38] Components of confrontation include (1) clarifying the issues with parties; (2) expressing feelings descriptively; (3) expressing facts and fantasies; and (4) resolution and agreement. It would appear, however, that third-party intervention should be utilized sparingly.

Participative Management

Participative management is a philosophy of management in which hospital employees and physicians participate in a meaningful way in the administration of the hospital. It is a philosophy espoused by Rensis Likert and by the late Douglas McGregor, who wrote of "theory X and theory Y."[39] Studies by Coleman, Gamson and Corwin support the view that broad participation in authority systems minimizes major incidents of conflict, although minor incidents may be more frequent.[40]

Management by objectives and comprehensive institutional goal setting are examples of participative management. The administrator does not abdicate his responsibility, he shares it. By sharing planning, coordination, control, and management information, the administrator can actually gain more control over his responsibilities.[41]

Sensitivity Training

Sensitivity training, with emphasis on institutional social system development, can help to overcome "hang-ups" related to concerns over status.[42] Laboratory training based on the more traditional group dynamics training is suggested rather than the recent individual self-awareness training which at times borders on therapy. It is the latter, personal development training, that has been maligned recently.

Training in a Team

Health workers are expected to function as a team, yet they are seldom trained for this role. Hospital administrators spend more time with physicians and nurses than any other group. It would be beneficial if they had meaningful dialogue in the formative educational period. This could be easily arranged through seminars or research projects on such subjects as ethics, legal problems, group dynamics, contemporary problems in health, to name just a few. Opportunities for informal as well as formal associations should be arranged. Interdisciplinary study or informal association can also be arranged through the work environment.

Combined degree programs between medicine and hospital administration and/or nursing and hospital administration should be considered seriously. In addition to improving team associations at the educational level, it would help to improve administrative skills of those who actually administer a large part of health service and health team.

In Summary

Conflict in hospitals is an incredibly complex issue. While it deserves considerably more research, much can be done to apply current knowledge of sources and mitigating activities. In general, increased demand for services and attempts to diagnose and lessen conflicts will result in new policies and procedures. Among these will be research studies to identify the impact of various conflict situations. In addition, one can expect to see changes in goal setting, planning, organizational relationships and training programs.

Notes

1. Among them are: Amitai Etzioni, *Complex Organizations* (New York: Holt, Rinehart & Winston, 1961), pp. 124–26; Mason Haire, *Modern Organization Theory* (New York: Wiley, 1965); and Robert L. Kahn, *Organizational Stress* (New York: Wiley, 1964).

2. Basil S. Georgopoulos and Floyd C. Mann, *The Community General Hospital* (New York: Macmillan Co., 1962), p. 400.
3. Alfred H. Stanton and Morris S. Schwartz, *The Mental Hospital* (New York: Basic Books, 1954), pp. 342–65; and William A. Caudill, *The Psychiatric Hospital as a Small Society* (Howard University Press, 1958), pp. 87–127, as reported by Peter M. Blau and Richard W. Scott, *Formal Organizations* (Chandler, 1962), pp. 53–54.
4. Richard Walton, *Interpersonal Peacemaking* (Addison Wesley, 1969), p. 5.
5. Amitai Etzioni, *Modern Organizations* (Englewood Cliffs, N.J.: Prentice-Hall, 1964), p. 95.
6. *Rx for Action,* Report of the Health Task Force of the Urban Coalition, John Gardner, Chairman (Washington, 1969).
7. Etzioni, op. cit., pp. 4–11.
8. Victor Thompson, "Hierarchy, Specialization & Organizational Conflict," *Administrative Science Quarterly,* p. 519, and Ronald Corwin, "Patterns of Organizational Conflict," *Administrative Science Quarterly,* December 1969, pp. 507–21.
9. Robert L. Kahn, *Organizational Stress* (New York: Wiley, 1964), p. 380.
10. Ibid., p. 144.
11. Ibid., pp. 362–71.
12. Ibid., pp. 225–335.
13. Walton, op. cit., p. 3.
14. Alan C. Filley and Robert J. House, *Managerial Process and Organization Behavior* (Glenview, Ill.: Scott, Foresman & Co., 1969, p. 55.
15. Ibid., p. 61.
16. Charles Perrow, "Goals and Power Structure," *The Hospitals and Modern Society,* Eliot Friedson, ed. (Free Press, 1963), pp. 112–46, and article in *Handbook of Organizations;* and Georgopoulos, op. cit., p. 567.
17. Georgopoulos, op. cit., p. 567.
18. "Trustee's View of Administrators Told," *Modern Hospital,* October 1968, p. 29.
19. Mary E. W. Goss, "Patterns of Bureaucracy Among Staff Physicians," *The Hospital,* p. 180.
20. Chris Argyris, *Diagnosing Human Relations in Organizations: A Case Study of a Hospital* (New Haven: Yale University, Labor and Management Center, 1965), p. 62; and W. G. Bennis et al., "Reference Groups and Loyalties in the Outpatient Department," *Administrative Science Quarterly,* March 1958.
21. S. H. Croog, "Interpersonal Relations in Medical Settings," *Handbook of Medical Sociology,* H. E. Freeman, S. Levine, and L. G. Reeder, eds. (Prentice-Hall, 1963), p. 256.
22. Secretary's Advisory Committee on Hospital Effectiveness, Department of Health, Education, and Welfare, 1967.
23. *Abstracts of Hospital Management Studies,* vol. IV (June 1968). University of Michigan, pp. 137–40 and 196.
24. R. G. Corwin and Marvin J. Taves, "Nursing and Other Health Professions," *Handbook of Medical Sociology,* pp. 187–212, and Argyris, op. cit.
25. Argyris, op. cit., p. 189.
26. Corwin and Taves, op. cit., note that studies in two states indicated teaching outranked nursing in prestige (p. 193).
27. Corwin and Taves, op. cit., p. 189.
28. Ibid., p. 206
29. W. Richard Scott, "Some Implications of Organization Theory for Research on Health Services," *Milbank Memorial Fund Quarterly,* XLIV, no. 4, Part 2 (October 1966), p. 52.
30. Argyris, op. cit., pp. 67–69.
31. Taves, op. cit., p. 51.
32. Ibid., p. 74 and p. 205; Georgopoulos, op. cit., p. 398; and Argyris, op. cit., p. 10.

33. Perrow, op. cit., p. 965. Perrow reported a study by Coser which found nurses giving only custodial care were alienated because they were "unable to implement a single goal."
34. Argyris, op. cit., p. 70.
35. *Goals for Dallas,* Dallas, Texas, 1966.
36. George Odiorne, *Management by Objectives* (Pitman, 1965).
37. Norman F. Maier, "Maximizing Personal Creativity Through Better Problem Solving," *Personal Administration* 27 (1964); and Alan C. Filley and Andre Delbecq, "On the Possibility of a Better World," University of Wisconsin (unpublished).
38. Richard E. Walton, *Third Party Consultation* (Addison-Wesley, 1969).
39. R. Likert, *New Patterns in Management* (McGraw-Hill, 1961); and D. McGregor, *The Human Side of Enterprise* (McGraw-Hill, 1960).
40. James S. Coleman, *Community Conflict* (Glencoe, Ill.: Free Press, 1957); William Gamson, "Rancorous Conflict in Community Politics," *American Sociological Review* 31, pp. 71–81; and Ronald G. Corwin, "Patterns in Organizational Conflict," *Administrative Science Quarterly,* December 1969, pp. 507–20.
41. A. S. Tannenbaum, "Control in Organizations: Individual Adjustment and Organizational Performance," *Administrative Science Quarterly,* September 1962, p. 236.
42. Paul C. Buchanan, "Laboratory Training and Organization Development," *Administrative Science Quarterly,* September 1969, pp. 466–77; Kurt Lewin, *Resolving Social Conflicts: Selected Papers on Group Dynamics* (Harper, 1948).

13

Conversation with Fletcher Byrom

William F. Dowling

*F*letcher Byrom is a man of many titles, which, in turn, bespeaks a diversity of interests and accomplishments—chairman of the board and chief executive officer of Koppers, chairman of the President's Export Council, chairman of the Committee for Economic Development, trustee of Allegheny College and the Carnegie Mellon University, and director of the Mellon National Bank, ASARCO, the Continental Group, and the Ralston Purina Company. The list is partial.

Titles, however, are unspecific. They indicate that their possessor is a high achiever, an unordinary man. But they tell next to nothing about what distinguishes him from the commonality of his kind, even from the commonality of an exceptional kind.

In reading about Byrom, in reading what he has written—more important, in talking to him—we get an intuition about his governing passion. He is a man convinced that the key role of the chief executive officer of any corporation is to act as a role model for the managers in the corporation and he is equally convinced of what that role model should be. His provocative talk, "Hang Loose: A Message to My Successor," which details his Nine Commandments, contains the mandatory disclaimer that he doesn't confuse himself with God. But a lawgiver, in the meaning personified by Solon, the living embodiment of the collective wisdom and conscience of the organization, that's a role we suspect he would find it difficult to disown.

According to Confucius, when the king inquired what to do about a large number of thieves, the reply was, "If you, sir, were not covetous, although you should reward them to do it, they would not steal." Just so. And the CEO is the king, the climate setter in his organization.

What kind of climate does Fletcher Byrom seek to create at Koppers? In a sense, that's what this whole conversation is about. We will attempt, however, to put a few points in relief.

SOURCE: Reprinted, by permission of the publisher, from *Organizational Dynamics,* Summer 1978, © 1978, by AMACOM, a division of American Management Associations.

Take the issue of corporate morality. Byrom displayed an instinct for the jugular in his letter of March 23, 1976, on corporate ethics. The letter was sent to all employees. We quote only the following lines:

> *The dictates of conscience for a person with a family might be to think whether you would be happy to tell your spouse and children or other family members the details of the actions you are contemplating.*
>
> *If you would not want to do so, Koppers would not want you to take the action.*

Like all organizations, Koppers seeks to recruit and keep young people with superior talent. Koppers has been unusually successful at both recruiting and keeping them. Why? Byrom's partial explanation is the company's attitude toward generalists and specialists: "We have found that the so-called generalist, is, in reality, a man with some very specialized training coupled with a very broad outlook on all aspects of the company's activities." Koppers' stance, in a nutshell, is to keep an open mind and to develop specialists into generalists.

Most distinctive is Byrom's conviction that an organization is best served by managers with a broad perspective and understanding of society's problems. To this end young managers are selected to participate in what Byrom calls "a general survey of the nation and the world, past, present, and future, as seen from the fifteenth floor of the Koppers building." Byrom feels so strongly about the seminars, so strongly about "insinuating some of my thoughts into their minds," that he devotes three hours a month to conducting these seminars during the first year. After that, other top managers take over.

A unique formal effort at climate determination and role setting by the man who counts today for the men who will count the day after tomorrow. We think that you will find much of what Byrom has to say unique, some of it controversial, but all of it stimulating.

Dowling: Let's begin with your Nine Commandments—I am amused that you were able to get along with nine. The one you put as the most important, hang loose, was, I gather, in part a reaction to the fact that formerly Koppers was anything but a hang-loose organization. Instead, it was extremely structured. You described some of your experiences with General Brehon Somervell when he was chief executive officer.

My question is, how do you, as chief executive officer, go about implementing your first Commandment?

Byrom: Leadership, in a sense, is example setting. Certainly that's one of its major components. Personally I believe that I'm not smart enough to be sure I'm right on everything. Of course, I do my best to try to be right, but every time I reach a decision, I try to remember that that decision may well be wrong. So I don't get imbued with the feeling that my decisions are extremely important. If you maintain a historical perspective, you recognize that your reactions at any given time aren't nearly as critical as they seem to be.

There is a timeliness about decisions, a point in time when you have to make them. You use all the time you have available to you to get as many facts as you can, to analyze the validity of your assumptions, and so forth. Then you make the decision on the basis of when it has to be made and on the basis of the best information available to you. Once you have made the decision, you ought to relax. It may be right; it may be wrong. In any case, you can't change the fact that the decision *has* been made.

Events may permit you, however, to alter the impact of the decision. You ought to be ready to do that if it was wrong. I'm not proposing that decision making be a sloppy, ill-formed, noncaring kind of process. The more important point is not to worry about the decision after the fact. That's what I mean by hang loose.

Dowling: You also make a point about learning to trust your intuition. You gave the very interesting example of the home-building field, where all the data indicated that Koppers should get into this area. Your intuition told you no—and your intuition happened to be correct. Part of the hypothesis of hanging loose, as you define it, seems to be learning to trust your intuition.

Byrom: That's right, because intuition actually is calling on the memory cells in your mind that, in effect, are data registers for previous experiences.

Dowling: And intuition, as Robert Greenleaf says, is the ability to see patterns based on what has happened previously. Also, both you and Greenleaf point out that there's always an information gap. If you waited until you had all the information you needed, you would never make a decision.

Byrom: That's what I mean about a timeliness in decision making. I've seen many cases of people wanting to wait another month, because they'll know that much more. Then, in another month, the opportunity will have passed. You grab the handle now or you miss it forever. People are not infallible. Also, I have come to believe that the things you can't control have more influence on what happens than the things you can control. Therefore, it's difficult, at a given point in time, to be sure whether what you've done is right or wrong.

Dowling: You don't seem to have much faith in the validity of long-range planning. You claim that it's very difficult to see more than two or three years ahead. If I understand you correctly, you feel a lot of companies waste a lot of brain power on "long-range planning."

Byrom: We do quite a bit of it ourselves, and we do it in a very sophisticated way, with a regression formula, input-output matrices, and so on, but to us, it's a discipline more than it is a guide to future decision making. It's a thought process that should help you to understand the environment better, to be able to evaluate events as they take place. You anticipated something and it went the other way. If you have taken the trouble of anticipating something, you should at least be able to recognize that it hasn't happened that way. If you hadn't done the planning, you wouldn't have realized that what happened was unexpected.

As a regimen, as a discipline for a group of people, planning is very valuable. My position is, go ahead and plan, but once you've done your planning, put it on the shelf. Don't be bound by it. Don't use it as a major input to the decision-making process. Use it mainly to recognize change as it takes place.

Dowling: Generally the longer the time span on a project from conception to completion, the less the chance that it's going to turn out the way you anticipated it. I remember reading about the construction of the St. Lawrence Seaway, for example. If what I read was correct, the St. Lawrence Seaway was really superseded by the time it was completed—it took about 20 years. By that time, you had containerization and other developments that made the seaway a waste of time and money.

Byrom: That's been particularly true since the Second World War. The events of World War II introduced a degree of revolution in technological development that fundamentally changed the requirements for social and political organization, a change to which they still have not adapted. The fact that these institutions have not adapted to the potential and realities of technological development since World War II is gradually destroying the system.

That's another part of planning. How do you undertake long-range planning if your principal customer is a failing railroad, like Penn Central? Do you decide that there's going to be no market? Or do you assume that something will happen to save that railroad because, in fact, we have to have it?

Dowling: Somehow or other it's going to continue to exist, even if as a last resort, it's a matter of public subsidy.

Byrom: Despite predictable difficulties with Penn Central, we built a very large "tie-treating" plant to supply its needs. It could have been considered a stupid move. As it is, Conrail is faced with the major task of rebuilding its roadbed, and we're sitting there with a plant that's ideally suited to its needs. You can call that long-range planning. I'm not certain what to call it. We did long-range planning in the sense that we examined the alternatives, but we had no reason to believe we were right, except that the inherent nature of the infrastructure in the society made Penn Central a necessity.

Dowling: Like New York City. Whether it goes bankrupt or not, it's going to have to provide essential services. Someone, somehow, somewhere is going to have to pick up the tab, since the city is not going to disappear.

Another one of your Commandments deals with the importance of increasing the number of interfaces. Have the decision, wherever possible, made at the same level as the problem. I assume this Commandment has both an efficient and an ethical side; the efficient side is that if the decision gets made where the problem is, it will be a better decision.

Byrom: And faster.

Dowling: And faster, right. Second, from an ethical point of view, it fosters the ethic of self-actualization and encourages people to grow.

Byrom: Very definitely. Peter McCullough [chairman of Xerox], some years ago, remarked that the organizations that will be successful in the future are the ones that have found the key to delegating freedom for decision making to the point in the organization at which the impact of that decision will be felt strongly.

Self-actualization, self-definition, challenge—whatever you want to call it—is highly desirable. We're reorganizing our company right now in recognition of how desirable it is. Our president is going to retire next February, a year from now. With normal organizational practice, you would replace the president with another chief operating officer. Had we done so, we probably would have affected three, four, or five jobs in the organization. As we looked at our organization, however, we recognized that we had a very large pool of highly qualified people who combined years of service with us with good educational backgrounds and broad experience that had come from having worked in line and staff. Right now they are aggressive, highly motivated, and capable. But how do you keep them that way?

Dowling: In other words, how do you provide maximum opportunities for career advancement and career maintenance?

Byrom: Our theory is that the best motivated person is a five-foot ten-inch non-swimmer in six feet of water. If you're doing as well as you should, everyone's head ought to be a little bit under water all the time. People perform best under conditions of moderate tension.

Dowling: You have to strike a balance.

Byrom: Sure. I was asked by a friend of mine who is the chief executive of another company to come and speak to his management last year. I followed Walter Menninger [a psychiatrist at the Menninger Clinic], who was describing to the same group what you should not do, in terms of stress, with your management team. When he was through, I got up and said, "I'm half afraid to speak before you, because everything I am about to say fundamentally contradicts what Menninger has just finished saying."

I recognized what he was saying. My feeling, though, is that we seek out tough, capable people who thrive under the tensions we quite deliberately try to maintain. There isn't any question about our people being under stress. For one thing, there's no book they can consult to find out what to do, no procedure bank. There's no organization chart to find out who's in charge.

We aim at putting people in a position where the have to think about what they're doing, where they feel that their prime responsibility is to themselves. After the fact, they can't say that the book said for them to do it this way.

Dowling: That's a prop they don't possess.

Byrom: That's right. They don't have any prop. If you ask Joe why he did it that way, Joe knows that he's got to explain the rationale behind his actions. It has to be a reasonable rationale. On the other hand, it doesn't have to be right. And it doesn't have to be the way I would have done it. We constantly challenge people to think for themselves.

Take the question of improper payments. We say you've got to think about it, you've got to decide whether it's the right thing to do. Don't say it was something you didn't want to do, but that it was in the best interests of the company. That's nonsense. If you don't want to do it, if you couldn't tell your children. . . .

Byrom's Commandments

1. Hang loose. That's the most important Commandment of all.
2. Listen for the winds of change.
3. Increase the number of interfaces.
4. Keep your intuition well lubricated, but
5. Make sure you know where the information is buried.
6. Use growth as a means of getting and keeping good people, and use those people as a means of achieving continued growth. The two are interdependent.
7. Avoid like the plague those specialists who are *only* specialists.
8. Set your priorities in terms of the probable, rather than the merely possible; but
9. Make sure you generate a reasonable number of mistakes. That's right—make sure you generate a reasonable number of mistakes.

Dowling: How would you explain the difference between thinking like a president and thinking like a division general manager?

Byrom: Let me explain it. By the end of this year, we'll probably have 30 division general managers instead of five. We want those division general managers to have the same authority the presidents had when they were general managers. So what we're saying is, the chief operating officers should start to manage after the fact. They're not supposed to make decisions on matters that are the responsibility of division general managers.

Their responsibility is to make sure they've got a sensing system so that after the fact they can understand what is going on. And it ought to be, essentially, on a real-time basis, so that they have the opportunity to question the person who has carried out a particular action when they feel it's wrong, and see to it that we don't repeat any errors.

The other point is that, increasingly, the president should not be a decision maker. As chairman of the board, I had pretty much already eliminated decision making as one of my responsibilities. I also suggested that our president move in that direction, and he has. Now, we're going to ask these five guys to do the same. That moves everyone in the organization up one level.

Dowling: Didn't you also add a vice-chairman level?

Byrom: The vice-chairman is the former president, who retires in a year. What we added were deputy chairmen. Now, the deputy chairmen have no authority of their own. They can act for me if I'm not around, but it is not a level. It is my level. They are an extension of me. It's the chairman and five presidents, and maybe 30 divisions, where we used to have a chairman, a president, and five divisions.

Dowling: How many deputy chairmen?

Byrom: Three.

Dowling: And they are an integral part of your office.

Byrom: The problem, frankly, is that we've got a whole lot of very good people. I suppose it's imprudent of me to mention all these good people, because the headhunters will start coming around. But I'm not really bothered about that, because all of us have challenging functions to perform.

One of the problems with having five presidents is that people on the corporate staff who have to report to the president ask who they report to. I say, "The president." They ask if I mean all five. And I say, "Yes."

How can you reconcile priorities among presidents? When the president had authority over the staff, he could tell which item had priority. Now priorities are determined by the facts surrounding them, not by someone in his infinite wisdom determining what they are. Sometimes the facts will be so obscure that reasonable people cannot arrive at the priorities. For those few occasions, I'm around, and I am ready and willing to mediate the question.

Another part of our organizational philosophy is that we believe organizational relationships depend on who is in what job at any particular time. No two people have the same characteristics. It's a little bit like a football team, and I've used this example before. Joe Paterno, the football coach at Penn State, is a friend of mine. I'm a Penn State graduate and I think he's great. Joe changes his offense from year to year, on the basis of the kind of players he's got. If you've got a guard who can pull out, and very quickly get out and knock the end out of play, and if you've also got a runner who can get behind that guard, the chances are that you can run a whole lot of plays off tackle.

But it doesn't matter how good the runner is. If you don't have a guard who can get that end blocked out of the play, there's no way you can depend on that running back. You'd better have a passer in that kind of situation.

I think an inflexible organizational chart, which assumes that anyone in a given position will perform exactly the way his predecessor did, is ridiculous. He won't. Therefore, the organization ought to shift and adjust and adapt to the fact that there's a new person in that spot. Given the right to do so, people will.

Dowling: One point bothers me a little. I'm thinking, in part, of Alfred P. Sloan and his policies. When Sloan took over from William C. Durant at General Motors, he centralized, in contrast to Durant. (It was a feudal system under Durant.) At the same time, he was exceedingly explicit about the authority that was left. In other words, I guess what I'm saying is that vagueness and centralization go hand in hand. If people don't understand their role, what they are empowered to do, they tend to be timid.

Byrom: We say that you have all the authority I have, in any area of the business you're responsible for. The one limit you have is to recognize that after the fact, you've got to be able to satisfy me that the action was a reasonable one to take. And if you aren't sure, you'd better talk about it beforehand so you understand the parameters of our philosophy. You will be judged on the number of times you waste your time and mine talking about things you should have known how to handle or, equally, the number of times you go ahead and do something and then, after the fact, can't demonstrate the understanding of the problem that allows you to create a decent rationale.

What you need is a sensing system on a real-time basis. I mentioned the sensing system needed by the new president. You've got to know what's going on so you can be of help. You know, following Greenleaf's idea, it isn't a matter of having authority and trying to find the guy who's making a mistake. The top executive functions as an enabler, as a catalyst, as the individual who's there to say, "Joe, you can get into real trouble doing that sort of thing. Did you think about this aspect of it?" "No, I never even heard of it," Joe may reply. "Well, let's talk about it."

The next time around, Joe's got the gist of your conversation buried somewhere in his brain. Now, if he does the same thing again, when he comes back, you say, "Joe, we talked about this." And maybe he says, "I forgot all about that conversation."

Dowling: He's in trouble.

Byrom: He isn't in trouble yet, but I say, "Joe, the purpose of these conversations is to be helpful to you, to put some information into your memory bank. Don't do the same thing again and tell me you forgot the conversation. Put it in your memory bank and think about it."

Now, to me, that isn't being authoritative. That's leadership. You know, it still leaves the guy with responsibility. No one is taking it away from him. No one is saying "You don't have the right to do that." But he's got to work at it, and he's got to know what's going on.

One of the heritages we have from General Somervell's era is a very good control system. He used it in an authoritative fashion; I use it in an information fashion. I have available to me a book that's this thick, and with the new organization it's going to be much thicker because we're going to have the same kind of information for 30 profit centers instead of for five.

We've got five-year "trendlines" and 12-month moving averages on every factor of our operation, including sales and overhead. We've got it expressed in terms of absolute numbers and in terms of ratios. There isn't a word of text in the whole book. It's nothing but charts and tables; the charts give you five-year and 12-month moving averages. The tables provide the detailed, month-by-month background of the charts. By the twentieth of every month I get the summary of what happened the previous month, and in three hours—I usually look at it on Sunday afternoons—I am, in effect, prepared to practice management by exception. I can come in on Monday morning and ask questions of ten people, and in an hour and a half I can satisfy myself about the state of the operation.

On top of that I've got all kinds of people who are happy to talk. There isn't any attempt to hide information. No one's seriously in trouble because they've got problems. They're supposed to have problems.

Dowling: Another one of your Commandments was the importance of making a reasonable number of mistakes. The making of mistakes is an inherent part of the growth process and has to be recognized as such.

Byrom: It certainly does.

Dowling: The concept that if you can't give a rational explanation for it after you've made a decision, for God's sake, don't decide until you come and talk to me first is, I suppose, a kind of built-in assurance that those mistakes aren't going to be too costly.

Byrom: That's right. Because if you give people the right to make mistakes, you have the responsibility toward them not to let them make a mistake that would be catastrophic. I'm in favor of putting the nonswimmer who is five foot ten inches in six feet of water, but not in 20 feet of water, where he is certain to drown. So it's not a case of just throwing someone overboard and saying, "Learn to swim." You try to bring him along and to put him in an area of responsibility that is reasonably consistent with his ability to reach up and handle the problem. But it's a challenge. You want managers who are slightly but not deeply over their heads.

Another point is that as computer science improves, and management information systems improve, we're gradually all going to be looking at the same terminals, and getting some real-time results. Instead of receiving data on the twentieth of each month, I'll get it on the second, because fundamentally our information is based on transaction data. Something is shipped and the transaction goes into the memory bank. As of a given moment, we can find out how many shipments we made to a particular customer so far this month and which salesman handled them. . . .

Dowling: One of the things you obviously believe in is job rotation as a career development technique. You stress the fact that your managers may be specialists, may have a very real technical competency, but they also need to have a general overall view of the organization, and this obviously doesn't come about accidentally. It comes about because they're purposely moved around from division to division and from staff positions to line positions.

Byrom: We don't do it as much as I would like, but we do it more than most companies. And here the computer should prove to be a big help. You want to know that you've considered everyone who should be considered for a job opportunity. When you get as big as we are, however, there is no way that human beings are going to be able to guarantee that they've covered everyone.

We have sent out—and I must admit that the first time around it didn't work very well—questionnaires to all our people, asking them what they think is important about their lives. If someone were going to judge them, what kinds of things have they done that they would like the judges to know about?

Dowling: Who received the questionnaires? How many people?

Byrom: All 7,000 salaried employees—including clerks as well as senior managers. We find talent in surprising places. Most people have better ideas of what they themselves can do well than other observers. What do you think you do best? Would you rather do something else? If so, what would you like to do in this company? What other kinds of jobs would you like? Are you looking for help in acquiring skills that you think with a little bit of help would qualify you for a significant change?

We put the answer into a computer. A job comes up. We hit the computer and say, "These are the job criteria; these are the skills, these are the motivations we'd like to have. Tell us who we ought to look at." . . .

Dowling: In talking about gathering information, you mentioned finding out where the information is buried. You used the phrase "nose-to-nose communication." I gather you're not a great believer in restricting communication to hierarchical channels.

Byrom: Action channels, I think, should be hierarchical. Informational channels should be completely free; I've always insisted on that. I've always made sure that everybody understood that they should not let their nose get out of joint if I talked to the lowest member of their management group about something he or she was doing. It is my responsibility not to misuse that kind of information. I can't override a manager's decision on the basis of something I heard from a subordinate three levels down in his organization.

On the other hand, I can say, "John, have you thought about this? I understand the following. . . ."

Dowling: John's going to have a pretty good idea where you got the information.

Byrom: I don't mind telling him. But woe to the guy who then goes back and says, "I don't want you talking to Byrom any more." I don't think anyone would do that. We don't have that kind of organization. Of course, I try very hard not to misuse the trust. If you're going to have information, you can't use it to negate somebody's delegated authority. You can use it to help him but not to supersede his authority.

As long as you can do that, I don't think people mind you talking, and at this stage of the game it's a tradition in our company.

Dowling: If they do mind, they're pretty insecure.

Byrom: That's right.

Dowling: They are not only insecure, but they have reason to be insecure.

Byrom: In almost every case. And we really don't want those kinds of people. Our company requires very tough people. That's what I said when I talked to Menninger. What you're talking about is stress caused by insecurity, and what we try to do is make sure that we don't have insecure people in the first place.

The interesting thing is that most people probably don't prefer this style. Given a choice, everyone would say that this is what they want, freedom to do their own thing. But if they were able to make the choices without making them publicly, they would opt instead for a style that provided maximum security. Everyone likes to have a merit evaluation, just so long as they are sure nobody else is getting any more than they are. . . .

Dowling: The question that inevitably arises is: Do you have an unusually high rate of executive turnover?

Byrom: No. In fact, we have almost no turnover.

Dowling: Even in the first few years with people who come in at the entry level?

Byrom: My memory is that it's 5 percent, and that's low. I'm talking about college graduates, M.B.A.s, and that type of new hire.

Dowling: They come in as managers and in many cases this is their first corporate job. And there's a 5 percent turnover in the first year?

Byrom: In the first year, it isn't even that high. I'm talking about the first five years. People don't leave in a year. One factor that accounts for the difference is our seminar program. It's now in its fifth or sixth year. These people hear about the seminar program during their first year. And after a year or two, they're eligible for it.

This year we're conducting three seminars: one in Chicago, one in Pittsburgh, and one in Baltimore. There are 25 people scheduled for each seminar. The first year I meet them 12 times, assign reading material, and moderate the discussion for two or three hours at each meeting. Frankly, how many corporations are there in which young managers have the opportunity to sit down with the chairman of the board and talk about something that has nothing to do with the company?

Dowling: It's the world as viewed from the fifteenth floor of the Koppers Corporation, as I recall your phraseology.

Byrom: We talk about world environments, world forces, the struggle and tensions of the world's economy. We focus on economics in the seminars.

Dowling: You mentioned that whatever John Kenneth Galbraith has just written is always on the reading list.

Byrom: That was true. Today, however, we really don't have much time for Galbraith. Other readings are much more important.

Dowling: How long do the seminars last?

Byrom: They start, normally at 4:30 and we'll break at 7:30. And we hold them monthly.

Dowling: How long do they run?

Byrom: I take them for a year. After that we get other senior executives to function as moderators. We must have five other top executives conducting seminars. And we're into the fifth year. By now close to 300 people are in this program every month.

After the first year, the seminars tend to be more self-directive. Participants indicate some of their interests, what they'd like to talk about. In fact, we tell them that if they want to hold the seminars without any of our senior executives there, that's fine with us. But they don't want to. The reason is very interesting. They claim that the reading is demanding, even though it's only one or two books a month.

With jobs and their family responsibilities and so forth, it is more reading of this type than most of them would do on their own. They are afraid that without the discipline the presence of the senior executive brings, they wouldn't do their homework.

It's a very interesting comment that I find frightening. In our society, we consider an education to be a terminal achievement. Once you leave the formal program, you're educated. I know that's not correct.

Also, from the standpoint of the company, a whole lot of people get to see what kind of a person Byrom is and what kind of people the other top executives are.

Our people use the seminars as a recruiting tool, because young college people are excited about this kind of an atmosphere. And we think that it's a kind of atmosphere that causes people to want to stick around.

Dowling: I'm thinking of a piece by Harry Levinson with a very tricky title, "Oedipus in the Boardroom," in which he maintains that the CEO sets the overall tone and climate of the organization. He gives a couple of examples. For instance, he considers, rightly or wrongly, that the Bell Telephone System as a system is—he doesn't say paternalistic, he says maternalistic. It gives its managers a great deal of security and encourages a great deal of dependency. The effect is that a particular kind of individual is attracted to the system, someone who puts a high value on security and is at home with dependency.

The man who is attracted to IBM is a very different kind of being. It's a very different kind of corporation with a very different kind of tone, and one that basically was set by Thomas Watson, Jr.

The prime explanation, it would seem to me, for your remarkably low turnover is that you obviously have established a kind of climate, a kind of tone, that appeals greatly to a certain kind of people. On the other hand, some people would run a mile from the Koppers organization.

Byrom: Another interesting point is that people who leave us frequently come back.

Dowling: You don't hold it against them. I have encountered organizations where the attitude is that the person who leaves is disloyal, an ingrate.

Byrom: We feel just the opposite. We say, "God bless you, and if it doesn't work out, don't have any inhibitions about coming back and talking to us."

The kinds of people who leave us usually leave for a job that pays them significantly more than we're willing to pay for their talents at that point in time. We expect them to go for that reason. Also, there are people who constantly hanker to do their own thing, who really believe that there is more opportunity for an entrepreneurial spirit to operate outside of the corporation, albeit one as loose as ours is. Still, there are too many checks, too many places that you have to go to get things approved, and so on. I've talked to some of these people and I say, "Don't kid yourself. If you're your own boss, you've got a banker. Bankers look over your shoulders, and they can be a lot less understanding than a senior manager."

People leave, however, for those two kinds of reasons, plus the fact that sometimes people don't feel they're moving as fast as they should. Sometimes that's true, and I don't blame anyone for leaving if the opportunities don't seem to be with us. This, of course is why we keep trying to maximize the number of opportunities. Otherwise, you'll lose the good people and keep the drones. We do everything in our power to keep young, aggressive, capable people.

You expressed surprise over our low turnover. Why should anyone want to leave?

Dowling: The question is a natural. First, because your people, as you concede, operate under an unusual level of tension and stress, and second, because at least in the early years of service, turnover among managers is traditionally very high. So Koppers is an unusual case.

I read that article of Harman's you sent me with great interest. To what extent—I'm thinking of your seminars, especially—do you define the mission of the corporation in the way Harman advocates? Do you talk about or advocate putting the development and growth of management and employees first, contributing to the overall social welfare system second, and profitability third?

Byrom: You aren't doing justice to Harman.

Dowling: That's a possibility. I'm simply stating the factors in the order that he lists them.

Byrom: If you look at it more closely, what Harman is saying is that the corporation of the future's primary responsibility will be to provide self-definition for all its employees, provided it recognizes that it must fulfill its mission, which includes operating as an economically viable institution.

In other words, you don't relegate profits to a back seat in relation to social responsibility or anything else. Profits are the means by which you maintain the viability of an institution that is a constructive contributor to the well-being of society. If you don't make adequate profits, the organization goes out of business. But you have to provide self-definition for employees at the same time. You cannot use profits as an excuse not to give self-definition activities to your employees.

Do you understand what I am saying? I'm saying that I'm responsible for running an economic institution that is viable. And all my decisions are reached on that basis. If a plant has an obsolete process and it's no longer strategically located under the logistics of supply, shipping, delivery, and so forth, I have no compunctions about shutting that plant down. Under our societal arrangements, I'm not responsible for providing employment for someone who, unfortunately, worked in the plant that had to be shut down.

On the other hand, to the degree that I can, I am going to give these workers opportunities to move and to take other jobs within the company. Society, I think, has a responsibility to these people. And if society wants to assign me that responsibility, then I've got to charge more money so that I can fund my ability to do what society is telling me I have to do.

Dowling: Or to use one of Harman's concepts—his concept of the forgiven tax, as he calls it—society, through the tax structure, can make allowances to you so that you can undertake these responsibilities.

Byrom: However, I should never be asked to make an economically nonviable decision in order to fulfill some social mandate. If I can fulfill a social mandate and still be economically viable, okay. Or if society tells me that I have to do it, I'm going to charge the prices that permit me to afford to be able to do what I've been told to do.

Charles Schultz has written a book called *The Public Use of Private Interests,* which consists of the Godkin lectures at Harvard this year, or last year. I commend the book to you because basically it says that we've got to use economic incentives as the means by which we accomplish objectives such as improving the quality of the environment.

Anyhow, getting back to the question of how much we get into the sort of thing in our seminars. We get into it a lot. The whole question of the nature of social change and its impact on economic institutions is a subject we examine closely.

In some of the seminars, for example, we read Daniel Bell's *Cultural Contradictions of Capitalism* and Arthur Okum's *The Big Trade-Off: Equality Versus Efficiency,* the Godkin lectures at Harvard a couple of year ago. We frequently talk in George Lodge's terms about the sense of entitlement that comes to us all simply as human beings.

Dowling: Bell uses the phrase, "revolution of entitlement" in *Cultural Contradictions of Capitalism.*

Byrom: That's right.

Dowling: The switchover from an emphasis on equality of opportunity to the demand for equality of results.

Byrom: And that leads to the question of what impact this is going to have on the Lockean concepts of property rights. Basically, what are property rights? We get into the question—as you probably read in one of the pieces I sent you—of whether, if you're born next to a cornfield in Iowa, you have more rights to corn than the starving peasant in the sub-Sahara.

That always starts a fascinating discussion. Then we examine some jobs in Koppers I happen to know about that are awful jobs—awful in the sense that they don't place any demands on people.

Dowling: If you think like Fred Herzberg, there's nothing necessarily wrong with the kinds of jobs you're talking about. Fred is fond of calling them Mickey Mouse jobs and he says that Mickey Mouse jobs are fine, if you can find enough Mickey Mouse people to fill them. He goes on to argue that there are more Mickey Mouse jobs than there are Mickey Mouse people. That's the rub.

Byrom: You used to have eighth-grade dropouts performing some of these jobs. Now they're done by high school graduates. There's no way that they're ever going to be self-defined in these responsibilities. There are two alternatives. You can replace them with robots—and that's what I think you ought to do—some jobs could use handicapped people, to whom, in fact, they might be a challenge. It would serve to bring them into the economic mainstream of society.

Dowling: Chris Argyris has a wonderful description of the happy morons at the Utica knitting mills. These were people who were hired during World War II because the rest of the labor force had disappeared. They enjoyed these very dull jobs. Their attendance records, their production records, were much better than those of the previous jobholders.

Byrom: I suggested that approach. We looked into it and the agencies didn't want the work done at our plant. They wanted us to ship the material out to their shops and then they would ship back the finished work. It ended up being economically impossible. As near as I can figure out the only reason they wanted to do it that way was that they wanted to be sure society understood who was doing good for these people.

A lot of people get upset when I say this—but I think that we have the ability to replace human beings almost completely with machinery in the next 25 years. I believe that the opportunity for improvement in the quality of life is an inverse function of the amount of human effort required to create material wealth. The less effort required, the greater the opportunity for improving the quality of life in this society.

Unfortunately, we are hung up on the petard of Calvinism—and I'm a Presbyterian—but we have theological mores that were good for society when you had to find some way of giving dignity to work. And the Puritan work ethic is great for developing countries, where you still need reasons to cause people to find dignity in work. . . .

Dowling: The percentage of GNP that we spend on R&D keeps dropping.

Byrom: That's true. It's not all that bad. We probably spent more on R&D than was productive. A lot of it wasn't true R&D. It was development for consumption products, and you can do that anytime. I'm more worried about the amount we spend on basic research. The CEO, I hope, is going to come up with a policy statement on innovation in technology.

I have a feeling—here I'm an optimist—that basic research doesn't cost that much and that it's still going on. What's happening, alas, is that as we understand nature better, we're starting to move into some areas that were previously inviolable in terms of religious mores and so forth.

Dowling: For example.

Byrom: Cloning, DNA research.

Dowling: Right.

Byrom: We're getting to the point where people are suggesting that maybe we have got to decide what research projects can be worked on and what can't. That to me is a horrifying development. The idea that human being is capable of deciding whether a particular investigation is in the best interests of humankind or not approaches the heretical position of trying to act like God. I don't believe that God worries about our understanding and finding new tools. I think what upsets God is when we presume to know the difference between good and bad and right and wrong, concepts I don't think human beings are capable of differentiating.

The search for knowledge is not an action against God. A lot of people think it is, however.

Dowling: Yes, when it involves a threat to what might be called their own "can't helps."

Byrom: Okay, that's book burning.

Dowling: It is. Justice Oliver Wendell Holmes once said, "I have my can't helps, but I refuse to inflict them on the universe." A lot of people fail to make that distinction. They have their "can't helps" and they want to inflict them on the universe.

Byrom: That's how we got in the Dark Ages, and we could go back to them.

I said that we are heading toward an authoritarian society. Why? Are we going to have an authoritarian society because of energy? We have an energy problem that requires long-range thinking, long-term projections—8, 10, 15 years—and the decisions have to be approved, if not made, by people who were elected on a two-year basis.

Dowling: Or at most elected on a six-year basis.

Byrom: There is no one who can get reelected on a platform of quadrupling the cost of the home heating bill. There is no way to get elected by introducing austerity to the discipline of a free society. So what we do instead is move further and further toward the crisis, which is already here but which we haven't recognized.

Eventually, people will recognize the crisis, and then everyone will be very happy to have an agency that will tell them how much they can have in order to make sure that you aren't getting more than I'm getting. Within five years, I predict that we will have a WPB (War Production Board) kind of agency that allocates energy according to what that agency perceives as the value to society of whatever product you produce. And if it determines that the product doesn't contribute very much, you won't get any energy.

If that isn't authoritarian, I'd like to know what is. But, of course, it will take place within a democratic framework.

Dowling: Don't you see any viable alternative?

Byrom: I think we're going down the drain. We'll just be less free and much poorer. It isn't going to be the end of the world.

The other point is that in a free-trading world, one in which much of the capital-intensive industry in other industrial societies is either state owned or state controlled, decisions are made on the basis of sociopolitical criteria rather than economic criteria. The question then becomes how a private enterprise system, trying to operate on economic criteria, competes in a world in which its competition uses sociopolitical criteria as the basis for making decisions. In the long run, that kind of competition would drive the private corporation into bankruptcy.

Can private enterprise survive in that kind of world? I doubt it, at least for capital-intensive industries. I agree with Boulding when he envisions a steady state in material terms. The value of living could still be enhanced greatly if we used machinery to make all our material goods so that we could be astronomers, wood-carvers, photographers, and teachers. That would be a pretty good life.

Dowling: You're talking about psychological substitutes for an improved standard of living.

Byrom: That's right. Now, that's all said as if we're dwelling in a vacuum—which we aren't. There is a developing world out there that needs everything we can possibly produce and needs all the help we can give it. If we were willing to produce to a maximum, beyond our requirements, and use the incremental cost advantages as a means of subsidizing the improvement of the developing nations' position, Boulding wouldn't have very much to worry about, because the world needs all the production of which we are capable. The problem is, as individuals, we don't know how to deal with distributing that kind of potential.

Dowling: Do you see any chance of developing institutions that will enable us to deal with this problem?

Byrom: Yes. I think our problem is the next 25 years. In 50 years or something close to that, the world will have recognized that the concept of the sovereignty of nation states is no longer reasonable. We're interdependent. We have to establish world institutions that would veto any attempts by previously sovereign nation states to put their self-interests ahead of those of the rest of the world. I think that will come about because we will have solved the energy problem and we will not be in the position of allocating scarcities. Technology will have given us the opportunity to fulfill the material wants of the whole world.

14

Managerial Work:
Analysis from Observation

Henry Mintzberg

*W*hat do managers do? Ask this question and you will likely be told that managers plan, organize, coordinate, and control. Since Henri Fayol [9]* first proposed these words in 1916, they have dominated the vocabulary of management. (See, for example, [8], [12], [17].) How valuable are they in describing managerial work? Consider one morning's work of the president of a large organization:

> *As he enters his office at 8:23, the manager's secretary motions for him to pick up the telephone. "Jerry, there was a bad fire in the plant last night, about $30,000 damage. We should be back in operation by Wednesday. Thought you should know."*
>
> *At 8:45 a Mr. Jamison is ushered into the manager's office. They discuss Mr. Jamison's retirement plans and his cottage in New Hampshire. Then the manager presents a plaque to him commemorating his thirty-two years with the organization.*
>
> *Mail processing follows: An innocent-looking letter, signed by a Detroit lawyer, reads: "A group of us in Detroit has decided not to buy any of your products because you used that anti-flag, anti-American pinko, Bill Lindell, upon your Thursday night TV show." The manager dictates a restrained reply.*
>
> *The 10:00 meeting is scheduled by a professional staffer. He claims that his superior, a high-ranking vice-president of the organization, mistreats his staff, and that if the man is not fired, they will all walk out. As soon as the meeting ends, the manager rearranges his schedule to investigate the claim and to react to this crisis.*

Which of these activities may be called planning, and which may be called organizing, coordinating, and controlling? Indeed, what do words such

*Bracketed numbers refer to *References* at the end of the article.

SOURCE: Reprinted by permission. Henry Mintzberg, "Managerial Work: Analysis from Observation," *Management Science,* October 1971. B 97–B 110.

as "coordinating" and "planning" mean in the context of real activity? In fact, these four words do not describe the actual work of managers at all; they describe certain vague objectives of managerial work. ". . . they are just ways of indicating what we need to explain." [1, p. 537]

Other approaches to the study of managerial work have developed, one dealing with managerial decision-making and policy-making processes, another with the manager's interpersonal activities. (See, for example, [2] and [10].) And some empirical researchers, using the "diary" method, have studied, what might be called, managerial "media"—by what means, with whom, how long, and where managers spend their time.* But in no part of this literature is the actual content of managerial work systematically and meaningfully described.† Thus, the question posed at the start—what do managers do?—remains essentially unanswered in the literature of management.

This is indeed an odd situation. We claim to teach management in schools of both business and public administration; we undertake major research programs in management; we find a growing segment of the management science community concerned with the problems of senior management. Most of these people—the planners, information and control theorists, systems analysts, etc.—are attempting to analyze and change working habits that they themselves do not understand. Thus, at a conference called at M.I.T. to assess the impact of the computer on the manager, and attended by a number of America's foremost management scientists, a participant found it necessary to comment after lengthy discussion [20, p. 198]:

> I'd like to return to an earlier point. It seems to me that until we get into the question of what the top manager does or what the functions are that define the top management job, we're not going to get out of the kind of difficulty that keeps cropping up. What I'm really doing is leading up to my earlier question which no one really answered. And that is: Is it possible to arrive at a specification of what constitutes the job of a top manager?

His question was not answered.

Research Study on Managerial Work

In late 1966, I began research on this question, seeking to replace Fayol's words by a set that would more accurately describe what managers do. In essence, I sought to develop by the process of induction a statement of managerial work that would have empirical validity. Using a method called "structured observation," I observed for one-week periods the

---

*Carlson [6] carried out the classic study just after World War II. He asked nine Swedish managing directors to record on diary pads details of each activity in which they engaged. His method was used by a group of other researchers, many of them working in the U.K. (See [4], [5], [15], [25].)

†One major project, involving numerous publications, took place at Ohio State University and spanned three decades. Some of the vocabulary used followed Fayol. The results have generated little interest in this area. (See, for example, [13].)

chief executives of five medium to large organizations (a consulting firm, a school system, a technology firm, a consumer goods manufacturer, and a hospital).

Structured as well as unstructured (i.e., anecdotal) data were collected in three "records." In the *chronology record,* activity patterns throughout the working day were recorded. In the *mail record,* for each of 890 pieces of mail processed during the five weeks, were recorded its purpose, format and sender, the attention it received and the action it elicited. And, recorded in the *contact record,* for each of 368 verbal interactions, were the purpose, the medium (telephone call, scheduled or unscheduled meeting, tour), the participants, the form of initiation, and the location. It should be noted that all categorizing was done during and after observation so as to ensure that the categories reflected only the work under observation. [Mintzberg's study] [19] contains a fuller description of this methodology and a tabulation of the results of the study.

Two sets of conclusions are presented below. The first deals with certain characteristics of managerial work, as they appeared from analysis of the numerical data (e.g., How much time is spent with peers? What is the average duration of meetings? What proportion of contacts are initiated by the manager himself?) The second describes the basic content of managerial work in terms of ten roles. This description derives from an analysis of the data on the recorded *purpose* of each contact and piece of mail.

The liberty is taken of referring to these findings as descriptive of managerial, as opposed to chief executive, work. This is done because many of the findings are supported by studies of other types of managers. Specifically, most of the conclusions on work characteristics are to be found in the combined results of a group of studies of foremen [11], [16], middle managers [4], [5], [15], [25], and chief executives [6]. And although there is little useful material on managerial roles, three studies do provide some evidence of the applicability of the role set. Most important, Sayles' empirical study of production managers [24] suggests that at least five of the ten roles are performed at the lower end of the managerial hierarchy. And some further evidence is provided by comments in Whyte's study of leadership in a street gang [26] and Neustadt's study of three U.S. presidents [21]. (Reference is made to these findings where appropriate.) Thus, although most of the illustrations are drawn from my study of chief executives, there is some justification in asking the reader to consider when he sees the terms "manager" and his "organization" not only "presidents" and their "companies," but also "foremen" and their "shops," "directors" and their "branches," "vice-presidents" and their "divisions." The term *manager* shall be used with reference to all those people in charge of formal organizations or their subunits.

Some Characteristics of Managerial Work

Six sets of characteristics of managerial work derive from analysis of the data of this study. Each has a significant bearing on the manager's ability to administer a complex organization.

Characteristic 1. The Manager Performs a Great Quantity of Work at an Unrelenting Pace

Despite a semblance of normal working hours, in truth managerial work appears to be very taxing. The five men in this study processed an average of 36 pieces of mail each day, participated in eight meetings (half of which were scheduled), engaged in five telephone calls, and took one tour. In his study of foremen, Guest [11] found that the number of activities per day averaged 583, with no real break in the pace.

Free time appears to be very rare. If by chance a manager has caught up with the mail, satisfied the callers, dealt with all the disturbances, and avoided scheduled meetings, a subordinate will likely show up to usurp the available time. It seems that the manager cannot expect to have much time for leisurely reflection during office hours. During "off" hours, our chief executives spent much time on work-related reading. High-level managers appear to be able to escape neither from an environment which recognizes the power and status of their positions nor from their own minds which have been trained to search continually for new information.

Characteristic 2. Managerial Activity Is Characterized by Variety, Fragmentation, and Brevity

There seems to be no pattern to managerial activity. Rather, variety and fragmentation appear to be characteristic, as successive activities deal with issues that differ greatly both in type and in content. In effect the manager must be prepared to shift moods quickly and frequently.

A typical chief executive day may begin with a telephone call from a director who asks a favor (a "status request"); then a subordinate calls to tell of a strike at one of the facilities (fast movement of information, termed "instant communication"); this is followed by a relaxed scheduled event at which the manager speaks to a group of visiting dignitaries (ceremony); the manager returns to find a message from a major customer who is demanding the renegotiation of a contract (pressure); and so on. Throughout the day, the managers of our study encountered this great variety of activity. Most surprisingly, the significant activities were interspersed with the trivial in no particular pattern.

Furthermore, these managerial activities were characterized by their brevity. Half of all the activities studied lasted less than 9 minutes and only 10 percent exceeded one hour's duration. Guest's foremen averaged 48 seconds per activity, and Carlson [6] stressed that his chief executives were unable to work without frequent interruption.

In my own study of chief executives, I felt that the managers demonstrated a preference for tasks of short duration and encouraged interruption. Perhaps the manager becomes accustomed to variety, or perhaps the flow of "instant communication" cannot be delayed. A more plausible explanation might be that the manager becomes conditioned by his workload. He develops a sensitive appreciation for the opportunity cost of his own time. Also, he is aware of the ever present assortment of obligations associated with his job—accumulations of mail that cannot be delayed, the callers that must be attended to, the meetings that require his participation. In other words, no matter what he is doing, the manager is plagued by what he must do and what he might do. Thus, the manager is forced to treat issues in an abrupt and superficial way.

Characteristic 3. Managers Prefer Issues That Are Current, Specific, and Ad Hoc

Ad hoc operating reports received more attention than did routine ones; current, uncertain information—gossip, speculation, hearsay—which flows quickly was preferred to historical, certain information; "instant communication" received first consideration; few contacts were held on a routine or "clocked" basis; almost all contacts concerned well-defined issues. The managerial environment is clearly one of stimulus-response. It breeds, not reflective planners, but adaptable information manipulators who prefer the live, concrete situation, men who demonstrate a marked action-orientation.

Characteristic 4. The Manager Sits between His Organization and a Network of Contacts

In virtually every empirical study of managerial time allocation, it was reported that managers spent a surprisingly large amount of time in horizontal or lateral (nonline) communication. It is clear from this study and from that of Sayles [24] that the manager is surrounded by a diverse and complex web of contacts which serves as his self-designed external information system. Included in this web can be clients, associates and suppliers, outside staff experts, peers (managers of related or similar organizations), trade organizations, government officials, independents (those with no relevant organizational affiliation), and directors or superiors. (Among these, directors in this study and superiors in other studies did *not* stand out as particularly active individuals.)

The managers in this study received far more information than they emitted, much of it coming from contacts, and more from subordinates who acted as filters. Figuratively, the manager appears as the neck of an hour-glass, sifting information into his own organization from its environment.

Characteristic 5. The Manager Demonstrates a Strong Preference for the Verbal Media

The manager has five media at his command—mail (documented), telephone (purely verbal), unscheduled meeting (informal face-to-face), scheduled meeting (formal face-to-face), and tour (observational). Along with all the other empirical studies of work characteristics, I found a strong predominance of verbal forms of communication.

Mail By all indications, managers dislike the documented form of communication. In this study, they gave cursory attention to such items as operating reports and periodicals. It was estimated that only 13 percent of the input mail was of specific and immediate use to the managers. Much of the rest dealt with formalities and provided general reference data. The managers studied initiated very little mail, only 25 pieces in the five weeks. The rest of the outgoing mail was sent in reaction to mail received—a reply to a request, an acknowledgment, some information forwarded to a part of the organization. The managers appeared to dislike this form of communication, perhaps because the mail is a relatively slow and tedious medium to use.

Telephone and Unscheduled Meetings   The less formal means of verbal communication—the telephone, a purely verbal form, and the unscheduled meeting, a face-to-face form—were used frequently (two-thirds of the contacts in the study) but for brief encounters (average duration of 6 and 12 minutes, respectively). They were used primarily to deliver requests and to transmit pressing information to those outsiders and subordinates who had informal relationships with the manager.

Scheduled Meetings   These tended to be of long duration, averaging 68 minutes in this study, and absorbing over half the managers' time. Such meetings provided the managers with their main opportunities to interact with large groups and to leave the confines of their own offices. Scheduled meetings were used when the participants were unfamiliar to the manager (e.g., students who request that he speak at a university), when a large quantity of information had to be transmitted (e.g., presentation of a report), when ceremony had to take place, and when complex strategy-making or negotiation had to be undertaken. An important feature of the scheduled meeting was the incidental, but by no means irrelevant, information that flowed at the start and end of such meetings.

Tours   Although the walking tour would appear to be a powerful tool for gaining information in an informal way, in this study tours accounted for only 3 percent of the managers' time.
   In general, it can be concluded that the manager uses each medium for particular purposes. Nevertheless, where possible, he appears to gravitate to verbal media since these provide greater flexibility, require less effort, and bring faster response. It should be noted here that the manager does not leave the telephone or the meeting to get back to work. Rather, communication is his work, and these media are his tools. The operating work of the organization—producing a product, doing research, purchasing a part—appears to be undertaken infrequently by the senior manager. The manager's productive output must be measured in terms of information, a great part of which is transmitted verbally.

Characteristic 6.   *Despite the Preponderance of Obligations, the Manager Appears to Be Able to Control His Own Affairs*

Carlson suggested in his study of Swedish chief executives that these men were puppets, with little control over their own affairs. A cursory examination of our data indicates that is true. Our managers were responsible for the initiation of only 32 percent of their verbal contacts and a smaller proportion of their mail. Activities were also classified as to the nature of the managers' participation, and the active ones were outnumbered by the passive ones (e.g., making requests vs. receiving requests). On the surface, the manager is indeed a puppet, answering requests in the mail, returning telephone calls, attending meetings initiated by others, yielding to subordinates' requests for time, reacting to crises.

However, such a view is misleading. There is evidence that the senior manager can exert control over his own affairs in two significant ways: (1) It is he who defines many of his own long-term commitments by developing appropriate information channels which later feed him information, by initiating projects which later demand his time, by joining committees or outside boards which provide contacts in return for his services, and so on. (2) The manager can exploit situations that appear as obligations. He can lobby at ceremonial speeches; he can impose his values on his organization when his authorization is requested; he can motivate his subordinates whenever he interacts with them; he can use the crisis situation as an opportunity to innovate.

Perhaps there are two points that help distinguish successful and unsuccessful managers. All managers appear to be puppets. Some decide who will pull the strings and how, and they then take advantage of each move that they are forced to make. Others, unable to exploit this high-tension environment, are swallowed up by this most demanding of jobs.

The Manager's Work Roles

In describing the essential content of managerial work, one should aim to model managerial activity, that is, to describe it as a set of programs. But an undertaking as complex as this must be preceded by the development of a useful typological description of managerial work. In other words, we must first understand the distinct components of managerial work. At the present time we do not.

In this study, 890 pieces of mail and 368 verbal contacts were categorized as to purpose. The incoming mail was found to carry acknowledgements, requests and solicitations of various kinds, reference data, news, analytical reports, reports on events and on operations, advice on various situations, and statements of problems, pressures, and ideas. In reacting to mail, the managers acknowledged some, replied to the requests (e.g., by sending information), and forwarded much to subordinates (usually for their information). Verbal contacts involved a variety of purposes. In 15 percent of them activities were scheduled, in 6 percent ceremonial events took place, and a few involved external board work. About 34 percent involved requests of various kinds, some insignificant, some for information, some for authorization of proposed actions. Another 36 percent essentially involved the flow of information to and from the manager, while the remainder dealt specifically with issues of strategy and with negotiations. (For details, see [19].)

In this study, each piece of mail and verbal contact categorized in this way was subjected to one question: Why did the manager do this? The answers were collected and grouped and regrouped in various ways (over the course of three years) until a typology emerged that was felt to be satisfactory. While an example, presented below, will partially explain this process to the reader, it must be remembered that (in the words of Bronowski [3, p. 62]): "Every induction is a speculation and it guesses at a unity which the facts present but do not strictly imply."

Consider the following sequence of two episodes: A chief executive attends a meeting of an external board on which he sits. Upon his return to his organization, he immediately goes to the office of a subordinate, tells of a conversation he had with a fellow board member, and concludes with the statement: "It looks like we shall get the contract."

The purposes of these two contacts are clear—to attend an external board meeting, and to give current information (instant communication) to a subordinate. But why did the manager attend the meeting? Indeed, why does he belong to the board? And why did he give this particular information to his subordinate?

Basing analysis on this incident, one can argue as follows: The manager belongs to the board in part so that he can be exposed to special information which is of use to his organization. The subordinate needs the information but has not the status which would give him access to it. The chief executive does. Board memberships bring chief executives in contact with one another for the purpose of trading information.

Two aspects of managerial work emerge from this brief analysis. The manager serves in a "liaison" capacity because of the status of his office, and what he learns here enables him to act as "disseminator" of information into his organization. We refer to these as *roles*—organized sets of behaviors belonging to identifiable offices or positions [23]. Ten roles were chosen to capture all the activities observed during his study.

All activities were found to involve one or more of three basic behaviors—interpersonal contact, the processing of information, and the making of decisions. As a result, our ten roles are divided into three corresponding groups. Three roles—labelled *figurehead, liaison,* and *leader*—deal with behavior that is essentially interpersonal in nature. Three others—*nerve center, disseminator,* and *spokesman*—deal with information-processing activities performed by the manager. And the remaining four—*entrepreneur, disturbance handler, resource allocator,* and *negotiator*—cover the decision-making activities of the manager. We describe each of these roles in turn, asking the reader to note that they form a *gestalt,* a unified whole whose parts cannot be considered in isolation.

The Interpersonal Roles

Three roles relate to the manager's behavior that focuses on the interpersonal contact. These roles derive directly from the authority and status associated with holding managerial office.

Figurehead As legal authority in his organization, the manager is a symbol, obliged to perform a number of duties. He must preside at ceremonial events, sign legal documents, receive visitors, make himself available to many of those who feel, in the words of one of the men studied, "that the only way to get something done is to get to the top."

There is evidence that this role applies at other levels as well. Davis [7, pp. 43–44] cites the case of the field sales manager who must deal with those customers who believe that their accounts deserve his attention.

Leader   Leadership is the most widely recognized of managerial roles. It describes the manager's relationship with his subordinates—his attempts to motivate them and his development of the milieu in which they work. Leadership actions pervade all activity—in contrast to most roles, it is possible to designate only a few activities as dealing exclusively with leadership (these mostly related to staffing duties). Each time a manager encourages a subordinate, or meddles in his affairs, or replies to one of his requests, he is playing the *leader* role. Subordinates seek out and react to the leadership clues, and, as a result, they impart significant power to the manager.

Liaison   As noted earlier, the empirical studies have emphasized the importance of lateral or horizontal communication in the work of managers at all levels. It is clear from our study that this is explained largely in terms of the *liaison* role. The manager establishes his network of contacts essentially to bring information and favors to his organization. As Sayles notes in his study of production supervisors [24, p. 258], "The one enduring objective [of the manager] is the effort to build and maintain a predictable, reciprocating system of relationships. . . ."

Making use of his status, the manager interacts with a variety of peers and other people outside his organization. He provides time, information, and favors in return for the same from others. Foremen deal with staff groups and other foremen; chief executives join boards of directors, and maintain extensive networks of individual relationships. Neustadt notes this behavior in analyzing the work of President Roosevelt [21, p. 150]:

> *His personal sources were the product of a sociability and curiosity that reached back to the other Roosevelt's time. He had an enormous acquaintance in various phases of national life and at various levels of government; he also had his wife and her variety of contacts. He extended his acquaintanceships abroad; in the war years Winston Churchill, among others, became a "personal souce." Roosevelt quite deliberately exploited these relationships and mixed them up to widen his own range of information. He changed his sources as his interests changed, but no one who had ever interested him was quite forgotten or immune to sudden use.*

The Informational Roles

A second set of managerial activities relates primarily to the processing of information. Together they suggest three significant managerial roles, one describing the manager as a focal point for a certain kind of organizational information, the other two describing relatively simple transmission of this information.

Nerve Center   There is indication, both from this study and from those by Neustadt and Whyte, that the manager serves as the focal point in his organization for the movement of nonroutine information. Homans, who analyzed Whyte's study, draws the following conclusions [14, p. 187]:

> *Since interaction flowed toward [the leaders], they were better informed about the problems and desires of group members than were any of the followers and therefore better able to decide on an appropriate course of action. Since they were in close touch with other gang leaders, they were also better informed than their followers about conditions in Cornerville at large. Moreover, in their positions at the focus of the chains of interaction, they were better able than any follower to pass on to the group decisions that had been reached.*

The term *nerve center* is chosen to encompass those many activities in which the manager receives information.

Within his own organization, the manager has legal authority that formally connects him—and only him—to *every* member. Hence, the manager emerges as *nerve center* of internal information. He may not know as much about any one function as the subordinate who specializes in it, but he comes to know more about his total organization than any other member. He is the information generalist. Furthermore, because of the manager's status and its manifestation in the *liaison* role, the manager gains unique access to a variety of knowledgeable outsiders including peers who are themselves *nerve centers* of their own organizations. Hence, the manager emerges as his organization's *nerve center* of external information as well.

As noted earlier, the manager's nerve center information is of a special kind. He appears to find it most important to get his information quickly and informally. As a result, he will not hesitate to bypass formal information channels to get it, and he is prepared to deal with a large amount of gossip, hearsay, and opinion which has not yet become substantial fact.

Disseminator Much of the manager's information must be transmitted to subordinates. Some of this is of a *factual* nature, received from outside the organization or from other subordinates. And some is of a *value* nature. Here, the manager acts as the mechanism by which organizational influencers (owners, governments, employee groups, the general public, etc., or simply the "boss") make their preferences known to the organization. It is the manager's duty to integrate these value positions, and to express general organizational preferences as a guide to decisions made by subordinates. One of the men studied commented: "One of the principal functions of this position is to integrate the hospital interests with the public interests." Papandreou describes his duty in a paper published in 1952, referring to management as the "peak coordinator" [22].

Spokesman In his *spokesman* role, the manager is obliged to transmit his information to outsiders. He informs influencers and other interested parties about his organization's performance, its policies, and its plans.

Furthermore, he is expected to serve outside his organization as an expert in its industry. Hospital administrators are expected to spend some time serving outside as public experts on health, and corporation presidents, perhaps as chamber of commerce executives.

The Decisional Roles

The manager's legal authority requires that he assume responsibility for all of his organization's important actions. The *nerve center* role suggests that only he can fully understand complex decisions, particularly those involving difficult value tradeoffs. As a result, the manager emerges as the key figure in the making and interrelating of all significant decisions in his organization, a process that can be referred to as *strategy-making*. Four roles describe the manager's control over the strategy-making system in his organization.

Entrepreneur The *entrepreneur* role describes the manager as initiator and designer of much of the controlled change in his organization. The manager looks for opportunities and potential problems which may cause him to initiate action. Action takes the form of *improvement projects*—the marketing of a new product, the strengthening of a weak department, the purchasing of new equipment, the reorganization of formal structure, and so on.

The manager can involve himself in each improvement project in one of three ways: (1) He may *delegate* all responsibility for its design and approval, implicitly retaining the right to replace that subordinate who takes charge of it. (2) He may delegate the design work to a subordinate, but retain the right to *approve* it before implementation. (3) He may actively *supervise* the design work himself.

Improvement projects exhibit a number of interesting characteristics. They appear to involve a number of subdecisions, consciously sequenced over long periods of time and separated by delays of various kinds. Furthermore, the manager appears to supervise a great many of these at any one time—perhaps 50 to 100 in the case of chief executives. In fact, in his handling of improvement projects, the manager may be likened to a juggler. At any one point, he maintains a number of balls in the air. Periodically, one comes down, receives a short burst of energy, and goes up again. Meanwhile, an inventory of new balls waits on the sidelines and, at random intervals, old balls are discarded and new ones added. Both Lindblom [2] and Marples [18] touch on these aspects of strategy-making, the former stressing the disjointed and incremental nature of the decisions, and the latter depicting the sequential episodes in terms of a stranded rope made up of fibres of different lengths each of which surfaces periodically.

Disturbance Handler While the *Entrepreneur* role focuses on voluntary change, the *disturbance handler* role deals with corrections which the manager is forced to make. We may describe this role as follows: The organization consists basically of specialist operating programs. From time to time, it experiences a stimulus that cannot be handled routinely, either because an operating program has broken down or because the stimulus is new and it is not clear which operating program should handle it.

These situations constitute disturbances. As generalist, the manager is obliged to assume responsibility for dealing with the stimulus. Thus, the handling of disturbances is an essential duty of the manager.

There is clear evidence for this role both in our study of chief executives and in Sayles' study of production supervisors [24, p. 162]:

> *The achievement of this stability, which is the manager's objective, is a never-to-be-attained ideal. He is like a symphony orchestra conductor, endeavoring to maintain a melodious performance in which contributions of the various instruments are coordinated and sequenced, patterned and paced, while the orchestra members are having various personal difficulties, stage hands are moving music stands, alternating excessive heat and cold are creating audience and instrument problems, and the sponsor of the concert is insisting on irrational changes in the program.*

Sayles goes further to point out the very important balance that the manager must maintain between change and stability. To Sayles, the manager seeks "a dynamic type of stability" (p. 162). Most disturbances elicit short-term adjustments which bring back equilibrium; persistent ones require the introduction of long-term structural change.

Resource Allocator   The manager maintains ultimate authority over this organization's strategy-making system by controlling the allocation of its resources. By deciding who will get what (and who will do what), the manager directs the course of his organization. He does this in three ways:

1. *In selecting his own time,* the manager allocates his most precious resource and thereby determines organizational priorities. Issues that receive low priority do not reach the *nerve center* of the organization and are blocked for want of resources.
2. In designing the organizational structure and in carrying out many improvement projects, the manager *programs the work of his subordinates.* In other words, he allocates their time by deciding what will be done and who will do it.
3. Most significantly, the manager maintains control over resource allocation by the requirement that he *authorize all significant decisions* before they are implemented. By retaining this power, the manager ensures that different decisions are interrelated—that conflicts are avoided, that resource constraints are respected, and that decisions complement one another.

Decisions appear to be authorized in one of two ways. Where the costs and benefits of a proposal can be quantified, where it is competing for specified resources with other known proposals, and where it can wait for a certain time of year, approval for a proposal is sought in the context of a formal *budgeting* procedure. But these conditions are most often not met—timing may be crucial, nonmonetary costs may predominate, and so on. In these cases, approval is sought in terms of an *ad hoc request for authorization*. Subordinate and manager meet (perhaps informally) to discuss one proposal alone.

Authorization choices are enormously complex ones for the manager. A myriad of factors must be considered (resource constraints, influencer preferences, consistency with other decisions, feasibility, payoff, timing, subordinate feelings, etc.). But the fact that the manager is authorizing the decision rather than supervising its design suggests that he has little time to give to it. To alleviate this difficulty, it appears that managers use special kinds of *models* and *plans* in their decision-making. These exist only in their minds and are loose, but they serve to guide behavior. Models may answer questions such as, "Does this proposal make sense in terms of the trends that I see in tariff legislation?" or "Will the EDP department be able to get along with marketing on this?" Plans exist in the sense that, on questioning, managers reveal images (in terms of proposed improvement projects) of where they would like their organizations to go: "Well, once I get these foreign operations fully developed, I would like to begin to look into a reorganization," said one subject of this study.

Negotiator The final role describes the manager as participant in negotiation activity. To some students of the management process [8, p. 343], this is not truly part of the job of managing. But such distinctions are arbitrary. Negotiation is an integral part of managerial work, as this study notes for chief executives and as that of Sayles made very clear for production supervisors [24, p. 131]: "Sophisticated managers place great stress on negotiations as a way of life. They negotiate with groups who are setting standards for their work, who are performing support activity for them, and to whom they wish to 'sell' their services."

The manager must participate in important negotiation sessions because he is his organization's legal authority, its *spokesman* and its *resource allocator*. Negotiation is resource trading in real time. If the resource commitments are to be large, the legal authority must be present.

These ten roles suggest that the manager of an organization bears a great burden of responsibility. He must oversee his organization's status system; he must serve as a crucial informational link between it and its environment; he must interpret and reflect its basic values; he must maintain the stability of its operations; and he must adapt it in a controlled and balanced way to a changing environment.

Management as a Profession and as a Science

Is management a profession? To the extent that different managers perform one set of basic roles, management satisfies one criterion for becoming a profession. But a profession must require, in the words of the *Random House Dictionary*, "knowledge of some department of learning or science." Which of the ten roles now requires specialized learning? Indeed, what school of business or public administration teaches its students how to disseminate information, allocate resources, perform as figurehead, make contacts, or handle disturbances? We simply know very little about teaching these things. The reason is that we have never tried to document and describe in a meaningful way the procedures (or programs) that managers use.

The evidence of this research suggests that there is as yet no science in managerial work—that managers do not work according to procedures that have been prescribed by scientific analysis. Indeed, except for his use of the telephone, the airplane, and the dictating machine, it would appear that the manager of today is indistinguishable from his predecessors. He may seek different information, but he gets much of it in the same way—from word-of-mouth. He may make decisions dealing with modern technology but he uses the same intuitive (that is, nonexplicit) procedures in making them. Even the computer, which has had such a great impact on other kinds of organizational work, has apparently done little to alter the working methods of the general manager.

How do we develop a scientific base to understand the work of the manager? The description of roles is a first and necessary step. But tighter forms of research are necessary. Specifically, we must attempt to model managerial work—to describe it as a system of programs. First, it will be necessary to decide what programs managers actually use. Among a great number of programs in the manager's repertoire, we might expect to find a time-scheduling program, an information-disseminating program, and a disturbance-handling program. Then researchers will have to devote a considerable amount of effort to studying and accurately describing the content of each of these programs—the information and heuristics used. Finally, it will be necessary to describe the interrelationships among all of these programs so that they may be combined into an integrated descriptive model of managerial work.

When the management scientist begins to understand the programs that managers use, he can begin to design meaningful systems and provide help for the manager. He may ask: Which managerial activities can be fully reprogrammed (i.e., automated)? Which cannot be reprogrammed because they require human responses? Which can be partially reprogrammed to operate in a man-machine system? Perhaps scheduling, information collecting, and resource-allocating activities lead themselves to varying degrees of reprogramming. Management will emerge as a science to the extent that such efforts are successful.

Improving the Manager's Effectiveness

Fayol's 50-year-old description of managerial work is no longer of use to us. And we shall not disentangle the complexity of managerial work if we insist on viewing the manager simply as a decision-maker or simply as a motivator of subordinates. In fact, we are unlikely to overestimate the complexity of the manager's work, and we shall make little headway if we take over simple or narrow points of view in our research.

A major problem faces today's manager. Despite the growing size of modern organizations and the growing complexity of their problems (particularly those in the public sector), the manager can expect little help. He must design his own information system, and he must take full charge of his organization's strategy-making system. Furthermore, the manager faces what might be called the *dilemma of delegation*. He has unique access to much important information but he lacks a formal means of disseminating it. As much of it is verbal, he cannot spread it around in an efficient manner. How can he delegate a task with confidence when he has neither the time nor the means to send the necessary information along with it?

Thus, the manager is usually forced to carry a great burden of responsibility in his organization. As organizations become increasingly large and complex, this burden increases. Unfortunately, the man cannot significantly increase his available time or significantly improve his abilities to manage. Hence, in the large, complex bureaucracy, the top manager's time assumes an enormous opportunity cost and he faces the real danger of becoming a major obstruction in the flow of decisions and information.

Because of this, as we have seen, managerial work assumes a number of distinctive characteristics. The quantity of work is great; the pace is unrelenting; there is great variety, fragmentation, and brevity in the work activities; the manager must concentrate on issues that are current, specific, and ad hoc, and to do so, he finds that he must rely on verbal forms of communications. Yet it is on this man that the burden lies for designing and operating strategy-making and information-processing systems that are to solve his organization's (and society's) problems.

The manager can do something to alleviate these problems. He can learn more about his own roles in his organization, and he can use this information to schedule his time in a more efficient manner. He can recognize that only he has much of the information needed by his organization. Then, he can seek to find better means of disseminating it into the organization. Finally, he can turn to the skills of his management scientists to help reduce his workload and to improve his ability to make decisions.

The management scientist can learn to help the manager to the extent he can develop an understanding of the manager's work and the manager's information. To date, strategic planners, operations researchers, and information system designers have provided little help for the senior manager. They simply have had no framework available by which to understand the work of the men who employed them, and they have had poor access to the information which has never been documented. It is folly to believe that a man with poor access to the organization's true *nerve center* can design a formal management information system. Similarly, how can the long-range planner, a man usually uninformed about many of the *current* events that take place in and around his organization, design meaningful strategic plans? For good reason, the literature documents many manager complaints of naive planning and many planner complaints of disinterested managers. In my view, our lack of understanding of managerial work has been the greatest block to the progress of management science.

The ultimate solution to the problem—to the overburdened manager seeking meaningful help—must derive from research. We must observe, describe, and understand the real work of managing; then and only then shall we significantly improve it.

References

1. Braybrooke, David. "The Mystery of Executive Success Re-examined," *Administrative Science Quarterly*, vol. 8 (1964), pp. 533–60.
2. Braybrooke, David, and Lindblom, Charles E. *A Strategy of Decision.* New York: Free Press, 1963.
3. Bronowski, J. "The Creative Process," *Scientific American,* vol. 199 (September 1958), pp. 59–65.
4. Burns, Tom. "The Directions of Activity and Communications in a Departmental Executive Group," *Human Relations,* vol. 7 (1954), pp. 73–97.
5. Burns, Tom. "Management in Action," *Operational Research Quarterly,* vol. 8 (1957), pp. 45–60.
6. Carlson, Sune. *Executive Behavior.* Stockholm: Strömbergs, 1951.
7. Davis, Robert T. *Performance and Development of Field Sales Managers.* Boston: Division of Research, Graduate School of Business Administration, Harvard University, 1957.
8. Drucker, Peter F. *The Practice of Management.* New York: Harper and Row, 1954.
9. Fayol, Henri. *Administration industrielle et générale.* Paris: Dunods, 1950 (first published 1916).
10. Gibb, Cecil A. "Leadership," Chapter 31 in Gardner Lindzey and Elliott A. Aronson, eds. *The Handbook of Social Psychology.* 2d ed. Reading, Mass.: Addison-Wesley, 1969, vol. 4.
11. Guest, Robert H. "Of Time and the Foreman," *Personnel,* vol. 32 (1955–56), pp. 478–86.
12. Gulick, Luther H. "Notes on the Theory of Organization," in Luther Gulick and Lyndall Urwick, eds. *Papers on the Science of Administration.* New York: Columbia University Press, 1937.
13. Hemphill, John K. *Dimensions of Executive Positions.* Columbus, Ohio: Bureau of Business Research Monograph on Number 98, The Ohio State University, 1960.
14. Homans, George C. *The Human Group.* New York: Harcourt, Brace, 1950.
15. Horne, J. H., and Lupton, Tom. "The Work Activities of Middle Managers—An Exploratory Study," *The Journal of Management Studies,* vol. 2 (February 1965), pp. 14–33.
16. Kelly, Joe. "The Study of Executive Behavior by Activity Sampling," *Human Relations,* vol. 17 (August 1964), pp. 277–87.
17. Mackenzie, R. Alex. "The Management Process in 3D" *Harvard Business Review,* November–December 1969, pp. 80–87.
18. Marples, D. L. "Studies of Managers—A Fresh Start?" *The Journal of Management Studies,* vol. 4 (October 1967), pp. 282–99.
19. Mintzberg, Henry. "Structured Observation as a Method to Study Managerial Work," *The Journal of Management Studies,* vol. 7 (February 1970), pp. 87–104.
20. Myers, Charles A., ed. *The Impact of Computers on Management,* Cambridge, Mass.: The M.I.T. Press, 1967.
21. Neustadt, Richard E. *Presidential Power: The Politics of Leadership.* New York: The New American Library, 1964.

22. Papandreou, Andreas G. "Some Basic Problems in the Theory of the Firm," in Bernard F. Haley, ed., *A Survey of Contemporary Economics,* Vol. II, Homewood, Ill.: Irwin, 1952, pp. 183–219.

23. Sarbin, T. R. and Allen, V. L. "Role Theory," in Gardner Lindzey and Elliott A. Aronson, eds., *The Handbook of Social Psychology,* Vol. I, 2d ed. Reading, Mass.: Addison-Wesley, 1968, pp. 488–567.

24. Sayles, Leonard R. *Managerial Behavior: Administration in Complex Enterprises.* New York: McGraw-Hill, 1964.

25. Stewart, Rosemary. *Managers and Their Jobs,* London: Macmillan, 1967.

26. Whyte, William F. *Street Corner Society.* 2d ed. Chicago: University of Chicago Press, 1955.

PART IV

Organizational Structure and Process

Editors' Summary Comments

*I*n Part IV, we will present selections that examine the concept of organizational structure and the process components of communication, decision making, performance evaluation, and reward systems. The effects of these components determine to a considerable degree the behavior of individuals in organizations.

The structure of an organization consists of relatively fixed relationships among jobs and groups of jobs. The decisions that managers must make in designing the structure relate to a five-step process: (1) diagnosing the organization's environment; (2) defining jobs; (3) grouping jobs into departments; (4) determining the size of the department; and (5) delegating authority to the manager. According to contemporary theorists, the most effective organization structure must be related to situational factors, such as environmental demands and technological parameters.

Individuals in organizations perform as members of a group within an organization structure and communicate for many reasons, one of which is to make decisions. One of the most important purposes of an organization structure is to facilitate the two fundamental processes of communications and decision making.

A crucial process in most organizations concerns the evaluation and rewarding of individual performance. Effective performance evaluation requires not only an accurate assessment of the content and requirements of jobs, but also the development of valid and reliable

175

performance criteria. The rewarding of behavior is an important process that acts to strengthen desired behavior or eliminate undesired behavior on the part of the individual.

In the first selection, "Organization-Environment: Concepts and Issues," Raymond Miles, Charles Snow, and Jeffrey Pfeffer examine the extent to which organizations are shaped by their environments. They point out that there is no doubt that organizations must and do adjust their strategies, technologies, structures, and processes to meet changing environment demands. However, they conclude that current theories fail to clearly indicate how environmental conditions place constraints on adjustment alternatives and how each adjustment decision constrains those that follow.

Tom Alexander's article, "Why Bureaucracy Keeps Growing," provides the reader with a practitioner's view of the realities of this organizational design form. He points out that bureaucracy has a number of inherent flaws that have contributed to its relative ineffectiveness. Most important of these are the lack of recognition of changes in the environment and the fact that most bureaucrats act in their own self-interest and for the survival of the bureaucratic system—points that many readers will easily relate to. The reader, however, must judge for himself or herself where bureaucracy as an organizational design form can be effective.

In "Organizational Design: An Information Processing View," Jay Galbraith presents a model of designing organizations that is based on the amount and quality of information that is required for effectiveness. He notes that reduction or increase in the capacity to process information must be accompanied by a change in the structure of the organization.

The matrix form of organizational design is a significant evolutionary trend in many organizations. In "Problems of Matrix Organizations," Stanley Davis and Paul Lawrence note that we should investigate the problems as well as the advantages, and they discuss economic pressures that can have dysfunctional effects on the success of this design.

The next selection, Victor Vroom's article "Can Leaders Learn to Lead?", focuses on the development of a normative or prescriptive decision-making model for leaders. Vroom links effective leadership—that is, successful decision making—to the degree to which the leader should share his or her decision-making power with subordinates. The author is optimistic about the leaders learning to enlarge their repertoire of styles as they become more aware of which style is appropriate in which situation.

Many ills in organizations have been attributed to problems with communications. The selection "When Productivity Lags, Check at the Top: Are Key Managers Really Communicating?" develops this point further and suggests ways of looking at the problems through diagnosis and proper implementation of an action plan.

Evaluating the performance of managers has become an important factor in most organizations. In "The Science of Telling Executives How They're Doing," Herbert Meyer points out that performance ratings have become the key factor in determining who gets raises and who gets promoted. Such systems have contributed to more open and candid relationships and have reduced uncertainty—an unsettling occurrence for some managers.

The *Business Week* selection "The Tightening Squeeze on White-Collar Pay" identifies some major compensation problems faced by many organizations—compression, inflation, and the motivational value of money. Improved performance evaluation and merit systems are stressed along with some examples from selected forms.

The final selection discusses how Sears has implemented a career planning program for its managerial staff. Built on its job description and compensation system, the program stresses flexibility and the all-important trend of cross-functional moves across the company.

15

Organization-Environment:
Concepts and Issues

Raymond E. Miles, Charles C. Snow,
and Jeffrey Pfeffer

To what extent are organizations shaped by their environments, that is, by the network of individuals, groups, agencies, and organizations with whom they interact? Are there organizational characteristics— strategies, technologies, structures, processes—which are appropriate for one environment but which may lead to failure in another? More pointedly, are there linkages across these characteristics which determine organizational success—are there, for example, particular structures and processes which fit certain technologies or strategies but not others?

Over the past two decades, an increasing number of studies have been aimed at these and related questions. At best, however, these efforts have been only modestly successful—the clear stream of association discovered in one study is frequently muddied in the next.

In part, this confusion concerning what is and is not known about organizational responses to environmental demands and the linkages among technology, structure, and process can be attributed to the usual set of definitional and measurement problems which plague research in all areas of organizational behavior and which are exacerbated here by the extreme complexity of the variables being examined. However, we believe that a more basic problem exists: the theory-map which should help us locate where organization-environment research is and the direction it should take is incomplete and in many areas obscure.

SOURCE: Raymond E. Miles, Charles C. Snow, and Jeffrey Pfeffer, "Organization-Environment: Concepts and Issues," *Industrial Relations,* October 1974, pp. 244–66. Reprinted by permission.

The purpose of this article is to take stock of the organization-environment literature to this point and to make some preliminary suggestions concerning future research on this topic. We will first briefly outline the route which research in this area appears to have taken to this point. Next we will describe the general requirements for a useful map or model of organization-environment relations by which we can measure progress and plan future research. Then, using this model as a conceptual framework, we will attempt to organize some of the salient contributions to theory and research in this area and, more importantly, to examine the points at which current theory and research fall short of the requirements of the complete model. Finally, these deficiencies will be used to plot out a tentative course for future theory building, data collection, and analysis.

An Overview of Organization-Environment Research

For the first half of this century, management and organization theorists tended to ignore the environment, or at least to hold it constant, as they sought universalistic principles of structure, planning, control, and the like. Weber, while aware of some of the dysfunctions of bureaucratic structures and processes, implied that these structures were appropriate for all organizational settings.[1] Similarly, Taylor viewed his principles of scientific management as universally applicable and treated environmental demands and organizational objectives as fixed in his search for the "one best way."[2] And, later developers of administrative principles gave little attention to environmental differences as they attempted to integrate experiences from the church, the military, and business into a common set of practical prescriptions.

Economists, of course, were concerned with organizational adjustments to the environment, but by and large these were treated simply as formal exercises in profit-maximizing logic. In their models, market forces set the prices for goods and services, and the entire organization was characterized as a production function whose blend of capital and labor was dictated by the quest for cost minimization. Entrepreneurial and marketing decisions were viewed as important, but little effort was made to specify the impact of these decisions on organizational structure and processes.[3]

Attacks on universalistic organization and management principles began in the thirties and forties and heated up in the fifties. The initial criticism concerned the alleged inability of bureaucracies to adapt to the needs of individuals and changes in the government. Gouldner provided case study evidence suggesting that bureaucratization could be efficacious in one setting (an office) but damaging in another (a mine).[4] Burns and Stalker extended this notion of contingent organizational responses by noting that successful firms in a stable environment tended to have "mechanistic" or highly bureaucratized structures and processes while successful firms in changing and uncertain environments tended to have "organic" or flexible structures and processes.[5] The impact of Burns and Stalker's work was augmented by the growing acceptance of the "systems" view of organizations which portrayed them as socio-technical mechanisms drawing resources from the environment at one end and exporting goods and services into the environment at the other.

Through the late fifties and the sixties, a series of increasingly elaborate models portraying the linkages among environment, technology, structure, and process were developed. Most of these, however, dealt with only a limited aspect of the full adjustment sequence (e.g., tying particular technologies to specific products or markets or relating types of production processes to organization structure and staffing), and most were content to describe the expected relationships without specifying how they were achieved—that is, the role of managerial choice in the adjustment process was seldom treated. Finally, most of these descriptive models failed to deal with the adjustment process over time, and, therefore, we have little understanding of how today's managerial decisions affect the ability of the organization to adjust to changing environmental demands in the future.

The deficiencies noted in this overview are, we feel, largely the result of misdirection. As suggested earlier, a clearer model of the crucial elements of the organization-environment relationship is needed. In the following section, we outline the dimensions of an improved "map."

A "Decision-Points" Map

In our view, the study of organizational adaptation to environmental demands should be focused on a series of intertwined "decision points":

1. The decisions by which the organization selects a portion of the total environment as its particular arena of activity (i.e., its *domain*) and chooses a basic strategy for managing the domain;
2. The decisions by which the organization establishes an appropriate *technology* for implementing its basic operating strategy;
3. The decisions by which the organization creates a *structure* of roles and relationships to control and coordinate technology and strategy; and
4. The decisions made to assure organizational *continuity*—the capacity to survive, adjust, and grow.

Focused specifically on these decision points, research should highlight those aspects of organization-environment relations which are "determined" or "fixed" either by the environment or by preceding decisions and those which allow for the exercise of managerial judgment. The examination of the demands and constraints which alternative choices at each decision point place on those which follow should provide evidence concerning the "feasible set" of choices available and the costs and benefits among these alternatives. Research directed to these decision points would both highlight the role of managerial judgment in the organization-environment adjustment process and provide guidance to managers faced with crucial choices in these areas.

Obviously by specifying these decision points we do not intend to imply that a particular individual or group in the organization makes *a* definitive decision or consciously chooses *a* specific course of action in each of the four areas listed here. Instead, we are saying that these broad categories provide a convenient way of grouping together numerous decisions and actions which, in the aggregate, define the organization's relationship to its environment.

In the following sections, we will examine some of the more important contributions to the existing organization-environment literature, structuring our selective review around the decision-point framework described above and noting the extent to which its requirements have been met by previous research.

The Organization and Environment Literature

Before we review the literature on organization and environment, following the decision-points map outlined above, it may be helpful to first consider the concept of environment itself—is there such a thing, and, if so, how has it been and how can it be described?

Organizational Boundaries

It is usually taken for granted that there is some boundary separating the organization from its environment, environment potentially being everything which is outside of the organization. Starbuck has compared the problem of finding the organization's boundary to that of finding the boundary of a cloud.[6] In defining a cloud, we can measure the density of its moisture and, by selecting some specific level of density, determine what properly "belongs" to the cloud and what "belongs" to its environment. But with organizations, as opposed to clouds, the boundary problem is more difficult. If, for example, we wish to measure the density of member interaction and involvement, we must specify the decisions or issues which concern us. Clearly, interaction patterns and degree of involvement of various individuals and groups, e.g., stockholders, unions, suppliers, etc., vary depending upon whether our concern is with long-range planning, wage and salary issues, or the imminent bankruptcy of the firm. Thus, while the density of interaction and involvement can be measured, it changes over time and across decision areas, thereby changing the determination of what is "in" the organization and what is "in" the environment.

Because organizations are open social systems, they are constantly changing, and their boundaries fluctuate accordingly. At a minimum— indeed perhaps it is the best that can be hoped for—the definition of the organization's boundary should be consistent with the problem under investigation.

Dimensions of Environment

Assuming that we can distinguish between the organization and its environment, how can the environment be described in a way that is analytically useful? Emery and Trist developed a typology of environments based on the degree of interconnectedness and the extent of change in the environment.[7] Other authors (e.g., Dill, Burns and Stalker, Thompson, Lawrence and Lorsch, Duncan, Osborn and Hunt) have also focused on change as an important environmental dimension, the general argument being that bureaucratic structures inhibit the organization's ability to perceive and adjust to rapid environmental change.[8]

Some authors, however, have not distinguished between rate of environmental change and degree of uncertainty (unpredictable change) and have, therefore, implicitly equated the two. It is possible to have rapid but largely predictable change in the environment, and, in such a situation, the organization does not really confront uncertainty, as it knows reasonably well what environmental conditions it will face in the future. A related problem involves treating the environment and the organization as global entities, as if somehow a monolithic environment produces uniform responses across the entire organization. However, it is quite plausible to think of a flexible technology with stable customer demands, changing credit and money market conditions with a stable technology, relatively constant patterns of external dependence with a flexible organization structure, etc. The failure to distinguish between change and uncertainty, and the failure to specifically address less global aspects of the environment and organization, have confounded attempts to link environmental dimensions to organizational characteristics.

Finally, theorists (particularly Thompson, Perrow, and Duncan) have stressed the heterogeneity of the environment.[9] Here it is argued that complex, differentiated environments are likely to require different organizational structures than do environments which are simple and homogeneous. Once again, however, some confusion develops. Thompson treats the dimensions of heterogeneity and change as independent, while Duncan views both as components of environmental uncertainty.[10]

The Enacted Environment

Regardless of the analytical dimensions used to describe the environment, there remains the issue of how the environment becomes known to the organization (i.e., its managers). Weick has argued that the important organizational environments are those which are *enacted* or created through a process of attention.[11] The organization responds only to what it perceives; those things that are not noticed do not affect the organization's decisions and actions. This focus on the process of attention means that the same "objective" environment may appear differently to different organizations, and this may be the main reason why previous research using so-called "objective" or "hard" (i.e., nonperceptual) measures of environmental variables has largely failed to predict organizational responses. Clearly, the organization will ultimately be victimized by perceptions which ignore or distort crucial environmental elements, but a wide range of "perceived environments" may be tolerable for lengthy periods in many real circumstances.

The emphasis on enactment also means that organizational information-processing systems are critical in determining how the organization adjusts to its environment. How organizations attend to various aspects of their environment and how this information is collected and processed are issues that are both unexplored and critical to our understanding of organizational adaptation. It is entirely conceivable that organization structure itself conditions the enactment process. Thus, one could argue that complex, differentiated organization structures will be more likely to produce complex, differentiated managerial perceptions of the environment. Therefore, structure may not only be a consequence of the environment but may also influence the environment through its effect on managerial attention processes.

Domain Definition and Strategic Response

In enacting its environment, the organization has, in part, defined its domain. An organization's domain consists of those activities it intends to pursue, and, in choosing a domain of activity, the organization simultaneously determines its pattern of interdependence with elements of the environment (suppliers, customers, unions, etc.). For example, if the organization decides to be a general hospital, it defines a pattern of interdependence with environmental elements that may be distinctly different from a hospital specializing in only a few major ailments. Unfortunately, there is little descriptive literature concerning the organization's strategic choice of a domain of activity—why, for example, within the same general environment some organizations choose to specialize while others diversify.[12]

Also, as Thompson has pointed out, the organization cannot unilaterally choose its domain. There must be some degree of consensus among those with whom the organization comes into contact—either resource providers or critics of the organization's proposed activities—regarding the desired arena of activity, and this process of attaining domain consensus frequently constrains what activities the organization undertakes.[13]

The patterns of interdependence established by the organization's choice of domain subsequently affect its behavior. Randall investigated the willingness of state employment offices in Wisconsin to undertake human-resources development activities.[14] He found that such activities were more likely to occur when the office had a community-action agency in its domain acting as a source of pressure. Pfeffer, in a study of Israeli managers' attitudes, found that managers were more willing to undertake activities favored by the government to the extent that their firms were (1) more dependent on the government for financial assistance; (2) sold a relatively greater proportion of their output to the government; and (3) had a higher proportion of foreign ownership.[15] He also found that managers in firms which were in poor financial condition claimed that their decisions were more influenced by bankers.

Managing the Environment

While organizations are clearly influenced by forces in their domain, they also have a wealth of available means for altering their environments to make them conform more closely to what the organization can manage. One strategy for dealing with environmental interdependence involves working directly with the groups or organizations concerned, using such means as long-term contracts, joint ventures, cooptation, or merger.[16] Another strategy works indirectly to influence or regulate interdependence, using third parties such as trade associations, coordinating groups, or government agencies (which may provide, for example, direct cash subsidies to the organization or legislation to restrict competition).[17] A third strategy is less clear-cut than the previous ones. Phillips has argued that in oligopolistic industries, firms behave as if they were in a small group, conforming to group norms and implicitly or explicitly coordinating their activities.[18] Perrow has described instances where corporations "willingly suspended" competition in the short run because of strong industrial norms of how business relations ought to be conducted.[19] Finally, if environmental factors prove difficult to "manage," the organization has the option of choosing another domain, avoiding uncertainty or dependence by getting into a new line of activity; consequently, diversification is another way of coping with the environment.

Establishing an Organizational Technology

Having determined a domain, or sphere of activity, the organization next requires a technology to produce the goods or services that it has decided to provide. Broadly defined, technology is the combination of skills, equipment, and relevant technical knowledge needed to bring about desired transformations in materials, information, or people.[20]

It should be emphasized that, as with domain definition, there is a good deal of choice involved in the selection of a technology, depending on how the organization perceives the environment and how it defines its activities. Perrow, for example, described two correctional institutions dealing with delinquent youths.[21] One was operated as if its primary goal were custody, and to simply confine people required only a very "routine" technology—a small custodial staff, centralized decision making, and generally uniform treatment of the raw materials (i.e., the youths). The other institution operated as if it were pursuing more therapeutic goals, with a "nonroutine" technology that permitted much more flexibility in dealing with the youths. Similarly, there is not much in common between the technology used by a large military kitchen and a fine gourmet restaurant, though in broad terms both have established a domain which involves providing meals.

Thus, depending on the organization's strategy for dealing with the domain, one type of technology may appear to be more appropriate than another, while others are disregarded as totally infeasible. Thus, within the feasible range of technologies, managers are free to choose some particular mix of skills, equipment, etc., and may have even greater discretion in deciding how this technology is to be operated.

Types of Technology

Several typologies of technology have been advanced. Woodward, the first to introduce technology as an important organizational variable, constructed a technological scale ranging from unit or prototype production, through small-batch, mass, and finally continuous-process production.[22] Each of these technologies differs in the degree to which it is labor or capital intensive and particularly in the extent to which it permits specialized handling. Other typologies have been offered (e.g., Perrow, Thompson, Hickson, et al.),[23] but Woodward's scheme allows us to make some broad comparisons across different types.

Comparisons among Technologies

The unit or small-batch production technology is labor intensive and highly flexible. Thus, it is not well suited to strategies involving standardized products and long production runs but rather to customized products. This type of technology can operate at low output levels or where there is considerable fluctuation in output. A unit technology is usually accompanied by an organization structure which utilizes general as opposed to specialized employee skills, and this technology may be relatively easily adjusted in order to experiment with new developments and work processes.

Mass-production technologies also tend to be labor intensive, although their more rigid forms, such as the automobile assembly line, are capital intensive. A mass-production technology, because it typically employs expensive limited-purpose equipment, is much less flexible than a unit technology and requires a very high volume of output in order to be economical. And, because of its rigid scheduling requirements, even small fluctuations in output are costly to this type of system. In contrast to unit production, the organization structure appropriate for a mass-production technology includes numerous standardized procedures and employees with limited and specialized skills who may be relatively interchangeable within the system but cannot be easily converted to new methods and processes.

Finally, continuous-process technology is highly capital intensive and requires a large output volume. Although this type of technology usually allows a diverse range of related products to be manufactured, the technology itself is quite inflexible—it can be adapted to produce other products only at great cost. Continuous-process technology requires relatively few individuals to monitor the machinery, but such employees frequently must have high levels of judgmental and technical skill.

Sealing off the Technical Core

Because of the variety in these technologies, each requires different means of protecting it from costly environmental disturbances. Woodward found different sequences of production (manufacturing cycles) for each type of system. In unit production, the organization first obtains a customer order and then develops and manufactures the product. In mass production, the organization spends a great deal of time developing and producing the product, then engages in extensive marketing efforts in order to sell it. Lastly, in continuous-process production, the most critical function is to continually develop and market new products amenable to the existing technology, while producing the present product mix.

The time span of managerial decision making also varies with each type of technology. Whereas in unit production, the time span of decisions is short, it is considerably longer in mass production, and in continuous-process production, the large capital investments involved mean that many decisions require ten to twenty years and more to implement. Put another way, each technology places a unique set of demands on the organization structure to maintain control and coordination.

Development of an Organization Structure

Organization structure refers to the decomposition of the entire organization into subunits and to the relatively enduring relationships among them, and, therefore, structure includes such major organizational (as opposed to individual) variables as complexity, formalization, centralization, and administrative intensity (the ratio of clerical and managerial employees to all other employees). As mentioned earlier, the organization's structure exists to control and coordinate the technology and serves as a buffer between the technical core and the environment. However, the relationship between technology and structure is more complicated than was once believed.

Relationship between Technology and Structure

Studies of technology and structure appear to have had two overriding concerns. First, there have been several attempts to determine whether or not there is a direct relationship between the organization's technology and its structure. Second, and more recently, there has been a research interest in determining whether technology or organization size has the greater impact on structure. Two reviews of the technology, size, and structure literature have summarized the research as follows: (1) the definition and measurement of both technology and structure have not been consistent across studies, and, therefore, these studies are not strictly comparable; (2) studies across several types of organizations may reflect interindustry differences and their impact on structure rather than the specific influence of technology; (3) a single organization may operate more than one technology, making the "dominant" technological influence on structure difficult to ascertain; (4) organization size appears to be a somewhat stronger determinant of structure than does technology—only in small organizations does technology appear to have a clear and consistent impact on structure; and (5) because technology and size together explain such a small amount of the variance in organization structure, other predictors of structure (e.g., measures of the environment and managerial ideologies) need to be investigated.[24]

Some recent research, however, has suggested that structure may not respond directly to technology per se but rather to the different demands for control and coordination associated with each type of technology. For example, Woodward found that as technology moves from unit to mass production and then to continuous process, there is an increase in mechanical over personal forms of control.[25] At the same time, as one moves through the technology classification, control systems tend to be unitary (i.e., applied throughout the organization) in unit technologies, fragmented (i.e., different control standards and mechanisms for each major organizational subunit) in mass-production technologies, and unitary once again in continuous-process technologies. Thus, Woodward argued, the different technologies require different forms of control, and these in turn place some demands on, but do not precisely determine, a particular organization structure (e.g., unitary control can be achieved by formalized rules or by centralized decision making).

Similarly, each type of technology must be coordinated differently, and these different coordination demands must be accommodated by the organization's structure. Although definitive empirical research remains to be done in this area, it is generally true that as the organization's technology becomes more routine, coordination tends to become more formalized. Thus, with a unit or small-batch technology, coordination by mutual adjustment—where the technological process is modified on an ad hoc basis to meet the transformation needs of the inputs—seems to be most appropriate. With mass and continuous-process technologies, however, it is possible to coordinate these production processes by standardized procedures and longer-range plans (a variety of which may be accommodated within particular organization structures).

Deficiencies in Current Theory and Research

As indicated in the review above, several of the decision points in our map of organization-environment relations have not been adequately researched. However, we should hasten to add that the areas which remain incomplete are obviously the most difficult ones, so the limitations of previous research are more often those of omission rather than commission. Three areas in particular need special attention in future research. First, although we frequently talk about managerial perceptions of the environment, we have no convenient way of describing or categorizing these perceptions, and we therefore tend to speak of managerial perceptions in global terms or ignore them completely. Secondly, previous research has primarily attempted to discover associations between environmental variables and particular *types* of organization structure, but we believe that this search for precise relationships is likely to prove futile. Instead we feel that future research should focus on the *demands* made by each decision point on the next decision point—the extent to which managerial choice is constrained —rather than on the ultimate adjustment(s) to these demands. Such a focus would permit us to account for the frequent observation that organizations adopt a variety of forms in response to apparently similar environmental demands. And, finally, by far the vast majority of previous organization-environment research has treated the organization as a static entity, leaving us with little understanding of how organizations adjust to their environments over time.

Managerial Perceptions

Child has argued that managerial perceptions and actions have a strong influence on organizational responses to the environment.[26] His concept of *strategic choice* corresponds closely to our concept of a decision point—at each stage of the adjustment process, managers have more or less discretion in guiding their organizations along different courses.

In a very preliminary way, Snow and Miles have attempted to categorize managerial perceptions of the environment and to describe how these perceptions are transformed into organizational responses.[27] From interviews with top managers in 16 college textbook publishing firms, these authors have developed four relatively distinct types of environmental enactment. Although the typology is crude, subsuming a number of variables in addition to managerial perceptions, each of the four types portrays a distinct pattern of organization-environment interaction. The four types of enactment are:

1. *Domain Defenders,* organizations whose top managers perceive little or no change and uncertainty in the environment and who have little inclination to make anything other than minor adjustments in organizational structure and processes.
2. *Reluctant Reactors,* organizations where top managers perceive some change and uncertainty in the environment but who are not likely to make any substantial organizational adjustments until forced to do so by environmental pressures.
3. *Anxious Analyzers,* organizations where top managers perceive a good deal of change and uncertainty in the environment but who wait until competing organizations develop a viable response and then quickly adopt it.
4. *Enthusiastic Prospectors,* organizations whose top managers continually perceive (almost create) change and uncertainty in the environment and who regularly experiment with potential responses to new environmental trends.

Subsequent decisions concerning strategy, technology, and structure appear to be quite consistent with each of these respective types (e.g., Domain Defenders, as opposed to Enthusiastic Prospectors, were more likely to have mass-production than unit technologies and to have "mechanistic" rather than "organic" organization structures). Moreover, the findings of this study suggest that the actions an organization takes in responding to its environment are much more likely to be consistent with top management perceptions of the environment than any "objective" indicator of environmental conditions is likely to predict.[28] We do not, however, mean to imply that the search for objective environmental measures be abandoned. Quite the contrary. Actual environmental conditions, as suggested earlier, clearly do influence organizational behavior, at least in the longer run. Moreover, measures of these characteristics are needed as a validity check for measures of managerial perceptions. We are arguing, as does Child, that perceptions guide the strategic choices managers make to achieve a better fit between their organizations and the environment and that these perceptions must be included in any model of organizational adaptation.

Adjustments to the Demands of Each Decision Point

A second major deficiency in the previous research concerns what we believe to be a somewhat misdirected research emphasis. As noted earlier, the typical study in this area attempts to correlate measures of predetermined environmental and organizational variables in the hope of discovering significant relationships among aspects of the environment and various forms of organization structure. Such a procedure, however, does not usually allow for the possibility that, across a particular set of organizations, a wide range of responses to similar environmental demands may be observed. For example, in the college textbook publishing study, two organizations whose top managements perceived a great deal of change and uncertainty in their environments nevertheless made substantially different adjustments to this environmental turbulence. One firm went through a major effort to restructure the organization while simultaneously creating a program to financially underwrite a small number of free-lance professionals who were to experiment with new publishing techniques. The other organization, by contrast, retained its current overall organization structure but set up several cross-functional project teams to develop publishing programs to deal with changing environmental demands. Conventional measures of organization structure might easily misrepresent what was occurring in either or both of these organizations and might show little relationship between uncertainty and structure. In fact, however, both organizations were responding, albeit differently, to the same set of environmental demands and with the same intended outcomes.

Two points are worth noting about this example. The first is that future research needs to investigate the *demands* which the choice of a domain makes on a basic operating strategy, the demands which strategy makes on technology, which technology makes on structure, etc. Once the demands which each decision point makes on the next are understood, then we can investigate the various responses which are made to each of these demands. Following the decision points map offered here, it is not necessary to demonstrate, for example, a specific set of structural features flowing from a given set of technological demands. Rather, it is important only to show that adjustments are or are not being made and to determine whether these appear to fall within some feasible set of responses. Secondly, we need more longitudinal studies of organizational adaptation. The management of the second publishing firm in the above example was, at the time of the study, tentatively considering some structural reorganizations, and its experimentation with cross-functional project teams may have been only the first step in a larger move resembling the changes made in the first publishing company. Cross-sectional studies utilizing static models cannot possibly capture the richness of the responses which organizations make to ensure their survival and foster growth.

A Deficiency in Dynamics

Despite the fact that the bulk of the theory and research discussed here deals with a dynamic process—the alignment of organizational strategy, structure, and process with environmental demands—surprisingly little specific attention has been given to the impact of current adjustment decisions on those which will (or should) follow as the environment changes and as the organization commits itself to a particular way of functioning. There is a body of literature on organizational growth, but to this point there has been little effort to integrate growth theories and research with the more recent flow of concepts and models attempting to link environmental demands with specific types of organizational technology and structure.[29] Dynamic models are, of course, far more difficult to build and test than static models, but it is our belief that such attempts must be made.

Original Strategy and Structural Decisions

Stinchcombe has shown that organizations are "imprinted" by the conditions existing in the industry to which they belong at the time the industry is "born."[30] He suggests that environmental conditions at any point in time not only specify the needs for particular goods and services but also determine many of the characteristics of the organizations created to provide them. Stinchcombe believes, for example, that the "railroad age" could occur only after society had developed the institutions, expertise, and means of legitimizing the organizational structures and processes necessary to develop and implement already existing technology.

More importantly, Stinchcombe argues that organizational structures, processes, and norms of behavior born (imprinted) in a given era tend to persist even though environmental conditions, including perhaps both the demands for different types of goods and services and the capacities for different forms of organizations to meet these, may have changed dramatically. He notes that this "imprinting" process appears to affect not only "first-born" firms but also those created as the industry expands— newer organizations imitate those already in existence. He further asserts that the "liability of newness" tends to restrict the adoption of new structures and processes unless the changes in environmental conditions are especially stark and dramatic. Thus, well into the twentieth century most railroad companies had structures, staffing patterns, managerial views of the market, etc., which may have been far more appropriate to the environmental conditions in the period of their birth.

"Nonrational" Adjustment Process

How then do organizations adapt to changing environmental conditions? Alchian has suggested that the process can be envisioned as essentially one of natural selection.[31] That is, given that imitation is never perfect, some organizations, by chance alone, will have characteristics more amenable to newly arising conditions than will their counterparts. Successful chance adaptations will be imitated as less fortunate organizations feel the pressure of their improper alignment with the environment, and a new cycle will begin. Alchian does not argue against the possibility of rationality in the adjustment process; he simply points out that it is not necessary to assume rationality in order to explain organizational growth and survival. In other words, one could build a model which, in effect, holds organizations constant and shifts the environment so that some organizations in a given group are more "favored" than others.

Taken together, the arguments of Stinchcombe and Alchian may appear to discourage efforts to describe relationships between organizations and their environments. That is, if, as Stinchcombe argues, organizational structures and processes are natural products of cultural norms and capabilities, then initial choices of domain, strategy, technology, etc. among organizations in older industries are greatly constrained. Moreover, if one adopts Alchian's view, chance variation in initial organizational form and process may well be the key to future success or failure. Thus, neither the original set of decisions nor subsequent adjustments would appear to turn on the correctness of managerial choice—in fact, what might first appear to be a poor adjustment could later prove to be a triumph of unintended foresight!

However well these notions fit reality, managers are not likely to be satisfied with theories which ignore or diminish the requirements of organizational rationality in the process of diagnosing environmental demands and choosing appropriate structures and processes to meet them. The image of various species of organizations originating simply by the grace of a benevolent environment and then growing by extending their existing forms and processes (to the limits of technological capacity), with certain of the species benefiting at random from environmental changes, may be accurate—but it is also discomforting.

Growth and Adjustment through Excess Managerial Capacity

A more palatable line of reasoning, but one difficult both to specify completely and to test, is offered by Penrose.[32] She argues that ignoring managerial decision making as an important factor in organizational growth and survival is as much at odds with observable behavior as is the economic assumption of perfect profit-maximizing decisions in response to environmental change. She urges the incorporation of managerial capability as a determinant of growth and survival—in fact, she offers a theory of organizational growth with excess managerial capacity as a prime ingredient. That is, Penrose believes that the organization whose managerial talent is fully employed in the operation of the existing technology and process is unlikely to perceive new environmental threats or opportunities, or, if they are perceived, to be able to respond beyond the simple extension of existing practices. She further contends that the organization with excess managerial capacity is not only able to take advantage of uncertainty but will be under strong internal pressure from this underemployed cadre of managerial talent to seek out and confront environmental uncertainty.

Penrose's model appears to fit nicely with our earlier characterizations of the types of environmental enactment and response among publishing companies. Those organizations and their top managerial groups characterized as Domain Defenders tend, by and large, to fully employ their existing managerial resources in the administration and improvement of their current operations. Managers in such organizations are typically greatly knowledgeable about the processes in their particular firm, but the demands of their jobs—highly standardized procedures and centralized decision making—offer little opportunity or incentive for search or innovation other than that linked closely to cost-cutting and other attempts to make existing practices more efficient. At the other extreme, the Enthusiastic Prospectors deliberately attempt to both develop and import managerial talent specifically for the purpose of searching out and responding to new environmental opportunities. It would appear to follow that while both types of organizations may succeed, there are more limits placed on the growth possibilities of the Domain Defenders than on the Enthusiastic Prospectors, and the latter have more insurance against the threat of disaster (or at least the requirement for some major adjustments) as the result of environmental changes than do their perhaps presently more efficient counterparts. This last point requires elaboration.

Adjustment Costs and Benefits

We have suggested, based on our research, that within the same "objective" environment both Domain Defenders and Enthusiastic Prospectors can apparently survive and even flourish, at least in the short run. Domain Defenders survive by working more intensively in a narrow segment of the environment, perhaps offsetting the loss of some potential gains in new areas by servicing their known area with increasing cost efficiency. Enthusiastic Prospectors, on the other hand, are less likely to invest their key talent in improving existing products or procedures and more likely to invest them in exploring new opportunities. They may thus operate on a higher cost curve but offset this by frequent successes in new areas. Note that, at a given point in time, both Domain Defenders and Enthusiastic Prospectors feel that the strategies, structures, and processes of their organizations fit the demands of their environment as it has been perceived and enacted by their managements.

What happens, however, if the environment becomes more or less turbulent? If the environment moves toward greater stability, the Domain Defenders would appear to be favored. Given their stable goals, they can build on their existing capabilities to improve efficiency and reap additional profit, while Enthusiastic Prospectors pay an even higher price for their excess coping capability. On the other hand, if environmental conditions become significantly more uncertain, the Enthusiastic Prospectors may be favored. They have a ready capacity for moving into new areas and experience in reshaping their structure and processes to meet new demands. Domain Defenders can survive under increasingly turbulent conditions only by (1) continuing to narrow the scope of their operations and concentrating on only the healthiest areas; or (2) attempting to move into new product or service areas (which they are likely to do hesitantly and clumsily). The first adjustment tack may ultimately prove impossible or unprofitable as the domain-narrowing process reaches its limits. Similarly, the second adjustment mechanism may prove extremely costly and time consuming, as it requires substantial restaffing and restructuring throughout the system. If the necessary changes are anticipated far enough in advance, a successful transition is possible. As suggested, however, Domain Defenders, in our research at least, typically do not maintain the sensing mechanisms necessary to identify and evaluate trends outside of their narrow domains and thus would be less likely to forecast environmental changes as effectively as would the Enthusiastic Prospectors. Consequently, it appears that if changes are particularly rapid or dramatic, Domain Defenders run the risk of major, perhaps disastrous losses. Our arguments here should not be construed as a blanket endorsement of growth and/or unconstrained diversification. Clearly not all "prospectors" strike gold and overextension of resources is a frequent cause of failure.

In sum, it appears that the price of excess adjustment capability is inefficiency, while the price of insufficient coping capacity is ineffectiveness. That is, an organization which adopts a flexible, highly adaptable structure and process in a stable environment may not minimize its costs (inefficiency), while an organization which maintains a bureaucratized structure and process in a highly turbulent environment runs the risk of major losses and even failure (ineffectiveness). Moreover, it would appear that it would be easier, particularly in the short run, to bureaucratize an organic structure than to develop coping capacity in a highly mechanized structure.

Extending this last point, Bennis has predicted the ultimate demise of all bureaucratic structures and processes in the face of ever-increasing environmental turbulence.[33] A more flexible argument seems to us more realistic—there are and will likely continue to be stable environments (or at least areas of stability) around many organizations which will prove quite amenable to specialized technologies, coordination by planning and standardized procedures, and control by policy and rule, but, at the same time, it seems likely that most organizations will also ultimately face the need for sizeable changes. Several available models (e.g., Perrow[34]) view organization structure and process as determined by, or contingent on, environmental and/or technological characteristics. A true contingency model, however, would not only describe the range of organizational structures and processes appropriate under various environmental conditions but also specify the costs, benefits, and means of maintaining an appropriate level of adjustment capability, given the choice of organizational structure and process.

Conclusions

We have attempted in this article to point out the areas where existing concepts and research concerning organization-environment relations appear to be deficient. Although we have no doubts that organizations must and do adjust their strategies, technologies, structures, and processes to meet changing environmental demands, we are convinced that current theories fail to clearly indicate how environmental conditions place constraints on adjustment alternatives and how each adjustment decision constrains those that follow. We are equally convinced that within these constraints there frequently exists the opportunity for managers to exercise considerable decision-making discretion (e.g., a variety of organizational structures and/or processes may meet the demands of a particular strategy or technology, and the choice among these is an exercise in managerial judgment). Thus, efforts to find direct linkages between, say, a given technology and a particular structural form are likely to be frustrated, with the possible unwarranted conclusion that no relationship exists.

We have also heavily emphasized managerial perceptions as a key variable at each of the decision points in the adjustment process. Top management clearly influences the process of domain definition, the choice of a basic operating strategy, the development of a core technology, and so on, and we believe that research in this area will make its largest contribution when it uncovers and displays for managers the implications of their current decisions for the longer-run adjustment capabilities of their organizations.

To provide information on the total adjustment process, researchers will most likely be forced out of their current mode of cross-sectional survey studies and toward longitudinal analyses. Particularly important will be attempts to contrast the behavior of those organizations which appear to be at the leading and lagging edges of their particular industry or grouping and which describe not only the nature of their adjustment to environmental demands but the process by which these adjustments came about.

Notes

1. Max Weber, *The Theory of Social and Economic Organization*, trans. by A. M. Henderson and Talcott Parsons (New York: Free Press, 1947), p. 34.
2. Frederick W. Taylor, *The Principles of Scientific Management* (New York: Harper & Brothers, 1911).
3. For a criticism of the economic theory of the firm from a behavioral standpoint, see Richard Cyert and James G. March, *A Behavioral Theory of the Firm* (Englewood Cliffs, N.J.: Prentice-Hall, 1963).
4. Alvin W. Gouldner, *Patterns of Industrial Bureaucracy* (New York: Free Press, 1954).
5. Tom Burns and G. M. Stalker, *The Management of Innovation* (London: Tavistock, 1961).
6. William H. Starbuck, "Organizations and Their Environments," in Marvin D. Dunnette, ed., *Handbook of Industrial and Organizational Psychology* (Chicago: Rand McNally, in press).
7. Fred E. Emery and Eric L. Trist, "The Causal Texture of Organizational Environments," *Human Relations* XVIII (February 1965): 21–32. The four types of environments are placid-randomized, placid-clustered, disturbed-reactive, and the turbulent field. These are arranged in ascending order of change and uncertainty, and Emery and Trist argue that each type of environment requires a different form of organization structure.
8. William R. Dill, "Environment as an Influence on Managerial Autonomy," *Administrative Science Quarterly* II (March 1958): 404–43; Burns and Stalker, op. cit.; James D. Thompson, *Organizations in Action* (New York: McGraw-Hill, 1967); Paul R. Lawrence and Jay W. Lorsch, *Organization and Environment* (Boston: Harvard Graduate School of Business Administration, 1967); Robert B. Duncan, "Characteristics of Organizational Environments and Perceived Environmental Uncertainty," *Administrative Science Quarterly* XVII (September 1972): 313–27; Richard N. Osborn and James G. Hunt, "Environment and Organizational Effectiveness," *Administrative Science Quarterly* XIX (June 1974): 231–46.
9. Thompson, op. cit.; Charles Perrow, "A Framework for the Comparative Analysis of Organizations," *American Sociological Review* XXXII (April 1967): 195–208; *Organizational Analysis: A Sociological View* (Belmont, Calif.: Wadsworth, 1970): and *Complex Organizations: A Critical Essay* (Glenview, Ill.: Scott, Foresman, 1972); Duncan, op. cit.
10. Other dimensions of the environment which have been investigated are: (1) concentrated-dispersed, (2) environmental capacity (rich-lean), (3) domain consensus-dissensus, and (4) mutability-immutability. See Howard Aldrich, "An Organization-Environment Perspective on Cooperation and Conflict Between Organizations in the Manpower Training System," New York State School of Industrial and Labor Relations Reprint Series, 1972.
11. Karl E. Weick, *The Social Psychology of Organizing* (Reading, Mass.: Addison-Wesley, 1969).
12. Drucker has offered perhaps the best discussions of how organizations define a domain of activity, but he does not go deeply into the effects of domain definition on organizational structure and process. See Peter F. Drucker, *The Practice of Management* (New York: Harper & Brothers, 1954) and

Management: Tasks, Responsibilities and Practices (New York: Harper & Row, 1974). For an excellent study of the effects of organizational strategy on structure, see Alfred D. Chandler, Jr., *Strategy and Structure* (Garden City, N.Y.: Doubleday, 1962).

13. See Thompson, op. cit., pp. 28–29. For two examples of research using the concept of domain consensus, see Sol Levine and Paul E. White, "Exchange as a Conceptual Framework for the Study of Interorganizational Relationships," *Administrative Science Quarterly* V (March 1961): 583–601; and Burton R. Clark, *The Open Door College* (New York: McGraw-Hill, 1960).

14. Ronald Randall, "Influence of Environmental Support and Policy Space on Organizational Behavior," *Administrative Science Quarterly* XVIII (June 1973): 236–47.

15. Jeffrey Pfeffer, "Interorganizational Influence and Managerial Attitudes," *Academy of Management Journal* XV (September 1972): 317–30.

16. Long-term contracts as a means of stabilizing the environment have been discussed by Harold Guetzkow, "Relations Among Organizations," in Raymond V. Bowers, ed., *Studies on Behavior in Organizations* (Athens, Ga.: University of Georgia Press, 1966), pp. 13–44. For joint ventures, see Michael Aiken and Jerald Hage, "Organizational Interdependence and Intraorganizational Structure," *American Sociological Review* XXXIII (December 1968): 912–30. For cooptation, see Philip Selznick, *TVA and the Grass Roots: A Study in the Sociology of Formal Organization* (Berkeley and Los Angeles: University of California Press, 1949). Merger activity has been investigated by, among others, Jeffrey Pfeffer, "Merger as a Response to Organizational Interdependence," *Administrative Science Quarterly* XVII (September 1972): 382–94.

17. On coordinating agencies, see Eugene Litwak and Lydia F. Hylton, "Interorganizational Analysis: A Hypothesis on Co-ordinating Agencies," *Administrative Science Quarterly* VI (March 1962): 395–420. Among the many sources on attempts to influence government agencies, see George J. Stigler, "The Theory of Economic Regulation," *Bell Journal of Economics and Management Science* II (Spring 1971): 3–21; Raymond A. Bauer, Ithiel de Sola Pool, and Lewis A. Dexter, *American Business and Public Policy* (New York: Atherton, 1964); Donald R. Hall, *Cooperative Lobbying: The Power of Pressure* (Tucson: University of Arizona Press, 1969).

18. Almarin Phillips, "A Theory of Interfirm Organization," *Quarterly Journal of Economics* LXXIV (November 1960): 602–13.

19. Perrow, *Organizational Analysis,* chap. 4.

20. This definition comes from Louis E. Davis, "Job Satisfaction Research: The Post-Industrial View," *Industrial Relations* X (May 1971): 180.

21. Perrow, *Organizational Analysis,* pp. 28–37.

22. Joan Woodward, *Industrial Organization: Theory and Practice* (Oxford: Oxford University Press, 1965).

23. Perrow, "A Framework"; Thompson, op. cit.; David J. Hickson, D. S. Pugh, and Diana C. Pheysey, "Operations Technology and Structure: An Empirical Reappraisal," *Administrative Science Quarterly* XIV (September 1969): 378–97.

24. Lawrence B. Mohr, "Organizational Technology and Organizational Structure," *Administrative Science Quarterly* XVI (December 1971): 444–59; John Child and Roger Mansfield, "Technology, Size, and Organization Structure," *Sociology* VI (September 1972): 369–93.

25. Joan Woodward, ed., *Industrial Organization: Behaviour and Control* (Oxford, England: Oxford University Press, 1970).

26. John Child, "Organizational Structure, Environment and Performance—The Role of Strategic Choice," *Sociology* VI (January 1972): 1–22.

27. Charles C. Snow and Raymond E. Miles, "Managerial Perceptions and Organizational Adjustment Processes," unpublished working paper.

28. In a criticism of Lawrence and Lorsch's Environmental Uncertainty Questionnaire, Tosi, et al. show that different objective measures of environmental uncertainty produce different results when they are correlated with organizational variables. Henry Tosi, Ramon Aldag, and Ronald Storey, "On the Measurement of the Environment: An Assessment of the Lawrence and Lorsch Environmental Uncertainty Questionnaire," *Administrative Science Quarterly* XVIII (March 1973): 27–36. (It should also be noted that different perceptual measures of environmental uncertainty might also produce results similar to those of Tosi et al. The concept of environmental uncertainty is badly in need of both theoretical and operational refinement.)

29. For a review of the literature on organizational growth (up to 1965), see William H. Starbuck, "Organizational Growth and Development," in James G. March, ed., *Handbook of Organizations* (Chicago: Rand McNally, 1965), pp. 451–533.

30. Arthur Stinchcombe, "Social Structure and Organizations," in March, op. cit., pp. 142–93.

31. Armen A. Alchian, "Uncertainty, Evolution, and Economic Theory," *Journal of Political Economy* LVIII (June 1960): 211–21.

32. Edith T. Penrose, *The Theory of the Growth of the Firm* (New York: Wiley, 1959). See, particularly, pp. 46–54 and 200–201.

33. Warren G. Bennis, *Changing Organizations* (New York: McGraw-Hill, 1966).

34. Perrow, *Organizational Analysis*.

16

Why Bureaucracy Keeps Growing

Tom Alexander

The first bureaucracy came into being in the early morning of civilization, and soon afterward, no doubt, somebody uttered the first complaint about bureaucrats. Complaining has been going on ever since, to little or no avail. In our day, the complaints have taken on a new intensity, yet bureaucracies are growing faster than ever. This paradox has attracted the attention of scholars, who have undertaken a more or less scientific examination of a phenomenon that is usually just railed against.

Unfortunately, they bring bad news. They tell us that the fungoid bureaucratic growth of our day is not a transitory reflection of contemporary political fashions, but a self-perpetuating affliction, a consequence of deep flaws in the design of most present-day democratic systems. On the other hand, these scholars are also concocting proposals for new checks and balances designed to bring bureaucratic behavior more into line with the public interest.

Practitioners in this field call it by an unhandy name, "public choice." This undescriptive label goes back to the beginnings of the discipline, which evolved from efforts in the 1960's to use economic theories and models to explain why voters vote as they do. By now public choice has extended concepts of economics to all kinds of non-market actors—not only political bodies but also religious organizations, foundations, universities, and criminals.

The pioneers were about half a dozen American economists, several of whom had either served in government themselves or analyzed government operations in think tanks such as the RAND Corporation or the Institute for Defense Analyses. Today the Public Choice Society has some 700 members, about half economists and half political scientists, with a few sociologists and philosophers.

SOURCE: Tom Alexander, "Why Bureaucracy Keeps Growing," *Fortune* (May 7, 1979), pp. 164–76. Reprinted with permission.

Public choice starts by assuming that politicians, bureaucrats, academics, criminals, and all others who make their living outside of ordinary industry and commerce behave pretty much like the consumers, tradesmen, and corporate managers who are the hidden actors beneath the abstractions of conventional economic analysis. That is, they generally act on the basis of self-interest. This leads them to deploy their resources so as to maximize their "utility," i.e., their personal welfare as they perceive it.

While ordinary economics uses money as the measure of utility, non-market economics considers all kinds of other rewards as well, including votes, power, prestige, perquisites of office, security of tenure, convenience, and even the pleasant feeling that comes with doing good according to one's own lights. Given this broad concept of utility, public choice holds that in a conflict between self-interest and public interest, bureaucrats will favor self-interest most of the time.

An Absence of Disciplines

This may appear to be a crashingly obvious notion. People in the private sector are assumed to act in accord with their self-interest. Why should anyone expect government bureaucrats to be different? But the point is precisely that we have not confronted this fact of life. The central problem with government bureaucracies in a modern democracy is not that they exist—we could hardly do without them—but that we have failed to subject them to disciplines like those that operate in the private sector.

In private business, the workings of self-interest are tempered and channeled by market disciplines, such as competition and consumer choice, and by public restraints, such as antitrust laws. Government bureaucracies are not subject to these constraints. Accordingly, the dynamics of self-interest tends to produce bureaucratic overgrowth, far in excess of what the public wants or what reasonable measures of social utility can justify.

An early analyst of this tendency was the economist Anthony Downs, who while working at RAND in the early 1960's wrote a pungent and entertaining book, *Inside Bureaucracy*. He pointed out that, for one thing, growth improves chances for promotion. Another incentive to growth is the general practice of awarding salaries and other perquisites primarily on the basis of the number of people an individual has under his supervision—a surefire formula for overmanning.

Downs also pointed out that in a bureau, growth triggers more growth. As an organization gets bigger, it necessarily adopts a hierarchical structure to control the flow of information and authority up and down the chain of command. The larger the organization, the more levels of command. But the more levels, the more information and authority get lost in passing through channels, the more they get distorted by the self-interest of people in the hierarchy, and the more time is spent in supervising or being supervised, coordinating or being coordinated. Therefore, the less time, on average, each person spends producing whatever useful output the organization is supposed to produce. "In any large multilevel bureau," Downs says, "a very significant portion of all the activity being carried out is completely unrelated to its formal goal or even the goal of the topmost officials."

Feeding Paper to the Monitor

Government bureaus have rather little incentive to improve efficiency. What they have plenty of is pressure for control and accountability: each echelon in the hierarchy is generally held responsible, ultimately by Congress and the public, for the deeds and scandals of all lower echelons. This generates a requirement for lots of internal and external monitoring and lots of internal procedures, regulations, reports, and forms. These monitoring activities, Downs observed, generally grow into a bureaucracy of their own. Furthermore, he pointed out, "any increase in the number of persons monitoring a given bureau will normally evoke an even larger increase in the number of employees assigned to deal with the monitors. This occurs because records can be read much faster than they can be compiled. To keep an additional monitor busy, the operating bureaucrat assigns two or more people to produce the report he demands."

Not being subject to market competition, government agencies often display behavior akin to that of private monopolies. Under competitive conditions, companies can generally maximize profits by pricing goods at fairly close to cost. The amount they produce will then probably tend to approximate the amount society wants, i.e., is willing to pay for. Classical private monopolies, in contrast, maximize profits by producing less than the optimum and charging higher prices. But public-sector monopolies are different, argues William Niskanen, another former RAND analyst. Niskanen, who is now chief economist at Ford Motor Co., observed bureaucracy close-up while serving in Robert McNamara's Pentagon and in the Office of Management and Budget. He points out that government monopolies are primarily interested in bigger budgets, not bigger profits. One consequence is that they tend to produce *more* than society wants, while still charging high prices.

The Washington Monument Game

A bureaucrat seldom gains any personal reward from saving the taxpayers' money. In fact, the incentives tend to run in the opposite direction: the less money an agency spends this year, the less it is likely to get next year. A periodic episode in bureaus is the spending spree that occurs near the end of their budget cycle if they discover that by ill chance they have failed to spend their full appropriation.

Most governments, to be sure, make efforts to impose limits on agency budgets. In the U.S., the controls include oversight by the Office of Management and Budget and by various committees in Congress. But this monitoring is never adequate, argues William Niskanen. In the first place, being a monopoly, the agency has plenty of opportunity to conceal information about its essential costs of doing business. While at OMB, Niskanen found that he really couldn't do a very effective job of monitoring the bureaus supposedly under his supervision, because they always knew a lot more about their departments than he did.

Though overseeing Congressmen usually have only skimpy knowledge of the internal needs of an agency, the agency has a finely tuned sense of the external pressures on the politicians. So it has the advantage of what public-choice experts call an "all or none" bargaining position: it can argue without effective contradiction that substantial budget cuts would disastrously cripple its operation. And if the economies are imposed anyway, the agency can act to maximize their impact on the government and the public. When the budget of the U.S. Customs Service was reduced some years back, for instance, the service responded by firing every customs inspector in the U.S., but not one other member of the agency.

While this ploy was somewhat more blatant than average, the tactic is a favorite of the bureaucracy's budget officers. They refer to it as "the Washington Monument game," in memory of the National Park Service official who in 1971 testified that the only feasible economy measure he could think of was to close the Washington Monument to tourists.

An even more devilish tactic is to hold down the initial budget request by asking for *too little* money for certain functions mandated by law, such as veterans' benefits or Medicare. Then, as the year progresses and a shortfall shows up, Congress is forced to come forward with a supplemental appropriation.

The Iron Triangle

Until fairly recently, public-choice theorists tended to focus on such bureaucratic maneuvering as the main explanation for government expansionism. But a newer line of theory and research puts most of the blame on Congress. With government's ever-widening role as a source of rewards and punishments, more and more of politics consists of responding to special-interest constituencies. A Congressman from a district where such a constituency is prominent has a powerful incentive to get on a committee that deals with those interests, so he will bargain and logroll for that appointment. Over time, therefore, committees tend to become dominated by Congressmen who favor generous appropriations for the agencies they oversee. Political scientists refer to the mutual bond that develops between interest groups, bureaucracies, and Congressmen as the "iron triangle."

Recently, some young theorists at the California Institute of Technology have been studying a disturbing new version of the triangle. These researchers, Morris Fiorina, John Ferejohn, and Roger Noll, began by exploring a well-known puzzle of political science: the decline of competition in national politics as reflected in the ability of congressional incumbents to remain in office for many terms. The turnover rate in the House of Representatives from one Congress to the next has dropped from an average of around 50 percent in the nineteenth century to around 15 percent at present. Since the 1960's, the turnover resulting from electoral defeat alone (leaving aside deaths and retirements) has declined from more than 10 percent to less than 5.

Many explanations have been offered for this most recent decline, including gerrymandering in the reapportionment of districts and the access that incumbents have to publicity and postal privileges. Fiorina, however, focused his attention on the decline in the number of "marginal" districts—those that have a history of very close congressional elections and frequent unseatings of incumbents. After extended visits to several newly safe districts, he outlined a mechanism to explain the mystery of the vanishing marginals.

The driving energy for this mechanism is the immense expansion in the level and variety of federal programs. By now, it is the rare company or citizen who doesn't have some kind of periodic encounter with a federal agency resulting in either a benefit or a nuisance. And the pork barrel, which once contained mainly river and harbor projects, is now full of grants for law enforcement, sewage treatment, education, hospitals, research facilities, housing, old-age programs, etc.

Since Congress ultimately controls access to budgets and new programs, the bureaucrats tend to be attentive to a Congressman's requests to bend a rule here, expedite a grant there. This kind of congressional favor-doing is well appreciated by constituents, while statesmanship in larger matters tends to be either invisible or controversial. One measure of the increase in such back-home services has been a fourfold growth since 1960 in the number of congressional staff members who take care of constituent "casework" in the districts.

Bureaucrats Vote Too

An incumbent's bank of gratitude for favors done can very well provide the margin of re-election. Many a Congressman who rails in public about bureaucracies and federal spending is perfectly aware that they are the basis for his newfound lock on public office. The bureaucrats cooperate in the charade as long as the votes keep coming in for the things they want.

Fiorina and his colleagues are not optimistic about the prospects of breaking up this "Washington system," as they term it. Says Fiorina: "We, the people, weed out those Congressmen whose primary interest is not re-election."

As government grows, still another self-propagating chain reaction comes into play. Economist Gordon Tullock, a former State Department bureaucrat who is now a professor at the Center for Public Choice at Virginia Polytechnic Institute, points out that, as voters, government employees have a lot more incentive than the average citizen to vote for new programs. And they have a lot of votes: these days about one American family in five has a member employed in the public sector. Surveys suggest that bureaucrats vote far more faithfully than members of any other occupational group, and that they are likely to vote for more government. The total effect, it seems, is that public-sector employees and their families account for nearly one vote in three, and provide a strong stimulus to further government growth.

From a public-choice perspective, some kinds of efforts at government reform are likely to be counterproductive. A notable example is the recurrent urge to make things tidier by placing all similar-sounding functions in one department, as President Carter wants to do with his proposed departments of Education and Natural Resources. The usual stated motives for such reforms are that government activity is "uncoordinated," "conflicting," or "redundant," and therefore wasteful. But William Niskanen maintains that to have some conflict and redundancy is probably beneficial, one reason being that government often is not clear about what is the best thing to do.

"In many areas," he says, "competition among bureaus has been the primary reason why the government did something right, rather than everything wrong." He argues that competition between the Navy and Air Force to develop aircraft and armaments has produced the best tactical-aircraft systems in the world. Niskanen participated in McNamara's efforts in the early 1960's to bring the feuding military services under centralized control, but he now suspects that the old bugaboo, "interservice rivalry," was a good thing. Such competition encouraged the military services to deliver public critiques of others' claims on national resources. This disseminated information about the defense bureaucracy's cost of doing business and thereby reduced its bargaining advantage. Confining interservice disputes within the walls of the Pentagon amounted in effect to transforming a competitive industry into a monopoly.

Contesting the belief that centralization promotes efficiency, Niskanen calculates that creating the departments of Defense and Health, Education and Welfare increased the costs of performing these agencies' functions by 34 and 25 percent. The creation of huge new departments, he adds, has certainly not brought any large gains in effectiveness. "Since the establishment of the Department of Defense, the U.S. has fought one war to a draw against a second-rate military power, lost another war to a third-rate military power, and lost its strategic nuclear superiority over the Soviet Union. Since the establishment of HEW, health costs have skyrocketed, educational test scores have progressively declined, and there have been perennial demands for welfare reform. Following the establishment of HUD, our major cities have experienced fiscal collapse and continued decay. Following the establishment of the Department of Transportation, a large part of the railroad system has gone through bankruptcy to nationalization. Many other conditions have contributed to these problems, of course, but there is no evidence that the establishment of these departments has reduced them."

The Rule of Two

Some public-choice analysts argue that it would be in the public interest to contract a good many government functions out to the private sector. Considerable evidence supports this view. For instance, studies in various areas show that it costs much less to have garbage collected by private companies than by municipal sanitation departments. In one study, the private haulers collected twice as much garbage per man-day as the sanitation departments did. In view of such findings. Tullock likes to cite what he calls the Bureaucratic Rule of Two: "The removal of an activity from the private to the public sector will double its unit cost of production."

But there are practical limits, of course, on the transfer of government functions to private contractors. The broader thrust on the prescriptive side of public choice is to try to construct checks and incentives to guard against or offset the antisocial tendencies of bureaucratic dynamics.

A lot of attention, for example, is going to the question of how to restrain the power of organized interest groups. Tullock proposes that two-thirds majorities be required in most votes in Congress, particularly for money bills. Recognizing that it is unrealistic to expect Congressmen to impose upon themselves such an increase in their cost of doing business, Tullock suggests that, if he wanted to, the President could achieve the same result by automatically vetoing all bills. A less radical suggestion for weakening the iron triangle is to select the membership of congressional committees by drawing lots.

Spurred by the increasing restiveness of voters, Congress itself has been searching for acceptable ways of disciplining both itself and the agencies it has been responsible for creating. Among the initiatives now being examined are "sunset" laws, which would make agencies justify their own existence every few years, and "sunrise" laws, which would require that precise goals be spelled out in advance for every new program, along with provisions for periodic review to see whether the goals had been met.

"I'm basically pessimistic," says Morris Fiorina. "Things like sunset and sunrise laws are useful, but ultimately they're only Band-Aids. They don't get to the heart of our problems, which have to do with the fact that a Congressman is elected from a single district by means of a simple plurality. He is not accountable to a national constituency and doesn't run on the basis of his party's record, but rather on how well he serves his district. Any effective reforms would have to go to the heart of our fundamental institutions."

The Too-High-Fever Aspect

Without strong countervailing forces of some kind, bureaucratic bloat will tend to get worse. The self-augmenting mechanisms that public-choice thinkers discern in government are disturbingly reminiscent of the phenomenon that scientists and engineers call "positive feedback." Most systems found in nature—physical and biological—exhibit negative feedback, in which a given action induces a stabilizing counteraction. In positive feedback, by contrast, a given action produces conditions that favor further action in the same direction.

An example is an extremely high fever that impairs the body's temperature-control mechanisms, with the result that the fever gets still worse, and so on, sometimes to the point of death. Another example is cancer. As these instances suggest, systems with positive feedback tend, in time, to destroy the host system they grow upon.

17

Organization Design:
An Information Processing View

Jay R. Galbraith

The Information Processing Model

A basic proposition is that the greater the uncertainty of the task, the greater the amount of information that has to be processed between decision makers during the execution of the task. If the task is well understood prior to performing it, much of the activity can be preplanned. If it is not understood, then during the actual task execution more knowledge is acquired which leads to changes in resource allocations, schedules, and priorities. All these changes require information processing *during* task performance. Therefore *the greater the task uncertainty, the greater the amount of information that must be processed among decision makers during task execution in order to achieve a given level of performance.* The basic effect of uncertainty is to limit the ability of the organization to preplan or to make decisions about activities in advance of their execution. Therefore it is hypothesized that the observed variations in organizational forms are variations in the strategies of organizations to (1) increase their ability to preplan, (2) increase their flexibility to adapt to their inability to preplan, or (3) to decrease the level of performance required for continued viability. Which strategy is chosen depends on the relative costs of the strategies. The function of the framework is to identify these strategies and their costs.

The Mechanistic Model

This framework is best developed by keeping in mind a hypothetical organization. Assume it is large and employs a number of specialist groups and resources in providing the output. After the task has been

SOURCE: Reprinted with permission from "Organizational Design: An Information Processing View," by Jay R. Galbraith, *Interfaces*, vol. 4, no. 3 (May 1974), pp. 28–36, published by the Institute of Management Sciences.

divided into specialist subtasks, the problem is to integrate the subtasks around the completion of the global task. This is the problem of organization design. The behaviors that occur in one subtask cannot be judged as good or bad *per se*. The behaviors are more effective or ineffective depending upon the behaviors of the other subtask performers. There is a design problem because the executors of the behaviors cannot communicate with all the roles with whom they are interdependent. Therefore the design problem is to create mechanisms that permit coordinated action across large numbers of interdependent roles. Each of these mechanisms, however, has a limited range over which it is effective at handling the information requirements necessary to coordinate the interdependent roles. As the amount of uncertainty increases, and therefore information processing increases, the organization must adopt integrating mechanisms which increase its information processing capabilities.

1. Coordination by Rules or Programs

For routine predictable tasks March and Simon have identified the use of rules or programs to coordinate behavior between interdependent subtasks [March and Simon, 1958, Chap. 6]. To the extent that job related situations can be predicted in advance, and behaviors specified for these situations, programs allow an interdependent set of activities to be performed without the need for interunit communication. Each role occupant simply executes the behavior which is appropriate for the task related situation with which he is faced.

2. Hierarchy

As the organization faces greater uncertainty its participants face situations for which they have no rules. At this point the hierarchy is employed on an exception basis. The recurring job situations are programmed with rules while infrequent situations are referred to that level in the hierarchy where a global perspective exists for all affected subunits. However, the hierarchy also has a limited range. As uncertainty increases the number of exceptions increases until the hierarchy becomes overloaded.

3. Coordination by Targets or Goals

As the uncertainty of the organization's task increases, coordination increasingly takes place by specifying outputs, goals or targets [March and Simon, 1958, p. 145]. Instead of specifying specific behaviors to be enacted, the organization undertakes processes to set goals to be achieved and the employees select the behaviors which lead to goal accomplishment. Planning reduces the amount of information processing in the hierarchy by increasing the amount of discretion exercised at lower levels. Like the use of rules, planning achieves integrated action and also eliminates the need for continuous communication among interdependent subunits as long as task performance stays within the planned task specifications, budget limits and within targeted completion dates. If it does not, the hierarchy is again employed on an exception basis.

The ability of an organization to coordinate interdependent tasks depends on its ability to compute meaningful subgoals to guide subunit action. When uncertainty increases because of introducing new products, entering new markets, or employing new technologies these subgoals are incorrect. The result is more exceptions, more information processing, and an overloaded hierarchy.

Design Strategies

The ability of an organization to successfully utilize coordination by goal setting, hierarchy, and rules depends on the combination of the frequency of exceptions and the capacity of the hierarchy to handle them. As the task uncertainty increases the organization must again take organization design action. It can proceed in either of two general ways. First, it can act in two ways to reduce the amount of information that is processed. And second, the organization can act in two ways to increase its capacity to handle more information. The two methods for reducing the need for information and the two methods for increasing processing capacity are shown schematically in Figure 1. The effect of all these actions is to reduce the number of exceptional cases referred upward into the organization through hierarchical channels. The assumption is that the critical limiting factor of an organizational form is its ability to handle the non-routine, consequential events that cannot be anticipated and planned for in advance. The non-programmed events place the greatest communication load on the organization.

1. Creation of Slack Resources

As the number of exceptions begin to overload the hierarchy, one response is to increase the planning targets so that fewer exceptions occur. For example, completion dates can be extended until the number of exceptions that occur are within the existing information processing capacity of the organization. This has been the practice in solving job shop scheduling problems [Pounds, 1963]. Job shops quote delivery times that are long enough to keep the scheduling problem within the computational and information processing limits of the organization.

Figure 1   Organization Design Strategies

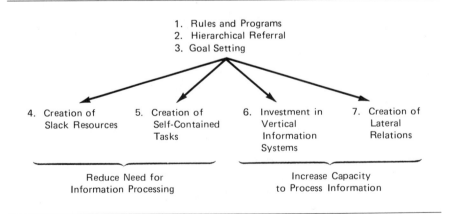

Since every job shop has the same problem standard lead times evolve in the industry. Similarly, budget targets could be raised, buffer inventories employed, etc. The greater the uncertainty, the greater the magnitude of the inventory, lead time or budget needed to reduce an overload.

All of these examples have a similar effect. They represent the use of slack resources to reduce the amount of interdependence between subunits [March and Simon, 1958, Cyert and March, 1963]. This keeps the required amount of information within the capacity of the organization to process it. Information processing is reduced because an exception is less likely to occur and reduced interdependence means that fewer factors need to be considered simultaneously when an exception does occur.

The strategy of using slack resources has its costs. Relaxing budget targets has the obvious cost of requiring more budget. Increasing the time to completion date has the effect of delaying the customer. Inventories require the investment of capital funds which could be used elsewhere. Reduction of design optimization reduces the performance of the article being designed. Whether slack resources are used to reduce information or not depends on the relative cost of the other alternatives.

The design choices are: (1) among which factors to change (lead time, overtime, machine utilization, etc.) to create the slack, and (2) by what amount should the factor be changed. Many operations research models are useful in choosing factors and amounts. The time-cost trade off problem in project networks is a good example.

2. Creation of Self-Contained Tasks

The second method of reducing the amount of information processed is to change the subtask groupings from resource (input) based to output based categories and give each group the resources it needs to supply the output. For example, the functional organization could be changed to product groups. Each group would have its own product engineers, process engineers, fabricating and assembly operations, and marketing activities. In other situations, groups can be created around product lines, geographical areas, projects, client groups, markets, etc., each of which would contain the input resources necessary for creation of the output.

The strategy of self-containment shifts the basis of the authority structure from one based on input, resource skill, or occupational categories to one based on output or geographical categories. The shift reduces the amount of information processing through several mechanisms. First, it reduces the amount of output diversity faced by a single collection of resources. For example, a professional organization with multiple skill specialties providing service to three different client groups must schedule the use of these specialties across three demands for their services and determine priorities when conflicts occur. But, if the organization changed to three groups, one for each client category, each with its own full complement of specialties, the schedule conflicts across client groups disappear and there is no need to process information to determine priorities.

The second source of information reduction occurs through a reduced division of labor. The functional or resource specialized structure pools the demand for skills across all output categories. In the example above each client generates approximately one-third of the demand for each skill. Since the division of labor is limited by the extent of the market, the division of labor must decrease as the demand decreases. In the professional organization, each client group may have generated a need for one-third of a computer programmer. The functional organization would have hired one programmer and shared him across the groups. In the self-contained structure there is insufficient demand in each group for a programmer so the professionals must do their own programming. Specialization is reduced but there is no problem of scheduling the programmer's time across the three possible uses for it.

The cost of the self-containment strategy is the loss of resource specialization. In the example, the organization forgoes the benefit of a specialist in computer programming. If there is physical equipment, there is a loss of economies of scale. The professional organization would require three machines in the self-contained form but only a large time-shared machine in the functional form. But those resources which have large economies of scale or for which specialization is necessary may remain centralized. Thus, it is the degree of self-containment that is the variable. The greater the degree of uncertainty, other things equal, the greater the degree of self-containment.

The design choices are the basis for the self-contained structure and the number of resources to be contained in the groups. No groups are completely self-contained or they would not be part of the same organization. But one product divisionalized firm may have eight of fifteen functions in the division while another may have twelve of fifteen in the divisions. Usually accounting, finance, and legal services are centralized and shared. Those functions which have economies of scale, require specialization or are necessary for control remain centralized and not part of the self-contained group.

The first two strategies reduced the amount of information by lower performance standards and creating small autonomous groups to provide the output. Information is reduced because an exception is less likely to occur and fewer factors need to be considered when an exception does occur. The next two strategies accept the performance standards and division of labor as given and adapt the organization so as to process the new information which is created during task performance.

3. Investment in Vertical Information Systems

The organization can invest in mechanisms which allow it to process information acquired during task performance without overloading the hierarchical communication channels. The investment occurs according to the following logic. After the organization has created its plan or set of targets for inventories, labor utilization, budgets, and schedules, unanticipated events occur which generate exceptions requiring adjustments to the original plan. At some point when the number of exceptions becomes substantial, it is preferable to generate a new plan rather than make incremental changes with each exception. The issue is then how frequently should plans be revised—yearly, quarterly, or monthly? The greater the frequency of replanning the greater the resources, such as clerks, computer time, input-output devices, etc., required to process information about relevant factors.

The cost of information processing resources can be minimized if the language is formalized. Formalization of a decision-making language simply means that more information is transmitted with the same number of symbols. It is assumed that information processing resources are consumed in proportion to the number of symbols transmitted. The accounting system is an example of a formalized language.

Providing more information, more often, may simply overload the decision maker. Investment may be required to increase the capacity of the decision maker by employing computers, various man-machine combinations, assistant-to, etc. The cost of this strategy is the cost of the information processing resources consumed in transmitting and processing data.

The design variables of this strategy are the decision frequency, the degree of formalization of language, and the type of decision mechanism which will make the choice. This strategy is usually operationalized by creating redundant information channels which transmit data from the point of origination upward in the hierarchy where the point of decision rests. If data is formalized and quantifiable, this strategy is effective. If the relevant data are qualitative and ambiguous, then it may prove easier to bring the decision down to where the information exists.

4. Creation of Lateral Relationships

The best strategy is to employ selectively joint decision processes which cut across lines of authority. This strategy moves the level of decision making down in the organization to where the information exists but does so without reorganizing around self-contained groups. There are several types of lateral decision processes. Some processes are usually referred to as the informal organization. However, these informal processes do not always arise spontaneously out of the needs of the task. This is particularly true in multinational organizations in which participants are separated by physical barriers, language differences, and cultural differences. Under these circumstances lateral processes need to be designed. The lateral processes evolve as follows with increases in uncertainty.

4.1. Direct Contact Between managers who share a problem. If a problem arises on the shop floor, the foreman can simply call the design engineer, and they can jointly agree upon a solution. From an information processing view, the joint decision prevents an upward referral and unloads the hierarchy.

4.2. Liaison Roles When the volume of contacts between any two departments grows, it becomes economical to set up a specialized role to handle this communication. Liaison men are typical examples of specialized roles designed to facilitate communication between two interdependent departments and to bypass the long lines of communication involved in upward referral. Liaison roles arise at lower and middle levels of management.

4.3. Task Forces Direct contact and liaison roles, like the integration mechanisms before them, have a limited range of usefulness. They work when two managers or functions are involved. When problems arise involving seven or eight departments, the decision making capacity of direct contacts is exceeded. Then these problems must be referred upward. For uncertain, interdependent tasks such situations arise frequently. Task forces are a form of horizontal contact which is designed for problems of multiple departments.

The task force is made up of representatives from each of the affected departments. Some are full-time members, others may be part-time. The task force is a temporary group. It exists only as long as the problem remains. When a solution is reached, each participant returns to his normal tasks.

To the extent that they are successful, task forces remove problems from higher levels of the hierarchy. The decisions are made at lower levels in the organization. In order to guarantee integration, a group problem solving approach is taken. Each affected subunit contributes a member and therefore provides the information necessary to judge the impact on all units.

4.4. Teams The next extension is to incorporate the group decision process into the permanent decision processes. That is, as certain decisions consistently arise, the task forces become permanent. These groups are labeled teams. There are many design issues concerned in team decision making such as at what level do they operate, who participates, etc. [Galbraith, 1973, Chaps. 6 and 7] One design decision is particularly critical. This is the choice of leadership. Sometimes a problem exists largely in one department so that the department manager is the leader. Sometimes the leadership passes from one manager to another. As a new product moves to the market place, the leader of the new product team is first the technical manager followed by the production and then the marketing manager. The result is that if the team cannot reach a consensus decision and the leader decides, the goals of the leader are consistent with the goals of the organization for the decision in question. But quite often obvious leaders cannot be found. Another mechanism must be introduced.

4.5. Integrating Roles The leadership issue is solved by creating a new role—an integrating role [Lawrence and Lorsch, 1967, Chap. 3]. These roles carry the labels of product managers, program managers, project managers, unit managers (hospitals), materials managers, etc. After the role is created, the design problem is to create enough power in the role to influence the decision process. These roles have power even when no one reports directly to them. They have some power because they report to the general manager. But if they are selected so as to be unbiased with respect to the groups they integrate and to have technical competence, they have expert power. They collect information and equalize power differences due to preferential access to knowledge and information. The power equalization increases trust and the quality of the joint decision process. But power equalization occurs only if the integrating role is staffed with someone who can exercise expert power in the form of persuasion and informal influences rather than exert the power of rank or authority.

4.6. Managerial Linking Roles   As tasks become more uncertain, it is more difficult to exercise expert power. The role must get more power of the formal authority type in order to be effective at coordinating the joint decisions which occur at lower levels of the organization. This position power changes the nature of the role which for lack of a better name is labeled a managerial linking role. It is not like the integrating role because it possesses formal position power but is different from line managerial roles in that participants do not report to the linking manager. The power is added by the following successive changes:

a. The integrator receives approval power of budgets formulated in the departments to be integrated.
b. The planning and budgeting process starts with the integrator making his initiation in budgeting legitimate.
c. Linking manager receives the budget for the area of responsibility and buys resources from the specialist groups.

These mechanisms permit the manager to exercise influence even though no one works directly for him. The role is concerned with integration but exercises power through the formal power of the position. If this power is insufficient to integrate the subtasks and creation of self-contained groups is not feasible, there is one last step.

4.7. Matrix Organization   The last step is to create the dual authority relationship and the matrix organization [Galbraith, 1971]. At some point in the organization some roles have two superiors. The design issue is to select the locus of these roles. The result is a balance of power between the managerial linking roles and the normal line organization roles. Figure 2 depicts the pure matrix design.

The work of Lawrence and Lorsch is highly consistent with the assertions concerning lateral relations [Lawrence and Lorsch, 1967, Lorsch and Lawrence, 1968]. They compared the types of lateral relations undertaken by the most successful firm in three different industries. Their data are summarized in Table 1. The plastics firm has the greatest rate of new product introduction (uncertainty) and the greatest utilization of lateral processes. The container firm was also very successful but utilized only standard practices because its information processing task is much less formidable. Thus, the greater the uncertainty the lower the level of decision making and the integration is maintained by lateral relations.

Table 1 points out the cost of using lateral relations. The plastics firm has 22 percent of its managers in integration roles. Thus, the greater the use of lateral relations the greater the managerial intensity. This

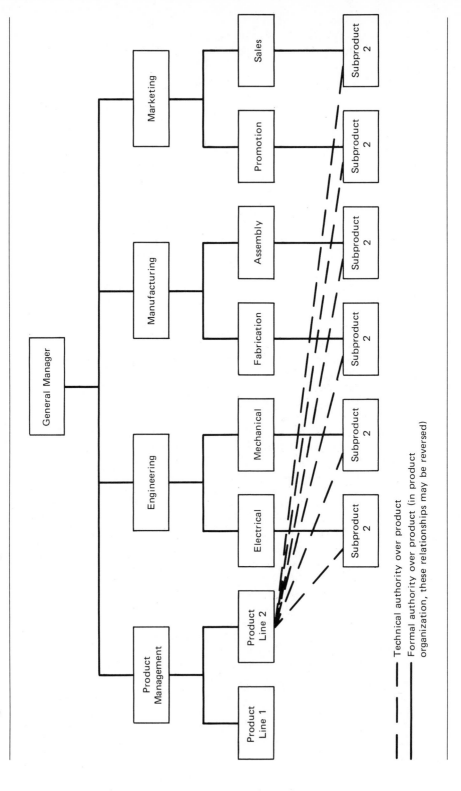

Figure 2   A Pure Matrix Organization

Technical authority over product

Formal authority over product (in product organization, these relationships may be reversed)

Table 1

	Plastics	Food	Container
Percent new products in last ten years	35%	20%	0%
Integrating devices	Rules	Rules	Rules
	Hierarchy	Hierarchy	Hierarchy
	Planning	Planning	Planning
	Direct contact	Direct contact	Direct contact
	Teams at 3 levels	Task forces	
	Integrating dept.	Integrators	
Percent integrators/managers	22%	17%	0%

SOURCE: Adopted from Lawrence and Lorsch, 1967, pp. 86–138 and Lorsch and Lawrence, 1968.

cost must be balanced against the cost of slack resources, self-contained groups and information systems.

Choice of Strategy

Each of the four strategies has been briefly presented. The organization can follow one or some combination of several if it chooses. It will choose that strategy which has the least cost in its environmental context. [For an example, see Galbraith, 1970.] However, what may be lost in all of the explanations is that the four strategies are hypothesized to be an exhaustive set of alternatives. That is, if the organization is faced with greater uncertainty due to technological change, higher performance standards due to increased competition, or diversifies its product line to reduce dependence, the amount of information processing is increased. *The organization must adopt at least one of the four strategies when faced with greater uncertainty.* If it does not consciously choose one of the four, then the first, reduced performance standards, will happen automatically. The task information requirements and the capacity of the organization to process information are always matched. If the organization does not consciously match them, reduced performance through budget and schedule overruns will occur in order to bring about equality. Thus the organization should be planned and designed simultaneously with the planning of the strategy and resource allocations. But if the strategy involves introducing new products, entering new markets, etc., then some provision for increased information must be made. Not to decide is to decide, and it is to decide upon slack resources as the strategy to remove hierarchical overload.

There is probably a fifth strategy which is not articulated here. Instead of changing the organization in response to task uncertainty, the organization can operate on its environment to reduce uncertainty. The organization through strategic decisions, long term contracts, coalitions, etc., can control its environment. But these maneuvers have costs also. They should be compared with costs of the four design strategies presented above.

Summary

The purpose of this paper has been to explain why task uncertainty is related to organizational form. In so doing the cognitive limits theory of Herbert Simon was the guiding influence. As the consequences of cognitive limits were traced through the framework, various organization design strategies were articulated. The framework provides a basis for integrating organizational interventions, such as information systems and group problem solving, which have been treated separately before.

Bibliography

Cyert, Richard, and March, James. *The Behavioral Theory of the Firm.* Prentice-Hall, Englewood Cliffs, N.J., 1963.

Galbraith, Jay. "Environmental and Technological Determinants of Organization Design: A Case Study," in Lawrence and Lorsch (eds.), *Studies in Organization Design.* Richard D. Irwin Inc., Homewood, Ill., 1970.

Galbraith, Jay. "Designing Matrix Organizations," *Business Horizons,* February 1971, pp. 29–40.

Galbraith, Jay. *Organization Design.* Addison-Wesley Pub. Co., Reading, Mass., 1973.

Lawrence, Paul, and Lorsch, Jay. *Organization and Environment.* Division of Research, Harvard Business School, Boston: 1967.

Lorsch, Jay, and Lawrence, Paul. "Environmental Factors and Organization Integration." Paper read at the Annual Meeting of the American Sociological Association, August 27, 1967, Boston, Mass.

March, James, and Simon, Herbert. *Organizations.* John Wiley & Sons, New York, 1958.

Pounds, William. "The Scheduling Environment" in Muth and Thompson (eds.) *Industrial Scheduling,* Prentice-Hall Inc., Englewood Cliffs, N.J., 1963.

Simon, Herbert. *Models of Man.* John Wiley & Sons, New York, 1957.

18

Problems of Matrix Organizations

Stanley M. Davis and
Paul R. Lawrence

No organization design or method of management is perfect. And
any form can suffer from a variety of problems that develop because of
the design itself. This is particularly true when a company tries a new
form. In this article we look at one relatively new organization form—the
matrix—which has gained considerable popularity in recent years but
which has some significant pathologies. Before discussing its ills, however,
let us look for a moment at matrix management and organization (see
ruled insert on page 218) and at how widespread the matrix is in U.S.
industry today.

The list of well-known companies that are using some form of a matrix
is becoming long and impressive. Take, for example, a company that has
annual sales of $14 billion and employs about 400,000 people in scores of
diverse businesses—General Electric. For decades, despite the diversity of
its businesses, GE used one basic structure throughout its organization:
five functional managers reporting to one general manager. Employing
the logic that a company must organize to meet the particular needs of
each business, some GE groups, divisions, and departments, which have
found the pyramid form cumbersome, have turned to the matrix as a
fundamental alternative.

In projecting its organization over the next ten years, GE management
states in its Organization Planning Bulletin (September, 1976):

"We've highlighted matrix organization . . . not because it's a
bandwagon that we want you all to jump on, but rather that it's a
complex, difficult, and sometimes frustrating form of organization to live

SOURCE: Stanley M. Davis and Paul R. Lawrence, "Problems of Matrix
Organizations," *Harvard Business Review*, May–June 1978, pp. 131–42. Reprinted
with permission. Copyright © 1978 by the President and Fellows of Harvard
College; all rights reserved.

with. It's also, however, a bellwether of things to come. But, when implemented well, it does offer much of the best of both worlds. And all of us are going to have to learn how to utilize organization to prepare managers to increasingly deal with high levels of complexity and ambiguity in situations where they have to get results from people and components *not* under their direct control. . . .

"Successful experience in operating under a matrix constitutes better preparation for an individual to run a huge diversified institution like General Electric—where so many complex, conflicting interests must be balanced—than the product and functional modes which have been our hallmark over the past twenty years."

Other major corporations, in diverse activities, such as Bechtel, Citibank, Dow Chemical, Shell Oil, Texas Instruments, and TRW, to mention a few, have also turned to the matrix. Based on our studies of the matrix in these companies, we believe that while some of the matrix's popularity is simply a passing fad, most uses of it are founded on solid business reasons that will persist. The matrix's most basic advantage over the familiar functional or product structure is that it facilitates a rapid management response to changing market and technical requirements. Further, it helps middle managers make trade-off decisions from a general management perspective.

Because the matrix is a relatively new form, however, the companies that have adopted it have of necessity been learning on a trial and error basis. The mistakes as well as the successes of these pioneers can be very informative to companies that follow their lead. Here, we present some of the more common problems that occur when a company uses a matrix form. For the sake of easy reference, we diagnose each pathology first, then discuss its prevention and treatment. By using this format, however, we do not mean to suggest that simple first-aid treatment of pathologies will cure them.

Ills of the Matrix

Many of the ailments we discuss do arise in more conventional organizations, but the matrix seems somewhat more vulnerable to these particular ones. It is wise, therefore, for managers thinking of adopting a matrix to be familiar with the diagnoses, prevention, and treatment of nine particular pathologies: tendencies toward anarchy, power struggles, severe groupitis, collapse during economic crunch, excessive overhead, sinking to lower levels, uncontrolled layering, navel gazing, and decision strangulation.

Tendencies toward Anarchy
A formless state of confusion where people do not recognize a "boss" to whom they feel responsible.

Diagnosis—Many managers who have had no first-hand familiarity with matrix organizations tend to have half-expressed fears that a matrix leads to anarchy. Are these concerns based on real hazards? Actually today, a considerable number of organizations are successfully using the matrix form, so we need not treat anarchy as a general hazard of the matrix. However, there are certain conditions or major misconceptions that could lead a company into the formless confusion that resembles anarchy.

Through firsthand experience we know of only one organization that, using a "latent" matrix form, quite literally came apart at the seams during a rather mild economic recession. Following a fast-growth strategy, this company used its high stock multiple to acquire, and then completely assimilate, smaller companies in the recreation equipment field. Within a period of about six months the company changed from an exciting success to a dramatic disaster. Its entire manufacturing, distribution, and financial systems went out of control leaving unfilled orders, closed factories, distressed inventories, and huge debts in their wake.

Of course, there are many possible reasons why this might have happened, but one perfectly reasonable explanation is that the organization design failed under stress. What was that design?

Essentially, the organization used a functional structure. As it acquired each small company, top management first encouraged the owners and general managers to leave, and then it attached the company's three basic functions of sales, production, and engineering to their counterparts in the parent organization. Within the parent marketing department, a young aggressive product manager would be assigned to develop for the acquired product line a comprehensive marketing plan that included making sales forecasts, promotion plans, pricing plans, projected earnings, and so forth. Once top management approved the plan, it told the selected product manager to hustle around and make his plan come true. This is where the latent matrix came in.

The product manager would find himself working across functional lines to try to coordinate production schedules, inventories, cash flow, and distribution patterns without any explicit and formal agreements about the nature of his relationships with the functional managers. Because he was locked into his approved marketing plan, when sales slipped behind schedule, his response was to exhort people to try harder rather than to cut back on production runs.

But once one or two things began to crumble, there was not enough reserve in the system to keep everything else from going wrong. As the product manager lost control, a power vacuum developed, into which the functional managers fell, each grabbing for total control. The result was that a mild recession triggered conditions approaching anarchy.

Prevention—We believe the lesson of this experience is loud and clear. Organizations should not rely too much on an informal or latent matrix to coordinate critical tasks. Relationships between functional and product managers should be explicit so that people are in approximate agreement about who is to do what under various circumstances. Properly used, a matrix does not leave such matters in an indefinite status; it is a definite structure and not a "free form" organization.

A useful "anarchy index" is how many people in an organization do not recognize one boss to whom they feel responsible for a major part of their work. In a study of five medical schools, which are notoriously anarchical, the one with the most explicit matrix structure was also the one with the least number of "bossless" people.[1]

Treatment—Should the worst happen and a company plunge into anarchy, true crisis management would be the best response. The crisis response is really no mystery. The CEO must pull all key people and critical information into the center. He or she must personally make all important decisions on a round-the-clock schedule until the crisis is over. Then and only then can he undertake the work of reshaping the organization so that is can withstand any future shock such as a minor recession.

Power Struggles

Managers jockey for power in many organizations, but a matrix design almost encourages them to do so.

Diagnosis—The essence of a matrix is dual command. For such a form to survive there needs to be a balance of power, where its locus seems to

---

What Is a Matrix?

The identifying feature of a matrix organization is that some managers report to two bosses rather than to the traditional single boss; there is a dual rather than a single chain of command.

Companies tend to turn to matrix forms:

1 when it is absolutely essential that they be highly responsive to two sectors simultaneously, such as markets and technology;
2 when they face uncertainties that generate very high information processing requirements; and
3 when they must deal with strong constraints on financial and/or human resources.

Matrix structures can help provide both flexibility and balanced decision making, but at the price of complexity.

Matrix organization is more than a matrix structure. It must be reinforced by matrix systems such as dual control and evaluation systems, by leaders who operate comfortably with lateral decision making, and by a culture that

can negotiate open conflict and a balance of power.

In most matrix organizations there are dual command responsibilities assigned to functional departments (marketing, production, engineering, and so forth) and to product or market departments. The former are oriented to specialized in-house resources while the latter focus on outputs. Other matrices are split between area-based departments and either products or functions.

Every matrix contains three unique and critical roles; the top manager who heads up and balances the dual chains of command, the matrix bosses (functional, product, or area) who share subordinates, and the managers who report to two different matrix bosses. Each of these roles has its special requirements.

Aerospace companies were the first to adopt the matrix form, but now companies in many industries (chemical, banking, insurance, packaged goods, electronics, computer, and so forth) and in different fields (hospitals, government agencies, and professional organizations) are adapting different forms of the matrix.

shift constantly, each party always jockeying to gain an advantage. It is not enough simply to create the balance, but there must also be continual mechanisms for checking the imbalances that creep in.

In business organizations that operate with a balance of power form, there is a constant tendency toward imbalance. As long as each group or dimension in an organization tries to maximize its own advantage vis-à-vis others, there will be a continual balancing struggle for dominant power. A power struggle in a matrix is qualitatively different from that in a traditionally structured hierarchy because in the latter it is clearly illegitimate. In the matrix, however, power struggles are inevitable; the boundaries of authority and responsibility overlap prompting people to maximize their own advantage.

Prevention—Most top managers will find it exceedingly difficult to forestall all power struggles. Equal strength on the part of the two parties, however, will prevent struggles from reaching destructive heights. Friendly competition should be encouraged, but all-out combat severely punished. Managers in a matrix should push for their advantages but never with the intention of eliminating those with whom they share power, and always with a perspective that encompasses both positions.

Treatment—The best way to ensure that power struggles do not undermine the matrix is to make managers on the power axes aware that to win power absolutely is to lose it ultimately. These managers need to see that the total victory of one dimension only ends the balance, finishes the duality of command, and destroys the matrix. They must see this sharing of power as an underlying principle, before and during all of the ensuing and inevitable power struggles.

Matrix managers have to recognize that they need worthy adversaries, counterparts who can match them, to turn the conflict to constructive ends. For this successful outcome three things are necessary.

First, matrix managers always have to maintain an institutional point of view, seeing their struggles from a larger, shared perspective. Second, they have to jointly agree to remove other matrix managers who, through weakness or whatever inability, are losing irretrievable ground. And, third, that they replace these weak managers with the strongest available people—even if to do so means placing very strong managers in weakened parts of the organization and reversing their power initiatives.

Another key element in stopping power struggles before they get out of hand and destroy the balance is the top level superior to whom the duelling managers report. Because of this element, the matrix is a paradox—a shared-power system that depends on a strong individual, one who does not share the authority that is delegated to him (say by the board), to arbitrate between his power-sharing subordinates.

The top manager has many vehicles for doing this: the amount of time he spends with one side of the matrix or the other, pay differentials, velocity of promotion, direct orders issued to one dimension and not to the other, and so forth. What he must do above all, however, is protect the weak dimension in the organization, not necessarily the weak manager in charge of that dimension.

Severe Groupitis

The mistaken belief that matrix management is the same as group decision making.

Diagnosis—The confusion of matrix behavior with group decision making probably arises from the fact that a matrix often evolves out of new project or business teams, which do suggest a group decision process. Under many circumstances, of course, it is perfectly sensible for managers to make decisions in groups. But managers should expect difficulties to arise if they believe group decision making to be the essence of matrix behavior.

We have seen one matrix organization that had a severe case of "groupitis." This multiproduct electronics company had a product manager and a product team, comprised of specialists drawn from the ranks of every functional department, assigned to every product. So far so good. But somehow the idea that the matrix structure requires that *all* business decisions be hammered out in group meetings became prevalent in the organization. To make decisions in other ways was considered illegitimate and not in the spirit of matrix operations.

Many of the decisions that had to be made about each product involved detailed matters with which only one or two people were regularly conversant. Yet all team members were constrained to listen to these issues being discussed until a decision was made, and were even expected to participate in the discussion and influence the choice. Some individuals seemed to enjoy the steady diet of meetings and the chance to practice being a generalist.

However, a larger number of people felt that their time was being wasted and would have preferred leaving the decisions to the most informed people. The engineers, in particular, complained that the time they were spending in meetings was robbing them of opportunities to strengthen their special competence and identities. As well as noting these personal reactions, senior managers reported a general disappointment with the speed and flexibility of organizational responses.

Prevention—Because the whole idea of a matrix organization is still unfamiliar to many managers, it is understandable that they confuse it with processes such as group decision making. The key to prevention is education. Top managers need to accompany their strategic choice to move toward a matrix with a serious educational effort to clarify to all participants what a matrix is and what it is not.

Treatment—In the case of the multiproducts electronics company, the problem came to light while we were researching the matrix approach. Once senior people had clearly diagnosed the problem, it was 90% cured. Top management emphatically stated that there was nothing sacred about group decisions and that it was not sensible to have all product team members involved all the time. Once the line between individual and group matters was drawn according to who had information really relevant to a decision, meetings became fewer and smaller and work proceeded on a more economical and responsive basis. The concept of teamwork was put in perspective: as often as necessary and as little as possible.

Collapse During Economic Crunch

When business declines, the matrix becomes the scapegoat for poor management and is discarded.

Diagnosis—Matrix organizations that blossom during periods of rapid growth and prosperity sometimes are cast away during periods of economic decline. On reflection, we can understand this. In prosperous times, companies often expand their business lines and the markets they serve. The ensuing complexity may turn them toward matrix management and organization.

However, if these companies follow the normal business cycle, there will be a period of two to five years before they experience another economic crunch which is more than enough time for the matrix concept to spread throughout a company. By that time the matrix occupies a central place in company conversations and is a familiar part of these organizations. Although there may still be some problems, the matrix seems there to stay.

When the down part of the economic cycle begins, senior management in these companies may become appreciably bothered by the conflict between subordinates as well as by the apparent slowness with which they respond to the situation. "We need decisive action" is their rallying cry.

In an authoritarian structure top management can act quickly because it need not consider the spectrum of opinion. Thinking there is no time for organizational toys and tinkering, the top level managers take command in an almost, but not quite, forgotten way, and ram their directives down the line. The matrix is "done in."

Prevention—Top management can prevent this kind of collapse of the matrix by employing general managerial excellence, independent of the matrix, long before the crunch arrives. Good planning, for example, can often forecast downturns in the economic cycle. Corporate structures such as the matrix should not have to change because of standard changes in the business cycle. When management planning has been poor, however, the matrix is a readily available scapegoat.

Companies that experience severe economic crunches often make drastic changes in many directions at once: trimming product lines, closing offices, making massive personnel and budget cuts, and tightening managerial controls. The matrix is often done in during this period for several reasons: it represents too great a risk; "it never really worked properly" and giving it the coup de grace can disguise the failure of implementation; and the quality of decision making had not improved performance sufficiently to counterbalance the hard times. Measures management can take to prevent this pathology do not lie within the matrix itself, as much as with improvements in basic managerial skills and planning.

A real estate and construction company provides an example of how a company can anticipate and flexibly respond to an economic crunch that demonstrates the strength rather than the weakness of the matrix. The company has developed a structure as well as procedures that are especially well suited to the economic uncertainties of the business. These include a set of fully owned subsidiaries each the equivalent of a functional department in a manufacturing company and each the "home base" for varied specialists needed to execute all phases of a major building project. The heads of the subsidiaries act as chief salesmen for their various services, and often head up the bidding teams that put together sophisticated proposals.

As a proposal project proceeds, the selected project manager is drawn into the team in anticipation of securing the contract. This ensures an orderly transition to the project management phase. The project office is given first-line responsibility for control of costs, schedules, and quality of the project, but the top management team from the parent company reviews the project regularly as a backup.

The company has used the matrix to advantage in weathering major shifts in both the availability of business by market segment, for example, from schools to hospitals, and the level of construction activity. It maintains a cadre of professional specialists and project managers, who can be kept busy during the lows of the cycle, which it rapidly expands during the highs by subcontracting for temporary services.

Treatment—This is one pathology that requires preventive treatment; we do not know of any cure. When the matrix does collapse during an economic crunch, it is very unlikely that it can be resurrected. At best, the organization will go back to its pendulum days, alternating between the centralized management of the crunch period and the decentralized freedoms of more prosperous times. Even if top management should try again, it is likely to get a negative response from lower level managers. "They said they were committed to the matrix, but at the first sign of hard times all the nice words about the advantages of the matrix turned out to be just that—nice words." If a company's conditioned response to hard times is to retrench, it should not attempt a matrix in the first place.

Excessive Overhead

The fear of high costs associated with a matrix.

Diagnosis—On the face of it, a matrix organization would seem to double management costs because of its dual chain of command. This issue deserves thoughtful consideration.

The limited amount of research on matrix overhead costs indicates that in the initial phases overhead costs do in fact rise, but that, as a matrix matures, these extra costs disappear and are offset by productivity gains.[2] Our experience supports this finding. In a large electronics company we observed in some detail how initial overhead increases not only necessarily occur in a matrix but also how they can inflate unnecessarily. In this case, the company decided to employ the matrix design from the outset in setting up its new operating division at a new plant site.

This unique organizational experiment had a number of positive attributes, but one of its problems was with overhead costs. In staffing the new division, top management filled every functional office and every product manager's slot with one full-time person. This resulted in a relatively small division having top level managers as well as full-time functional group and full-time product managers. Within months, however, this top heavy division was pared down to more reasonable staffing levels; by assigning individuals to two or more slots, management got costs under control.

Prevention—The division's problem was caused by top management's assumption that each managerial slot requires a full-time incumbent. Overstaffing is much less liable to occur when an organization evolves gradually from a conventional design into a matrix, and managers perform as both functional and product managers. While this technique can be justified as a transition strategy, it also has its hazards. A safer route is to assign managers roles on the same side of the matrix (i.e., two functional jobs or two product management jobs).

As a final argument against the fear of overhead costs, consider that no well-run organization would adopt a matrix structure without the longer run expectation that, at a given level of output, the costs of operations would be lower than with other organizational forms. In what way can such economies be achieved?

The potential economies come from two general sources: fewer bad decisions and less featherbedding. First and most important, the matrix can improve quality of business decisions because it helps bring the needed information and emphasis to bear on critical decisions in a timely fashion. The second source, less featherbedding, is not so obvious, but potentially of greater significance. How can it work?

Treatment—Perhaps the clearest example of the matrix's potential to reduce redundancies in human resources is the way some consulting organizations employ it. These firms usually set up a matrix of functional specialists against client or account managers. The body of other consultants are grouped with their fellow specialists but are available for assignment to projects under the leadership of account or client managers.

From an accounting standpoint, therefore, consultants' time is directly billed to clients' accounts when they are working for an account or engagement manager. Otherwise, their time is charged against the budget of their function manager. The firm's nonbillable costs are, therefore, very conspicuous—both by department and by individual consultant. Of course, some time charged to functional departments, such as background study, research work, and time between assignments should by no means be thought of as wasted. But management can budget such time in advance so that it can scrutinize the variances from the budget.

As one senior manager in a consulting firm put it, "There is no place to hide in a matrix organization." This fact makes clear-cut demands on middle level people and consequently puts pressure on them to produce. For the long-term good of both the people involved and the organization, top managers need to keep such pressures from becoming too strong. Because it is perfectly possible to get too much as well as too little pressure, a creative tension is sought.

Sinking to Lower Levels

The matrix has some difficulty in staying alive at high levels of a corporation, and a corresponding tendency to sink to group and division levels where it thrives.

Diagnosis—Sinking may occur for two reasons. Either senior management has not understood or been able to implement the matrix concept as well as lower level managers, or the matrix has found its appropriate place. For example, if a company sets up a matrix between its basic functional and product groups, the product managers never truly relinquish their complete control, and the matrix fails to take hold at the corporate level.

But, say, one or two of the managers find the idea to be useful within their divisions. Their own functional specialists and project leaders can share the power they delegate and the design can survive within subunits of the corporation. For example, Dow Chemical's attempt to maintain the product/geography balance at the top failed, but the function/product balance held within the geographic areas for several years.

When sinking occurs because of top management misunderstanding, it is likely to occur in conjunction with other pathologies, particularly power struggles. For instance, if many senior executives consider adopting the matrix idea, but only one or a few really become convinced of its worth, there is a danger: those at the top who espouse a philosophy and method they did not employ themselves will be pitted against those who are able to show that it does work.

Prevention—If the corporate top management thinks through which dimensions of the company it must balance, and at what level of aggregation, it can keep the matrix from sinking. For example, top managers should ask themselves if all the business units need to be balanced by central functional departments. If the answer is no, then some business units should operate as product divisions with the traditional pyramid of command, while others share functional services in a partial matrix. However, sinking is not always bad and should be prevented only when it indicates that an appropriate design is disintegrating.

Treatment—Before matrix management can run smoothly, it must be in the proper location. As often as not, when a matrix sinks, it may simply be experiencing a healthy adjustment, and ought to be thought of as settling rather than as sinking. Settling is likely to occur during the early stages of a matrix's evolution and leads to manageable matrix units.

The question of size is a great concern for many managers who ask, in effect, "That sounds great for a $250-million company with a few thousand employees, but can it work for a $2-billion or $3-billion company with 50,000 employees? Its entire company is the size of one of our divisions." Out experience indicates that matrix management and organization seems to function better when no more than 500 managers are involved in matrix relationships. But that does not rule out the $2-billion to $3-billion company. In a company of 5,000 only about 50 managers are likely to be in the matrix; so in a company with 50,000 employees only about 500 may need to be involved in dual reporting lines. With that number, the people who need to coordinate regularly are able to do so through communication networks that are based on personal relations.

Whatever the size unit in which the matrix operates, the important thing is for management to have reasoned carefully from an analysis of the task to the design of the organization. Then, if settling occurs, it should be seen not as pathology but as a self-adjustment that suggests the organization's capacity to evolve with growth.

Uncontrolled Layering

Matrices which lie within matrices which lie within matrices result frequently from the dynamics of power rather than from the logic of design.

Diagnosis—Sometimes matrices not only sink but also cascade down the organization and filter through several levels and across several divisions. This layering process may or may not be pathological. In fact, it may be a rational and logical development of the matrix, but we include it briefly here because it sometimes creates more problems than it solves. In terms of the metaphor we have used in this article, layering is a pathology only if the matrix begins to metastasize. When this occurs, organization charts begin to resemble blueprints for a complex electronic machine, relationships become unnecessarily complex, and the matrix form may become more of a burden than it is worth.

Prevention and treatment—The best remedies for uncontrolled layering are careful task analysis and reduced power struggles. We have seen a few cases where one dimension of a matrix was clearly losing power to the other, so, adapting an "if you can't beat 'em, join 'em" philosophy, it created a matrix within its own dimension. A product unit, for example, developed its own functional *expertise* distinct from the functional *units* at the next level up. The best defense was a good offense, or so it seemed.

In two other cases, the international divisions of two large companies each created its own matrix by adding business managers as an overlay to its geographic format, without reconciling these with the managers who ran the domestic product/service groups. In each case, adequate conceptualization by top managers would probably have simplified the organization design and forestalled the layering, which occurred because of power maneuvers. Management can treat this unhealthy state best by rebalancing the matrix so that no manager of one dimension is either too threatened or pushed too hard toward a power goal.

Matrix design is complex enough without the addition of power struggles. A well-conceptualized matrix is bound to be less complex and easier to manage than one that is illogically organized.

Navel Gazing

Managers in a matrix can succumb to excessive internal preoccupation and lose touch with the marketplace.

Diagnosis—Because a matrix fosters considerable interdependence of people and tasks and demands negotiating skills on the part of its members, matrix managers sometimes tend to get absorbed in internal relations at the expense of paying attention to the world outside the organization, particularly to clients. When this happens, an organization spends more energy ironing out its own disputes than in serving its customers. The outward focus disappears because the short-term demands of daily working life have yet to be worked through.

The navel gazers are not at all lethargic; rather they are involved in a heated fraternal love/hate affair with each other. This inward preoccupation is more common in the early phases of a matrix, when the new behaviors are being learned, than in matrices that have been operating for a few years.

Prevention—Whatever other pathologies develop in a matrix, attention to their cure is bound to increase the internal focus of the members; so prevention of other pathologies will certainly reduce the likelihood of this one occurring. Awareness of the tendency will also help. Since the product dimension of the organization generally has a more external focus than the resource dimension, the responsibility for preventing an excessive introspection is not equally distributed. The product dimension people can help the others keep perspective, but a strong marketing orientation is the best preventative of all.

Treatment—If the managers in the matrix are navel gazing, the first step in the treatment is to make these managers aware of the effects. Are customers complaining a lot, or at least more than usual? Managers need to confront internal conflict, but also to recognize that confrontation is secondary to maintaining effective external relationships. Navel gazing generally occurs when the matrix has been fully initiated but not yet debugged. People accept it, but they are engrossed in figuring out how to make it work.

The second step is to treat the inward focus as a symptom of the underlying issue: how to institutionalize matrix relationships so that they become familiar and comfortable routines, and so that people can work through them without becoming obsessed by them. Finally, it must always be remembered that any form of organization is only a means and should never become an end in itself.

Decision Strangulation

Too much democracy, not enough action?

Can moving into a matrix lead to the strangulation of the decision process, into endless delays for debate, for clearing with everybody in sight? Will decisions, no matter how well thought through, be made too late to be of use? Will too many people have power to water down all bold initiatives or veto them outright? Such conditions can arise in a matrix. We have in mind three situations—constant clearing, escalation of conflict, and unilateral style—each calling for slightly different preventive action and treatment.

Constant clearing—In one company we know of, various functional specialists who reported to a second boss, a product manager, picked up the idea that they had to clear all issues with their own functional bosses before agreeing to product decisions. This meant that every issue had to be discussed in at least two meetings, if not more. During the first meeting, the specialists and the product manager could only review the facts of the issue, which was then tabled until, at the second meeting, the specialists cleared the matter with their functional bosses—who by this process were each given a de facto veto over product decisions.

This impossible clearing procedure represented, in our view, a failure of delegation, not of the matrix. One needs to ask why the functional specialists could not be trusted to act on the spot in regard to most product decisions in ways that would be consistent with the general guidelines of their functional departments. Either the specialists were poorly selected, too inexperienced and badly informed, or their superiors were lacking in a workable degree of trust of one another. Regardless, this problem, and its prevention and treatment, needs to be addressed directly without making a scapegoat of the matrix.

Escalation of conflict—Another possible source of decision strangulation in matrix organizations occurs when managers frequently or constantly refer decisions up the dual chain of command. Seeing that one advantage of the conventional single chain of command is that two disagreeing peers can go to their shared boss for a resolution, managers unfamiliar with the matrix worry about this problem almost more than any other. They look at a matrix and realize that the nearest shared boss might be the CEO, who could be five or six echelons up. They realize that not too many problems can be pushed up to the CEO for resolution without creating the ultimate in information overload. So, they think, will not the inevitable disagreement lead to a tremendous pileup of unresolved conflict?

Certainly, this can happen in a malfunctioning matrix. Whether it does happen depends primarily on the depth of understanding that exists about required matrix behavior on the part of managers in the dual structure. Let us envision the following scene: a manager with two bosses gets sharply conflicting instructions from his product and his functional bosses. When he tries to reconcile his instructions without success, he quite properly asks for a session with his two bosses to resolve the matter. The three people meet, but the discussion bogs down, no resolution is reached, and neither boss gives way.

The two bosses then appeal the problem up a level to their respective superiors in each of the two chains of command. This is the critical step. If the two superiors properly understand matrix behavior, they will first ascertain whether the dispute reflects an unresolved broader policy issue. If it does not, they know their proper step is to teach their subordinates to resolve the problem themselves—not to solve it for them. In short, they would not let the unresolved problem escalate, but would force it back to the proper level for solution, and insist that the solution be found promptly.

Often, conflict cannot be resolved; it can, however, be managed, which it must be if the matrix is to work. Any other course of action would represent management's failure to comprehend the essential nature of the design.

Unilateral style—A third possible reason for decision strangulation in a matrix system can arise from a very different source—personal style. Some managers have the feeling they are not truly managing if they are not in a position to make crisp, unilateral decisions. Identifying leadership with decisive action, they become very frustrated when they have to engage in carefully reasoned debates about the wisdom of what they want to do.

Such a manager is likely to feel frustrated even in regard to a business problem whose resolution will vitally affect functions other than his own, such as in a company that is experiencing critical dual pressure from the marketplace and from advancing technology. A matrix that deliberately induces simultaneous decision making between two or more perspectives is likely to frustrate such a person even further.

If managers start feeling emasculated by bilateral decision making, they are certain to be unhappy in a matrix organization. In such cases the strangulation is in the eye of the beholder. Such people must work on their personal decision-making style or look for employment in a nonmatrix organization.

At Last, Legitimacy

We do not recommend that every company adopt the matrix form. But where it is relevant, it can become an important part of an effective managerial process. Like any new method it may develop serious bugs, but the experiences that many companies are acquiring with this organization form can now help others realize its benefits and avoid its pitfalls.

The matrix seems to have spread despite itself and its pathologies: what was necessary was made desirable. It is difficult and complex, and human flexibility is required to arrive at organizational flexibility.

But the reverse is also true; success has given the form legitimacy, and, as the concept spreads, familiarity seems to reduce the resistance and difficulties people experience in using the matrix. Managers are now beginning to say, "It isn't that new or different after all." This familiarity is a sign of acceptance, more than of change or moderation of the design.

For generations, managers lived with the happy fiction of dotted lines, indicating that a second reporting line was necessary if not formal. The result had always been a sort of executive ménage à trois, a triangular arrangement where the manager had one legitimate relationship (the reporting line) and one that existed but was not granted equal privileges (the dotted line).

As executives develop greater confidence with the matrix form, they bring the dotted line relationship out of the closet, and grant it legitimacy.

Each time another organization turns to the matrix, it has a larger and more varied number of predecessors that have charted the way. The examples of wider applicability suggest that the matrix is becoming less and less an experiment and more and more a mature formulation in organization design. As more organizations travel the learning curve, the curve itself becomes an easier one to climb. Similarly, as more managers gain experience operating in matrix organizations, they are bound to spread this experience as some of them move, as they inevitably will, into other organizations.

We believe that in the future matrix organizations will become almost commonplace and that managers will speak less of the difficulties and pathologies of the matrix than of its advantages and benefits.

Notes

1 From the forthcoming article by M. R. Weisbord, M. P. Charns, and P. R. Lawrence, "Organizational Dilemmas of Academic Medical Centers," *Journal of Applied Behavioral Science,* Vol. XIV, No. 3.

2. C. J. Middleton, "How to Set Up a Project Organization," HBR March–April 1967, p. 73.

19

Can Leaders Learn to Lead?

Victor H. Vroom

*L*ike my fellow authors, I start with certain preconceptions. These preconceptions—some may call them biases—influence the way in which I view issues of leadership, particularly leadership training. I have tried to depict these preconceptions in Figure 1.

Figure 1   Schematic Representation of Variables Used in Leadership Research

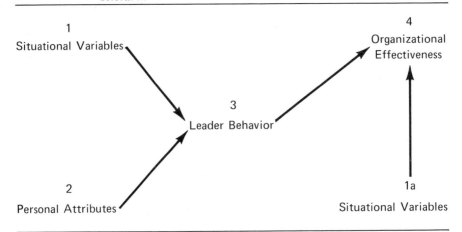

The central variable in this figure is the behavior of the leader, which I believe is determined by two classes of variables, attributes of the leader himself and attributes of the situation he encounters. Furthermore, I assume that many of the differences in the behavior of leaders can be explained only by examining their joint effects, including interactions between these two classes of variables.

SOURCE: Victor H. Vroom, "Can Leaders Learn to Lead?" *Organizational Dynamics.* Reprinted by permission of the publisher from *Organizational Dynamics,* Winter 1976, © 1976 by AMACOM, a division of American Management Associations. All rights reserved.

The left-hand portion of the diagram is the descriptive side of the leader behavior equation. Much of my research has focused on these relationships in an attempt to understand the ways in which managers actually respond to situations that vary in a number of dimensions. If you examine the right-hand side of Figure 1, however, you encounter issues that are potentially normative or prescriptive in character. They deal with the consequences of leader behavior for the organization, and here I share with Fiedler (and probably disagree with Argyris) a conviction that a contingency model is required. I do not see any form of leader behavior as optimal for all situations. The contribution of a leader's actions to the effectiveness of his organization cannot be determined without considering the nature of the situation in which that behavior is displayed.

Working with the Contingency Model

I am going to assume that most of you are familiar with the model that Phil Yetton and I developed and have described in detail in our recent book. As a normative model, it deals with the right-hand side of Figure 1, but it is a limited model because it deals with only one facet of leadership behavior—the extent to which the leader shares his decision-making power with his subordinates.

Figure 2 shows the latest version of our model. For purposes of simplicity, the presentation here is restricted to the model for group problems, that is, problems or decisions that affect all or a substantial portion of the manager's subordinates. At the top of the figure are problem attributes—that is, situational variables that ought to influence the decision process used by the leader—specifically, the amount of opportunity that the leader gives his subordinates to participate in the making of a decision. To use the model, one first selects an organization problem to be solved or decision to be made. Starting at the left-hand side of the diagram, one asks oneself the question pertaining to each attribute that is encountered, follows the path developed, and finally determines the problem type (numbered 1 through 12). This problem type specifies one or more decision processes that are deemed appropriate to that problem. These decision processes are called the "feasible set" and represent the methods that remain after a set of seven rules has been applied. The first three of these rules eliminate methods that threaten the quality of the decisions, while the last four rules eliminate methods that are likely to jeopardize acceptance of the decision by subordinates.

For those who are unfamiliar with the Vroom-Yetton model, let me point out that the decision processes are described here in a kind of code. AI and AII are variants of an autocratic process. In AI the manager solves the problem by himself using whatever information is available to him at that time; in AII he obtains any necessary information of a specific nature from his subordinates before making the decision himself. CI and CII are variants of a consultative process. In CI he shares the problem with relevant subordinates individually, getting their ideas and suggestions before making the decision; CII is similar, but the consultation takes place within the context of a group meeting. Finally, GII corresponds with Norman Maier's concept of group decision in which the manager's role is

Figure 2 Decision Process Flowchart (Feasible Set)

A. Does the problem possess a quality requirement?
B. Do I have sufficient information to make a high-quality decision?
C. Is the problem structured?
D. Is acceptance of the decision by subordinates important for effective implementation?
E. If I were to make the decision by myself, am I reasonably certain that it would be accepted by my subordinates?
F. Do subordinates share the organizational goals to be attained in solving this problem?
G. Is conflict among subordinates likely in preferred solutions?

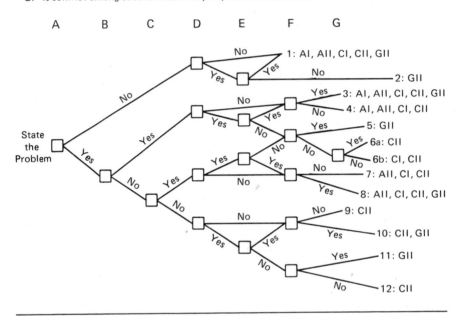

that of a chairperson of a group meeting aimed at reaching consensus on the action to be taken.

The part of the model described so far specifies how decisions should *not* be made, not how they should be made. For most problem types, there exist more than one decision process consistent with the rules and therefore contained in the feasible set. We have also been concerned with the consequences of various ways of choosing from these alternatives. There is considerable evidence that the time required to make the decision (defined either as the elapsed time or the number of man-hours needed to make the decision) increases with the intensity of involvement or participation of subordinates. Thus a time-efficient model (which we term Model A) would select the most autocratic alternative within the feasible set, a choice that would be clearly indicated in crisis or emergency situations and in situations in which one seeks to minimize the number of man-hours that enter into making the decision.

Of course, time is not the only dimension to include in deciding the degree to which the leader should encourage the participation of his subordinates in decision making. In addition to the possibilities that participation may increase decision quality or its acceptance (considerations that are incorporated into the rules referred to previously), there are also grounds for believing that participation contributes to individual and team development and is likely to result in more informed and responsible behavior by subordinates in the future. Hence Model B, which could be thought of as a time-investment or developmental model, dictates the choice of the most participative process within the feasible set. It is important to note that Models A and B are consistent with the same rules (to protect decision quality and acceptance) but represent extremely different ways of operating within these rules. Model A maximizes a short-run value—time; Model B maximizes a long-run value—development.

What is the image of the effective leader portrayed by this normative model? He is neither universally autocratic nor universally participative but utilizes either approach in response to the demands of a situation *as he perceives them*. Above all, he is a flexible leader who has thought through his values and who has a repertoire of skills necessary to execute effectively each of the decision processes.

Validating the Model

When Philip Yetton and I wrote our book, we had no evidence validating the model other than the consistency of our rules with existing empirical evidence concerning the consequences of alternative approaches. During the past six months, Art Jago and I have been working to remedy this deficiency. We have asked managers, all of whom were unfamiliar with the model, to select two decisions that they had made—one that proved to be successful and one that proved to be unsuccessful. Each manager wrote up each decision situation as a case and specified the decision process he used in solving the problem. Later these managers were trained in the problem attributes and went back over each of these two cases, coding each in a manner that would permit the researcher to determine the problem type and the feasible set of methods for that problem type.

The data for this study are still coming in. To date, we have written accounts of 46 successful decisions and 42 unsuccessful ones. (It seems that some managers have difficulty in recalling the decisions they made that did not turn out too well!) Figure 3 shows the results available so far. These results clearly support the validity of the model. If the manager's method of dealing with the case corresponded with the model, the probability of the decision's being deemed successful was 65 percent; if the method disagreed with the model, the probability of its being deemed successful was only 29 percent.

Figure 3   Relationship Between Model Agreement and Decision Outcome

	Percent Successful	Percent Unsuccessful	Total
Method used agrees with feasible set	65	35	100%
Method used disagrees with feasible set	29	71	100%

It is important to note, however, that behavior that corresponds with the model is no guarantee that the decision will ultimately turn out to be successful—nor is behavior outside the feasible set inevitably associated with an unsuccessful decision.

To create a model of decision processes that completely predicts decision outcomes (that is, which generates 100 percent observations in upper left and lower right cells) is an impossibility. Any fantasies that we may have entertained about having created a model of process that would completely determine decision outcomes have been permanently dashed against the rocks of reality! Insofar as organizations are open systems and decisions within them are made under conditions of risk and uncertainty, it will be impossible to generate complete predictability for a model such as ours. To be sure, we may be able to use the data from the study I have described to improve the "batting average" of the model, but the limit of success must be less than perfection.

Implications for Training

I would now like to turn to the central issue of this symposium, the use of the model in leadership training. Over the past few years, several thousand managers have received training in the concepts underlying the model. The workshops have ranged from two to over five days in length, and the participants have included admirals, corporation presidents, school superintendents, and senior government officials. I have been personally involved in enough of this training to have learned some important things about what to do and what not to do. And because I believe that there are substantial but understandable misconceptions about how training based on the Vroom and Yetton model works, I would like to describe the things I have learned.

It would have been possible to build a training program around the model that was completely cognitive and mechanistic. Participants would be sold on the model and then trained in its use through intensive practice—first on standardized cases and later on real problems drawn from their own experiences. Such an approach would represent a new domain for Taylorism and could even be accomplished through Skinnerian programmed learning. I believe that, at best, this behavioral approach would influence what Argyris calls espoused theories and would not have any long-lasting behavioral effects.

Our methods have been much more influenced by Carl Rogers than by B. F. Skinner. We have assumed that behavioral changes require a process of self-discovery and insight by each individual manager.

One method of stimulating this process is to provide the participant with a picture of his own leadership style. This picture includes a comparison of his style with that of others, the situational factors that influence his willingness to share his power with others, and similarities and differences between his own "model" and the normative models.

In advance of the training program, each participant sits down with a set of cases, each of which depicts a leader confronted with an actual organizational problem. We call these cases "problem sets," and the number of cases in different problem sets ranges from 30 to 54. The common feature in each of the eight or nine problem sets that have been developed is that the cases vary along each of the situational dimensions used in the construction of the normative model. The set is designed so that the variation is systematic and that the effects of each situational attribute on a given manager's choice of decision process can be readily determined. This feature permits the assessment of each of the problem attributes in the decision processes used by a given manager.

The manager's task is to select the decision process that comes closest to depicting what he would do in each situation. His responses are recorded on a standardized form and processed by computer along with other participants' responses in the same program.

Instead of writing about information contained on a printout, I thought that it might be more efficient to let you see what it looks like. The next figure reproduces three of the seven pages of feedback that a manager recently received. Examine the first page of the printout shown in Figure 4. Consider A first in that figure. The first row opposite "your frequency" shows the proportion of cases in which the manager indicated he would use each of the five decision processes. The next row (opposite "peer frequency") shows the average use of these processes by the 41 managers constituting his training group. A comparison of these two rows indicates the methods he used more and less frequently than average.

The third row shows the distribution of decision processes that would be used by a manager using Model A, the time-efficient model in the 30 cases. The final row shows a distribution for Model B, the developmental or time-investment model.

To obtain an overall picture of how participative this manager's responses are in relation to other members of his training group and to Models A and B, it is necessary to assign scale values to each of the five decision processes. The actual numbers used for this purpose are based on research on the relative amounts of participation perceived to result from each process. AI is given a value of 0; AII a value of 1; CI a value of 5; CII a value of 8; and GII a value of 10.

With the aid of these scale values a mean score can be computed for the manager his peers, and both models. These are obtained by multiplying the percentage of times each process is used by its scale value and dividing by 100. These mean scores are shown in B along with the standard deviation (SD), a measure of dispersion around the mean—that is, an indicator of how much behavior is varied over situations.

These mean scores are shown graphically in the figure at the bottom. Each asterisk is the mean score of one of the group members. The symbol X is printed underneath this manager's mean score, the symbol P under the group average, and the symbols A and B show the location on the scale of Models A and B respectively.

D through F in Figure 4 are on the second page of the printout. As we previously mentioned, the normative model identifies 12 problem types corresponding to the terminal nodes of the decision tree shown in Figure 2. There is at least one case within the set of 30 problems that has been designated by the authors and most managers as representative of each type. The problem types and corresponding problem numbers are shown in the two left-hand columns of D. In the third and fourth columns, the prescriptions of Models A and B are given, and the fifth column shows the feasible set for that problem type. The last column, marked "your behavior," indicates the manager's responses to each of the cases of the indicated problem type. If there is more than one case of that type, the

Figure 4 Page 1 of Printout

NAME OR I.D. — JOHN DOE

A — PROPORTION OF CASES IN WHICH
EACH DECISION PROCESS IS USED

	AI	AII	CI	CII	GII
YOUR FREQUENCY	43%	3%	23%	30%	0%
PEER FREQUENCY	25%	14%	19%	27%	15%
MODEL A (MINIMIZE PARTICIPATION)	40%	13%	3%	23%	20%
MODEL B (MAXIMIZE PARTICIPATION)	0%	0%	0%	40%	60%

B — SCALED PARTICIPATION
SCORES

	MEAN	SD
YOUR RESPONSES	3.60*	3.48
PEER AVERAGE	4.73	3.66
MODEL A	4.17	4.31
MODEL B	9.20	0.98
* YOUR SCORE IN FIGURE 1		

C — FREQUENCY DISTRIBUTION OF SCALE SCORES
(MEAN LEVELS OF PARTICIPATION)

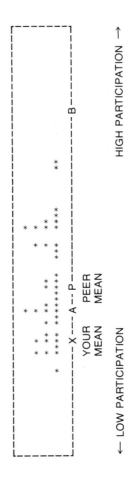

```
                                        *
            *                       *   *
        *   *   *    **        *    **
      * *** * ** **           ***   ****
    * **** **********       ***     ****          **
    ----X----A--P--------------------------------B-----
      YOUR    PEER
      MEAN    MEAN

←— LOW PARTICIPATION                    HIGH PARTICIPATION —→

              P A R T I C I P A T I V E N E S S
```

Figure 4   Page 2 of Printout

D — BEHAVIOR BY PROBLEM TYPE

PROBLEM TYPE	PROBLEM NUMBERS	MODEL "A"	MODEL "B"	FEASIBLE SET	YOUR BEHAVIOR
1	14, 15, 17, 28	AI	GII	AI, AII, CI, CII, GII	AI AI AI AI AI
2	3, 5,	GII	GII	GII	CII AI
3	2, 22, 27, 30	AI	GII	AI, AII, CI, CII, GII	AI AI CI AI CII AI
4	12, 25, 26, 29	AI	CII	AI, AII, CI, CII	CI CI CI CII
5	7, 8, 20	GII	GII	GII	CI CI AI
6A	1, 10	CII	CII	CII	CI CI
6B	11	CI	CII	CI, CII	CII
7	21, 24	AII	GII	AII, CI, CII	CII AI
8	19, 23	AII	GII	AII, CI, CII, GII	CI AII
9	4, 16	CII	CII	CII	AI CI
10	6, 9	CII	CII	CII, GII	CII
11	13	GII	GII	GII	AII
12	18	CII	CII	CII	CII

E — FREQUENCY OF AGREEMENT WITH THE NORMATIVE MODEL

	YOUR MEAN	PEER AVERAGE
AGREEMENT WITH FEASIBLE SET	17 (57%)	20.8 (69%)
AGREEMENT MODEL A (MINIMUM PARTICIPATION)	12 (40%)	12.1 (40%)
AGREEMENT WITH MODEL B (MAXIMUM PARTICIPATION)	4 (13%)	6.3 (21%)

F — FREQUENCY OF RULE VIOLATIONS

RULE	RESPONSES IN VIOLATION	YOUR FREQUENCY	PEER AVERAGE	PROBLEM NUMBERS
1 LEADER INFORMATION RULE	AI	3.0 (25%)	0.7 (6%)	6 19 24
2 GOAL CONGRUENCE RULE	GII	0.0 (0%)	1.3 (10%)	0
3 UNSTRUCTURED PROBLEM RULE	AI, AII, CI	3.0 (50%)	2.8 (47%)	6 9 16
4 ACCEPTANCE RULE	AI, AII	1.0 (10%)	1.3 (13%)	5
5 CONFLICT RULE	AI, AII, CI	3.0 (60%)	1.9 (39%)	1 5 10
6 FAIRNESS RULE	AI, AII, CI, CII	2.0 (100%)	1.3 (63%)	3 5
7 ACCEPTANCE PRIORITY RULE	AI, AII, CI, CII	4.0 (100%)	2.9 (72%)	7 8 13 20

*— PROBABILITY OF RULE VIOLATION (THAT IS, FREQUENCY OF VIOLATION EXPRESSED AS A PERCENTAGE OF RULE APPLICABILITY)

Figure 4   Page 3 of Printout

Leadership Style Analysis

| YOUR MEAN = X | MODEL A MEAN = A |
| PEER MEAN = P | MODEL B MEAN = B |

G — MAIN EFFECTS OF PROBLEM ATTRIBUTES

PARTICIPATIVENESS ON PROBLEMS WITH ATTRIBUTE

PROBLEM ATTRIBUTES	Level	< LOW PARTICIPATION	Participativeness chart (low → high)	HIGH PARTICIPATION >	PROBLEMS WITH ATTRIBUTE
IMPORTANCE OF THE QUALITY OF THE FINAL SOLUTION (ATTRIBUTE A)	HIGH	X=4.97 P=4.17	XA ···· P	B	(1, 2, 4, 6, 7, 8, 9, 10, 11, 12, 13, 16, 18, 19, 20, 21, 22, 23, 24, 25, 26, 27, 29, 30)
	LOW	X=1.33 P=3.75 A=4.38	X ···· A ···· P		(3, 5, 14, 15, 17, 28)
ADEQUACY OF MANAGER'S INFORMATION AND EXPERTISE (ATTRIBUTE B)	HIGH	X=3.67 P=4.24 A=2.75	A ···· X ···· P	B	(1, 2, 8, 11, 12, 20, 22, 25, 26, 27, 29, 30)
	LOW	X=4.67 P=5.71 A=6.00	X ···· P ···· A	B	(4, 6, 7, 9, 10, 13, 16, 18, 19, 21, 23, 24)
DEGREE OF STRUCTURE IN PROBLEM (ATTRIBUTE C)	HIGH	X=3.67 P=4.97 A=3.67	X ···· A ···· P	B	(7, 10, 19, 21, 23, 24)
	LOW	X=5.67 P=6.46 A=8.33	X ···· P ···· A ·· B		(4, 6, 9, 13, 16, 18)
IMPORTANCE OF SUBORDINATE ACCEPTANCE (ATTRIBUTE D)	HIGH	X=3.80 P=5.30 A=5.35	X ···· P ···· A	B	(1, 3, 5, 6, 7, 8, 10, 11, 12, 13, 14, 15, 16, 18, 20, 22, 24, 29, 30)
	LOW	X=3.20 P=3.59 A=1.80	A ·· X ·· P	B	(2, 4, 9, 17, 21, 23, 25, 26, 27, 28)
PROBABILITY OF LEADER'S SELLING HIS OWN SOLUTION (ATTRIBUTE E)	HIGH	X=1.30 P=3.68 A=1.80	X · A ·· P	B	(6, 12, 14, 15, 16, 19, 22, 24, 29, 30)
	LOW	X=6.30 P=6.91 A=8.90	X ···· P ···· A	A · B	(1, 3, 5, 7, 8, 10, 11, 13, 18, 20)
DEGREE TO WHICH SUBORDINATES SHARE GOALS (ATTRIBUTE F)	HIGH	X=3.58 P=5.45 A=4.83	X ···· A ···· P	B	(2, 6, 7, 8, 9, 13, 19, 20, 22, 23, 27, 30)
	LOW	X=4.75 P=4.49 A=3.92	A ·· P ·· X		(1, 4, 10, 11, 12, 16, 18, 21, 24, 25, 26, 29)
PROBABILITY OF CONFLICT AMONG SUBORDINATES (ATTRIBUTE G)	HIGH	X=3.27 P=3.99 A=4.27	X ···· P ·· A	B	(1, 2, 5, 8, 9, 10, 13, 15, 16, 19, 21, 22, 26, 28, 29)
	LOW	X=3.93 P=5.47 A=4.07	X ···· A ···· P		(3, 4, 6, 7, 11, 12, 14, 17, 18, 20, 23, 24, 25, 27, 30)

* * * * * *   NOTE: THE THREE ATTRIBUTES WITH THE GREATEST EFFECT ON YOUR RESPONSES ARE A, C, AND E.   * * * * * *

methods used are shown in the same order as the problem numbers at the left-hand side.

E reports the frequency with which the manager's behavior agreed with the feasible set, with Model A, and with Model B. For comparison purposes, the average rates of agreement for members of the manager's training group are also presented.

Each time our manager chose a decision process that was outside the feasible set, he violated at least one of the seven rules underlying the model. F in Figure 4 reports the frequencies with which each rule was violated both by this manager and by his peer group. The right-hand column shows the specific cases in which the rule violations occurred. It should be noted that each manager understands the seven rules by the time he receives the feedback, and it is possible for him to reexamine the problems with the appropriate rule in mind.

We have previously noted that the cases included in a problem set are selected in accordance with a multifactorial experimental design. Each of the problem attributes is varied in a manner that will permit the manager to examine its role in his leadership style. Figure 4 (page 3 of printout) depicts these results. Consider problem attribute A—the importance of the quality of the final solution. The problem set contains cases that have a high quality requirement and those without a quality requirement (the identifying numbers of these cases are shown at the right-hand side of this table).

The mean scores for the manager's behavior on these two sets of cases are specified at the left-hand side of each row and are designated by the symbol X. They are also designated by the symbol X on each of the scales, and the slope of the line made by connecting the two letters (X) provides a visual representation of that difference.

If the score opposite "high" is greater (that is, more toward the right-hand side of the scale), it means that the manager encourages more participation from his subordinates on important decisions than on so-called trivial ones. However, if the score opposite "high" is lower, it means that the manager is willing to use more participative methods on problems for which the course of action adopted makes little difference and is more autocratic on "important" decisions.

The letter P shown on both scales designates the average effects of this attribute on the manager's peer group, and the letters A and B designate the effects on Models A and B respectively.

A similar logic can be used in interpreting the effects of each of the other attributes in the model. At the bottom of the page, the computer prints out the three attributes that have the greatest effect on the manager's behavior—magnitude of effect referring to the amount of difference the attribute makes in his willingness to share his decision-making power with subordinates.

The results shown in Figure 4 pertain to only one manager and to his peer group. Similar data have been obtained from several thousand managers, a sufficient number to provide the basis for some tentative generalizations about leadership patterns. One of our conclusions is that differences among managers in what might be termed a general trait of participativeness or authoritarianism are small in comparison with differences within managers. On the standardized cases in the problem sets, no manager has indicated that he would use the same decision process on all problems or decisions—and most use all methods under some circumstances.

It is clear that no one score computed for a manager and displayed on his printout adequately represents his leadership style. To begin to understand his style, the entire printout must be considered. For example, two managers may appear to be equally participative or autocratic on the surface, but a close look at the third page of the printout (Figure 4) may reveal crucial differences. One manager may limit participation by his subordinates to decisions where the quality element is unimportant, such as the time and place of the company picnic, while the other manager may limit participation by his subordinates to those decisions with a demonstrable impact on important organizational goals.

In about two-thirds of the cases we have examined—both those used in the problem sets and those reported to us by managers from their experiences—the manager's behavior was consistent with the feasible set of methods given by the model. Rules that helped ensure the acceptance of or commitment to a decision tend to be violated much more frequently than rules that protect the quality of the decision. Our findings suggest strongly that decisions made by typical managers are more likely to prove ineffective because subordinates don't fully accept decisions than because decision quality is deficient.

Let me now turn to another thing that we have learned in the design of this training—the usefulness of the small, informal group as a vehicle in the change process. The first four or five hours in the training process are spent in creating six- to eight-person teams operating under conditions of openness and trust. Each participant spends more than 50 percent of the training time with his small group before receiving feedback. Group activities include discussing cases in the problem set and trying to reach agreement on their mode of resolution, practicing participative leadership styles within their own groups, analyzing videotapes of group problem-solving activities; then group members give one another feedback on the basis of predictions of one another's leadership styles.

After feedback, group members compare results with one another and with their prior predictions and share with one another what they have learned as well as their plans to change. The use of small, autonomous groups greatly decreases the dependence of participants on the instructor for their learning and increases the number of people who can undergo the training at the same time. I have personally worked with as many as 140 managers at the same time (22 groups), and 40 to 50 is commonplace.

One criticism that has been correctly leveled at the Vroom and Yetton work stems from the fact that the data on which the feedback is based are, at best, reports of intended actions rather than observations of actual behavior. While we have evidence that most managers honestly try to portray what they think they would do in a particular situation rather than what they think they should do, I am persuaded by Argyris's evidence that many people are unaware of discrepancies between their espoused theories and their actions. Small groups can be helpful in pointing out these discrepancies. I have seen managers who were universally predicted by other group members to have a highly autocratic style, who were provided with very specific evidence of the ground for this assumption by other group members, but who later received a printout reflecting a much more participative style. I am less concerned about the relative validity of these discrepant pieces of data than I am about the fact that they are frequently confronted and discussed in the course of the training experience.

In fact, we have begun using a different source of potential inconsistencies, and it is logical to assume that this source will have more information about a manager's behavior than do the other members of his small group. I am referring to the manager's subordinates.

In a recent variant of the training program, subordinates were asked to predict their managers' behavior on each of the cases in the problem set. These predictions were made individually and processed by computer, which generated for each manager a detailed comparison of his perceptions of his leadership style with the mean perception of his subordinates. Not surprisingly, these two sources of information are not always in perfect agreement. Most managers, as seen by their subordinates, are substantially more autocratic (about one point on the 10-point scale) and in substantially less agreement with the model. Once again, I am less concerned with which is the correct description of the leader's behavior than I am with the fact that discrepancies generate a dialogue between the manager and his subordinates that can be the source of mutual learning.

We are still experimenting with methods of using the Vroom-Yetton model in leadership training and, I believe, still learning from the results of this experimentation. How effective is the training in its present form? Does it produce long-lasting behavioral changes? I must confess that I do not know. Art Jago and I are in the first stages of designing an extensive follow-up study of almost 200 managers in 20 different countries who have been through a four- or five-day version of the training within the past two and one-half years. If we can solve the incredible logistical and methodological problems in a study of this kind, we should have results within a year.

On the basis of the evidence, I am optimistic on two counts: first, as to the leader's potential to vary his style to meet the requirements of a situation; second, as to the leader's ability, through training and development, to enlarge the repertoire of his styles. In short, like Argyris and unlike Fiedler, I believe that managers can learn to become more effective leaders. But like Fiedler (and unlike Argyris), I believe that such effectiveness requires a matching of one's leadership style to the demands of the situation. I also am confident that 50 years from now both contingency models will be found wanting in detail if not in substance. If we are remembered at that time, it will be for the kinds of questions we posed rather than the specific answers we provided.

20

When Productivity Lags, Check at the Top:
Are Key Managers Really Communicating?

Stewart L. Tubbs
Robin N. Widgery

*A*l Stone was the frustrated manager of a manufacturing plant with over 6,000 employees. Even with 30 years of experience, he was not getting the results he knew the plant was capable of.

Although the plant was profitable, absenteeism had steadily increased over the past five years. Also, he felt special concern about the performance of his immediate management team—the heads of the major departments. In spite of his repeated efforts to improve communication, there seemed to be less and less free and open information exchanged between him and the group. Moreover, he believed a similar communication problem existed generally within and between all departments.

Adding to Al's frustrations was his realization that orders and directives from his office were evoking only sluggish or minimal response. And finally, he was particularly annoyed that the expenditure of $50 million on tools and equipment only two years earlier had produced less than a one percent increase in production efficiency, not enough to improve his plant's ranking of 15th best in the company. Some kind of organizational improvement program was clearly called for, and after consultation with appropriate division and corporate officials, Al finally got one underway.

The results were not immediate, of course. But within two years, Al's

SOURCE: Stewart L. Tubbs and Robin N. Widgery, "When Productivity Lags, Check at the Top: Are Key Managers Really Communicating." Reprinted, by permission of the publisher, from *Management Review,* November, 1978, pp. 20–25. © 1978 by AMACOM, a division of American Management Associations. All rights reserved.

frustrations began to ease, and he was able to report dramatic gains in four principal problem areas:

Absenteeism began to slack off significantly.

Relations between Al and his management team improved greatly, and he saw tremendous improvements in the attitude and performance of his departmental managers.

Production efficiency recorded a 7 percent increase, enough to move the plant up to third place in company rankings (highest in the history of the plant).

Savings of some $7 million were recorded as a result of reduced production costs, and new machinery requirements totaled only a fraction of one percent of the big investment made only a few years earlier.

The Development Plan

Al started his development program by calling in a team of two communications consultants. Both the consultants and the plant manager spent several weeks investigating the general dimensions of the problems plaguing the management team. It was agreed that the strategy would be simple and direct, following the plan outlined in Figure 1.

Al's advisors avoided a pitfall common to many organizational improvement programs by establishing a steering committee representing all departments and levels that would be affected. This group's role was to help design procedures that were practical within its members' work environments.

The steering committee accepted several strategic assumptions that were to guide every phase of the improvement activity:

Plant ownership of the project must be ensured. The committee spent much time briefing every level of supervision on every work shift. It was agreed that there should be a consensus

Figure 1   Development Plan

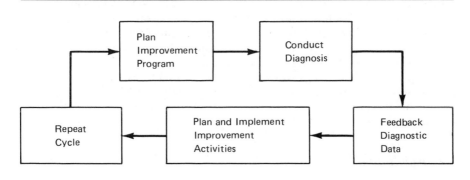

for the program, and a go/no-go philosophy was followed at each level of management. If the supervisors in any department or shift decided not to participate, they were free to bow out. None did.

Efforts to bring about organizational improvements should start at the top of the organization and move progressively to lower levels of management. Although this strategy is not subscribed to universally, the committee believed that for long-lasting improvements in human interaction, improved managerial behavior had to be taught by example down the organization.

Feedback of organizational and managerial performance data is an effective method for helping to bring about improvements in leadership behavior and human interaction in general. It was the consensus of the management team that the consultants should examine the "health" of several variables that determine organization effectiveness. Questionnaires and in-depth interviews were administered to everyone in the management group.

Organizational improvements are more likely to occur if plant personnel participate in developing their own solutions. It was assumed that those closest to the problem would be most likely to identify the causes correctly and to design effective solutions. Moreover, those who participated in the design of corrective plans would feel a heightened sense of commitment and a greater feeling of ownership.

The consultant team can best be relied upon to assist with the technology of diagnosing organizational problems, assessing changes in the system, and making sound recommendations. The committee hoped to avoid any appearance that the program was either the consultants' "baby" or just a strategy by the plant manager to make himself look good in the eyes of corporate management.

Conduct Diagnosis

Two hundred and forty managers at top and middle levels were surveyed, using a questionnaire developed at the Institute for Social Research at the University of Michigan and modified by the consultants. The survey measured several social elements within the organization, that is, supervisory and peer leadership, communication, coordination, motivation, problem solving, decision making, and satisfaction.

The profiles of the organization are shown in Figures 2 and 3. Note that these figures indicate conditions at the times of both the first and second measurements. The improvements occurring by the time of the second measurement were significant.

Feedback Diagnostic Data

Results of the survey were systematically fed to each level of supervision. These feedback presentations included: (1) an explanation of

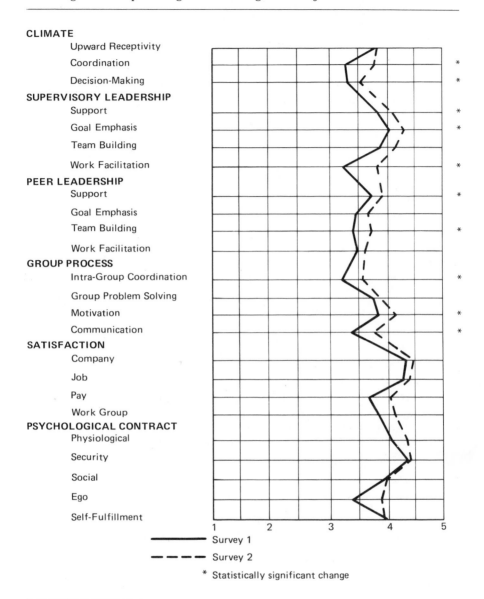

Figure 2   Top Management: A Diagnostic Profile

CLIMATE
Upward Receptivity
Coordination
Decision-Making

SUPERVISORY LEADERSHIP
Support
Goal Emphasis
Team Building
Work Facilitation

PEER LEADERSHIP
Support
Goal Emphasis
Team Building
Work Facilitation

GROUP PROCESS
Intra-Group Coordination
Group Problem Solving
Motivation
Communication

SATISFACTION
Company
Job
Pay
Work Group

PSYCHOLOGICAL CONTRACT
Physiological
Security
Social
Ego
Self-Fulfillment

——— Survey 1

– – – – Survey 2

* Statistically significant change

diagnostic profiles; (2) and identification of problem elements by level, department, and shift; (3) in-depth discussions of what might have caused the various problems; and (4) group discussions of what might be done to solve these problems.

After the feedback of the diagnostic data, the plant manager and his staff requested that the consultants conduct in-depth interviews with supervisors in order to get more specific information and suggestions about the most severe problems.

Figure 3 Middle Management: A Diagnostic Profile

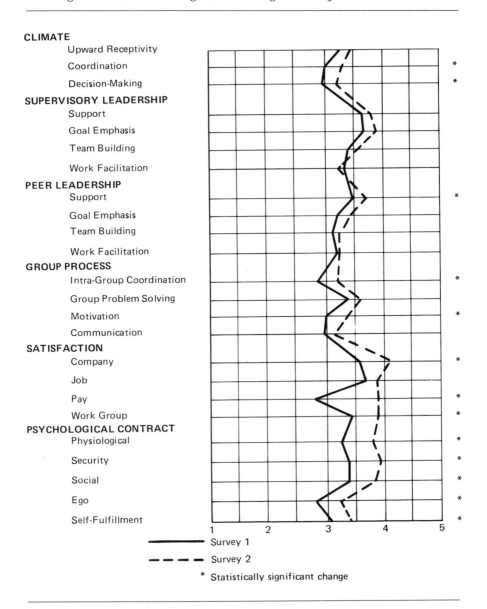

The interview data were summarized in a brief report that included a list of recommendations based on the interviews and the perspectives of the consultants. This report was presented to the plant manager and all department heads. Besides providing anonymous comments from the interviewees, it included recommendations designed to improve the human climate of the plant.

Plan and Implement Improvement Activity

After the interview report, the plant manager and all department heads held a series of offsite action-planning conferences. These were used to improve communication between the plant manager and his immediate staff and to plan further communication improvements. Problems identified in the survey and interviews were discussed in great depth, with an emphasis on constructive ideas for improving the effectiveness of the entire management team.

It was decided that each department would hold regular weekly meetings for the purpose of improving coordination and communication among the various functions. Not only were task problems discussed at these meetings, but the agenda was structured to provide opportunities for the discussion of relationship problems. To stimulate the latter discussions, generally only supervisors and their immediate subordinates met.

Moreover, these meetings allowed the plant manager to communicate directly corporate and divisional information pertinent to employee needs. (During interviews at the time of the repeat diagnosis, most supervisors agreed that these regular meetings had been highly useful in improving their departments' human climate and efficiency.)

Repeat Cycle

The second diagnosis was made 19 months after the first in order to measure the kind and degree of improvements. A second round of interviews was also conducted to probe the perceived causes for the changes further. The improvements were significant from both statistical and financial points of view.

This project, along with hundreds of others, indicates that even effective organizations can improve their performance by using their human resources better. Basically, the program described above improved the quality and quantity of organizational communication. By doing so, it greatly improved coordination of effort. Moreover, improved employee satisfaction and motivation were translated into improved efficiency and profitability.

Not all organizational change programs have such positive results. Let's take a look at some of the features we think can help make the difference between success and failure.

Learning through Feedback

Anyone who has ever had a lesson with a golf or tennis pro knows that old habits are comfortable, but not always the most effective. Through the use of survey feedback, we were able to help top and middle managers see the anonymous reactions and ratings of their subordinates. These quantitative survey data and qualitative interview comments were two very informative types of feedback that motivated the managers to improve. For example, one interviewed employee complained that,

"Apparently, I never do anything right around here. The only time I ever hear from my boss is when I screw up." When the boss heard this, he realized that it was probably true for a lot of his subordinates.

Without this type of feedback from subordinates, we all have a tendency to feel that the jobs we are doing are good enough and perhaps don't need improvement. But with feedback, we are better able to learn which of our management behaviors consistently succeed with the majority of our subordinates and which indicate room for improvement.

Improving Management Style

The primary focus of the program was to improve management style. Many writers have devoted space to this concept. Rensis Likert summarizes it well with his idea of Systems 4 management style, which has four behavioral elements: (1) supportive relationships, (2) strong emphasis on goals, (3) the building of team effort, and (4) helping to facilitate the work of subordinates. In the initial diagnosis of the management team, the consultants found that although supervisors generally rated their superiors slightly higher than the national average for "work facilitation," superiors scored far below average for "support," "goal emphasis," and "team building."

Through offsite conferences and many consultation meetings, the consultants continually stressed the importance of these four management behaviors. They also coached the managers in interpersonal communication skills and in conducting group meetings.

Although they did not believe that there is necessarily one best style of management for all situations, they did believe that the four principles of Systems 4 management are valuable in *many* widely varying situations. Also, the efforts they made to establish top management support played a critical part in making this program work. Organizational improvement programs that do not have the support of top management are likely to show less dramatic improvement.

Managers who would like to bring about results like those described in this article can do so by supporting their consulting team, as Al Stone did. His open-minded support and his willingness to admit shortcomings and to try new behaviors served as a model for those below him. His whole-hearted commitment was one of the key ingredients to the program's success.

Managers who would help their organizations achieve higher levels of management efficiency would do well to observe a few important improvement guidelines:

Teach sound management behaviors down the organization by example.
Be open to your own need for improvement—do not ignore your own growth.
Establish benchmarks and quantify progress for every important management behavior.

Ensure that every level of management is a full partner in the creation of those ideas necessary for organizational improvement.

Establish the improvement effort as an ongoing process rather than as a one-shot program.

Most important to the success of any organizational improvement effort is the support of the person at the top—not in word, but in deed.

21

The Science of Telling
Executives How They're Doing

Herbert E. Meyer

*I*t is a universally acknowledged truth that uncertainty is bad for business. It is not so often observed that uncertainty is also bad for businessmen—bad for their health, their peace of mind, even bad for their performance as executives. And of all the uncertainties that have kept executives from sleeping peacefully at night, probably none are quite so unsettling as those related to the difficulty of figuring out their boss's real opinion of them.

It is partly—but only partly—to relieve executives of such anxieties that American business has developed a remarkable institution called "performance evaluation." Formal, regularized evaluation programs are now more or less omnipresent in large U.S. corporations. Not all corporations do it in precisely the same way, but the exercise ordinarily includes a face-to-face meeting, held at least once a year, at which each executive gets a fairly explicit judgment of his performance from his immediate superior.

Typically, this verdict has been approved at least two levels above the man or woman being judged—i.e., the executive doing the judging clears it with his own superiors. The evaluations are ordinarily recorded on special forms, which then become part of the executive's permanent employment record. At most companies, these systems are used to judge the performance of virtually all executives, from the lowest-ranking recruit up to and often including the chairman of the board (whose performance is evaluated by the directors).

SOURCE: Herbert E. Meyer, "The Science of Telling Executives How They're Doing," *Fortune,* January 1974, pp. 102–12. Reprinted with permission.

Good Marks for the Losers

While just about all corporations have adopted performance-evaluation systems, their effectiveness is still a matter of dispute. It is not always clear that the judgment delivered to executives reflects the true sentiments of their superiors. At Xerox Corp. there is a rule that no one who has been with the company for more than eight years may be fired without the approval of Chairman C. Peter McColough. In almost every instance, says McColough ruefully, he discovers that the candidate for firing has for years been rated highly in the company's evaluations.

All of which suggests that for an evaluation to be useful and meaningful it must be delivered by someone who's capable of imparting some painful truths. The worst mistake an evaluator can make is to let some executive who's barely making it leave the session harboring delusions about great prospects in his future.

At the same time, the evaluator has to be careful not to make the event too painful: he doesn't, presumably, want to crush the executive being judged under an avalanche of devastating criticisms. Finally, it is important that the judgments being delivered really do concern performance—and do not reflect the personal preferences and prejudices of the evaluator.

Getting a Line on the Judges

Performance evaluation is, then, something of an executive art and science in itself. Indeed, one important benefit of the system is that it helps top management to make some further judgments about the executives who judge others.

American business got into performance evaluation for several reasons. One reason, plainly, had to do with salaries: by providing the corporation with a structured, detailed record of each executive's performance during the preceding year, the evaluations made it possible to put salary administration on a rational basis. (See "A Computer May Be Deciding What You Get Paid," *Fortune,* November, 1973.)

In addition, the evaluation systems are used to help identify the executives who have some real potential for moving into the higher-ranking jobs in their companies. Supervising executives often include in their evaluation reports an outline of the preparation and experience a lower-level executive requires for his next promotion. For example, a supervisor might recommend that bright executives whose experience is limited to the U.S. market be given some exposure to international operations. Or he might recommend that a production man tapped for higher things be shifted for a while into sales.

In short, performance evaluation is being linked increasingly to companies' long-range planning efforts. And quite a few chief executives these days find the time to read hundreds, even thousands, of evaluation reports in an effort to see what's going on down there among the troops. The man at the top can get a sense from the reports of where the talent is, and where it isn't, and which parts of the company are likely to need the most executive-development help in the years ahead.

The system can also be rather helpful to the executives being evaluated. For one thing, the meetings with a supervisor can provide an occasion on which it is natural and possible for an executive to get on the record some views of his own about his job and about the possibility of handling it differently. At some companies—Texas Instruments, for example—this opportunity to get an executive's own views about his situation is considered to be as important a part of performance evaluation as the delivery of the superior's judgment.

Amazing Honesty at Citibank

At the First National City Bank one supervising executive has gone about as far as it is possible to go in giving his subordinates a chance to express themselves in performance evaluation. E. Newton Cutler Jr., a Citibank senior vice president, simply hands his subordinates their own blank evaluation forms and tells them to fill in their ratings themselves. "It's amazing how honest people are," Cutler marvels. "They put things in that are detrimental to their own progress and promotion." The procedure, which represents Cutler's own variation on the bank's evaluation system, has a built-in safeguard against things getting out of hand: Cutler himself makes a final review of the ratings.

Performance-evaluation systems also tend to protect an executive from being held back or treated unfairly. Virtually every system requires that supervisors justify their conclusions, both to their own supervisors and to the executive being evaluated; hence the chances of discrimination based on race, sex, taste in clothing, or plain old-fashioned personality conflicts are minimized.

And, of course, evaluations do a great deal to end the awful uncertainty that comes from not knowing what the boss thinks. Dr. Abraham Zaleznik, a psychoanalyst and a professor of social psychology and management at the Harvard Business School, is among those who believe that this uncertainty really is bad for businessmen. "It's important to know that your own image of yourself, and of your performance, squares with your boss's image," Zaleznik says. "Disparities between the two can lead to personal stress and do real physical damage."

It Started with Loyola

Formal performance-evaluation systems are not at all unique to American business. In fact, a system remarkably similar to many being used today was developed by Saint Ignatius of Loyola some time after he founded the Society of Jesus in the sixteenth century. Saint Ignatius used a combination reporting-and-rating system that was intended to provide a comprehensive portrait of each Jesuit's activities and potential. The system consisted of a self-rating received from each member of the order, reports by each supervisor on his subordinates' performance, and special reports sent directly to the society's Father-General from any Jesuit who believed he had information relating to his or his colleagues' performance that the Father-General might not otherwise receive.

In the U.S., however, the performance-evaluation systems being used by business have been influenced mainly by some systems first developed in the federal government. In 1842 the Congress passed a law requiring the heads of executive departments to make an annual report "stating among other things whether each clerk had been usefully employed and whether the removal of some to permit the appointment of others would lead to a better dispatch of the public business."

When James Polk became President in 1845, he ordered that these annual reports be sent directly to him. During the following decades a multitude of evaluation systems were tried and then abandoned—one system developed in 1879 by Carl Schurz, for the Pension Office, attempted to measure employees' performance simply by counting the errors they made in a year.

Some Obeyed More than Others

But as the century entered its final decade, it was the military that had developed the most precise, workable performance-rating system. In 1889, President Benjamin Harrison, impressed by what the War Department had accomplished, suggested that civilian agencies adopt similar techniques. His suggestion was generally ignored, and so Harrison issued an executive order *requiring* agencies to adopt the military system. The order was obeyed in some agencies more than others, and the inability of any President to establish a comprehensive, standard system of performance appraisals for the executive branch has continued right down to the present.

In part, the Presidents' difficulties reflect a powerful reluctance by members of Congress to let any chief executive have too much power over the presumably nonpartisan civil service. At the moment, the government's most recent task force on performance evaluation is hard at work in Washington, evaluating the performance of its scores of predecessors and preparing some recommendations on how agency heads might improve their evaluation systems.

American business has proceeded with greater dispatch. Exactly which corporation was the first to develop a formal evaluation system for executives, or when, is unknown. General Motors Corp. had a formal evaluation system for its executives as early as 1918, but G.M. doesn't know if it was first. The real trend toward formal, regularized, written systems didn't begin in earnest until after World War II.

The procedures vary quite a bit from one company to another. Sometimes the evaluator doesn't put anything on paper until after the judgment has been delivered—the written record becomes, in effect, a report on the meeting with the executive being judged. At White Motor Corp., on the other hand, the supervising executive calls in his subordinate only after completing the rating form and then clearing his conclusions with his own superior. Thus when an executive is invited in for a friendly chat, the verdict on his performance has already become a matter of record.

The form presented to the White Motor executive being evaluated includes, in addition to the traditional photograph and biographical data, a series of questions the supervisor has answered regarding the executive's major strengths and weaknesses. Also, the supervisor has placed a check next to one of the following phrases: outstanding, satisfactory plus, satisfactory, marginal, or "unsatisfactory—must be replaced." At White Motor, supervisors are required to state how soon their subordinates will be ready for promotion, and to outline to each subordinate what steps should be taken to prepare for future jobs with the company.

He Should Want to Improve

After being presented with the company's opinion of him, the executive is asked literally to sign on the dotted line. (His signature signifies awareness, not necessarily agreement.) The interview concludes with a discussion of the executive's performance; according to the White Motor Corp. supervisors' manual, he should leave the session "with a sincere desire to improve."

If an executive feels that he has been treated unfairly—more precisely, if he thinks he should be rated higher—he is encouraged to protest during the course of the interview itself. According to H. Herbert Phillips, the company's vice president for personnel and industrial relations, most differences of opinion are resolved right then. But if the executive is still not satisfied, he is entitled to appeal his rating directly to the company's personnel department. Someone will be assigned to hear both sides, then either back up the supervisor or suggest to him that the subordinate might actually have a point, and that his rating be reconsidered. "If it's the sort of personality conflict that just can't be resolved," Phillips says, "we usually wind up suggesting that the subordinate transfer to another department."

The questions dealt with on Sperry Rand Corp.'s performance-evaluation forms deal mainly with "promotability." Once a year, at evaluation time, the company's managing executives (about 1,000 in all) fill out "replacement charts," in which each supervisor lists the two or three subordinates he considers most qualified to replace him. Then, when the evaluations take place, the supervisor is supposed to be clear about any steps that must be taken to prepare these executives for their eventual promotions. The supervisor himself is rated on how well he plans the promotions.

At the heart of Sperry Rand's evaluation system is the so-called AROT column, in which four kinds of data are listed: the A refers simply to the executive's age; the R represents a performance rating (on a scale from 60 to 100); O is organizational data, e.g., the supervisor states whether the subordinate should be kept within his division or might work elsewhere in the corporation; and T stands for the time required to prepare the executive for his next promotion.

John Grela, Sperry Rand's vice president for organization and development, says the emphasis on promotions makes it easier for a supervisor to point out flaws in an executive's performance when the two sit down for the annual interview. "I knew we couldn't get people to sit down and say, 'You are bad here,' but a supervisor can deliver criticisms more easily when he's recommending a plan for future promotions." Grela says proudly, "It works."

The completed forms are shown to the executive being evaluated after they've been cleared with the supervisor's own superior. At Sperry Rand each executive's performance-evaluation forms are reviewed at least once a year by a committee consisting of the company's chairman, its president, and Grela. They meet with the supervisors to discuss the executives they've rated, and in effect rate the supervisors on how well they're doing in preparing subordinates for promotions. "We feel that part of a manager's salary is based on how well he develops people," Grela says. "If he isn't doing that, he hasn't earned that portion of his salary."

The Peers Vote at TRW

At TRW Inc., performance evaluations involve not only an executive's supervisors, but his peers as well. Before the judgments about an executive are made, his supervisor solicits the opinion of the men and women who work alongside him. "It's a regular part of our procedure," explains Stanley C. Pace, a TRW executive vice president, "but we do it informally. What happens is that at some time during the year—usually not just before the evaluations are written—I make it a point to chat with each subordinate's colleagues to see what they think about his performance. Everyone here knows that this is done, and the purpose of it is to encourage teamwork. We don't want anyone around here to think he can get away with being nasty or unhelpful to everyone except his boss."

Pace believes that checking informally around the office from time to time is the sort of thing that should be done by any good manager, regardless of whether a formal, annual evaluation interview is held with each executive. "One benefit of having these annual interviews," Pace adds, "is that they force me to get off my duff and talk to people."

Rating by the Numbers

At Worthington Corp., a subsidiary of Studebaker-Worthington, Inc., the man personally in charge of performance evaluation is Chairman Edward C. Forbes. His system is about as precise and quantitative as any in existence; it actually measures an executive's performance out to the second decimal place.

Once a year, every top-echelon Worthington executive drafts a list of his objectives for the coming twelve months, then sends the list directly to Forbes. He and the executive decide how important each objective is to the company and assign numerical priorities to them, ranging from three for the highest down to one for the lowest. At the end of the year, Forbes sits down again with the list (and with the executive), decides how well the executive did on each of his various objectives, and rates the man's success in achieving each objective on a scale of one to fifteen.

Each of these scores is then multiplied by the priority previously attached to it. The resulting numbers are added together and, finally, divided by the total number of weighted objectives for the executive's numerical rating. (When events beyond the control of any executive—such as a natural disaster in a particular marketing area—render an objective meaningless during the course of the year, Forbes simply eliminates that objective from the equation.)

The number that emerges from all this arithmetic is then worked hard by salary-administration officials at Worthington. It is combined with a variety of other numbers, reflecting, for example, the division's profit, the executive's current salary grade, his position within that grade, and his age, in order to determine the future salary.

In gauging an executive's promotability, Forbes relies on a curiously (for him) unmathematical evaluation system. He calls it RUST—an R means the executive must retire within a year, U means his performance has been unsatisfactory, S stands for satisfactory, and T, which is in there for reasons more euphonic than logical, signifies a potential for promotion. The same system Forbes uses to rate his top-echelon executives is also used, by them, to rate their own subordinates. The evaluations they perform may then be reviewed by Forbes—whose judgment on all executives at Worthington is the final one.

A Shortage of Bastards

Ultimately, of course, all those quantified results in performance-evaluation systems come back to somebody's personal judgment. The point of forcing evaluators to be quantitative is to ensure that the judgment is as objective as it can possibly be. White Motor Corp.'s Herbert Phillips, for example, considers it among his primary responsibilities as chief of personnel to ensure that each supervising executive focus attention on his subordinates' results—and not on their personalities.

There is no doubt that the main problem about objectivity is the powerful desire of most executives to be nice guys. To hear personnel men complain about it, there's an acute shortage of real bastards in American business. "Everybody likes to be a nice guy and hand out outstanding-performance ratings," says George Foote, a director of McKinsey & Co. "It's very difficult to get enough supervisors to be hard enough to make the system really work."

Some supervisors have managed to avoid hurting their subordinate's feelings, while still conveying some sense of the sad realities to top management, by using a king of Aesopian language. Over the years a sort of code has developed that tips off personnel directors and company chairmen to the supervisor's real opinion. For example, a supervisor writing about "a diligent, reliable worker" may well be sending up a signal that the executive in question is totally devoid of imagination. An executive credited with "a cheerful attitude toward work," who is said to "get along well with fellow employees," may just be an amiable fellow who hasn't produced a tangible result all year.

The Problem of Halos

Any distortions in executives' evaluation records can be perpetuated by a phenomenon called the "halo effect." What happens is that an executive, once rated as outstanding, tends to keep on receiving that rating regardless of how badly his performance may have slipped. It takes some courage for an evaluator to dissent from the judgments of his predecessors (whose past evaluations are always available to him). The phenomenon can, of course, also work to perpetuate a poor rating by executives who have been working hard to do a better job.

It is partly to counter the halo effect that Western Electric Co. has begun insisting that supervisors award outstanding ratings to no more than 20 percent of their subordinates. Norman Lucas, Western Electric's evaluation chief, says that the company's system forces an annual weeding out that makes it difficult for a once outstanding performer to coast along on the strength of earlier ratings.

Lowering the Temperature

The powerful link between performance evaluation and salary administration—in other words, money—can also work to prevent evaluation systems from functioning the way they're supposed to. It is, admittedly, hard to be objective when money is involved, and both the supervisor and the executive he's evaluating are apt to share the blame for the distorted results. The subordinate executive knows that the rating he receives is the major determinant of whether he receives a raise, and of how large that raise will be. Not surprisingly, it is often money, rather than any concern about "areas of weakness and potential," that is uppermost in an executive's mind as he heads in for that annual interview.

Once shown his rating, furthermore, an executive is often more interested in finishing the interview, so that he can get busy computing his raise, or celebrating it, than in paying attention to any message his supervisor is trying to deliver. And an executive whose rating denies him a raise will likely be too blinded by disappointment or resentment to listen, just then, to any friendly criticism of his work.

The connection between money and performance evaluation tends to distort the system in another way. The problem is that many evaluators, aware of the connection, have evolved a game called "playing the system." What they do is work backwards—that is, they decide first how large a raise they want to give an executive, then give him whatever rating will draw that raise from the company's salary-administration tables. Thus a supervisor who wants to give a raise (because, for example, the executive's wife has just had twins) may be led to distort the evaluation system so that the results seem to justify his a priori decision.

One obvious way to minimize system-playing is to separate the evaluation interview from decisions about salary. At International Paper Co., for example, it is now very difficult to get a raise simply on the basis of a supervisor's report. Instead, raises are linked to results. Each supervisor sits down with every employee for whom he is responsible and gets an agreement on objectives for the coming quarter and the long term—e.g., with respect to the man's sales. The two then sit down again at the end of the quarter and measure the extent to which the objectives they had agreed on were attained. Says William J. Connolly, who directs I.P.'s performance-evaluation programs, "When the annual salary review comes up, the decision doesn't come as a shock to the employee. He knows right along how he's been doing."

One difficulty with performance-evaluation systems stems directly from their success. That is, by creating a format in which it is natural to tell subordinates exactly what the company thinks of them, companies have given their supervisors an excuse for not delivering the message at other times. Supervising executives sometimes have a tendency to conceal their opinions for 364 days, and then to announce them in one huge dose. McKinsey's George Foote emphasizes that the annual interview is meant to complement, not replace, daily criticism and praise.

"Performance evaluation is actually less time-consuming when it's done daily," Foote says. "If you put the whole job off to the end, it takes more time to explain what's on your mind. The comment should be made when the event occurs. To save it until the end of the year is not only meaningless, it's divisive."

The New Environment at Chase

The need for formal performance-evaluation systems seems to be just about universally accepted in American business today. There is, however, some continuing controversy about the emphasis on forms and ratings. Some executives contend that the procedures have become bureaucratized to a point at which they actually represent an obstacle to useful communication between executives and their bosses. Many students of the subject, and many executives, seem to agree with William R. Hinchman Jr., a senior vice president of the Chase Manhattan Bank and the man in charge of its evaluation program. "Frankly," says Hinchman, "I'm not nearly so impressed with our actual reporting procedures as I am by the environment our performance-evaluaton system has given us. There's a more open and candid interaction among people here than we've had before, and this is where it counts. Not the forms."

That a system exists at all at Chase is a reflection of the bank's swift growth during the past decade, a period during which the number of executives soared, from around 1,000 in 1963 to 2,700 now. Hinchman concedes that it's too early to tell how successful the bank's present performance-evaluation system will be. But whatever happens, it probably can't be worse than the non-system the bank used to have.

A Dinner Jacket in the Drawer

This non-system, which disappeared some four decades ago, consisted pretty much of one Chase official with a little book in his bottom drawer. Once a year he'd pull it out and decide on all the raises in the company. Only when he received his raise and promotion could a Chase executive count on knowing what his bosses thought of him.

And, for all the tensions associated with performance evaluations nowadays, they're a breeze compared to the rather stunning method by which Chase used to tell some executives that they were being promoted. The executives got the news of their promotions on a day at the end of which they were invited to the bank's annual officers' dinner, a black-tie event. Anyone who thought he might get a promotion brought a dinner jacket to work, then hid it in a closet or desk drawer and hoped for the best. Those who were promoted donned their dinner suits and proceeded triumphantly to the gala. Those who weren't promoted stuffed their tuxedos into bags or attaché cases and smuggled them, and themselves, out the door as unobtrusively as possible.

22

The Tightening Squeeze on White-Collar Pay

*T*he merit pay system, which U.S. industry has used for decades to motivate and reward its managers and professionals, is in trouble. Pounded by inflation and rising into ever higher tax brackets, the upwardly mobile white-collar worker, from first-line supervisor to executive, is finding that the substantial "merit" raises he has won over the past five years often add up to one big zero.

A vast stratum of middle management, in fact, is beginning to see itself not only as one of the victims of society's shrinking expectations, but as the primary victim. "There is a great deal of sensitivity in this area now," says David Weeks, compensation director of the Conference Board, "because managers feel they are changing their relative position in society."

Some corporate pay administrators agree. "The slope of the wage curve is continuing to flatten in this country as in most of the world," says a personnel director at one of the largest U.S. corporations. "This means managers' salaries have less spread over other workers."

Business Week calculations, based on actual tax returns as compiled by the Joint Committee on Taxation, show what happens to taxpayers in the middle-management levels as they rise into a higher tax bracket with an 8% raise, the average merit increase these days. Even at a base of $15,000, the increase after additional taxes and 6.5% inflation (which is projected for this year) really amounts to only $202. At $75,000, the real increase is only $5, and in some salary ranges the net change is actually a loss.

The phenomenon of "compression" is at work both at the bottom and the top, squeezing the middle. It occurs at the low end when people newly hired are paid more than one-year and two-year employees or when hourly workers make more than their supervisors. Machine operators in one pulp mill now earn more than $30,000 a year with overtime. Supervisors at the mill have, in turn, been given a 10% differential. The trouble is, such differentials cannot be pushed on up through the organization.

"The company that doesn't recognize compression as a problem is naive," says Mel Shulman, vice-president of administration at Fibreboard Corp. "Every company has the problem."

Compression from the top occurs when corporate officers, increasingly under attack for their well-publicized high salaries, push more and more of their compensation into bonuses, options, perquisites, and other incentives often not available to managers down the line. Thus their salaries—not a true measure of their total compensation—keep a lid on the salaries below. The *Business Week* survey of top executive compensation, gleaned from proxy statements, showed that executives' salaries and bonuses combined soared 27.2% in 1976, driven up by 67.1% increases in bonuses. Dorothy Byrne, surveys manager at Hay Associates, a management consulting firm, says bonuses in the senior management group (which can include about 10 executives in a large company) averaged about 41% of base salaries. Other noncash items can add the equivalent of 50% to 100% of base salary, she adds.

If discontent is breaking out in the middle ranks, it is as much the companies' problem as that of their employees. White-collar workers have traditionally been rewarded—and motivated—under a merit system, flawed though it might be. But now companies find themselves in the uncomfortable position of trying, within the limits of burgeoning budgets for salaries and benefits, to balance rewards for those who perform, and particularly for those who directly influence profits, against just keeping everyone else whole. Nor can the problem be viewed any longer as temporary. Despite periodic assurances that inflation soon will be coming under control, prices have risen an average of 7.5% annually for the past five years, and the likelihood is that 1977 will not be much different. Couple that with higher taxes and it is plain that most white-collar workers cannot expect to be kept whole, much less get ahead.

A company's problem is particularly acute as it concerns white-collar professionals and managers, because rewarding performance is becoming increasingly difficult. Companies are experimenting with dozens of new pay plans, incentives, benefits, and appraisal systems designed to attract and hold the personnel they want, but the problems persist. "The systems are fouled up, they haven't kept pace," says David J. McLaughlin, a compensation specialist at McKinsey & Co. "The net of it is that very few companies can afford to grant increases radically different from what they're granting now, whatever system they use."

Says Marvin Schiller, vice-president of the consulting firm of A. T. Kearney Inc.: "The pressures for substantial adjustment are more than some companies can handle. There's the domino factor. Increase compensation on one level and you have to do it all the way up." Indeed, most companies interviewed by *Business Week* indicate they will try to hold salary increases in 1978 to this year's levels, unless inflation heats up even more than expected.

Testing New Incentives

But companies are involved in all kinds of new efforts to make those salary dollars count. "More companies are giving more merit raises now," says Robert W. Race, vice-president at Robert H. Hayes & Associates, Chicago. "They want to move key employees ahead more rapidly, maybe even with reviews every three months. And they're not hiring at the minimum range of their salary program, either, which could create long-term problems."

"Younger people expect more frequent reviews," says Morley P. Thompson, president of Cincinnati-based D. H. Baldwin Co., who acknowledges that Baldwin has been forced to upgrade its white-collar compensation program. "We had gotten pretty sloppy. We had to wake up." Thompson says Baldwin realized it had a problem not because people were leaving but because of employee comments. Its response has been to increase the frequency of salary reviews (high-potential managers are now reviewed twice a year) and to expand significantly the number receiving incentive compensation.

"White-collar employees are more ready to complain about salary than in the past," says Gerald H. Hoag, a vice-president at Robert H. Hayes. "That used not to be the thing to do, but salaries are more known than they used to be. Many companies are feeling the pressure to change, but some are trying to resist that pressure."

But more and more companies are experimenting with new incentives. Pitney-Bowes Inc. will begin a six-month trial program of granting overtime pay to exempt employees all the way up to senior executives. "You can be making $35,000 a year and still be eligible for overtime," says Raymond F. Sasso, manager of corporate compensation. There are restrictions: The extra pay will be only for mandated overtime beyond 45 hours a week on four consecutive weeks, but it will apply to professionals, such as engineers, and to managers as well.

Other companies are offering new incentives tied at least to the company's performance, if not the individual's. Last month, for example, Citicorp introduced a new concept into its staff incentive plans that allows employees to choose "book-value stock" rather than common stock, making them less vulnerable to the whims of the stock market. The new plan enables employees to participate in the bank's growth if the book value grows, even though the price of the common stock may play dead. Citicorp book-value stock over the past 10 years would have returned 13.4% a year, had it been available, says Lawrence Small, senior vice-president at Citibank. And Wang Laboratories Inc. last year introduced a stock option plan for all employees. Each six months they are granted options equal to 3% of their earnings for that period. The options are completely vested after five years and can be exercised at age 60.

Indeed, most companies are attempting to overhaul or at least fine-tune their pay programs. To motivate employees, companies are trying as

Adjusted Gross Income		After Tax Income		Effective Federal Tax Rate[a] 1977	After tax Income Adjusted for 6.5% Inflation 1977	Net Change After Taxes and Inflation 1976–77
1976	1977	1976	1977			
$15,000	$16,200	$13,339	$14,421	10.98%	$13,541	$+202
20,000	21,600	17,454	18,759	13.15	17,614	+160
25,000	27,000	21,335	22,833	15.43	21,439	+104
30,000	32,400	24,990	26,744	17.46	25,112	+122
35,000	37,800	28,636	30,531	19.23	28,668	+ 32
40,000	43,200	32,237	34,252	20.71	32,162	− 75
45,000	48,600	35,850	37,743	22.34	35,439	−411
50,000	54,000	38,880	41,022	24.03	38,518	−362
55,000	59,400	41,981	44,813	24.56	42,078	+ 97
60,000	64,800	45,112	46,973	27.51	44,106	−1,006
65,000	70,200	47,382	50,738	27.72	47,641	+259
70,000	75,600	50,579	54,169	28.35	50,863	+284
75,000	81,000	53,731	57,229	29.35	53,736	+ 5

[a] Average derived from actual returns
Data: Effective tax rates supplied by Joint Committee on Taxation; *Business Week* adjustments.

never before to make distinctions as to who should be rewarded and who should not. This involves wider variations in the amount of increases as well as in their timing. Making such distinctions requires better appraisal systems than most companies now have. "Performance evaluation is a lot more subjective than many companies would like to think," says Kearney's Schiller. "It requires hard decisions on the part of managers. It's easier to follow a formula." The increasing willingness of companies to provide employees with information about salaries and pay ranges poses problems, too. "For some, that can be an incentive. For others, it will be a frustration," says Schiller.

Robert D. Gray is director of the California Institute of Technology's Industrial Relations Center, which conducts discussion programs on compensation for managers at more than 50 member companies, including Bank of America, Atlantic Richfield, Kaiser Industries, and Safeway. "Even at companies that have had good, sound merit systems for 30 years, there is more interest than ever in measuring and rewarding performance," he says. Gray says salary ranges are broadening, and increases are more frequent because "for maximum motivation, rewards should follow closely upon performance." And he says that more employees have salaries above the mid-point of their range, and job posting and job bidding is on the rise. Some of the center's member companies now post job openings with salaries up to $60,000.

Some companies may have been complacent about compensation problems because, by and large, managers have not been hard to come by in recent years. The most recent compensation surveys, which massage the figures on competitors' pay into ever more precise numbers, indicate that it is not a tight market. Still, there are enough complaints

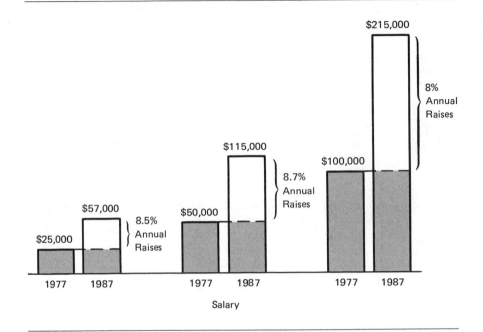

Salary

coming to the surface, enough compression problems arising, sufficient turndowns of promotion and defections of superior managers to make senior executives anxious. "Inflation creates such a pressure to keep people whole," says Schiller, "that the additional amount to discriminate for performance is just not there. This is one of the main causes of discontent at the middle-management level."

Status at Stake

Complicating the issue is the perception among white-collar personnel—and middle managers in particular—that their traditional status is being eroded. A series of studies by the Bureau of Labor Statistics called *Employment Cost Index,* which was started in the last quarter of 1975, shows that between March, 1976, and March, 1977, straight-time hourly earnings (including production bonuses and cost-of-living allowances) for white-collar workers increased 6.2% while those of blue-collar workers rose 7.4%. Within the white-collar group, managers' and administrators' earnings were up 6.3%, less than clerical workers' 6.6%.

Most managers still are far better off than the average citizen, of course, but their take-home pay has been hard hit by increasing taxes, the result of chronic jumps into ever higher tax brackets. "When a family's money income increases just enough to offset inflation, its real income stays the same," explain Emil H. Sunley Jr. and Joseph A.

Pechman in the Brookings Institution's *Inflation and the Income Tax*. "But as its money income increases, the family is thrown into higher tax brackets. And the fixed-dollar deductions, exemptions, and credits eliminate a lesser fraction of income otherwise subject to tax. The result is that tax liabilities increase faster than inflation and take away an increasing percentage of the family's real income."

Over the past few years—and this year, too, in the tax law that passed this spring—Congress has adjusted total tax collections to compensate for inflation. But since 1969, it has not reduced rates. Instead, it has cut the total tax load by increasing the standard deduction, or by fattening individual exemptions. This means the benefits for the most part are greatest for those with low and lower-middle incomes—less than $25,000—and for those with incomes of more than $200,000.

Further contributing to the general flattening of the pay structure is the proliferation of company benefits, such as dental care, home and automobile group insurance, legal aid, and eye care. Benefits now run to about one-third of payroll cost and have been growing at a faster rate than salaries in many companies. Hercules Inc.'s compensation manager, Robert E. Herzog, points out that for every Hercules payroll dollar an additional 50¢ goes toward benefits costs, if the employer's contribution to Social Security is included. But Herzog does not see much further escalation of benefits. "We've already taken care of everything from their teeth to their feet," he says.

The biggest "flattener" is compression, and it is the one companies find most ticklish to deal with. It can happen when a new B-school graduate comes in making as much as the MBA with two years experience and a couple of raises under his belt. Or it can happen when hourly employees' salaries push against those of their supervisors, a problem that many companies fix by raising the supervisor's pay and offering him overtime. But adjustments above that level—except in the auto industry, where even cost-of-living allowances extend high into the management structure—tend to be progressively smaller.

This is why plant managers at one major oil company say they are finding it hard to make hourly workers accept promotion to supervisor since the company eliminated its set differential for supervisors. And it explains why a senior auditor at a large accounting firm is reluctant to lose his substantial overtime pay—which he planned to take next year as a two-month vacation—to take a promotion to a first-line management job. Only the firm's up-or-out policy is causing him to even consider accepting the promotion.

"One of the principal reasons for compression in our business," says David L. Bartlett, personnel director at Houston's Pullman Kellogg, a division of Pullman Inc., "is the supply-demand situation in college recruiting. We don't have much influence on the 'going rate' for each mechanical engineer in 1977, for instance." For the last three or four years, the company has had to pay about 6% to 7% more each year for entry-level engineers. "This means," says Bartlett, "we know we're going to have to look at our one-year people and determine their merit and cost-of-living increases, with enough extra to leapfrog the new people."

The problem often occurs in companies with some of the most advanced policies because they tend to be the ones with some of the brightest young managers jockeying for position. A young Citibank MBA, on board for two years, sums up the problem. "Salaries of incoming MBAs are a function of the market," he says. "But once here, your salary is a function of internal policy." In his two years with the bank he has had a 15% promotional raise and a 10% merit increase, but new hires are starting at salaries within a whisker of his own. "Some of those who came in with me are worse off than I am," he says. "We are at a point now where we are really contributing and taking on a great deal of responsibility. But we get the feeling we are expendable, that they feel we can be replaced by new MBAs. It's causing a lot of people to reevaluate their position in the organization. My own superior is complaining about his differential over me, because he started at an even lower level than I did. It goes throughout the organization."

The pressure that increases in hourly pay put on supervisors' salaries is what troubles manufacturing companies. "Our biggest problem has been in the first- and second-level of supervision at sites where there have been rather large union wage settlements," says Hercules' Herzog. "It's particularly difficult along the Gulf Coast [where plants represent such large investments that labor costs are a relatively small part of total costs]. They can afford to pay high wages. But this puts pressures on the lower exempt salaries." Herzog estimates compression from the wage rolls occurs at 30% to 40% of Hercules' plants.

The Compression Factor

Compression has always been a problem, but persistent inflation aggravates it. "At the supervisory level, it's probably getting a little worse each year," says Hay Associates' Byrne. "It's becoming more and more of a problem. Companies had been trying to do something about it. But now they're trying to do something about it with a straight-forward policy. If you push salaries up in the supervisory ranks, you have to push them up farther. But the farther you go, the ripple is less and less."

The squeeze can be most acute in such high labor-cost areas as the West Coast, Chicago, and Detroit. The reason: Hourly wages typically are based on the local market, while exempt salaries tend to be set nationally.

To treat the problem, most companies offer 10% to 30% differentials to first-line supervisors. Aluminum Co. of America, with 43,000 employees, has a constantly changing pay scale. James H. Davis, general manager of personnel services, believes this helps to elminate the problem of compression. The competition is surveyed every three months, and pay scales are adjusted accordingly. Furthermore, the company attempts to keep at least a 20% differential in pay between an employee and his supervisor. The system also ensures that last year's hire will be better paid than this year's, says Davis. One reason is Alcoa's system of short intervals between raises, so that a new hire probably will receive a raise within four months. Many managers at Alcoa now receive raises more often than every year.

The auto companies also take care of the problem, simply by pushing the big hourly increases won by the workers up the line in some form.

Besides merit pay, many exempt employees at Ford Motor Co. receive a cost-of-living increase under other guises. "The point to be made is that people in the auto industry are compensated substantially higher than their counterparts in other industries," says a Ford executive, noting that secretaries of upper-middle managers not uncommonly earn $18,000 a year, compared with a national mean of about $10,600 for executive secretaries.

But the theory of the merit system, even if it has not been the practice, is to reward those who perform—and that means making distinctions. Those distinctions must be made within the limits of "ranges," which in turn must be separated by a differential reflecting different levels of jobs. In a large company, which may have three times as many management levels today as it had 10 years ago, those spreads must be maintained despite compression at the bottom—and sometimes at the top.

In spite of the problems, many companies today are making big distinctions in the raises they give. Digital Equipment Corp.'s merit increases run from nothing to 30%, Westinghouse Electric Corp.'s from nothing to 19%, Xerox Corp.'s from nothing to 13%. The pay raise differential between "good" and "adequate" performers in one large corporation has doubled in the past five years to 30% from 15%. Timing is a factor, too. At Pullman Kellogg, the former annual raise is now given at intervals varying from 6 to 18 months, depending on performance.

"Merit" systems are rarely based exclusively on merit, of course. "Companies may call their programs merit pay, but if you survey them, you'll find they had merit budgets of 9% to 12% during high inflation but only 5% during noninflationary periods," says Fibreboard's Shulman. "Most companies recognize inflation in their merit budgets but won't own up to it."

The Merit System

Atlantic Richfield, which is regarded by compensation specialists as having a "real" merit system, demonstrates the problem. "Even in our system, the range is fairly short between the satisfactory and the excellent performer," acknowledges Blair A. Hyde, Arco's compensation manager. "Add to this the natural reluctance of managers to reward one employee substantially more than another, and you see that while we do not just give out sweeping across-the-board increases, neither do we have wide swings that might be expected in a true merit system. There is no easy solution." Arco's target this year: an average increase of 10%, up from 8% last year. The lowest increase is targeted at 4%, the top one at 15%.

In the effort to reward the deserving, companies are using a variety of tactics. Security Pacific National Bank has been using a "performance zone" system for the past five years. Progressively higher zones mean fatter and quicker raises. Last May the system was altered so that high performance was further rewarded. A Zone 5, or "outstanding," performer may now receive an increase in 8 months instead of 10, and he can expect it to be 12% to 15% instead of 10% to 12%.

"We don't have any commitment to keep people whole in times of inflation," says Citicorp's Small, although he admits that ranges rise enough to keep "average" performers whole. But the emphasis clearly is on rewarding winners. A Citibank manager theoretically can receive up to four merit increases a year, and some actually do receive three. "We believe in smaller, more frequent increases rather than large rewards with a long time in between," says Small.

Many companies are also driven to making more exceptions to their own compensation rules so as to reward the people they do not want to lose, at whatever level. The traditional bell curve distribution, which gave a few people no increase, most people an average increase, and a few people large, 10% to 12% increases, has been supplemented with another small curve representing star performers, who receive raises of as much as 25%, says McKinsey's McLaughlin. "Companies are willing to override the system to keep the better person," he says. "Some are even giving promotional increases to keep them."

Most compensation executives say that granting phony promotions is dangerous, but many admit the practice is increasing. "Promotion is one way to keep people whole," says a personnel director for one of the 10 largest U.S. companies. "It gives you an excuse to give more money and a title with more prestige. Managers say, 'What can I call this today that I didn't yesterday to justify more pay?' Every company tries to avoid this, but every company has this pressure, and sometimes the pressure breaks out."

The Conference Board's Weeks says other kinds of exceptions, such as an unofficial differential for employees working in New York City, are cropping up more often because line managers find they cannot operate any other way. "The personnel guy is screaming," says Weeks. "But the division vice-president is putting on all the pressure he can to get it done. And sometimes the salary people would rather live with the exceptions than build something into the system that could be an administrative nightmare."

Some exceptions are built right into the system. Pitney-Bowes has set up "solo categories" for situations "where we need to do something for the individual or for a family of jobs," says Sasso. "We'll pull them out of their category and put them in the solo category." The ploy is used rarely, but Sasso says the company would have lost some key employees without it.

Incentive awards are another form of exception being built into the system. Awards are sometimes granted to managers far down the line. "The trend toward more incentive programs has been going on for the last five years, but it really accelerated in the last two," says Security Pacific's Senior Vice-President Irving Margol. "Right now we're looking at any job that might possibly lend itself to incentive pay."

The one-time award also is coming into fashion. It has two advantages: It can be given for a specific contribution (and therefore is applicable to more than just those managers who have a direct influence on profits), and it does not make the extra pay permanent. "If someone has demonstrated some absolutely unusual kind of performance and we want to reward him," says Xerox's personnel vice-president, Robert D. Firth, "we can give him a special merit award. At one time that was baked into their base salary forever. We're changing that and leaning more in the last two years toward the lump-sum, one-time payout. It's usually 10% of the individual's salary."

The one-shot award is spreading through middle and lower management, especially in such industries as paper, chemicals, and packaged goods. "Its pluses are that it's discretionary, it doesn't bind you for the long term and it serves as a goal for those who did not receive it as well as for those who did," says Kearney's Schiller. Adds Weeks: "More companies are doing this than are talking about it. Some are experimenting with it within eligible groups, so the companies don't broadcast it."

The Award System

At Pitney-Bowes, in a year-old program, the lump-sum payment is even used to motivate and reward those who have reached the top of their range. "We won't increase the range," says Pitney-Bowes' Sasso, "but if someone displays exceptional performance, they will receive a payment equal to 15% of their annual earnings." Each division can give the extra pay to no more than 15% of its employees, though actual awards run to only about 8% of personnel. And the award must be earned all over again each year. "This recognizes that sometimes in a job that's worth $30,000, some one is performing it $40,000 worth," says Sasso.

But some companies are simply pushing the kind of incentive awards they have long given to senior executives down to managers at lower levels. International Harvester Co. has one goals-oriented plan tied to the company's financial performance, the group's performance, and, finally the individual's performance. That plan, reviewed by the board each year, applies to only 200 senior executives and grants awards that can range from 15% to 60% of pay. But another incentive program is carried down to 2,400 managers, including plant managers, administrators, marketing personnel, and engineers. The incentives range from 10% to 35% of salary, based on much the same criteria as is the program for top executives.

At Baldwin, President Thompson's incentive program has been expanded to include division, plant, and operating managers. "It used to be just our corporate officers," says Thompson. "Now more people feel like they are part of management."

Some companies have had to pull back on incentive programs after they extended them to managers who do not directly influence profits and then discovered that there was no realistic way to measure their contribution. One large Southern company, where the incentive program typically pays 20% to 25% of senior executives' compensation, already has reduced those eligible for the program by 20% and is trying to restrict it even further. Those being eliminated from the program are having their salaries raised to compensate.

Alcoa also has changed its options and incentive programs in a way that limits rather than expands them. Participants in the option plan, limited to about 5% of the white-collar force, are a more homogeneous group than before—a "profit impact group," says Alcoa's Davis. And an incentive plan, which goes to about 12% of the white-collar force, also has been restructured. "It has been limited to protect people at a lower level from some of the risk of variability of the stock market and the business, allowing people at higher levels to accept more of the risks and more of the benefits of business swings," says Davis.

Measuring Performance

The risk factor is a real one, especially when incentives begin to loom large in the total compensation of relatively low-level managers. A Hay survey shows that middle-management base salaries rose a relatively stable 7.1% in 1976 and 7.5% in 1977. But the increase in base and bonus combined was far more mercurial. In 1976 the rise was 4.6%; this year it is 10%. At the top-management level the swing was even wider in base pay and bonus combined: 3.2% in 1976 compared with 14.6% in 1977.

There is a more fundamental problem with paying for performance, whether that means incentive pay or merely fatter than ordinary increases. To reward for performance, a company must first measure performance, and companies are finding that this is no easy task. "I don't know of any company that is satisfied with its performance appraisal system," says one personnel director. "It's a very serious problem."

"One of the things that became very obvious during 1975 and 1976 was that more effective ways of measuring performance had to be developed," declares Richard J. Battista, vice-president of First Pennsylvania Bank. "So the emphasis swung away from payment systems to performance systems." First Pennsylvania dropped its system tying evaluations to management by objectives because employee ratings varied too much and seemed too dependent on the manager's bias and the type of job involved.

First Pennsylvania is now instituting a behavior standard scale that breaks the job into skills such as communications, administration, and human relations. Each of these skill categories is further divided into "subsets," such as listening, follow-up and control, and assertiveness. And instead of a scale composed of terms such as "outstanding" or "superior," the rater must choose among descriptions such as "understands and learns new tasks quickly."

One unforeseen benefit of the system, which has already been applied to nonexempt employees, is a reduction in suits brought by disgruntled employees. "We went from more than 30 suits in 1975 down to essentially nothing," says Battista. "A lot of employee concern is resolved in the appraisal system."

Another tactic becoming increasingly common is a requirement that the appraisal be in narrative form. Pitney-Bowes chucked its check-off system two years ago to adopt narrative appraisals. "People with 20 or 30 subordinates have a tough time with it," says Sasso. "It's a nuisance, I won't deny that. But it forces more thought."

At Westinghouse, the evaluation program was revised recently to focus more on work objectives than on such generalities as "energy" and "judgment." And now the employee must sign his evaluation—a practice that is becoming more and more common.

The real problem is how the manager feeds back the evaluation to the employee. "Most people perceive their performance higher than their manager does," notes Fibreboard's Shulman. One way to solve that problem is to have both employee and manager evaluate performance, which is just what has been happening at Hercules, which, says Herzog, "systemized and formalized the relationship between compensation and performance" two years ago. Now manager and employee compare notes.

But the major flaw in appraisal systems is that managers are unwilling to criticize their employees. "The very hardest thing of all is to tell someone he's unacceptable," says Crocker National Bank's vice-president for cash compensation, Carl D. Herington. Says Hercules' Herzog: "Evaluating employees is one of the most difficult things managers have to do. There is a natural tendency on the part of managers to want to be liked, and this makes a negative evaluation difficult for them." This makes a real merit pay system that much harder to implement.

One answer is training. "Performance appraisal can't be reduced to a cold mathematical formula," says Citibank's Small. "More and more time is being given every year to coaching people down the line on the appraising process. And every year the environment gets more candid, more constructive, and more positive."

Opening the Books

If Citibank is becoming more candid about pay, so are most other companies. More openness about salaries, ranges, and even the way the company perceives the employee's potential may be the single most striking change in corporate pay policy in the past few years. Whereas employees once knew little more than what their own salary was, today in many companies they are told not only their range but the next one up. And the increasingly common practice of posting jobs, along with salary, gradually spreads the word even in close-mouthed companies. Aetna publishes a salary manual that lists all job classes and the salary ranges that go with them. One year ago, Crocker began giving employees access to all salary ranges except those at the executive level. "It certainly increases our credibility, because nobody is hiding anything," says Herington. "Also, the supervisors now know the employees have access to this information, so this influences the small percentage of supervisors who might want to play games." As Hay Associates' general partner Daniel L. Stix says: "You have to clean up your act before you can communicate what you're doing."

At Security Pacific National Bank, where employees are now given wallet-sized cards that spell out their job level and salary range, a pilot program is under way that asks employees what job they aspire to and then describes that job fully, including salary range. "We're reaching a point where there are very few secrets about salaries in this company. Today the emphasis is on spelling out the job up front, and that includes the salary," says Security Pacific's Margol.

The job up front is what more and more white-collar employees are counting on for some relief from the pay squeeze. "In a general sense, the only ones who have been able to better their position are the ones who have done it by promotion," says J. A. Riordan, director of Hay Associates' compensation center. And McKinsey's McLaughlin adds: "Merit has a hollow ring when even top performers making 10% increases only remain whole. Promotion is their real merit increase."

Promotion Pays Off

Citibank, the quintessential fast-track organization, where more than one in five are promoted each year and where promotion increases range to 20%, offers a good example. "The way to make substantially more money is to be promoted," says Small. "At the end of a 10-year period, people starting together can be 100% apart. Promotion is the real clincher."

Promotion pays off two ways. First, there is the promotion increase. Second, someone who receives regular promotions will tend to be continually in the bottom of his salary range, which means fatter merit raises, too. "The real question," says McLaughlin, "is whether managers can continue to move through their organizations."

It is a question as significant to companies as to managers. As discontent over the emptiness of merit raises in a prolonged period of inflation crops up more and more frequently, it is likely to be troublesome in companies without the growth to support high ratios of promotions. And companies in areas with high living costs and high local taxes will be even harder pressed to attract and hold employees than they already are. Statistics compiled by McKinsey show that managers making from $25,000 to $100,000 must receive annual raises of 8% to 8.7% just to stay even when inflation runs at 7%. But they indicate that in New York City, the manager in those brackets must receive increases of between 9% and 10% to stay even. In short, the companies that already have a problem motivating superior managers will find that problem accentuated.

"The pay problem is going to be less susceptible to a total group approach, less susceptible to a group cure," says the Conference Board's Weeks. "The problem will require more executive involvement. It's just not a problem the technicians can solve."

23

Planning Job Progression for Effective Career Development and Human Resources Management

Harry L. Wellbank, Douglas T. Hall,
Marilyn A. Morgan, and W. Clay Hamner

*T*here are three important problems with the way many career development and human resources management systems are currently designed and operated. First, there is rarely any connection between career planning and development, aimed at individual employees, and corporate human resources planning and management, aimed at organizational staffing needs. Second, much career development activity takes place in isolation or in classroom settings and is unrelated to actual job needs and experiences. Much career development has little connection with either the employee's organizational career or actual development. Third, many career development systems are unnecessarily complex, consisting of exotic planning exercises, computerized self-assessment instruments, or mathematical models.

To overcome these problems, Sears, Roebuck and Co. is developing a new method of job-based career development and human resources management, which it thinks will resolve these critical career management problems. To do this, it is using a highly potent, but very common, everyday training and development instrument: the job.

Sears has a long history of using job assignments for management development, though perhaps the "new" methods aren't really so new. For example, for years college recruits at Sears started on the back dock and rotated through six or eight other job assignments during the first

SOURCE: Harry L. Wellbank, Douglas T. Hall, Marilyn A. Morgan, and W. Clay Hamner, "Planning Job Progression for Effective Career Development and Human Resources Management. Reprinted, by permission of the publisher, from *Personnel,* March–April 1978, pp. 54–64. © 1978 by AMACOM, a division of American Management Associations. All rights reserved.

12 to 18 months. At the end of this period, the individual was assigned to his or her first supervisory position, as a department manager. During ensuing years, if the individual was still considered promotable, he or she was assigned to a variety of store staff positions—perhaps as many as five, six, or seven—ending with assistant store manager and store management.

All of these moves were made by the corporation on the basis of a feeling for what would be appropriate in terms of the company's past experience, that is, on the basis of "what worked." But with the human resources needs of today, unanalyzed past experience is not an adequate basis on which to proceed, and so Sears is adopting new methods.

Job Assignment Sequences for Career Development

To provide the foundation for the new approach, Sears is proposing several critical principles of career development:

> *The most important influences on career development occur on the job.* As the work at AT&T indicates, everyday job challenges and demands are powerful socializing and skill-building devices. The job itself undoubtedly has more influence on development than formally planned development experiences, such as classroom training and workshops.
>
> *Different jobs demand the development of different skills.* A supervisory job, for example, stimulates the development of greater human relations skills, while a staff specialist's job may stretch the person's technical skills.
>
> *Development occurs only when the person has not yet developed the skills demanded by a particular job.* If a person is put into a job that demands skills the person has already mastered, little or no new learning will take place. For a job to provide development experiences, it must stretch the person to learn new skills or improve existing ones. This principle seems painfully obvious, but it often is violated in many corporate personnel moves.
>
> *By identifying a rational sequence of job assignments for a person, the time required to develop the necessary skills for a chosen target job can be reduced.* If one job produces a certain amount of skill development, then a series of job assignments can be selected to produce even more development over the course of the person's career.

This last point is the key principle in the new Sears system—the use of a well-planned sequence of job assignments to maximize career development. Without a systematic way of analyzing job demands, job assignments often overlap greatly. Even promotions, if they are within the same functional area, often do not encourage the learning of new skills. But with a systematic method of evaluating job content, job progressions can be planned to minimize the overlap in job demands and maximize skill stretching.

Using a Job Evaluation System for More Rational Job Progression

Although job evaluation systems are generally used for compensation purposes, they also have great potential in career development since they provide systematic procedures for assessing the skills required in a particular job. The Hay system is used at Sears. However, the career management process to be discussed here can be used with various job evaluation systems, not just the Hay method.

The Hay system measures three basic competencies for each job: know-how, problem solving, and accountability. Know-how can be further broken down into three kinds of job knowledge: technical, managerial, and human relations. Problem solving and accountability also have several dimensions. Scores for each of these three competencies are assigned to each job, and a total value for each job is then computed. Thus, for any planned job transfer, the amount of increase (or decrease) the next job represents in each of the component skill areas, as well as in the total point value, can be computed. At Sears, any future job that is one scale unit or more above the previous job on any skill dimension requires significant learning on that dimension. Similarly, any transfer to a job representing a 10 percent or greater increase in total points is a growth-demanding assignment. Further, it is also desirable at Sears for a person to have a combination of experiences in different functional areas. Using these criteria, developmental career paths can be constructed to provide the following experiences:

> An increase in at least one skill area on each new assignment.
> An increase of at least 10 percent in total points on each new assignment.
> Assignments in several different functional areas.

Achieving Multiple Objectives in a Job Progression Development Program

Once an organization has a way to evaluate the skill requirements of different job assignments, job progression plans can be designed to achieve a number of objectives for both the organization and the employee. Several different objectives of a job progression development program and how each one might be achieved follow.

1. Identifying rational paths to target jobs. One of the most important purposes of a systematic job progression plan is to identify all of the logically feasible paths to any target job, such as store manager, a key job in a retailing organization. In most organizations, certain paths become established as the "best" routes to a particular job without a clear reason. Putting together rational career paths on the basis of an objective assessment of the skills that the paths will impart is a way of moving from folklore to facts about what jobs will best aid career growth.

Having done this, an organization may find that the range of rationally possible career paths to a given target job is wider than those paths in present use. A comparison of rationally feasible paths with actual paths (based upon job histories of present employees) may suggest alternative routes for developing employees who may have been overlooked in the past. This can increase both the organization's flexibility in meeting staffing needs and employees' development needs at the same time.

The set of rational paths should be screened carefully, of course, since it is possible that some make no sense because of practical constraints and needs. For example, it may be possible, in terms of the three previously mentioned criteria, to move a person from a merchandise manager to store manager in two moves, but the company would probably want to give the person more interim assignments just to learn more about the organization. To be most useful, the rational paths should be screened by many personnel specialists and managers in different functional areas to eliminate those that are unworkable. (However, paths should be screened out only for rational reasons; they should not be eliminated just because they have never been tried before. Those are exactly the paths an organization may *want* to try!)

2. Identifying rational "fast tracks" to a target job.   Once a set of feasible rational paths to a target job has been identified, the paths that entail the fewest moves—that is, those that prepare the person for the target job in the shortest period of time—can be identified. For example, many Sears personnel believe that it takes from 14 to 16 years to "grow" a store manager. However, preliminary analyses using job evaluations indicate that it is technically feasible to develop store managers in far less time.

This kind of analysis has great value for affirmative action purposes or for high-potential employees whom the organization may desire to move up as fast as their abilities will permit. Rapid promotions call for especially careful analysis on each job move, and the job evaluation system can reduce the risk of hurting the person's career through a series of inappropriate assignments that do not adequately prepare him or her for the responsibilities of the target job.

3. Identifying rational lateral moves (that is, slower career growth).   Many organizations in today's economy are not as much concerned about rapid promotions as they are about slower promotions. If an organization is in a fairly stable state—not growing, growing very slowly, or perhaps shrinking—it can be difficult to provide satisfying career experiences to bright, ambitious young employees when there are few promotion opportunities opening up. Are there alternatives to promotion that can provide career growth and fulfillment?

One viable alternative to promotions is increased use of lateral transfers, moves to jobs at the same level that demand quite different skills and therefore require career growth. Unfortunately, lateral moves as practiced in many firms now are simply reassignment to the same kind of job in a new location; this provides all the disadvantages of a geographical transfer (uprooting the family and so on) with no compensating benefits in the job itself. Therefore, lateral moves are not eagerly anticipated by many employees. In the eyes of many employees—and many executives, too—the only good move is an upward move.

But lateral moves can be used more creatively. With a job evaluation system, an organization can identify many jobs at about the same rank and pay level that represent a wide range of skills and responsibilities. At Sears, there are ample numbers of jobs at the same level that require acquisition of significant new skills in human relations, technical know-how, managerial competence, or problem solving. For example, movement from the job of merchandise manager in a medium-size store to operating superintendent would result in an increase in both managerial responsibilities and the kind of technical skills used. If organizational realities demand that promotions in a firm be slower, it will become especially important to plan for other methods of providing career fulfillment and maintaining employee commitment. Job progression planning is a useful tool for well-managed lateral transfers that maintain a high level of stimulation from the intrinsic features of the job itself.

4. Identifying rational downward moves.   Why not make more conscious, if sparing, use of downward moves as a way of developing people and meeting organizational needs better? If an organization had the option of moving people down just one level, imagine how much more flexibility it would have in its human resources planning.

One reason a downward move may be needed for employee development is that the organization wants to move a person into a new functional area, such as from finance to marketing. The person may be at too high a level for a lateral move into a marketing job at the same level; he or she simply may not have the technical skills to be able to handle that job. So, with the job evaluation data, the organization can look for a lower-level marketing job in which technical skill demands are more within the person's reach. Rather than make a guess at which job is at the appropriate level, the organization uses job evaluation scores to help it make a better informed decision. It can then put the person in this lower-level job for, say, six or eight months until he or she masters the new area, and then it can start advancing the employee in the marketing department.

Another situation that may occur is that a lower-level job may make significantly greater skill demands on one or two job dimensions than the job the person currently holds and the development of that skill may be critical to the person's career development. For example, consider a person who has advanced to a fairly high-level job in a technical staff function (for example, marketing research or engineering) but who has had no supervisory or management experience. In many cases like this, the next career move up for talented people is to be a manager of a technical group. But the promotion may be based on demonstrated technical proficiency, not managerial skill. Rather than risk a major promotion into management, the organization can identify a lower-level supervisory job in line management that may have lower total job points than the person's previous technical job but which demands considerable human relations skills. Using this job, the organization would try the person out for a year or so. Then if it wants to promote him or her to a management job, it can do it on the basis of demonstrated supervisory performance. But first it must use its job evaluation system to identify a good supervisory "trial" job.

5. Identifying career path clusters.   One problem with analyzing individual career paths, especially in large organizations, is information overload—there may be simply too many feasible paths available. Once an organization knows the characteristics of individual jobs, it can identify clusters of similar jobs. Then it can identify paths connecting various clusters of jobs on the way to the target job.

Similarly, the organization can identify paths within particular functions, departments, or specialties. For example, at Sears some people specialize in marketing and merchandising, which may involve a series of staff positions in territorial or corporate headquarters. Others take a store management route with positions mainly in the stores rather than in headquarters. These career specialties are actually more general concepts, and they provide a way to comprehend a larger set of job progression paths.

This kind of general information on job clusters and career specialties is usually clear and simple enough to be presented in recruiting or orientation literature. In fact, showing the recruit what the various career ladders are in the company seems to be a recent trend in the recruiting practices of many companies. ARCO's recruiting booklet does an especially good job of illustrating career ladders and of giving a recruit a short, self-directed career planning exercise as well.

6. Identifying good development moves from a given job.   Once an organization has identified the complete paths from present job to target job, it can move in for a close-up. This means identifying all the possible next jobs that are available and that provide either a 10 percent increase in total points or a significant increase in at least one job skill. The information display may include the total profile on all job dimensions for each of the possible next jobs. An example of this information is shown in Figure 1.

Figure 1 identifies nine jobs to be considered as reasonable next moves that would be considered promotions for someone who is the merchandising manager of a smaller store (sales volume $4 to $8 million). If the individual needs more merchandising experience, he or she may be assigned to the position of merchandising manager in a larger store to gain greater technical responsibilities. Assignment to the job of operating superintendent, personnel manager, or group advertising manager would provide the opportunity to develop a different set of technical skills. Selection of the most reasonable next assignment would be worked out with both the individual and his or her supervisor. Such factors as previous experience, identified target job, and job availabilities would have to be considered.

7. Identifying Training Needs for Future Jobs.   Another important use for the job evaluation data when next moves are being planned is to focus on the job dimensions where very large increases in skill will be needed. If the person is being stretched to an unusual degree on any one dimension, this may be a "red flag" that training is needed to support and supplement the on-the-job learning that will be taking place. In this way an organization can do a better job of integrating training activities with the actual training needs indicated by the job evaluation data in the new

Figure 1   Sears, Roebuck and Co.; Career Counseling Information:
Possible Job Moves (Current Job: Merchandise manager; store
volume, $4 to $7.9 million. Job Ratings*: Technical, D;
Managerial, II; Human relations, 3; and Challenge, 3.)

Possible Job Moves	Change in Job Dimensions
Percent change = 7.13	
Group advertising manager	+T†, −M
Store volume = Over $400 million	
Technical, E; Managerial, I; Human Relations, 3	
Percent change = 14.73	
Merchandise manager	+T
Store volume = $8 to $14.9 million	
Technical, E; Managerial, II; Human Relations, 3	
Percent change = 14.73	
Auto center manager	+T
Store volume = $1 to $2.9 million	
Technical, E; Managerial, II; Human Relations, 3	
Percent change = 7.13	
Group display manager	+T
Store volume = Under $76 million	
Technical, E; Managerial, II; Human Relations, 3	
Percent change = 14.73	
Operating superintendent, 1	+T
Store volume = Under $4 million	
Technical, E; Managerial, II; Human Relations, 3	
Percent change = 7.13	
Group installation manager	+T
Store volume = Under $5 million	
Technical, E; Managerial, II; Human Relations, 3	
Percent change = 14.73	
Operating superintendent, 2	+T
Store volume = $4 to $7.9 million	
Technical, E; Managerial, II; Human Relations, 3	
Percent change = 4.04	
Personnel manager, 1	+T
Store volume = $8 to $14.9 million	
Technical, E; Managerial, II; Human Relations, 3	
Percent change = 4.04	
Personnel manager, 2	+T
Store volume = $15 to $29.9 million	
Technical, E; Managerial, II; Human Relations, 3	

NOTE: *These are the job evaluation ratings on these four factors using the Hay system.
†Increases or decreases in the technical, managerial, and human relations demands of the job in comparison with the present job are shown in this column.

assignment. This analysis of the increments between the new and old job profiles can also help an organization avoid wasting training in areas where it is *not* needed.

    8. Identifying "People Pools" for Open Jobs: Staffing.   Career management also has a more "macro" or corporate objective: providing a pool of people who are developed and ready to assume increased job responsibilities. A job evaluation system can also be used to identify the pool of candidates for any given job. In other words, a job evaluation system can be used to select people for jobs as well as to select jobs for people.

When a position becomes open, for example, it would be possible to search the organization's personnel files and identify the people for whom the job would represent career growth, that is, people for whom the job would represent a gain of at least 10 percent in total job points or a significant stretching of skill on at least one job dimension. The organization would obviously supplement this information with other data, such as the employee's career preferences and performance appraisals. But the basic process of matching people to career-growing jobs is the same, whether the organization is looking at the employee's career planning objectives or its human resources planning and selection needs.

Implementation

How should this kind of job evaluation/job progression system be put to use in a corporate setting? Carefully, very carefully. Career management involves working with important information about people's work histories that will affect their future careers. An acceptable system, therefore, must have the following features:

Checks on the accuracy of the information used.
Opportunity for the employee to examine data on his or her
   work history and to remove incorrect information.
Provisions for inputs from the employee when decisions about
   his or her career are made.
Safeguards for the confidentiality of the data.

There are three likely users or consumers of the information provided through such a system. First, individual employees may use it in thinking about their own careers. Second, line managers and employee development and training specialists may use it for developing managers. Job progression can be related to performance appraisal and advancement potential to provide the most stretching experiences possible for the organization's most talented employees. And, last, corporate and human resource planning experts may use the information for present and future staffing activities.

More specifically, information about job progressions may be used in the following ways:

For Job Posting.   Along with possibly posting vacant jobs, an organization may also post the skill profile for each job and the various paths from each posted job to some generally valued target job.

For Widespread Dissemination of Basic Career Paths.   An organization may want to identify general clusters of paths, or career specialties. These can be printed and disseminated on posters, in pamphlets, in the company newspaper, or in other media for distribution to all employees to give them some clear, simple information about advancement possibilities in different parts of the organization. Such information is in extremely short supply in most organizations—but in high demand. The result is that the need for information is filled with rumors, myths, and other inaccuracies. Like pay, careers are the subject of much secrecy and much dysfunctional rumor in most organizations. Accurate, useful information on basic career paths can be quite easy to provide.

For On-line Computer Access. An organization may also want to store information on job evaluations and employees' career histories in an interactive computer system. The employee, a personnel specialist, or a manager can enter the number of a particular job and then request to have different kinds of information displayed: various career paths from that job to a target job, possible next jobs, their job evaluation profiles, training required, and perhaps salary ranges. A list of people for whom the job in question represents a significant growth experience can also be generated.

For Input to Employees, Line Managers, and Personnel Specialists. The three parties most interested in this information are the individual employee, the line manager, and the personnel specialist. The employee can use the data for his or her own career planning, and the manager and the personnel specialist can use the information to aid and counsel the employee in that process. The manager and personnel specialist can also use the information to assist in making different personnel decisions: hiring, transfers, promotions, demotions, and so on.

For Input to and from Corporate Planning. Organizations need to have as much coordination as possible between corporate planning, human resources planning, and individual career planning. Usually, these three kinds of planning operate in isolation, although they are all quite dependent on one another. For example, an employee may map out a career path in automotive sales, but the company may plan to get out of the automotive business. Similarly, an organization may plan a large expansion of its engineering operations, but it may lack qualified engineers and they may be in very short supply in the external labor market. A high-level planning committee that includes corporate planning, human resources planning, and career planning is one method of achieving this degree of integration.

Conclusion

The notion of using job evaluation schemes for purposes other than compensation is still in the early stages of application. Although the system is used at Sears, other point systems for evaluating jobs can be used for career planning. The important thing is to have an objective method of measuring the skills demanded by various jobs and of putting them together in a way that will stimulate growth in desired directions. This kind of system can lift career planning out of the informal corporate "old boy" network and reduce the employee's dependence upon a well-informed boss. Although there are many pitfalls in any centralized information system, if used carefully a job evaluation-based job progression system can be a useful way of increasing the employee's self-direction and career fulfillment and of providing for a more efficient utilization of the organization's human resources.

PART V

Organizational Change and Development

Editors' Summary Comments

*D*uring the latter part of this century we have witnessed remarkable and rapid changes in our life styles, institutions, and values. The advances of modern techniques; the geometric expansion of available scientific, personal, and financial information for reaching decisions; and the questioning of social structures, values, and the institutions of industrialized nations have been evident to even the most casual observer. Whether we approve of such changes is of course a moot question after they are made.

The modern organization needs to cope with changes in the environment and among its employees. The static or totally reactive organization will have a difficult time serving in a society that is changing. Yesterday's successes mean very little in a changing environment that wants, needs, and uses products and services that were not available last month or last year. In order to survive, organizations must develop a program that enables them to cope with change.

There is some disagreement among practicing managers and researchers about how organizational change can best be studied. A part of this disagreement centers on the exact interpretation of the term organizational development or "OD." The term as interpreted by most individuals refers to a planned, systematic program initiated by management, designed to make the organization more effective through methods that change knowledge, skills, attitudes, processes, and behaviors, based upon the assumption that organizational performance is enhanced when the program facilitates integration of individual and organizational objectives. This statement essentially captures the essence of organizational development and is definitely an "eclectic approach."

A current theme in the literature that discusses organizational change and development is that the scientific method needs to be considered, applied, and utilized whenever change and development is necessary. As such, we cast our interpretation of OD in the language of the behavioral scientists as follows:

1. What is the problem? (Diagnosis)
2. What are the alternative solutions to the problem? (Methods)
3. How should the appropriate methods be implemented? (Implementation)
4. Did the implemented solution work? (Evaluation)

The seven articles selected for this part deal with organizational change and development from a scientific and practitioner perspective. They focus on diagnosis, methods, implementation, and evaluation.

In the first article, "Organizational Development: Some Problems and Proposals," Robert L. Kahn reviews the current state of OD in terms of its research base. He questions the validity of much of the research that has sought to determine the outcome of OD programs. Kahn's discussion provides the reader with an overview of many of the popular OD methods and with encounter groups. He also distinguishes between the target and the means of organizational change, a distinction that allows for an integration of the process-structure dichotomy.

An ever-increasing problem in many organizations is the issue of managerial stress. In "Managing for a Healthier Heart," John Ivancevich and Michael Matteson examine both the sources and outcomes associated with the stress component, particularly heart disease. Various methods of reducing the negative forms of stress initiated by organizations are discussed.

The article "Goal Setting: The Tenneco Approach to Personnel Development and Management Effectiveness" discusses the most dominant change intervention found in contemporary organizations—goal setting, or management-by-objectives. The authors point out that the success attained by Tenneco can be attributed to the importance that the organization placed on diagnosis, top management commitment, goal-setting training, and external evaluation.

Thomas Patten has presented an organization's experience with the team building concept in "Team Building Part 1. Designing the Intervention." He discusses how certain firms have designed training and action research programs that can eventually lead to improvements in both morale and productivity.

Our last *Business Week* selection, "Stonewalling Plant Democracy," presents the negative—or maybe more realistic—side of a large-scale change program. The General Foods plant, initially designed around the concepts of challenging jobs and worker participation and democracy, has fallen on hard times. The reasons for the current state of this once highly successful program are both enlightening and important.

Charles Burck's article, "What's Good for the World Should Be Good for G.M.," is an interesting examination of the complexity of organizational change. In the discussion of G.M.'s recent "downsizing" to the "X" car, the reader will note that this change involved environmental analysis in addition to people, task, technology, and design changes.

Finally, in "One Firm's Family," the behavior of employees in I.B.M. is examined in multiple situations. It is an interesting discussion of how employees shape an organization, and how organizations shape the behavior of people.

24

Organizational Development:
Some Problems and Proposals

Robert L. Kahn

Introduction

Advising people in power about how they can better attain their goals is a very old occupation. Organizational Development (OD), on the other hand, is a new label for a conglomerate of things an increasing number of consultants do and write about. What that label refers to depends to a considerable extent upon the doer or writer. Among the critics and practitioners of organizational development, who are often the same people, there is a continuing argument over the state of the art, its proper definition, and the requisite skills for practicing it.

For example, Harry Levinson (1972), a clinical psychologist writing in the journal *Professional Psychology,* criticized OD practice for its neglect of diagnostic procedures, along with other theoretical and methodological shortcomings. He was answered in the same journal by Marshall Sashkin (1973a) and by Warner Burke (1973b), both of whom undertook a specific rebuttal of Levinson's criticisms and a general defense of organizational development as practiced. Levinson (1973a) responded; Sashkin (1973b) replied; Burke (1973a) commented further; and Levinson (1973b) offered summary comments, which included the inarguable observation that the discussion had reached the point of diminishing returns.

Such exchanges reveal a good deal about current practice and preference, and several recent review articles provide more comprehensive statements. One of the most instructive is Friedlander and Brown's chapter in the current *Annual Review of Psychology* (1974), which is built around the familiar dichotomy between people-oriented ("human processual") and technology-oriented ("technostructural") approaches to organizational change. Comprehensive reviews have also been written by Alderfer (1974), Sashkin et al. (1973), Strauss (in press), and Hornstein et al. (1971). Leavitt's earlier chapter (1965) speaks in terms of applied organizational change rather than development, but the difference is more terminological than substantive, and the review remains a useful commentary on what is now called OD.

More numerous than such reviews are books and articles that describe a preferred approach to organizational development, sometimes in very general terms, sometimes with a good deal of theoretical elaboration, occasionally with some substantiating empirical data. Examples are provided by Argyris (1970, 1971) on intervention theory, Blake and Mouton (1968, 1969) on grid organization development, Schein (1969) on process consultation, Schmuck and Miles (1971) on the OD Cube, and others.

My present purpose is neither to rehearse the OD arguments nor to review the reviews. Much less do I wish to dispute whether the practice of organizational development has been nearly completed, is well en route, or has barely begun the long transition from being a miscellany of uncertain devices to becoming a mature, usable set of principles and procedures for organizational change. I want instead to cite some problems, the resolution of which will facilitate that transition and thus make organizational development better than it is, in theory and practice.

Omissions and Redundancies

No reasonable person can complain that written material on organizational change and development is meager. In 1962 Everett Rogers (Rogers & Shoemaker, 1962, 1971), working in an admittedly broader area, the communication of innovations, generated a bibliography of some 1,500 items. In 1968 Ronald Havelock (Havelock et al., 1968, 1972) found almost 4,000 titles in the area of planned innovation, and offered the terrifying bibliographic projection that the number was increasing at the rate of 1,000 per year. Such volume invites specialization; in the more circumscribed area of organizational development, Jerome Franklin (1973) lists about 200 books, chapters, and articles. That is the body of material most relevant for our present purposes; what does it tell us?

About 15 years ago, March and Simon (1958) observed that rather little had been said about organizations, but that little had been said repeatedly and in many different ways. In the years since then, I believe that caustic judgment has become less accurate for organizational research in general, but it remains unhappily true of writings on organizational development. A few theoretical propositions are repeated without additional data or development; a few bits of homey advice are reiterated without proof or disproof, and a few sturdy empirical generalizations are quoted with reverence but without refinement or explication.

For example, Kurt Lewin's (1974a, b) suggestion that the process of planned change be conceptualized in terms of three successive phases—unfreezing, moving, and freezing—is often quoted or paraphrased as a preamble to research, but seldom with any clear indication of how that formulation determined the design of the research that follows its invocation. The Lewinian concept of quasi-stationary equilibrium (1947c) is also frequently mentioned, but without any systematic conceptualization or measurement of the alleged opposing forces. Gordon Lippitt (1969) presents this model as "force-field analysis," and 40 driving and restraining forces are represented by opposing arrows in a diagram (p. 156). The forces, however, are unidentified; their identification and measurement is left to the reader. Such presentations are common. The Lewinian schema thus remains not only unelaborated and untested, but really unused. It deserves more serious attention.

The OD literature contains other slogans, less theoretical but recited no less often. Consider, for example, the advice that the "change agent" should "start at the top" of the organization he intends to change. Beckhard (1969) makes "management from the top" one of five defining characteristics of organizational development; Blake and Mouton (1969) assert that "to change a company, it is necessary for those who head the company to lead the change of it." Argyris' recent cases (1971) begin with discussions between the author and chief executives of the companies described.

I have neither experience nor data to challenge the advice that one should start at the top, and certainly it has a pleasant ring. Nevertheless, it would benefit from specification and test. Does it mean that the top of the organization must change before any other part can do so? Does it mean that the people at the top of the organization must actively support the proposed program of change without necessarily becoming "trainees" themselves? Or does it mean merely that some degree of top-echelon sanction for the new enterprise of organizational development must be visible in order for others to accept the proposed changes? One can readily imagine research to answer these questions, but it has yet to be done. Nor can it be, until the homily about starting at the top is stated with enough specificity to be tested.

As an example of a third sort of redundancy without development, empirical generalization, let us take the proposition that organizational changes are more likely to be accepted by people who have had a voice in determining their content. This is the principle of participation, perhaps the best established and most widely accepted empirical generalization in the literature of organizational change. The research pedigree for this principle dates back at least to 1948, when Coch and French published their classic article on overcoming resistance to change. Their experiment demonstrated that varying degrees of employees' participation in changes of work methods were related to their expressed acceptance of the new methods, to the rapidity with which they learned those methods, and to their decision to remain as employees of the company.

As good research should, the Coch and French experiment not only answered old questions; it raised new ones. Some of them—the interaction of participation with individual personality differences, for example—have been the subject of subsequent investigations

(Tannenbaum & Allport, 1956; Vroom, 1960). Others remain unstudied; for example, the important question of distinguishing the motivational effects of participation from substantive effects of participative decisions.

It would be exciting to see an organizational development program that included research designed to obtain separate estimates of the effects of identical substantive changes generated under participative and nonparticipative conditions. Such data could be provided, I think, by means of a design using "master" and "slave" groups. (I use the terms only in their figurative, mechanical sense.) Work groups would be chosen in sets of three, one in each set randomly designated master, one slave, and one control. If one of the master groups decided in the course of an OD program that the group should have the authority to set its own standards or choose its own methods of work or have access to current cost data, these same changes would be initiated in the slave group, but by conventional managerial instruction. An increase in productivity or satisfaction in the master groups, as compared to control groups, would be interpreted as the combined consequence of the participative experience and the substantive participative decisions. An increase in productivity or satisfaction in the slave groups, as compared to control groups, would be interpreted as the effect of the substance of the decisions without the motivational effect of participation. The difference in criterion changes in a master group as compared to the matched slave group would be interpreted as reflecting the effect of participation alone, the effects of decision content having been held constant experimentally within each such pair of groups.

Whether or not readers share my enthusiasm for this particular case of unexplored research is not important. The foregoing examples of omission and redundancy in the literature of organizational development and change are not intended to urge some particular research project. Rather, they are intended to rouse in the reader a thirst for movement —for elaboration and strengthening of old theoretical formulations, for systematic test of old injunctions, for the refinement and extension of old empirical generalizations. Argument by example, however, is always judgmental; let us state the criticism of redundancy in more objective terms. Of the 200 items in the Franklin (1973) bibliography of organizational development, only 25 percent include original quantitative data; the remaining 75 percent consist for the most part of opinions, narrative material, and theoretical fragments. No branch of science can long afford such a ratio. Ideas and personal impressions need desperately to be tested by collision with facts. The mill of science grinds only when hypotheses and data are in continuous and abrasive contact.

Packages and Concepts

Organizational development is not a concept, at least not in the scientific sense of the word: it is not precisely defined; it is not reducible to specific, uniform, observable behaviors; it does not have a prescribed and verifiable place in a network of logically related concepts, a theory. These statements hold, I believe, in spite of some serious efforts to provide a workable definition and a meaningful theoretical context.

Lawrence and Lorsch (1969) provided one such example, building on their earlier work on differentiation and integration (1967) and describing organizational development in terms of activities at three interfaces—organization and environment, group to group, and individual in relation to organization. Argyris (1970) provides another example, in his sustained effort to conceptualize and describe his own experience in organizational change. His emphasis is on the autonomy and "health" of the client organization, and on OD as a means of increasing those valued characteristics by increasing the capacity of the organization to generate and utilize valid information about itself.

Argyris, like Lawrence and Lorsch, is stating his own definition and theoretical position; he is not attempting a formulation that accommodates everything that goes by the name of organizational development. Attempts at such broader and more eclectic statements sacrifice a good deal in precision and theoretical connectedness. For example, Bennis (1969) says that "organization development is a response to change, a complex educational strategy intended to change the beliefs, attitudes, values, and structure of organizations so that they can better adapt to new technologies, markets, and challenges, and the dizzying rate of change itself." His co-editor, Richard Beckhard (1969) says that "organizational development is the name that is being attached to *total-system*, planned-change efforts for coping with the above-mentioned conditions." (These conditions include four assertions about "today's changing world," five about "today's business environment," and six about "today's changing values.") I find those definitions too inclusive to be helpful, and others go still farther. Margulies and Raia (1972) offer a definition broad enough to include everything from market research to industrial espionage. They define organizational development as consisting of "data gathering, organizational diagnosis, and action interventions."

Other authors give us other descriptions, and their variety serves to underline my assertion that *organizational development* is not a concept. This assertion is in itself neither praise nor damnation; it merely reminds us that the term is a convenient label for a variety of activities. When we remember that fact about the term *OD,* we benefit from its convenience, as we do from the convenience of other colloquial terms—*mental health* and *illness,* for example. Scientific research and explanation, however, require concepts that get beneath convenient labels and represent explicitly defined and observable events and behaviors. The literature of organizational development is disappointing in this respect; it is tied too closely to the labels in terms of which the varied services of organizational development are packaged and marketed.

Moreover, this criticism holds even when we consider more specific terms. *Sensitivity training,* for example (also known as *laboratory method* or *T-Group training,* and partially inclusive of such variants as *encounter groups* and *personal development groups*), is itself a convenience term for a number of activities that probably vary as much with the preferences of the trainer as with anything else (Back, 1972). *Grid organization development* is another such term; it refers to those consulting and training activities marketed by Blake and Mouton and their colleagues (1964, 1968, 1969). Indeed, their firm has registered the term as a trademark or brand name—the antithesis of scientific conceptualization.

One of the persisting problems with research on organizational development is that it has incorporated such colloquial and commercial terms as independent variables. I have noted that of the more than 200 bibliographic entries on organizational development, about 25 percent (53) present quantitative data. Within that subset, more than 65 percent (35) utilized independent variables that must be considered packages rather than concepts. In most of those, the package was "the T Group," variously employed and mingled with lectures, skill-practice, and other training activities. In about 10 percent of the data-reporting articles, the "independent variable" was "Managerial Grid Training."

In a few cases the experimental treatment was simply—or rather, complicatedly—"Organizational Development." And a few others offer as the independent variable a sort of omnibus treatment in which the social scientist and management seem to have done a variety of things—T Groups, consultation, lectures, surveys, explicit changes in formal policies, and the like, which they hoped might produce wanted changes in employee attitudes and behavior. Evidence of such changes is presented, but we are left in doubt as to the potent ingredient or synergistic combination of ingredients that produced the effect.

Such aggregate treatments need not be bad, but they can be made scientifically good only when the package treatment is sufficiently described to permit replication and "dissection" of its ingredients. I have found no examples of sustained refinement of independent variables in the articles that make up the bibliography of organizational development, although some beginnings have been made from time to time. In 1965, Bunker, for example, showed that conventional T-Group experience produced changed interpersonal behavior in the back-home work situation, as measured in terms of the perceptions of co-workers, not merely the perceptions of the trainees themselves. Shortly thereafter, Bunker and Knowles (1967) replicated those findings, with variations in the duration of the experimental treatment. They compared the effects of two-week with three-week T Groups, and found that the latter generated the greater perceived changes in behavior. We could wish for more work along these lines, especially in view of the tendency toward shorter and more intensive use of T Groups and encounter groups—a tendency that appears to be based on administrative convenience rather than evaluative research.

There is another encouraging sign in the research that uses packages as independent variables: a few experiments or quasi-experiments have compared packages. Perhaps the best example of such comparative work is Bowers' (1973) article "OD Techniques and Their Results in 23 Organizations." This research is based on data from 14,000 respondents in 23 industrial organizations and reports gain scores (before and after treatment) for four patterns of developmental activity—Survey Feedback, Interpersonal Process Consultation, Task Process Consultation, Laboratory (T Group) Training—and two "control" treatments, "data handback" and "no treatment." Bowers found that "Survey Feedback was associated with statistically significant improvements on a majority of measures, that Interpersonal Process Consultation was associated with improvement on a majority of measures, that Task Process Consultation was associated with little or no change, and that Laboratory Training and No Treatment were associated with declines."

These findings are not definitive, nor are they presented as such. There are the now-familiar problems with raw gain scores (Cronbach et al., 1972), although Bowers has done supplementary analyses to control for initial differences in the several treatment groups and to test for the plausibility of the alternative hypothesis that his results merely reflect the regression of extreme scores toward the mean. There are other explicit limitations: the treatments are defined only approximately; there is confounding of change agents with treatment differences (since each change agent conducted the treatment of his choice); there is some self-selection of treatments by populations as well as change agents; and there is the absence of hard criteria of organizational change (productivity, profit, turnover, and the like). Finally, a sociologist of knowledge might express some lurking skepticism that Survey Feedback had been discovered by its proponents to be the most effective form of organizational development. Nevertheless, the comparison of treatments is most welcome; I applaud it and only wish that it were more frequent.

Friedlander and Brown (1974), in a careful review article of some 18 pages, require only three paragraphs to summarize comparative studies of OD interventions. Moreover, of the three studies summarized, two (Greiner, 1967; Buchanan, 1971) do not evaluate alternative interventions; the third study cited is that of Bowers.

Even such comparative studies, however, leave us with needs for explanation that can be satisfied only by research that clarifies the nature of the independent variable, the experimental treatment itself. Such conceptualization and explicit definition of the experimental treatment is well illustrated in three field experiments that are widely regarded as classics in organizational change—Coch and French's (1948) work on the effects of participation, Morse and Reimer's (1956) on hierarchical locus of decision-making power, and Trist and Bamforth's (1951) on changes in sociotechnical structure. There are other and more recent examples, of course, but the list remains short. Let us hope that it will lengthen.

Autobiography and Organization

My third criticism of research on organizational development may seem to include a contradiction in terms: the research on organizational development is not sufficiently organizational. It is too autobiographical a literature, too concentrated on the experience of the trainees and change agents. It is a literature of training episodes, and those episodes are often nonorganizational or extra-organizational.

Research that carries the term *organizational* in its title often consists of the group experience of a few people, far from the organizations that are allegedly being developed. More often than not, the criteria by which the success of the developmental process is judged are the reactions of these participants to the temporary group experience. Let us be specific: of the projects (in the Franklin [1973] bibliography) reporting empirical data interpreted in terms of organizational development, about 60 percent are based on data from the training episode only; 40 percent include some measure of the persistence of the training effect to some later time. A much smaller proportion, 15 percent, trace the training effect in terms of behavior in the organization itself. Forty percent measure the effect of the experimental treatment only in terms of self-report, and an equal proportion include no control or comparison group, either as part of an experimental design or in the statistical analysis of a larger population.

Friedlander and Brown (1974) report similar conclusions in the three kinds of process-oriented intervention that have been most researched—survey feedback, group development, and intergroup development. They find "little evidence that survey feedback alone leads to changes in individual behavior or organizational performance," but considerable evidence for reported attitudinal change, at least in the short run. They speak of research on group development intervention in comparable terms: "There remains a dearth of evidence for the effects of team building external to the group developed." As for intergroup relations development—

> . . . there is very little systematic research on the effectiveness of such interventions in the field. Case studies abound (e.g., Blake, Mouton, and Sloma [1965]), but they leave many questions about the efficacy of the intervention unresolved.

Most OD activities seem to emphasize process rather than structure as the primary target of change, and most research describing the effects of structural changes in organizations seems to exemplify a different tradition from organizational development. However, definitional distinctions are difficult to make when definitions are unclear. If one includes in the realm of organizational development those studies that Friedlander and Brown call "technostructural," the evidence for persisting organizational effects increases. Certainly such effects were attained in the coal-mine experiments of Trist and his colleagues (1951, 1963) and in the textile-mill experiments of Rice (1958, 1969). Thorsrud (1969), working in the same theoretical tradition, reported still broader and more ramifying changes in a series of Norwegian field experiments. In all these cases, the primary aim was to improve the goodness of fit between the social and the technical aspects of the work organizations. The improvement involved changes in both organizational aspects.

Significant increases in performance, attendance, and satisfaction have also been accomplished by organizational changes that begin with the division of labor, the definition of individual jobs. Such approaches include job design, job enlargement, and job enrichment, the distinctions among which are not always clear. All three share the assumption that many industrial jobs have been fragmented beyond the point of maximum efficiency, and that gains in performance and satisfaction are obtainable by reducing the fragmentation and increasing the variety of content. Results of such work are described by Davis and Taylor (1972) and Ford (1969), and are summarized by Stewart (1967) and Friedlander and Brown (1974). The findings are not uniform, nor are the changes in job content that serve as independent variables or the organizational circumstances in which the experiments were attempted. One must conclude, nevertheless, that the content of the job makes a difference, and that intervention in terms of job content is likely to have effects.

Our present point, however, is not where OD intervention should begin but rather where it should end. As the term *organizational development* reminds us, the organization is the major target of change. Persisting change in the organization must therefore be the criterion of OD success or failure.

Structure and Process

The penultimate problem that I wish to raise about organizational development is the separation of structure and process. It is a familiar enough distinction in organizational theory and in writings on organizational change. Friedlander and Brown (1974) classify all efforts at organizational development as either "technostructural" or "human processual." Leavitt (1965) had earlier proposed a trichotomy: a similar distinction between structure and process, and an additional distinction between technological structure and social structure. As classifications that remind us of the different emphases or starting points of various approaches to change, I find these schemes useful. As classifications that imply the separation of organizational process and structure, however, I find them misleading.

We have argued elsewhere (Katz & Kahn, 1966) that human organizations be viewed as a class of open systems which lack the usual properties of physical boundedness and therefore lack structure in the physical or "anatomical" sense of the term. The structure of an organization can thus be said to consist in the pattern of interdependent events or activities, cyclical and repetitive in nature, that in combination create the organizational product or service. Organizational structures can therefore be well described in terms of roles, those activities expected of persons occupying certain positions in a network of such expectations and behaviors.

The structure of the living organization is not the charts and job descriptions and work-flow diagrams usually employed to describe those roles and the relationships among them. The structure of an organization is the pattern of actual behaviors as that pattern is created and recreated by the human beings we call members of the organization.

It may be useful for some purposes to distinguish this actual organization from some idealized or preferred structure, to distinguish the paper organization from the living organization, for example. There are many ways of making such distinctions—formal versus informal organizational behavior, role prescriptions versus role elaborations, and the like. But the central point remains: the structure of the organization *is* the pattern of actual recurring behaviors.

If we are agreed on that point, the issue of structural versus processual approaches to organizational development takes on a new and clearer form. To change an organization means changing the pattern of recurring behavior, and that is by definition a change in organizational structure. For example, suppose that an OD practitioner somehow gets all the supervisors in an organization to tell employees in advance about any developments that may affect their jobs. Suppose that the giving of such advance information becomes a continuing supervisory practice, a norm among supervisors, and an expectation on the part of subordinates. It will then be part of the role structure of the organization.

Providing such information may or may not be written into the job descriptions of supervisory duties, may or may not be included among criteria for promotion of supervisors. Likelihood of providing such information may or may not be built into the selection procedures for supervisors. To the extent that these things are also done, the giving of advance information becomes more a part of the "formal" structure of the organization, by which I mean management's representation of the organization. The incorporation of some change into the formal structure of the organization—that is, into the management-prescribed roles—has its own significance. But the main issue is change in the enactment of roles; if there is change in those recurring behavior patterns, then the structure of the living organization has changed. Organizational development, if it implies change at all, must change those behaviors, regardless of whether it calls itself structural or processual.

I believe that these issues become clearer if we discuss separately the target and the means of organizational change, and if we do so in terms of role concepts. There is by now some consensus about these concepts and their definition. A role consists simply of the expected behaviors associated with a particular position or office. The people who occupy positions somehow interdependent with that office typically hold and communicate expectations about the behaviors they want enacted by its occupant. The job description thus becomes a special case of such role expectations, probably sent to the occupant by someone in the personnel department acting as a surrogate for upper management. The actual behavior of a person in a role is likely to be a complex combination of responses to the expectations of relevant others and spontaneous activities that are neither prescribed nor proscribed by others. These latter activities are referred to as role elaborations, in contrast to role prescriptions.

Now let us use these terms to discuss first the target of change and then the means of change. I assume that when people speak of the target as structural change, they mean changing the roles and the official or formal expectations associated with them. The number of jobs, their formally prescribed activities, and their prescribed relationships to other positions are examples of such changes.

When people speak of changes in process rather than structure, I assume that they are referring to aspects of role behavior that are not usually prescribed but left to the discretion of the occupant—role elaborations rather than role prescriptions. For example, in most organizations, the extent to which supervisors express consideration and interest toward workers is a matter of role elaboration—unspecified in the formal description of the supervisory job and not included in the role expectations expressed by the workers themselves. If an OD program increases supervisory consideration, the changes might ordinarily be referred to as processual. It might be argued, of course, that what the OD program has done is to move certain consideration-expressing behaviors from role elaborations (options) to role prescriptions (managerial expectations, in this case), and that the target is therefore the formal structure of the organization, after all. I would not disagree, except to point out that the observation illustrates my point about the special meaning of structure in human organizations, and the ultimate fusion of structure and process.

A similar distinction and unity with respect to structure and process is involved in the means of organizational change. One can, for example, attempt to bring about change by altering the formal role prescriptions, introducing new technology, new written policies, new division of labor, and the like. Or one can attempt to bring about change by means of process interventions—counseling, consultation, encounter groups, and the like.

But in the means of change, as in the target, we see some blurring of the usual dichotomy between structure and process. Even Frederick W. Taylor (1923), that classic exemplar of the structural approach to organizational change, began with process-like persuasion and interaction, first at the top of the company and then with the immortal Schmidt. Morse and Reimer (1956) used counseling, role playing, T Groups, and other process-emphasizing activities to bring about and anchor the systematic organizational change they sought.

On the other hand, the most process-oriented OD practitioner necessarily enters the organizational structure in which he hopes to encourage change. He creates a role for himself in that structure, and probably changes the role expectations and prescriptions of the people with whom he meets—if only because they are expected to speak with him, attend the group sessions he arranges, and the like. Moreover, his processual interventions, to the extent they are successful, are likely to lead to changes in formal policies, role prescriptions, and other representations of organizational structure.

The process-oriented OD specialist is likely to avoid specifying what structural changes he prefers; he expects those decisions to emerge from the heightened sensitivity and problem-solving abilities of the individuals and groups with which he has worked. He thus illustrates a certain complementarity with his structure-emphasizing counterpart. One OD specialist speaks in terms of process and says little about the structural end-state that he hopes to see the organization attain. The other concentrates on advocated changes in formal structure (job size, division of labor, and the like) and tells us little about the process by which changes are to be attained.

If there is a lesson for us as researchers and as observers of organizational development, it is to avoid being too absorbed with terminological distinctions and to concentrate instead on what is actually done by the change agent, what subsequent behavioral changes in the organization can be identified, their duration, and their ramifying or receding effects.

Changing the Unwritten Contract

I believe that the body of material on organizational development, with its distinctive strengths and weaknesses, is itself the product of special conditions—the concentration of developmental experience in business and industry, and the nature of the role relationship between managements and researcher-consultants. A management, typically concerned with the productivity and profitability of its enterprise, with secondary interests in job satisfaction and the meaningfulness of work, pays a specialist in organizational development to do certain agreed-upon things in expectation of improved productivity and profit. If these results can be brought about with concomitant gains in satisfaction and worker identification with task and mission, all the better; hence the special appeal of approaches that promise some explicit linkage of satisfaction and productivity. Management also assumes in most cases that the process of organizational development will not alter or infringe traditional managerial prerogatives in matters of personnel, resource allocation, and the like.

The change agent, in his writings about organizational development, gives more emphasis to humanistic values in organizational life. He accepts his role in relation to management in the hope of contributing to the realization of those values, in the hope of increasing the satisfaction and meaningfulness of work. He also wishes to add to the store of things known about human organizations and to learn how they can be influenced. He usually enters into the relationship with management as a paid consultant, and with implied agreement about areas of activity and reservation. Too often, in my view, that implies agreement to induce some changes in satisfaction, motivation, and productivity without becoming involved in resource allocation, availability of equipment, choice of supervisors, content of jobs, allocation of rewards, and the like. In the extreme case, the organizational developer agrees to leave the role structure alone and to induce changes in role elaboration—those activities and stylistic characteristics that are left to the discretion of individuals.

Progress in organizational change and the knowledge about change has been made sometimes in spite of those limitations, and sometimes because of welcome exceptions to them. Now there are numerous signs that the contract between management and behavioral science is being redrawn. Managements are less insistent on tangible results from intangible manipulations, and behavioral scientists are less willing to attempt such legerdemain. As one visible sign of this tendency, I welcome the work on job design (Davis & Taylor, 1972), which approaches organizational improvement through change in one of the major aspects of organizational structure—the division of labor. I hope that more research is done on job design, and that comparable lines of research develop on other aspects of formal organizational structure. Not only will this strengthen the practice of organizational development; it will also bring the language of organizational development into the larger realm of organizational theory and research. It is a long awaited convergence.

References

Alderfer, C. P. "Change Processes in Organizations." In *Handbook of Industrial and Organizational Psychology*, edited by M. D. Dunnette. Chicago: Rand McNally, 1974.

Argyris, C. *Intervention Theory and Methods*. Reading, Mass.: Addison-Wesley, 1970.

———. *Management and Organizational Development: The Path from Xa to Yb*. New York: McGraw-Hill, 1971.

Back, K. W. *Beyond Words*. New York: Russell Sage, 1972.

Beckhard, R. *Organizational Development—Strategies and Models.* Reading, Mass.: Addison-Wesley, 1969.

Bennis, W. G. *Organization Development: Its Nature, Origins, and Perspectives.* Reading, Mass.: Addison-Wesley, 1969.

Blake, R. R., and Mouton, J. S. *Corporate Excellence through Grid Organizational Development.* Houston: Gulf Publishing Co., 1968.

————. *Building a Dynamic Organization through Grid Organization Development.* Reading, Mass.: Addison-Wesley, 1969.

————, and Sloma, R. "The Union-Management Intergroup Laboratory: Strategy for Resolving Intergroup Conflict." *Journal of Applied Behavioral Science* 1 (1965): 25–57.

————; Barnes, L.; and Greiner, L. "Breakthrough in Organizational Development." *Harvard Business Review* 42 (1964): 37–59.

Bowers, D. "OD Techniques and Their Results in 23 Organizations: The Michigan ICL Study." *Journal of Applied Behavioral Science* 9 (1973): 21–43.

Buchanan, P. C. "Crucial Issues in OD." In *Social Intervention: A Behavioral Science Approach,* pp. 386–400. New York: Free Press, 1971.

Bunker, D. R. "Individual Application of Laboratory Training." *Journal of Applied Behavioral Science* 1 (1965): 131–47.

————, and Knowles, E. S. "Comparison of Behavioral Changes Resulting from Human Relations Training Laboratories of Different Lengths." *Journal of Applied Behavioral Science* 3 (1967): 505–23.

Burke, W. W. "Further Comments by Burke." *Professional Psychology,* May 1973, pp. 207–8. (a)

————. "Organization Development." *Professional Psychology,* May 1973, pp. 194–99. (b)

Coch, L., and French, J. R. P., Jr. "Overcoming Resistance to Change." *Human Relations* 1 (1948): 513–33.

Cronbach, J.; Gleser, G.; Nanda, H.; and Rajartnam, N. *The Dependability of Behavioral Generalizability for Scopes and Profiles.* New York: John Wiley, 1972.

Davis, L. E., and Taylor, J. C., eds. *Design of Jobs.* New York: Penguin Books, 1972.

Ford, R. N. *Motivation through Work Itself.* New York: American Management Association, 1969.

Franklin, J. L. "Organizational Development: An Annotated Bibliography." Ann Arbor, Mich.: Center for Research on the Utilization of Scientific Knowledge, Institute for Social Research, University of Michigan, 1973.

Friedlander, F., and Brown, L. D. "Organization Development." *Annual Review of Psychology* 25. Palo Alto, Calif.: Annual Reviews, 1974.

Greiner, L. E. "Patterns of Organizational Change." *Harvard Business Review* 45 (1967): 119–28.

Havelock, R., et al. *Bibliography on Knowledge Utilization and Dissemination.* Ann Arbor, Mich.: Institute for Social Research, 1968. Rev. 1972.

Hornstein, H. A., et al. "Some Conceptual Issues in Individual and Group-Oriented Strategies of Intervention into Organizations." *Journal of Applied Behavioral Science* 7 (1971): 557–67.

Katz, D., and Kahn, R. L. *The Social Psychology of Organizations.* New York: John Wiley, 1966.

Lawrence, P. R., and Lorsch, J. W. *Organization and Environment.* Boston: Division of Research, Harvard Business School, 1967.

————. *Developing Organizations: Diagnosis and Action.* Reading, Mass.: Addison-Wesley, 1969.

Leavitt, H. J. "Applied Organizational Change in Industry: Structural, Technological, and Humanistic Approaches." In *Handbook of Organizations,* edited by J. G. March. Chicago: Rand McNally, 1965.

Levinson, H. "The Clinical Psychologist as Organizational Diagnostician." *Professional Psychology* 3 (1972): 34–40.

―――. "Levinson's Response to Sashkin and Burke." *Professional Psychology*, May 1973, pp. 200–204. (a)

―――. "Summary Comments." *Professional Psychology*, May 1973, p. 208. (b)

Lewin, K. "Frontiers in Group Dynamics I." *Human Relations* 1 (1947): 5–41. (a)

―――. "Frontiers in Group Dynamics II." *Human Relations* 1 (1947): 143–53. (b)

―――. "Group Decision and Social Change." In *Readings in Social Psychology*, edited by T. M. Newcomb and E. L. Hartley. New York: Holt, 1947. (c)

Lippitt, G. L. *Organization Renewal.* New York: Appleton-Century-Crofts, 1969.

March, J., and Simon, H. *Organizations.* New York: John Wiley, 1958.

Margulies, N., and Raia, A. P. *Organization Development: Values, Process, and Technology.* New York: McGraw-Hill, 1972.

Morse, N., and Reimer, E. "The Experimental Change of a Major Organizational Variable." *Journal of Abnormal and Social Psychology* 52 (1956): 120–29.

Rice, A. K. *Productivity and Social Organization: The Ahmedabad Experiment.* London: Tavistock, 1958.

―――. "Individual Group and Intergroup Processes." *Human Relations* 22 (1969): 565–84.

Rogers, E., and Shoemaker, F. *Communication of Innovations.* New York: The Free Press, 1962. Rev. 1971.

Sashkin, M. "Organization Development Practices." *Professional Psychology*, May 1973, pp. 187–92. (a)

―――. "Sashkin's Reply to Levinson." *Professional Psychology*, May 1973, pp. 204–7. (b)

―――, et al. "A Comparison of Social and Organizational Change Models: Information Flow and Data Use Processes." *Psychological Review* 80 (1973): 510–26.

Schein, E. H. *Process Consultation: Its Role in Organization Development.* Reading, Mass.: Addison-Wesley, 1969.

Schmuck, R. A., and Miles, M. B., eds. *Organization Development in Schools.* Palo Alto: National Press, 1971.

Stewart, P. A. *Job Enlargement.* Iowa City: College of Business Administration, University of Iowa, 1967.

Strauss, G. "Organization Development." In *Handbook of Work Organization in Society*, edited by R. Dubin. Chicago: Rand McNally. In press.

Tannenbaum, A., and Allport, F. H. "Personality, Structure and Group Structure: An Interpretative Study of Their Relationship through an Event Structure Hypothesis." *Journal of Abnormal and Social Psychology* 53 (November 1956): 272–80.

Taylor, F. W. *The Principles of Scientific Management.* New York: Harper, 1923.

Thorsrud, E. "A Strategy for Research and Social Change in Industry: A Report on the Industrial Democracy Project in Norway." *Social Science Inform* 9 (1969): 65–90.

Trist, E. L., and Bamforth, R. "Some Social and Psychological Consequences of the Long Wall Method of Coal-Getting." *Human Relations* 4 (1951): 3–38.

―――; Higgin, G. W.; Murray, H.; and Pollack, A. B. *Organizational Choice.* London: Tavistock, 1963.

Vroom, V. *Some Personality Determinants of the Effects of Participation.* Englewood Cliffs, N.J.: Prentice-Hall, 1960.

25

Managing for a Healthier Heart

John M. Ivancevich
Michael T. Matteson

*W*ithin a year over 400 readers of *Management Review* will die from cardiovascular disease. Such is the pervasive nature of this killer.

Each year, approximately one million Americans die from various forms of cardiovascular disease, about 650,000 from heart attacks or coronary heart disease (CHD). For the past 60 years, there has been a steady, significant increase in recorded death rates from heart attacks. Although the precise causes of this increase are poorly understood, one partial explanation points to the increasing complexity and stress of modern life.

A major portion of this stress may have its genesis in organizational forces, called "stressors." These are present any time people are in situations in which their usual behaviors are inappropriate or insufficient, and in which negative consequences can result from not dealing with the situation properly.

It has been suggested that if such factors as blood pressure, cholesterol, and smoking were completely controlled, no more than 25 percent of heart disease would be eliminated. There is strong evidence that organizational stress plays an important role in the development of the remaining 75 percent of heart disease!

It has not been easy for management to accept that, for some, organizational stress contributes to coronary and other disease. However, in recent years medical journals have devoted increasing space to studies dealing with the relationships between organizational stress and CHD. From these studies, one finding shows up again and

SOURCE: John M. Ivancevich and Michael T. Matteson, "Managing for a Healthier Heart." Reprinted, by permission of the publisher, from *Management Review*, October 1978, pp. 14–19. © 1978 by AMACOM, a division of American Management Associations. All rights reserved.

again: organizational stressors can and do cause changes in the physiological and psychological makeups of some people. Further, these changes can contribute to CHD, as well as to other ailments, such as ulcers, migraines, asthma, sexual dysfunctions, and alcoholism.

The Stress Puzzle

Stress is a popular topic of conversation. Dr. Hans Selye first borrowed the English word from physics to describe the body's responses to everything from flu and cold temperatures to emotions such as fear and anger. Today, stress is often broadly defined as a consequence of any action, situation, or force that places special physical and/or psychological demands upon a person.

Stress creates an imbalance within a person. This imbalance manifests itself in many negative symptoms, such as insomnia, sweating, nervousness, and irritability. However, stress symptoms can also be positive, such as an increased state of self-motivation and more commitment to finish a job. What makes the pieces of the stress puzzle so difficult to fit together is that negative and positive stress symptoms are not the same for everyone.

All of us vary in our capacities to cope with stress. Personality characteristics, emotional balance, physical condition and health, and past experiences are major factors that determine our responses. Some amount of stress is good and has positive, productive consequences. Unfortunately, generalizing about how much organizational stress is optimal or needed for high job performance is impossible.

Some organizational stressors, such as being demoted, losing a job, or receiving conflicting demands from more than one superior, have negative consequences for most employees. On the other hand, some stressors, such as being passed over for promotion or not being allowed to participate in decision making, do not produce negative reactions in some individuals. There are even some stressors, such as a difficult job or numerous job assignments, that can have positive consequences.

One striking theme of Selye's research is that some people enjoy stress, and are only happy with a vigorous, fast-pace life. They are "racehorses." Others prefer a peaceful, quiet, tranquil environment. They are "turtles." Selye contends that both categories require a certain amount of stress, but the degrees and the sources differ. And the same stress that motivates racehorses to high levels of performance may be brewing subtle internal transformations that will cause some of them to become "unexpected" CHD statistics.

The main question is how much stress is enough. An optimum level of organizational stress can improve job performance, whereas excessive stress can retard performance and ruin health. When stress has positive consequences for an individual, job performance will in most cases improve, at least in the short run. Being overburdened by stress-producing forces or situations, however, can hurt performance. The relationship between organizational stress and individual performance often follows a bell curve.

From a job performance standpoint some stress is good, but excessive stress is bad. As organizational stress increases, so does individual performance—up to the optimum point. Beyond this level, stress causes a rapid decrease in individual performance.

The Stress Connection

A framework may be helpful to you as a manager in identifying individual stress problems and taking necessary corrective action. At a minimum, such a framework should include: major organizational *stressors*; the manner in which stressors are *perceived*; the *responses* or *outcomes* to the perception of stressors; and important *results* or *consequences*.

The variables in Figure 1 have been identified by medical and behavioral researchers as potentially significant for understanding the stressor and CHD link. However, a variety of other stressors may operate to bring about the same outcomes.

Conflicting and too many work demands can create role ambiguity, conflict, and overload. Cohesiveness and relations with others are group factors that may serve either as stressors or stress reducers. For example, low cohesion in a work group may create stress, whereas high cohesion may serve to offset the effects of other stressors by providing the employee with a great deal of psychological support.

For some people, a potential major stressor is underutilization. Lack of management attention may compound the situation by adversely affecting employee satisfaction. A perceived lack of career progress and inequity in reward systems are two other powerful stressors.

We carry "psychological baggage" into an organization just as we export our job problems into our personal lives. The impact of extraorganizational stressors should never be underestimated. About the best any manager can do about extraorganizational stressors is to be aware of their potential significance, to be alert to their presence, and to show compassion, interest, and understanding. Attempting to intrude on such stress-filled situations as marital problems or child-rearing practices is definitely not recommended. Well-meaning managers who attempt to play amateur psychiatrist may find that the only thing they have accomplished is to elevate *their own* stress levels!

The chart (opposite page) points out that individual perceptions are important in understanding outcomes and consequences. Whether a stressor actually provokes stress or not depends a great deal on how the employee perceives it. That perception in turn is influenced by a variety of individual differences, all of which affect both the physiological and the behavioral outcomes.

Organizational stressors do not always result in coronary heart disease. They can also improve performance and increase motivation and creativity. In many cases, their physiological impacts are minor. What Figure 1 attempts to do is introduce the notion that individual differences may play a major role in unraveling the mysteries of why organizational stressors contribute to an increased incidence of CHD for *some* individuals.

Figure 1   Organizational Stressors and Heart Disease: A Managerial Perspective

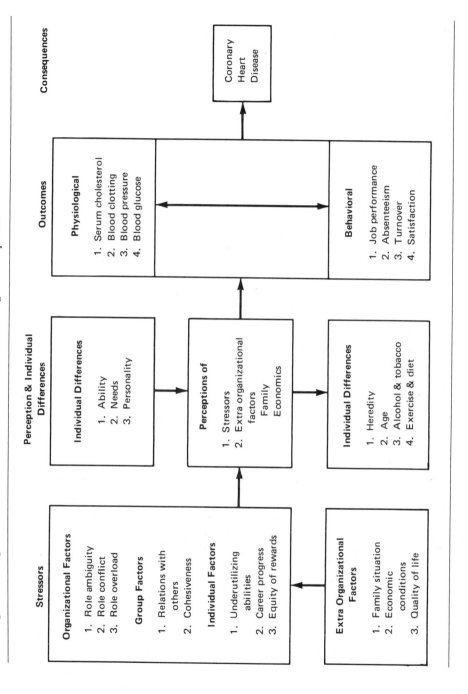

How We Respond to Stress

Employees may react to stress emotionally, behaviorally, and physiologically. The emotional reactions are the ones many people associate with stress. These range from anger and fear to anxiety and hostility. In some cases, the employee suffering from severe stress may act irresponsibly and irrationally.

The behavioral reactions can be either positive or negative. Moderate stress can result in improved levels of job performance. However, people suffering from excessive organizationally related stress tend to be absent more, to quit their jobs frequently, and to make more frequent errors in carrying out job tasks. They may also increase cigarette and/or alcohol consumption, turn to ill-advised medications, and, in severe cases, exhibit paranoid behavior.

Underlying all reactions to stress are physiological responses. These can lead to a wide variety of physical ailments, including migraines, ulcers, hypertension, and heart attacks.

Stressors such as role overload, poor relations with others, deadlines, and family arguments stimulate our glands and nervous system to produce hormones that equip us to combat the stress. These physiological reactions prepare the body to "fight" or "flee." As either route is taken, the system eventually restores itself to a position of balance. A problem within organizational settings—one that managers need to be aware of—is that the stressors build up rather slowly, and most people do not take a total fight or flight stance. *Therefore, stress reactions tend to accumulate and persist for long periods of time.*

This is where organic problems such as coronary heart disease enter the picture. Frequently, CHD gives few obvious early warning signals. Unless the best physiological predictors of coronary heart disease are monitored, there is little hope of reducing the widespread tragedy of a heart attack.

Stress and Occupations

Everyone has heard of the person who boasted, "I'm a top-level executive and I have an ulcer to prove it." Unfortunately, there is abundant evidence in the medical literature to indicate that people in some occupations have a higher incidence of such physical ailments as ulcers, heart disease, and high blood pressure. Human resources must be regarded as an irreplaceable asset in any company, and the relationship between occupational stressors and heart disease can provide important information for developing action programs. Examples of organizational stressors related to three occupational groups may illustrate this point.

Business Executives Successful executives are generally described as driving, ambitious, intense, and task oriented. They are company oriented and job centered and, therefore, are more prone to coronary problems, especially if all their personal interests are narrowly based.

Cardiologists Meyer Friedman and Ray H. Rosenman have correlated the traits of some hard-driving executives to produce a coronary-prone profile. The profiles are called Type A and Type B personalities. The Type A personality belongs to an executive with intense ambition, competitive drive, a sense of urgency, and restlessness. The Type A executive may have a higher probability of developing coronary heart disease or suffering a fatal heart attack.

Despite the pioneering work of Friedman and Rosenman, there is concern about labeling the Type A personality as coronary prone. In fact, some Type A business executives appear to be very healthy and thrive on fast-paced challenges. It seems more feasible to consider executives individually to establish their personal stress conditions and their abilities to cope with stressors.

The executives who have not attained their goals or ambitions may be the ones reporting the highest degree of stress. The 35-year-old comer who is still in the same position at 40 is the one who feels high stress. Less stress is reported by top-level executives who, after working hard and long, have achieved their career goals. The executive who has risen to the top appears to be able to channel new pressures and challenges into productive stress.

Accountants Much medical research has suggested that cholesterol is a factor in coronary heart disease. Cholesterol levels *do* appear to be a valid indicator of accountants' stress.

In one study, the effects of occupational stress upon levels of serum cholesterol was monitored. The accountants in the study had fairly routine work schedules except during urgent tax deadlines. Each accountant's highest level of cholesterol occurred during the points of highest stress or right before the deadlines. That is, cholesterol levels rose as tax deadlines approached. (One might question whether that phenomenon is restricted to accountants!) The lowest level of serum cholesterol occurred at times of minimal stress. This study suggests that cholesterol is extremely sensitive to stress associated with job conditions such as overload, urgency, and task completion.

Operating Employees A number of research reports indicate that job pressures at the operating employee level affect job satisfaction and, consequently, various physiological factors such as blood pressure and cholesterol. In fact, job satisfaction has been found to be inversely related to the frequency of heart attacks for telephone operators, manufacturing employees, sales personnel, and other occupational groups. Job pressures are caused by such factors as unclear requests from supervisors, emphasis on completing job tasks in unrealistic amounts of time, misunderstanding of the reward system being used, inability to accomplish challenging goals, and underutilization of abilities.

Prescriptions for Reducing Stress

Since potentially harmful stressors exist in every organization, at all levels, and for every occupation from the chief operating officer to the window washer, it is important to understand stress, reactions to it, and methods of reducing the negative forms of stress. Fortunately, numerous techniques, ranging from psychotherapy to transcendental meditation, are available for reducing negative stress reactions.

Individual Methods

Ultimately employees must assume the responsibility for their health. *Awareness* and then *action* are needed to reduce potentially harmful stress. As part of awareness, employess should arrange for a physical examination. Typically, the doctor will evaluate such factors as blood pressure, cholesterol level, smoking and drinking habits, coronary history and heredity, electrocardiogram, weight, physical activity record, and cardiorespiratory fitness index.

A growing number of physicians are recommending that in addition to getting the customary resting electrocardiogram, individuals should undergo a stress EKG, usually taken while undergoing strenuous levels of activity on a treadmill. Stress electrocardiograms are detecting coronary abnormalities in about 15 percent of patients with normal resting EKGs.

The results of this type of examination will provide the employee with specific information on current and projected health. Although the medical exam is discussed here under individual methods, special programs may be set up within the company's medical department or employees may be urged to take a physical by an outside preventive medicine clinic.

Beyond taking the physical exam, people should become intimately acquainted with themselves and the organizational and life stressors that make them tense or uncomfortable. Essentially a task of introspection, it is a necessary antecedent to any individually initiated action and its importance cannot be underestimated.

Medical records show that many heart attack survivors report becoming more introspective and reflective *after* their attacks. An unknown number of these might have averted their heart attacks altogether if they had shown the same degree of insight into their activities much earlier.

Once the employee is aware of his or her physical condition and organizational life, that person should take some *action*. Many techniques are available. Some involve nothing more than a decision to repattern certain activities, such as various inter-personal relationships within the company, or a resolve to seek clarification of ambiguous aspects of the organizational role.

Some research indicates that diet and exercise programs supervised by qualified medical professionals can be beneficial in reducing stress. For example, the National Jogging Association reports that many joggers say running relieves mental tension and depression and seems to add to their ability to react to stressors in more positive ways.

More exotic individual stress control techniques include yoga, transcendental meditation, and biofeedback. The scientific evidence of the benefits of such practices is scant, but some people definitely seem able to alter both psychological and physiological factors through such activities. Perhaps the day will soon be upon us when the coffee break is replaced by the exercise break or the meditation break!

Organizational Methods

The issue of the organization's responsibility for the health and fitness of employees is somewhat controversial. Some say that health is a personal matter and therefore the responsiblity of the individual. However, others feel that work, life, and health are so interrelated that the management of any organization must be concerned.

Whether viewed from the pragmatic standpoint of productivity or simply humane interest, it would seem that since all employees at all levels are the human resource core of any organization, management must do its part to minimize potentially harmful stress. Thus the preservation of health by managerial action can serve not only to protect the human assets of the organization, but also to bring about a worthy social goal.

As stated earlier, such stressors as role ambiguity, role conflict, role overload, underutilization of abilities, and poor working relations with others appear to be potentially harmful both for individual health and for organizational effectiveness. Through clear communication, the establishment of unambiguous job demands, and properly planned division of labor, managers can reduce some of these job stressors. Discussions between each subordinate and supervisor about the job and its range and depth could reduce ambiguity and conflict.

It is possible to change the overall climate of the organization by managerial action focusing on stressor reduction. Chief contributors to the type of climate prevailing in a company are the day-to-day practices and philosophy of its managers. Better managerial practices could include methods of early identification of stress-related problems so that employees under high stress can be helped. If the manager is viewed as an important resource for seeking help, employees may be more likely to recognize their own stress problems and more willing to ask for help.

Managers must be aware that organizational stressors can endanger their own health and that of their employees. Therefore, working at changing conditions in the organizational climate that can contribute to increased physical ailments is an important, sound, and worthy managerial practice. Being attuned to the different reactions to stress and following up when signs of stressful response appear are part of the awareness program. Asking, listening, and observing are three actions that will improve a manager's understanding of subordinate stress factors.

Another managerial action with potential for reducing stress effects is the use of increased participation in decision making (PDM). Some research indicates that low PDM is related to excess job stress. Attempts to decrease stress by PDM should be legitimate and require an analysis of important decision situations. Encouraging participation only in routine and trivial decisions is quite transparent and liable to result in even more stress. Also, employee participation should be considered a long-term endeavor. Research clearly demonstrates that involving employees in PDM and suddenly stopping participation after a short period can create negative emotional, behavioral, and physiological reactions.

Job enrichment is another potential strategy for reducing job stress. Through enriched jobs, employees may feel more important and satisfied with the activities they perform. Job enrichment may also remedy or minimize underutilization.

Of course, not all jobs can be enriched, nor do all employees want enriched jobs. There is also the problem of continual enrichment or later efforts to redesign jobs. How many times can a job be enriched? After the initial stimulation of an enriched job wears off, employees may again feel bored, dissatisfied, or underutilized.

Summing Up

Individuals react differently to stress at different times. For this and other reasons, the precise relationship between stress and heart disease and other health ailments is not—and may not ever be—known. However, it is equally clear that stress is taking its toll in organizational effectiveness, efficiency, productivity, and, more importantly, in human lives.

Some of the things we do know about stress are:

Stress is inevitable in organizations, and it has positive and negative consequences.

Stress is created by failure to accomplish career goals.

Organizations create stress by making ambiguous and conflicting requests and by overloading employees with work.

Reactions to stress can be emotional, behavioral, or physiological. Managers need to become more astute at detecting emotional and behavioral reactions both in themselves and in others.

Many of the popular stress-reduction techniques have not been evaluated rigorously to determine their effectiveness. Also, a technique that is an effective stress reducer for one employee may not work for another employee.

Methods to reduce stress can be individually and/or organizationally initiated. The correct sequence for a manager combating excessive organizational stress is to become aware of it first and then to select the best action for the situation and subordinates.

Increased attention to organizational stress may be the most important step a manager can take to ensure both organizational effectiveness and employee health.

26

Goal Setting:

The Tenneco Approach to Personnel Development and Management Effectiveness

*John M. Ivancevich, T. Timothy McMahon,
J. William Streidl, and Andrew D. Szilagyi, Jr.*

*A*pplying goal setting to an organization is intuitively appealing and seems seductively simple, but it is fraught with potential problems. The testimonials of goal-setting advocates are meaningless when an organization is attempting to implement, evaluate, and integrate such a program.

If we want to be able to develop managerial personnel to the limit of their potential, we have to ask ourselves a number of questions. Does each manager really have a clear understanding of his or her job responsibilities? Are superiors providing enough feedback on performance? Are managers given the opportunities and guidance to master their work, increase their skills and knowledge base, and receive promotions and move up to jobs with greater responsibility?

In this article we will examine the efforts of Tenneco Inc. to apply a goal-setting program for management development across relatively autonomous divisional and affiliated companies. By standing back and examining the sequence of activities implemented at Tenneco, we can acquire both a conceptual and an empirically based picture of the strengths and weaknesses of its effort. An analysis of the Tenneco

SOURCE: John M. Ivancevich, J. Timothy McMahon, J. William Streidl, and Andrew D. Szilagyi, Jr., "Goal Setting: The Tenneco Approach to Personnel Development and Management Effectiveness." Reprinted, with permission of the publisher, from *Organizational Dynamics,* Winter 1978, pp. 58–80. © 1978 by AMACOM, a division of American Management Associations. All rights reserved.

experience provides insight into the use of a goal-setting system in a company in which top management is committed to such use. The initial results of the Tenneco program indicate that the goal-setting system has been successful in many areas, although a continual monitoring effort is needed to determine long-run performance changes.

Traditional Goal-Setting Practices

When discussing an organization's goal-setting program, a person may have a number of different approaches in mind. Terms used to describe goal setting include management by objectives (MBO), management by results, work planning and review, and the charter of accountability concept. As George Odiorne emphasizes, goal-setting techniques involve:

> ... a process whereby the superior and subordinate managers of an organization jointly identify common goals, define each individual's major area of responsibility in terms of the results expected of him and use these measures as guides for operating the unit and assessing the contribution of each of its members.

The different terminology used has led to some confusion concerning the basis of goal setting, where it is implemented, and how it works. The major implication, however, is that through discussions and active involvement in goal setting, a subordinate will be motivated to work harder and consequently improve his or her performance.

The philosophical rudiments of goal setting provide the basis for a process that includes a series of interrelated and interdependent steps taken by the superior and subordinate. These steps are illustrated in Figure 1. They include: (1) a *diagnosis* to assess the needs, job, personnel, and technology; (2) *preparation* via communicating what goal setting is, training in the process, establishing objectives, making action plans, and evolving criteria to assess whether the goals of the process are being accomplished; (3) *goal setting*, with special attention paid to goal clarity, superior-subordinate participation, and the establishment of relevant goals and goal priorities; (4) an *intermediate review* of the original goals, which is a form of feedback and provides an opportunity to modify the original goals; and (5) a *final review* or discussion and analysis of the results, which are used to initiate the next complete cycle of objective setting. The anticipated result of the planning, control, and organization goal-setting process is improved and motivated involvement that is based on accomplishments rather than personality or popularity. In addition, managers are encouraged .o develop their skills and abilities within the framework of their jobs.

A number of important principles of action emerge from a close examination of this process:

Principle I: Diagnosis. The crucial first step in any goal-setting program should be a thorough diagnosis of the job, the participants, and the needs of the organization.

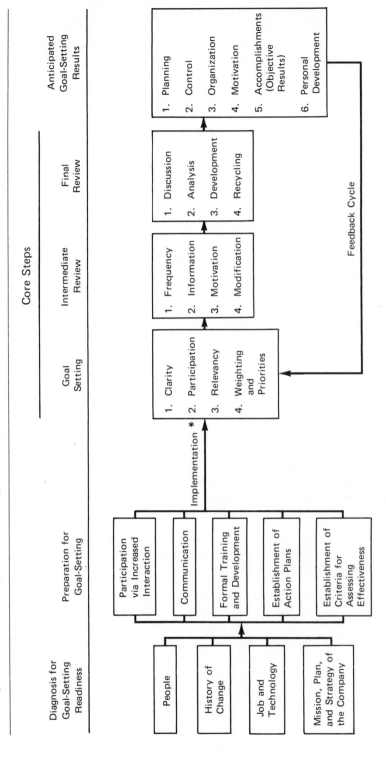

Figure 1 Goal-Setting Model for Superior-Subordinate Objective Setting

Diagnosis for Goal-Setting Readiness

Preparation for Goal-Setting

Core Steps

Goal Setting

Intermediate Review

Final Review

Anticipated Goal-Setting Results

People

History of Change

Job and Technology

Mission, Plan, and Strategy of the Company

Participation via Increased Interaction

Communication

Formal Training and Development

Establishment of Action Plans

Establishment of Criteria for Assessing Effectiveness

Implementation *

1. Clarity
2. Participation
3. Relevancy
4. Weighting and Priorities

1. Frequency
2. Information
3. Motivation
4. Modification

1. Discussion
2. Analysis
3. Development
4. Recycling

1. Planning
2. Control
3. Organization
4. Motivation
5. Accomplishments (Objective Results)
6. Personal Development

Feedback Cycle

* After the preparation phase is completed it is necessary to develop a systematic plan for implementation.

Principle II: Commitment. Goal setting requires the frequent and intensive involvement and participation of superiors and subordinates.

Principle III: Meaningful Goals. Goals should be established that, if attained, benefit organizational effectiveness *and* the personal growth and development of the participants.

Principle IV: Feedback. Goal setting relies heavily on feedback results, which should be as closely connected to behavior and performance as possible.

Principle V: Counseling. The superior should be competent in counseling subordinates on the achieved results and the expected or agreed-to results for the next cycle.

These principles are based on a review of the empirically based goal-setting literature, which has been quite sketchy and limited considering the worldwide use of organizational goal setting. The vast majority of goal-setting literature that espouses its virtues is based primarily on testimonial claims of consultants, academicians, and convinced practicing managers. These advocates propose an attractive list of benefits that can accrue and, in certain instances, have accrued to organizations that implement and monitor goal-setting programs. Some of these benefits include:

> Improved short- and long-range planning.
> A procedure for monitoring work progress and results.
> Improved commitment to the organization because of
>   increased motivation, loyalty, and participation of employees.
> Improved clarity in the manager's role.
> Improved communication between superiors and subordinates.

These and other benefits are certainly attractive to any manager. Unfortunately, some advocates assume that not only do these benefits flow easily from a goal-setting effort, but they do so in a relatively short time. These erroneous assumptions have not been evaluated in most reviews of goal-setting programs, and false claims have sometimes been made for the superiority of these programs. In addition, inflated expectations can emerge and have emerged that are impossible to fulfill in a short time.

A less vocal, but equally important, group of managers has experienced some of the negative consequences of goal-setting programs. Some of their complaints are:

> Goal-setting programs are used as a whip, particularly when
>   they are closely tied to wage and salary programs.
> Many programs not only fail to receive continual top
>   management commitment and support but do not reach the
>   lower managerial levels.
> There is an overemphasis on production and productivity, or
>   what are called "hard" performance indicators.
> Many superiors are not adequately trained in the goal-setting
>   process or in the most effective manner of coaching and
>   counseling subordinates.

Goal-setting programs fail to provide adequate personnel incentives to improve performance—the emphasis is only on the benefits to the organization with seemingly little concern for the development of the participating managers.

The advocates of goal setting in organizations project the impression that it is the panacea for motivation, leadership, change, development, and personal development problems. Because many organizations fail to recognize that goal setting is a comprehensive management process, they attempt to superimpose it on their existing structures, climates, and untrained personnel. This unfortunate imposition leads to some of the problems cited above, which probably account for the limited number of scientifically based success stories reported. Too, there is often a tendency to overemphasize hard performance factors in goal-setting programs. This type of focus fails to capture the developmental potential of goal setting. Another major block to creating a successful goal-setting system is the lack of top management involvement and support. The evidence is so clear cut that top management must be involved in each phase of the program that it is difficult to fathom why this issue is not a number-one priority.

Concern for Development

Many goal-setting systems have been introduced with an emphasis on only the hard performance indicators for managerial jobs. The Tenneco emphasis on development that resulted from the task force efforts described below put a new definition on work development. Tenneco's goal-setting system recognized the importance of being able to measure the quality and quantity of work performed, but it also stressed the fact that measurements exist that will help meet manager development objectives at each level of the managerial/professional organization. Several management experts have recognized the need for making manager development the building block of all organization units. The catalyst is the manager-employee relationship and the degree of support for continuing development that comes from such a relationship. In addition, there is the recognition that true development occurs over a period of time in an atmosphere that is related to the everyday work life of the employee and his ability to continue to improve, whether or not he is promoted (see Figure 2).

Tenneco's definition of development, as depicted in Figure 2, suggests that the basis for continued development is the ongoing dialog between manager and employee at every level of the organization. This dialog is expected to result in the development of hard performance indicators (defining what a good job is), while considering the manager's role, his or her unique qualifications, the formal organization structure, and the results expected from that employee. The result should be an emphasis on the individual employee's role in both providing his contribution (hard performance indicators) and obtaining personal satisfaction and self-fulfillment from that

Figure 2   Development Goal

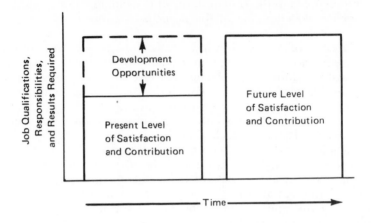

contribution. Concurrently, it should create a group of employees who are striving for perfection on their jobs and who will therefore become qualified to be considered for positions of greater responsibility.

Tenneco, like most organizations, utilizes hard performance indicators to determine whether results are being achieved. What is unique in the Tenneco approach is the attempt to tie in such achievement with the overall development objective, thereby pointing out how each employee contribution places the manager, employee, and organization as a whole in "win–win" positions.

Emphasis on Top-Management Support at Tenneco

A task force that represented each divisional company in Tenneco was appointed by the office of the president. Each company had at least one representative (vice-president or director) on the task force. The task force established some important objectives for its work in instituting a goal-setting system. The task force decided that it would be necessary to (1) secure and maintain management commitment, starting with top levels of the company and moving through each succeeding level of management, to ensure that the new performance planning and evaluation (PP&E) system would be used and would become a "managerial way of life" rather than a personnel program; (2) ensure that a minimum of additional procedure and paperwork would be used in introducing and implementing the system; (3) ensure that the system was understood conceptually and that the managers who had to use it had the basic skills necessary for system implementation; and (4) attempt to communicate the system effectively so that participants—superior and subordinate—recognized the need for continual interface, dialog, and commitment to goals by both at each level of the organization to achieve the development objectives of the organizations as a whole.

One form of top management support for the PP&E system is identified in the foreword to a booklet describing Tenneco's approach to goal setting with the following excerpted statement from Wilton E. Scott, chairman of the board and chief executive officer of Tenneco:

It is my utmost concern that among our thousands of employees there may be highly capable people whose talents we do not recognize or to whom we do not give maximum opportunity. And if we fail to do that, in fact, if we fail to offer maximum opportunity to any one person in our organization, we are failing in one of our basic management responsibilities . . . accordingly, I expect this philosophy and method of management to receive enthusiastic support at all levels within Tenneco.

Tenneco Inc. has an active office of the president. The above and similar statements of top management support were reinforced by the active participation of the office of the president in the formation of the task force and in the introduction of the PP&E system through initial training efforts. Members of the office of the president did, in fact, participate in the same basic training workshops as other members of management. This type of involvement is often bypassed in less effective goal-setting efforts.

Simply stated, Tenneco's philosophy of goal setting suggests that a maximum opportunity for personal satisfaction and personal contribution to the organization can occur only when the job is well defined in terms of the outputs expected from it. These outputs can be defined only through an ongoing relationship between manager and employee at every level of the organization, and the discussion of such development opportunities provides a basis for continual development. Figure 2 illustrates the long-run goal of personal development that manifests itself in the form of improved satisfaction and increased organizational and individual contribution.

Tenneco Preparation Phase

The top-management cadre was knowledgeable about problems encountered in other organizations with goal-setting systems. By studying the literature carefully, attending professional meetings, visiting with peers in other companies, and discussing goal setting with experts, the Tenneco team developed a set of scenarios of the crucial problems to avoid in implementing a goal-setting system within the company. This set included the following:

Commitment

Failure to get top management's commitment and involvement is a quick way to lose the influence of a goal-setting system. Lack of support from the top causes goal setting to deteriorate into another futile bureaucratic exercise. It becomes something for middle managers who are expected to represent top management to fiddle with. The middle-level executive writes a set of objectives, looks it over, and files it deeply into a desk drawer to simmer for at least a year. These objectives are retrieved one year later and looked at before the next year's cycle begins. Thus goal setting is reduced to filling out a report, filing it away, and looking at it a year later in a casual fashion. Instead of an exercise, this sequence of events can more appropriately be called "a game."

Evaluation

Many managerial processes and change interventions, such as goal setting, tend to have consultants carry out a diagnosis and evaluation of the system. This dual role of consultant and researcher is difficult to perform. The person or team performing the dual roles is likely to conclude that what ails the system can be treated by "their" package. Thus an organizational change expert finds that the problems can be remedied through goal setting; the transactional analysis specialist finds that TA is the answer; and the career planning advocate suggests that performance problems can be solved by developing career plans.

Tenneco decided to have an external group evaluate its goal-setting intervention. The roles of implementer and evaluator were separated on purpose. The internal task force decided to implement goal setting in the divisional companies. The preparatory steps for Tenneco's goal setting were conducted by representatives of the company and not by trainers from an institute or university. Although Tenneco was responsible for the preparation, evaluation was placed totally in the hands of John M. Ivancevich, J. Timothy McMahon, and Andrew D. Szilagyi, Jr., of the Department of Organizational Behavior and Management at the University of Houston.

Status of Goal Setting

Many companies treat the goal-setting system as an appendage that is not too important. The status of the program is ambiguous and questionable. If more than marginally acceptable improvements in personal development are to accrue, goal setting must become one of management's top priorities. If not, it often begins to suffer from a lack of attention. When this happens, the program disintegrates rapidly and ends up on a back burner or as a "wooden" set of notebooks that adorns each manager's shelf and collects dust.

Lack of Integration

Everyone always hopes that the goal-setting effort will be integrated with performance appraisal, managerial planning and controlling, and management development. Unless more than hoping is done the program becomes little more than useless. Integration with the normal managerial processes must be accomplished from the top down.

These four crucial issues were considered carefully by the task force. The task force produced specific strategies, policy suggestions, and action plans that addressed each issue. In working through their suggestions, the task force paid particular attention to failures reported by other companies that seemed to ignore the importance of commitment, evaluation, status, and integration.

Training Phase

An early suggestion by the development task force was that the PP&E system be field tested through initial introductory training activities and implementation in two companies. Concurrently, one of the other companies, which had eight years' experience with a comparable goal-setting system, could continue to operate within that system. The knowledge gained by the pilot companies and the experienced goal-setting company would, in turn, be used to build a better overall system for Tenneco.

The company with eight years' goal-setting experience provided a director-level manager to serve on the overall corporate task force during initial PP&E system-design activities. At the same time, that task force member, along with Tenneco corporate staff members, worked to develop an overall training package that could be used throughout all the Tenneco companies to introduce the system. Strengths and weaknesses found in the approch to introducing goal setting in the experienced company and that company's training materials provided additional input for both the task force and the subgroup that was assigned to develop the initial training package.

The pilot companies—one in a process industry, the other in manufacturing—were asked to carry out initial PP&E introductory activities before the total corporate training package was developed. The diversity and geographic spread of these companies provided an opportunity to field test some of the concepts built into the overall PP&E system, so that an introductory training package could be developed that was acceptable and effective across a wide range of industries.

The task force efforts and the specific training and introductory plans provided a conceptual basis of understanding and skill practice appropriate to each of the widely diverse companies within the Tenneco family of companies. Materials and "train the trainers" seminars for each divisional company were provided that set broad parameters for such training and had built-in flexibility to make the training and implementation suitable for each company. For example, in one large division of one of the companies, over 90 line managers were trained as PP&E trainers; in a smaller company with widely decentralized locations, one training and development specialist carried out the initial basic training.

The "train the trainers" sessions and the follow-up sessions in each divisional company resulted in the completion of basic goal-setting training for over 15,000 managerial and professional employees during 1976 in both the United States and overseas. This segment of the training concentrated on the individual identification of major responsibilities and goals (performance planning). It did not attempt to provide detailed knowledge on performance evaluation, coaching, and counseling. Another PP&E training segment is being carried on now on a highly flexible and decentralized basis for the approximately 5,000 managers of other managers and professional employees. These managers of managers must be skilled in completing the PP&E cycle through performance evaluation, coaching, and counseling activities.

Integrating PP&E with Normal Managerial Processes

The sheer size, diversity, and geographic spread of the Tenneco companies have provided some of the strengths of the Tenneco approach to date. At the same time, they could cause system weaknesses in terms of overall integration with its present and future management systems. As mentioned, the system has been installed throughout the various companies, utilizing basic training materials prepared at Tenneco's headquarters.

The corporate policy statement permits a considerable amount of divisional flexibility:

> The PP&E system represents a minimum standard to be achieved by all divisional companies and all Tenneco Inc. corporate staff groups. The minimum standard requires the continual use of formalized goal setting resulting from face-to-face meetings for the purpose of discussing, defining and recording responsibilities, expected results, priorities and target dates.

Tenneco has standard reporting systems (largely in the financial area), but there is considerable divisional autonomy in terms of other operating practices, procedures, policies, and systems. To date, each company continues to effect the integration of the PP&E system into its organization units in a manner appropriate for that unit. For example, within one of the larger manufacturing units, training methods, document flow procedures, audit and control activities, and so on are different for the international unit than they are for some of the domestic units. In fact, there are some variations between the major domestic units. This flexibility of approach ties back to making development the major objective. Currently, Tenneco corporate programs are being developed that will assist divisional managers to integrate their activities, but the approach will be through training and information rather than executive order.

Tenneco System in Action

In recent years many executives have accepted the principle that the health and growth of their enterprise depend, in part, on the growth and development of employees. Tenneco's management believed that goal setting via a performance planning and evaluation system could be a vehicle for such growth and development. In its most basic sense, the PP&E system represents a program for improving work performance and management development for managerial and professional-level employees in all Tenneco corporate staff groups and divisional companies.

A number of objectives have been established for the PP&E system. The first is improved on-the-job effectiveness by each employee in his or her present position by requiring planned attention to goals and priorities. The second is self-development to assure each employee's future effectiveness and career growth. The final objective is to locate managerial personnel with the ability to handle greater responsibility. A pool of such personnel assures management continuity from within the organization. Taken together, the objectives of the PP&E system are intended to provide each employee with the maximum opportunity for personal development and advancement and to provide a tool for more effective management. In its most basic form, the PP&E system is as shown in Figure 3.

The PP&E system is composed of several sequential steps. Each has a specific purpose and is essential to the program.

Performance Planning

In this first phase, the job and situation are diagnosed, and the employee states his or her job responsibilities and objectives for the year. The process includes:

> Broadly defining the key responsibilities of the job.
> Expressing specific objectives to be achieved for each key responsibility.
> Assigning relative priorities to the desired results.

This first step is important because it allows the employee to discuss specific job aspects with his or her supervisor and to obtain agreement on goals. The agreed-upon plans are recorded on a form and reviewed periodically by the superior and subordinate to check progress, discuss ways to improve, and agree on changes in activities that may be necessary to adapt to changes in the business climate or other related conditions.

Performance Evaluation

After one year, the results of the employee's actual performance are measured against stated objectives and priorities. The employee finds out exactly how well he or she is doing and any opportunities to contribute better results are fully identified. The evaluation phase has three basic parts.

> The supervisor completes a tentative evaluation of the subordinate's performance.
> The supervisor's superior reviews the tentative evaluation to assure consistency, equity, and quality.
> The supervisor discusses the evaluation with the subordinate, with a focus on developing the subordinate.

Development

During the performance evaluation session, the subordinate is told how well he or she is doing, and specific plans for development are made, based on a discussion of:

> Strengths and weaknesses of past performance.
> Potential performance improvement opportunities.

Figure 3   Philosophy of the Basic PP&E System (Goal Setting)

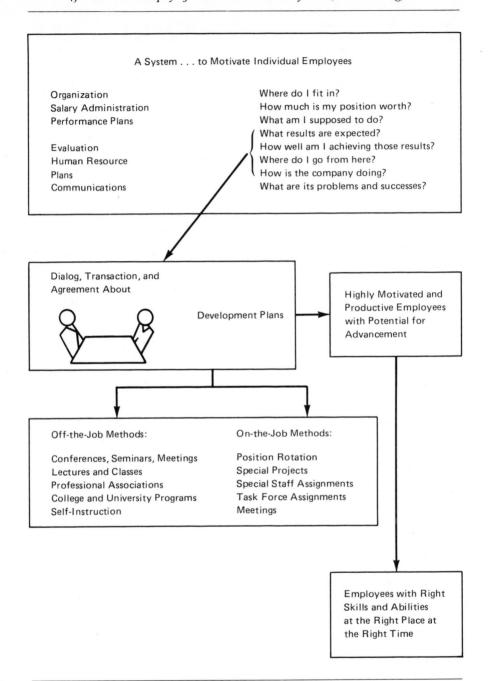

A System . . . to Motivate Individual Employees

Organization
Salary Administration
Performance Plans

Evaluation
Human Resource
Plans
Communications

Where do I fit in?
How much is my position worth?
What am I supposed to do?
What results are expected?
How well am I achieving those results?
Where do I go from here?
How is the company doing?
What are its problems and successes?

Dialog, Transaction, and
Agreement About

Development Plans

Highly Motivated and
Productive Employees
with Potential for
Advancement

Off-the-Job Methods:

Conferences, Seminars, Meetings
Lectures and Classes
Professional Associations
College and University Programs
Self-Instruction

On-the-Job Methods:

Position Rotation
Special Projects
Special Staff Assignments
Task Force Assignments
Meetings

Employees with Right
Skills and Abilities
at the Right Place at
the Right Time

The subordinate's interest in development and aspirations for advancement.

After the performance evaluation session, the supervisor completes an assessment of the employee's potential for development. The report includes:

Overall performance rating during the last period.
Development needs and mutually satisfactory action plans.
Progress and achievement from previous development plans.
Interests and aspirations.
Present promotability and potential for future achievement.
Possible replacements.

This assessment is reviewed by the supervisor's superior and is maintained within each division and at corporate headquarters to serve as a source for locating employees with advancement potential.

Experience and research reveal that there should be a relationship between how well a job is performed and the financial rewards allocated. Many companies have found, however, that little employee development takes place in salary review sessions. Because of this, the PP&E system requires salary discussion interviews to be separate and distinct from progress reviews and development/evaluation sessions. The PP&E system is designed to plan for good performance, correct performance problems, achieve the goal plan, assist the employee in developing his or her optimal skills, and, most important, increase the job effectiveness and long-run career development of each managerial and professional employee. PP&E-related discussions take place many times during the review year, as plans are modified, different goals are achieved and new ones developed, and the supervisor assumes the role of a coach in assisting the employee to develop his or her skill utilization.

The proper procedure for determining what impact, if any, the PP&E system is having on the participants is to perform a continuous evaluation. One source of information is the participants themselves. What do they feel about the program? What do they like or dislike? How are they conducting goal-setting sessions? These are some of the questions that can be examined in the evaluation phase.

Evaluation Phase

The scientific evaluation of the PP&E system focuses on five basic objectives:

1. Initially, to trace changes in attitudes throughout the PP&E system. After full implementation, to trace performance or on-the-job effectiveness.
2. To isolate problems participants are having with the PP&E system.

3. To determine how PP&E is being utilized on the job.
4. To gather scientific data so that modifications and changes in the PP&E system based on more than personal opinions or intuitive judgments can be initiated.
5. To compare Tenneco results with those in similar organizations that have implemented goal-oriented programs.

A survey methodology was used by external organizational researchers to achieve the evaluation objectives. The responses described attitudes about goal-setting activities, job characteristics, organization climate, and what it was like to set PP&E plans with a superior. It was assumed that positive and negative reactions to and attitudes about PP&E had to be studied over a period of time to acquire a picture of what was happening within the units and divisions. Studying reactions and attitudes over a short period is not recommended; goal-setting initiated changes often take time to appear.

The timing for assessing reactions and attitudes is spelled out in Figure 4. The first time frame for taking measurements is referred to as the *baseline*. Baseline measures were taken during April–July, 1976. From late 1977 on, similar evaluations will be conducted at Tenneco, so that each of the five objectives can be accomplished with scientifically based data.

Because of the diversity of type of division and geographic location in the overall PP&E introductory effort, a wide range of approaches were considered and used to determine how well the system was meeting development needs. Personal visits and consultations with line and staff personnel responsible for system introduction and implementation have been carried out continually since the system was introduced.

Ideally, of course, it would have been appropriate to attempt to measure attitudes before any changes had been introduced to Tenneco or its individual companies by training and by establishing the task force. This approach was not used because the high interest in getting the PP&E system introduced and implemented generated its own momentum, and it was felt that the need for the system in terms of overall developmental objectives far outweighed any concern for getting pure baseline measurements.

This article reports only the attitude data; it does not cover development or performance indicators. These measures will eventually be combined with the attitude data to provide a comprehensive picture of the impact of the PP&E system. Goal-setting results from other organizations suggest that changes in attitudes typically precede improvements in performance. Thus the initial research spotlight centers on attitudes of Tenneco managers toward PP&E.

Driver and Secondary Variables and Process Indicators

The Tenneco PP&E system appears to be stimulating, challenging, and pervasive enough to cause things to happen. It was assumed that after PP&E implementation, improvements would occur in such areas as job

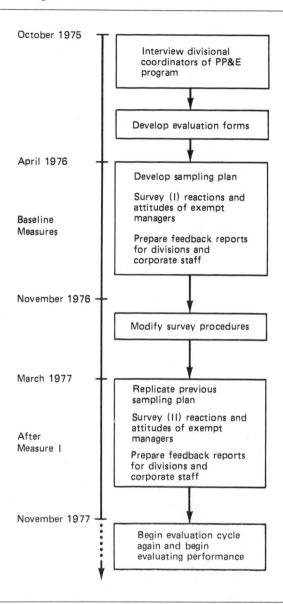

Figure 4   Goal-Setting Process: Tenneco PP&E Evaluation Program

October 1975

Interview divisional coordinators of PP&E program

Develop evaluation forms

April 1976

Baseline Measures

Develop sampling plan

Survey (I) reactions and attitudes of exempt managers

Prepare feedback reports for divisions and corporate staff

November 1976

Modify survey procedures

March 1977

After Measure I

Replicate previous sampling plan

Survey (II) reactions and attitudes of exempt managers

Prepare feedback reports for divisions and corporate staff

November 1977

Begin evaluation cycle again and begin evaluating performance

clarity, job tension, feedback, need satisfaction, and the linking of performance and rewards. The survey was designed to determine whether these attitudinal improvements were actually occurring.

Driver variables is the term used to describe the central attitude changes, after PP&E is implemented, in such areas as goal feedback, participation, role clarity, job autonomy, and job tension. It was assumed that the driver variables would provide the impetus and starting point for performance and self-development improvements.

The *secondary variables* were assumed to be important, but were expected to take longer to show improvements. Included in this set were such variables as job satisfaction, organizational climate, and job characteristic variables such as autonomy, feedback, and uncertainty. Again, previous research on goal setting in other organizations has indicated that these factors would begin to show significant changes after a program such as PP&E was functioning smoothly.

Process indicators was used to refer to measures that assess what goes on between superior and subordinate in PP&E planning and performance evaluation sessions. Unfortunately, it is extremely difficult to determine exactly what does happen when a boss and a subordinate meet to discuss the subordinate's goals. A number of survey questions were aimed at learning more about these important processes.

A few sample questions from the *driver, secondary,* and *process* portions of the survey questionnaire are listed in Table 1. The responses to the attitude questions were used to create the baseline measures. A similar survey will be conducted annually to generate measures subsequent to baseline PP&E implementation. The monitoring of attitudes will enable Tenneco managers to investigate soft spots in PP&E implementation more thoroughly.

Selected Results: Lots of Promise

The volume of data collected is too large to present in an article. However, a sample of the baseline results will provide some indication of the nature of PP&E at Tenneco. During the months of April-July 1976, over 4,500 out of a randomly selected sample of 5,300 surveyed at Tenneco responded to an attitude survey. These 5,300 were selected from a list of approximately 15,000 eligible managers. When the baseline data were collected, some managers were already using the PP&E system and others were not. A total of 2,131 respondents indicated that at the baseline point they were using the PP&E system; 2,395 respondents said they were not. Thus they were divided into two groups: *user of PP&E* and *nonuser of PP&E*.

User and Nonuser: Driver Results

In analyzing each driver variable score, the user managers responded more favorably than the nonusers. All references to "more" and "less" in discussing results refer to statistically significant differences $\leq .05$. In other words, the probability of the differences being due to chance is 5 percent or less. The users report more goal feedback, more goal participation, more goal clarity, more role clarity, less job tension, and more job autonomy.

User and Nonuser: Secondary Results

The positive improvements found in the driver variables were expected to be present to a lesser degree in the secondary variables. More time is generally needed to alter job satisfaction, organizational climate, and job characteristics. The users reported more pay satisfaction, training orientation, work group cohesion, and job variety. Of the 18 secondary variables measured, the users reported more favorable attitudes on 16,

Table 1 Sample of Survey Questions

Specific Portion of Questionnaire	Sample Questions
Driver Variables*	
Goal Feedback	I receive a considerable amount of feedback concerning my overall performance on the job.
Goal Participation	My superior usually asks for my opinions and thoughts when determining the results expected for my work.
Need Satisfaction	There is good opportunity for advancement.
Role Clarity	I feel certain about how much authority I have on my job.
Job Tension	I am unclear about just what the scope and responsibilities of my job are.
Secondary Variables*	
Pay Satisfaction	Considering the work required, the pay for my job is good.
Fringe Benefit Satisfaction	In general, I am satisfied with the personal protection (for example, hospitalization, surgical, and major medical) benefit plans I receive.
Organizational Climate	The organization places great emphasis on improving individual performance through training and development activities.
Job Characteristics	There are different types of work to do every day in my job.
Process Issues	
Time	How much time did you take to prepare your last set of PP&E plans?
Coverage	How many of your job duties were covered in your last PP&E session?
Involvement	To what extent were your PP&E plans determined by you?

*NOTE: The driver and secondary variable responses were made on a five-point Likert-type scale. An example would be a question to which the respondent marks one of the following: always, often, sometimes, rarely, never.

more than anticipated for the baseline period. For one of the other variables, job difficulty, the mean scores were the same for users and nonusers. Only for satisfaction with co-workers was the nonuser score more positive, but the difference was not statistically significant.

Process Results

Only the user managers completed this section of the survey. A profile of the results indicate the following:

About 20 percent of the PP&E session with the superior was spent on a discussion of results. (Given the age of this effort, 20 percent is acceptable We expect this figure to rise later.)

The majority of managers believed that they had more say than their superiors in establishing their individual PP&E plans.
PP&E plans were arranged according to priorities.
On the average, the PP&E participants met formally with superiors approximately two times to finalize their PP&E plans. The average meeting lasted about one hour.

The process results at Tenneco were compared with those obtained by user managers in other manufacturing companies using programs similar to PP&E. Answers from 800 managers responding to similar process questions were gathered from three non-Tenneco manufacturing organizations. The comparisons indicated that Tenneco managers were more satisfied with their goal-oriented program, but spent less time preparing for the planning sessions (one day versus several days) and focused slightly less on personal development during the sessions.

Overall Picture at the Baseline: Positive

For Tenneco as a whole, the best way to describe the baseline results is "positive." The profile that emerges when the data are analyzed shows that users of PP&E display more positive attitudes about their jobs, company, and supervisor. These improvements emerged shortly after implementation of the PP&E program.

If the word "positive" is used to describe the Tenneco picture at the baseline, another word is needed, and that is "caution." The results focused on driver and secondary variables that were attitudinal and process indicators, which are subjective. The reactions, attitudes, and performance of PP&E participants must continue to be monitored. The missing links at the baseline are the performance measures. These are needed to complete the picture of Tenneco PP&E. If the positive results in attitude changes associated with PP&E are duplicated in the future with positive performance and personal development changes, the Tenneco approach may well serve as an important model for other organizations.

Although the performance indicators have not been tapped because it is too early to look for changes, the findings are positive. The 800 goal-setting participants in the three non-Tenneco manufacturing companies completed a number of driver, secondary, and process questions in earlier surveys. They were used as a comparison sample to judge the differences between PP&E and similar programs in other companies. The users in the comparison companies were at approximately the same point of implementation and experience in goal setting when the measurements were taken. The Tenneco findings are quite similar to the comparison findings. This is impressive, because each of the comparison companies reported significant quality, quantity, cost, and safety performance improvements approximately 15 to 18 months after full implementation of their goal-setting systems. There is every reason to assume that Tenneco performance changes will be just as positive.

Some Weaknesses and Potential Problems

It would be exciting to be able to report that the Tenneco system has no weaknesses at its present stage of development. Unfortunately, this is not possible. First, because of the sheer size, diversity, and differences in processes used within each company it might be necessary to monitor or evaluate at different points in time. However, to encourage the evaluation of PP&E at all companies, it had to be done at a specific time by external parties. This has created some frustration among company executives, and may result in a decreased willingness to participate further in the evaluation. Managers whose divisions were not far along in the program felt anxious and threatened by the fact that they would not look as good on the reports evaluators submitted to corporate headquarters. Second, because of the flexibility purposely built into the programs within each company, some managers are not devoting the necessary time and energy to the PP&E system. Thus there is some unevenness across companies on how much they encourage managers to take the time to do a thorough job. The flexibility of the present arrangement may mitigate against correcting this defect.

In Tenneco's approach to goal setting, the flexibility is in the areas of policy, procedures, and training. Corporate policy is to establish minimum standards for the continual use of formalized goal setting. These standards provide a degree of continuity to the process of discussing, refining, and recording responsibilities, expected results, priorities, and target dates without being unduly restrictive. As a practical matter, Tenneco's policy gives divisional companies an opportunity to approach the goal-setting process in ways that will be the most helpful and applicable to them. For example, PP&E forms used by divisional companies differ in terms of general format and the categories of goals enumerated.

Flexibility is also reflected in the area of PP&E procedures. For example, the procedure requiring superior-level review (face to face) of performance evaluation made by a supervisor before it is discussed with the affected employee is not always adhered to. In some cases the physical separation of the evaluating supervisor and his or her superior makes the face-to-face review impractical because of unavoidable time lags. Where this is a problem, divisional companies have developed their own procedures for handling hierarchical review.

Flexibility in training covers variation in the length of training programs used by divisional companies and in several cases modifications in the training materials developed at Tenneco headquarters to meet the specific needs of the different companies. In addition, some companies have used line people as trainers, others have used staff, and some have used a combination of the two.

Another important part of evaluation is that feedback from it can be provided to make important modifications. Because of the flexibility built into PP&E no specific feedback strategy is used across companies. Research indicates that systematic feedback is an important priority in establishing a program such as goal setting. Presently, each company is able to develop its own feedback plans. Some participants have commented that they have not received any feedback on the evaluation.

Unless these complaints are remedied, cooperation between the PP&E participants and evaluators may become strained. It is a natural reaction after participating in a survey study to want some feedback on what was discovered.

There are no plans to allow each company eventually to tailor its own PP&E system. But because these companies have different customers, technologies, and problems, the PP&E efforts in each are expected to become more individualized. Initially, the objective was to get the companies involved in goal setting to use a common base—the PP&E system. However, it is becoming more obvious as the system becomes embedded that each company will have to make modifications.

Implications

A number of implications for practicing managers can be derived from the Tenneco approach to goal setting and management development and the corresponding research effort to evaluate the effectiveness of the system. This experience with goal setting is unique for reasons other than its scope and the large numbers of participants. First, although performance goals are not ignored, the focus is on manager development. The usual goal-setting approach is just the opposite; development is totally ignored. Second, the effectiveness of the system is determined by external evaluators employing a detailed survey research methodology. Unfortunately, in many situations, the degree of goal-setting effectiveness is determined by managers' and/or consultants' (internal and external) testimonials. Third, the reports of the external evaluations provide the basis for an ongoing feedback system that focuses on specific variables and dynamics of the goal-setting system. In most instances managers faced with a sputtering goal-setting system must base their diagnosis and remedial action on intuition, hunches, or selected feedback from participants. The external evaluations have raised the level of the feedback, making it a valuable commodity for managers.

1. *Organizational goal-setting systems need participants to look closely at personal development goals and avoid the relegation of these goals to a second-class citizenship role in the program. Personal development goals may be the key to an improvement in the quality of work life.* It's no secret that most goal-setting systems focus on performance goals, with little if any attention paid to personal development. If goal setting is to be a proactive program that makes the concept of sound human resource management operative and is intrinsically satisfying because the goals are meaningful, personal development goals have to be included. In fact, personal development goals may be more important than performance goals; they are surely not less important. Development goals are closely related to performance; they represent a medium for management improvement that will be reflected in performance. They serve as a major building block in a sound management resources program. And they can improve the quality of work life. Also, their value in terms of motivation and psychological involvement is important. Employees pay little attention to personal development goals because of the

overemphasis on performance goals. Feelings of increased responsibility, growth, challenge, and achievement can all flow from the establishment of personal development goals.

2. *Top-management support needs to be conveyed by actual involvement in training, implementation, and integration efforts.* Information that points to the necessity of top-management support of and seriousness about goal setting is plentiful and there is no need to repeat it here. However, the intent of top management is reinforced by appointing a development task force, attending the actual goal-setting training, and engaging external evaluators. The probability that goal setting will be perceived as "just another program" is reduced by each of these actions. The seriousness of top management is conveyed when it participates actively, then subjects the program to objective evaluation, using evaluation results to solve problems and identify needed modifications. It also shows it means business when it involves people throughout the organization in the process. No one at Tenneco has complained that top management is not involved in the PP&E system. In fact, all members of the office of the president participated in goal-setting training, and all employees seemed to understand that the very top level of Tenneco was committed and active.

3. *A critical issue is how the goal-setting system is implemented. In many cases, the method of implementation can make a difference between positive and negative effects.* Tenneco diagnosed before it acted; it appointed key people from each divisional company as representatives; it established a development task force to work out the problems; and it trained participants and educated them before the program was initiated. Each of these steps was taken carefully so that complaints, discomfort, and misunderstandings would be minimized. In many companies there is a tendency to rush into goal setting without establishing the necessary foundation. The task force was the foundation that addressed the issues so commonly faced in an intervention such as goal setting. It served as an information processing unit and as the hub of PP&E activities.

4. *The use of external evaluators minimizes the probability of bias creeping into assessments because the psychological (ego) involvement of the internal evaluator and the economic motivation of the consultant are eliminated.* With all the time and money many organizations spend in implementing goal-setting systems it is surprising how seldom evaluations are made and with what lack of rigor in following scientific procedures. Perhaps the investment was too high to make any criticism palatable. Or the people involved may have gotten so wrapped up in the "means"— gaining acceptance, developing forms and manuals, and establishing training programs—that the "end"—an effective, well-integrated system—got lost. Another possibility is that managers saw implementing a goal-setting system as a one-shot deal rather than an ongoing process that requires modification and an effort to sustain the system.

In any event, hiring qualified external evaluators on a contract basis has a number of advantages. Since these evaluators are not involved in the program design or implementation, they are not emotionally attached to its success and can be more objective. The scientific methodology they employ—data collection methods, data analysis, and standardized reporting formats—facilitate their objectivity. For example, the fact that participants can send unsigned questionnaires directly to the evaluators is likely to generate more honest responses than if they had to deliver them to the personnel manager, their immediate superior, or some executive committee.

Not only can the evaluation be more thorough and objective, but the management and responsibility for evaluation are removed from those directly involved. The result is that the evaluation is more likely to be completed on time. It is always advisable to separate implementation from evaluation for the reasons cited above, but it is also true from a pragmatic point of view that both processes will not be managed with the same vigor and rigor if they are handled by the same group.

External evaluators are also more likely to acquire and disseminate knowledge about goal setting in the form of research studies. There are exceptions, but internal evaluators usually limit distribution of their findings to managers within the organization (especially if the findings are unfavorable). External evaluators are typically more interested in adding to the body of knowledge. Their contribution to the knowledge base can stimulate further research, which should have positive payoffs for those interested in implementing and sustaining effective goal-setting systems.

5. *Previous research clearly projects the message that a system such as PP&E needs to be monitored over time. In fact, any major intervention needs to be traced longitudinally so that false or sleeper improvements can be identified.* An accurate assessment of the impact of a goal-setting program must include a strong interest in identifying cause-and-effect relationships. The only way to do this scientifically is to collect and analyze data at specific intervals over a period of time. Any other method leaves the validity of the findings open to question because of halo errors, extraneous influences, and other factors that cloud the cause-and-effect issue.

Continuing evaluation effort over time also forms the basis for problem identification and feedback of information to managers for problem solving. Managers become more deeply involved in the goal-setting program; they see themselves as more than just employees carrying out requisite procedures. In addition, the longitudinal nature of the evaluation gives managers an opportunity to see the impact of modifications in the program; they can see to what degree changes in the system are reflected at the next data collection point.

Estimates by "experts" in the area of goal-setting systems indicate that the time required to make a smooth-functioning, effective system fully operational may be as long as five years. If this is the case, it stands to reason that one evaluation, six months after implementation, is insufficient.

Conclusion

This report describes Tenneco's use of goal setting in nine divisional companies. Additional evaluations, testing, and modifications are to come. The preliminary findings, however, are encouraging and indicate that if goal setting is planned properly, implemented carefully, and evaluated, it has a potentially positive effect on employee attitudes. It is hoped that this article encourages organizations (1) to explore the options available to them for initiating and sustaining top-management involvement in goal setting carefully; (2) to consider emphasizing personal development goals at least as much as performance goals; and (3) to consider using external evaluators who can assess the strengths and weaknesses of an organization's goal-setting system objectively.

Selected Bibliography

Management by objectives or goal setting has been the subject of books and articles for more than 20 years. The early perspective of management by objectives is captured in Peter Drucker's *The Practice of Management* (Harper and Bros., 1954) and George Odiorne's *Management by Objectives* (Pitman, 1965). More recently two very informative books that trace MBO in organizational settings are Stephen J. Carroll and Henry L. Tosi's *Management by Objectives: Applications and Research* (Macmillan, 1973) and Anthony P. Raia's *Management by Objectives* (Scott, Foresman, 1974).

There are numerous descriptive articles on MBO or goal setting in organizations. Some of the more informative are Harry Levinson's "Management by Whose Objectives?" *Harvard Business Review* (July/August 1970, pp. 125–134); John M. Ivancevich, James H. Donnelly, Jr., and James L. Gibson's "Evaluating MBO: The Challenge Ahead," *Management by Objectives* (Winter 1975, pp. 15–23); Wendell French and Robert Hollmann's "Management by Objectives: The Team Approach," *California Management Review* (Spring 1975, pp. 13–24); and Dale D. McConkey's "MBO—Twenty Years Later, Where Do We Stand," *Business Horizons* (August 1973, pp. 25–36).

An outstanding review article that examines research on goal setting is Gary Latham and Gary Yukl's "A Review on the Application of Goal Setting in Organizations," *Academy of Management Journal* (December 1975, pp. 824–843). Examples of scientific evaluations of goal setting in organizations appear in Gary Latham and James Baldes's "The Practical Significance of Locke's Theory of Goal Setting," *Journal of Applied Psychology* (February 1975, pp. 122–124) and John Ivancevich's "Changes in Performance in a Management by Objectives Program," *Administrative Science Quarterly* (December 1974, pp. 563–574).

27

Team Building Part 1.
Designing the Intervention

Thomas H. Patten, Jr.

*H*ow can an organization increase employee satisfaction while improving overall effectiveness? Team building, a highly popular organization development technique, often produces such a happy result.

Why Team Building?
A Look before the Leap

By and large, managements recognize the interdependence of employees and the need for cooperation among people to accomplish work. This is one major reason for the emphasis on building strong managerial teams. But several conditions must exist before effective teams can be developed. First, the group must have a natural reason for working together that makes sense—whether in a department, an *ad hoc* committee or task force, or a top management team. Second, the members of the group must be mutually dependent on each other's experience, abilities, and commitment in order to fulfill mutual objectives. Third, group members must be committed to the idea that working together as a group, rather than in isolation or in opposition, leads to more effective decisions. Last, the group must be accountable as a functioning unit within a larger organizational context.

Key to the concept of the team is communication within the group. There has to be a singleness of mission and a willingness to cooperate. The mere fact of regular reporting relationships within organizational

SOURCE: Thomas H. Patten, Jr., "Team Building Part 1. Designing the Intervention." Reprinted, by permission of the publisher, from *Personnel*, January–February 1979, pp. 11–21. © 1978 by AMACOM, a division of American Management Associations. All rights reserved.

structures does not necessarily constitute a team, even if people appear to be grouped that way on the organization chart. Boxes and arrows symbolize neither the technical and interpersonal coordination nor the emotional investment—the commitment—that go into the true team. While managers and their subordinates might be able to improve their overall relationships, coordination, and communication in many situations, the word team should be reserved for a special type of work group.

It isn't possible to create a team in every group, even when there is singleness of mission and an absolute need to cooperate. People have different motivations—some are ambitious, devious, and uncooperative, while others are abrasive, self-seeking, and complacent. Some organizations contain many loners too uncomfortable and unskilled at working in groups to ever make the transition to becoming team players. Thus team building is not a viable intervention strategy for every group. Even where it is organizationally practicable, it might not take hold with people who have certain antithetical personality traits.

Personality traits are one thing, but issues are quite another. Specific programs and joint projects, for example, can bring labor and management forces together in a mutual effort in which leaders from both sides cooperate in achieving mutual objectives despite other fundamental differences. Workshop sessions conducted by a competent neutral human resources consultant often can help these individuals listen to each other, reduce tension, and reach agreement on some areas.

The basic purpose of team building, then, is to provide a means whereby groups or teams of managers can come together in a learning setting to acquire interactive skills for accomplishing tasks. The results of such successful team-building activities can be classified in three categories:

> *Results specific to one or more individuals.* Most team-building efforts improve the team members' understanding of the way in which authority, control, and power affect problem solving and data gathering. Consequently, the team can begin to experiment with new alternatives.
> *Results specific to the group's operation and behavior.* Team-building activities are sometimes preceded by sessions held to clarify the team's purpose and to establish workable long-term and short-term priorities and objectives.
> *Results that affect the group's relationships with the rest of the organization.* As the team members examine their own operation, studying communication and problem-solving techniques applicable to their own interpersonal processes, they come to see the big picture and to clarify their roles within the organization as a whole. Thus a successful team-building effort can go beyond the group; it can facilitate role negotiation between team members and interfacing organizational units, opening the door to possibilities of cross-functional communication within the organization.

Analysis of two case studies of team building will illustrate the theoretical concepts. The common denominator in both cases is the goal of knitting together a group of people sharing task responsibilities in a tense sociotechnical situation. The team-building models employed involved sustained efforts, the first effort having extended over a period of five years in thirty separate one-week workshops, and the second case being an ongoing effort of more than two years that shows promise and will probably receive managerial support for at least another year.

The Fedmil Study—Federal Civil Service and Military Managers

The first of the two case studies is called Fedmil, signifying that it involves federal civil service managers and military managers (U.S. Army officers) holding key positions in a major military command that operates throughout the world. The specific tasking of fedmil need not concern us especially, although it is worth noting that Fedmil is not a line organization, such as the infantry or the artillery, but is composed largely of highly educated engineering, electronic, scientific, and support personnel. The mix of specialisms predominant among managers in Fedmil is not unlike those found at AT&T, RCA, Raytheon, Honeywell, or IBM. Indeed, many Fedmil people had prior work experience in these organizations.

The participants in the Fedmil team-building effort were high-ranking civilian managers (model grade, GS-14) and military managers (modal rank, lieutenant colonel).

The need for the series of team-building workshops had previously been established by data gathered on relationships among three classes of managers at Fedmil—managers who were civilians, but not retired military personnel; managers who were civilians, but were also retired officers; and managers who were Army officers on active duty. The need was determined by observation, reports from top management, and a fiat and mandate from the top, rather than by the use of such empirical tools as questionnaires and interviews.

Frequently, noncombat units in military organizations are headed by a military officer whose immediate subordinate is a civilian. This one-over-one relationship (in a sense, two persons for one job), is based on the fact that the officer is subject to rotation every three years. The civilian subordinate remains to provide continuity in the direction of the organization's activity. Often the activity is technical or highly specialized, necessitating increased reliance on the civilian subordinate, at least when a high-ranking officer has been newly assigned to the job. Even so, the top job in the activity is typically reserved for a military officer, and a civilian cannot aspire to it. That many civilians are retired officers exacerbates the problem, as they may consider themselves more knowledgeable than the mobile officers on active duty or the younger, mobile career civil servants. When collaboration among these three types of managerial employee is impaired, an organization development (OD) intervention is warranted. In such circumstances, team building, perhaps in the form of a small-group training experience conducted by an outside consultant, often has substantial promise.

In this case, the different organizational components nominated the executives who would participate in the team-building effort. Most attendees were white men, 35 to 55 years of age. Very few minority-group members or women attended, because at the time the OD seminar/workshops were offered, few such individuals had become upwardly mobile enough to reach the high-ranking military and executive levels the program was designed to assist.

The seminar/workshops were called Organization Development Through Team Building (ODTTB). The program was initially conceived as a special set of interrelated seminars and workshops designed to aid Fedmil management in developing its team skills, ability to plan and control work, and competence in motivating subordinates. The program was designed to educate or develop top executives for team building. Participants were those who could be given time off the job and who were willing to attend. The major sessions of the team-building workshops and seminars are exhibited in Figure 1.

Built around a theoretical model and strategy for organizational change, ODTTB made use of both originally developed and commercially available material. It involves pulling the right levers in a strategy for change, which can be depicted linearly as:

Organization development → *management by objectives* → *rewards*
  through self-awareness
  and team building
  (OD₁)   (MBO)   (R)

The basic premise of the strategy is that in order to change executive behavior, the executives' awareness of their personal managerial styles must be raised to the point where they want to develop and improve the management of their organization. They are provided with an opportunity to learn skills as team members in reaching decisions based on consensus and resolution of interpersonal conflict. Next, the workshop provides them with practice in goal setting, work planning and review, problem solving, and time management—all basic to MBO. The final step in the process ties application of their new skills in with the organization's reward system. Working with the MBO processes in which they have been trained, and using their new interpersonal skills, managers can relate to employees and reward them, both financially and nonfinancially, to motivate them to perform assigned work to high standards. The Lewinian notion of unfreezing, changing, and refreezing is implicit in the seminar/workshop design. The goals of the team-building seminar/workshops were as follows:

To help participants establish a sense of teamwork and mutual trust in their respective organizational components.

To enable participants to develop skills in resolving conflicts with persons and groups, communicating openly with others, confronting issues, and conducting interpersonal

Figure 1 Design of the Team-Building Seminar/Workshop

	Monday	Tuesday	Wednesday	Thursday	Friday
	Self-Awareness as a Manager	*Group Decision Making and Consensus Building*	*MBO and Problem Solving*	*MBO, Interpersonal Communication Issues, and Delegation Skills*	*OD, MBO, and Reward Administration*
8:30–12:00	Theory input on OD	Theory input on team building	Theory input on MBO	Theory input on rational and emotional issues in MBO problem solving	Theory input on OD, MBO, and rewards and penalties
	Johari Window	Desert survival problem	MBO exercise on regular objectives	MBO exercise on innovative goals	MANDOERS* exercise on development and rewards
	FIRO-B exercise; form teams	Debriefing and relating exercise to job	Debriefing of exercise	Debriefing of exercise	Debriefing of exercise
12:00–1:00	Lunch	Lunch	Lunch	Lunch	Lunch

Figure 1   *Design of the Team-Building Seminar/Workshop (continued)*

1:00–3:30				
Theory input on behavioral science	Theory input on consensus	Theory input on problem solving and innovative MBO	Theory input on the management of managerial time	Theory input on the helping relationship in management and feedback
Managerial style	Interpersonal conflict management exercise	MBO exercise on problem-solving goals	Time management and delegation exercise	Team peer evaluations
System intervention exercise				
Debriefing of exercise	Debriefing of exercise	Debriefing of exercise	Debriefing of exercise	Seminar/Workshop evaluations
Unfreezing		*Changing*		*Refreezing*

NOTE: *MANDOERS is an acronym for management development, organizational effectiveness, and reward systems.

relations with peers, subordinates, counterparts, and
superiors.

To assist participants in understanding how to motivate others
and promote dedication to getting the job done.

To review and examine basic managerial skills in such areas as
work planning, setting managerial objectives, controlling
activities so that goals are attained, managing the use of
time, solving problems, and getting employees on the team.

To connect ideas about manager and employee behavior and
motivation with the administration of salaries and
nonfinancial rewards.

The program was designed to implement these goals and to provide
flexibility for the addition of modules at a later date, if desired, or for
teams requiring further work in, for example, MBO, role negotiation,
time management, and career life planning. Thus the design of the
program was sufficiently structured to permit learning, but flexible
enough to allow for any other necessary OD interventions.

Participants in the ODTTB seminar/workshops were given the option
to work in teams that included the boss and subordinates either in a
direct line relationship or in a functional staff relationship. Thus there
were several cases in which the teams fit the team-building requisite of
a natural, intact group, but most were artificial, composed of high-level
managers who split their time between working together closely and
working apart from the group.

If we step back from ODTTB, we are able to examine the difference
between team building itself and an executive seminar/workshop on
team building. The latter is concerned with learning about learning,
while the former is used to translate the learning into action on the job.
Learning about learning—the phenomenon of adults coming to realize
that they are responsible for their own growth and can best learn many
complex skills by working together on developmental tasks—has always
been one of the primary goals of the T-group in laboratory training. Yet
the findings demonstrate that team-building seminar/workshops can
also provide an opportunity for learning about learning. For the most
part, however, team building used in organizations for group
development appears to center on creating an awareness of the realities
of unequal power accountability and the participants' relationships to
the larger system rather than on personal growth *per se.*

An interesting contrast to the Fedmil team-building study is the
Basmanco model, the second of the two studies.

The Basmanco Study—Basic Manufacturing Company

The Basmanco team-building study is part of a continuing effort at a basic
manufacturing plant in one division of a *Fortune* 500 firm. The data
pertain to 35 participants, representing 10 percent of a total population
of 350 employees. The mix consists of the plant manager, all managers

reporting directly to him, plus about 25 unionized office employees supervised by the plant manager's managerial subordinates.

Rooted in an action research methodology, the Basmanco study is governed by the $OD_1 \rightarrow MBO \rightarrow RS$ theoretical stance described for Fedmil. The sequence of steps carried out at Basmanco is summarized in Figure 2. This OD effort was slowly implemented over two years, and several interventions are projected for the future. The ability of Basmanco to absorb the OD interventions and move toward behavioral and organizational change governed the tempo of the implementation effort.

Figure 3 portrays the nature of the interrelationships among the management consultant, or external change agent; the plant personnel manager, or internal change agent; and the client, who was the plant manager. The interrelationships shown are typical of many OD change efforts in the United States, whether they are used for team building or for other purposes. The double arrows in the triad suggest that all three principals in the change effort will continue to communicate and trust one another over time.

Returning to the Basmanco team-building effort described in Figure 2, we see that the change activity has evolved around offsite meetings, as opposed to the laboratory setting of seminar/workshops. The meetings dealt with live organizational problems and appear to be as close as we can come to the real-life, on-the-job situation. This setting is less conducive to learning about learning than to a desire to solve problems that will have an impact on the way in which employees and managers interact.

The activities presented in Figure 2 were supplemented by the plant personnel manager's intercession. Committees set up by action planning met during the workday several times monthly. These task forces zeroed in on the problem areas and proposed solutions for implementation that did not conflict with any provisions of the collective bargaining agreement. This was to avoid any allegation that an OD intervention was being used to undermine the union or to organize for union busting. Indeed, our goal was the opposite: to help the union develop more solidarity, to unify labor–management relations, and to give union members insights into union structure, philosophy, and dynamics.

In essence, the task approximated trying to catch a bucket of smoke. The problem as identified by the plant manager and personnel manager was an insidious atmosphere of interpersonal animosities; deep-rooted hard feelings of employees, in some cases going back a decade or more; leadership rivalry in the virtually all-female office union; and managerial chicanery and game playing in the grievance procedure.

There were several other complicating factors as well. The office was about 75 years old, dirty, poorly maintained, hot in the summer, cold in the winter, and physically unattractive. The office had once been a divisional headquarters, but the location had been downgraded to plant status within a larger division, with many employees unable or unwilling to accept the real consequences of the loss in status, and behaving as if it had never happened.

Figure 2   Basmanco Action Research Chronology

Date	Activity and Purpose	Result
August 1976	Two days of diagnostic interviewing and data gathering to identify problems and issues.	Formulation of report to be used for offsite meeting.
September 1976	One-day offsite meeting, attendance of 35, to react to data and plan preliminary actions.	Establishment of four labor-management committees (informal task forces or teams) focused on: —Trust and communication in management —Trust and communication in union —Discipline —Grievance procedure
January 1977	One-day offsite meeting similar to September meeting.	Report of committees and redesignation of committees to: —Efficiency committee working on problems of a new management information system (MIS) —Union committee —Labor education committee —Grievance committee
May 1977	Similar to the January 1977 effort.	Reduction of four committees to one interdepartmental committee to deal with MIS.
September 1977	One-day meeting with plant manager and personnel manager to check progress and plan extension of OD effort to plant union and lower-level plant department managers.	Diagnostic interviewing and beginning of extension of OD to the plant.
September 1977	Presentation of OD effort to divisional VP and other executives.	Obtained corporate expression of interest.
October 1977	One-day offsite meeting for 12 key managers only (office and plant).	Informed of corporate meeting, reviewed motivation and aspirations.

Most of the employees had at least ten years' service; some had been on the job 30 to 40 years. Nothing had ever been done before to deal with the physical and interpersonal office problems. Petty jealousy and resentments had simmered interminably. No one ostensibly wanted change, and yet when interviewed on an individual basis, many employees expressed feelings of hurt and pain.

Figure 3   The OD Change-Effort Triad

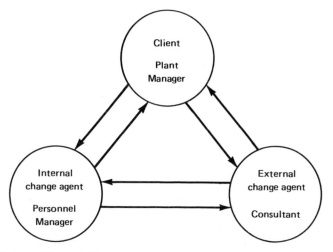

The In-house Manager's Side

- Knowledge of specific sociotechnical systems

- Perspective limited to organization (local outlook)

- Dependency on organization for financial rewards

- Company-person career bond

What the Consultant Brings

- Knowledge of OD techniques

- Experience in many organizations, variety of perspectives (cosmopolitan outlook)

- Independence

- No bond; easily dispensable relationship

Determined to try something to improve the climate, the plant manager had hired a well-qualified young personnel manager to analyze what was going on and what might be done about it. Several older, long-service key managers felt the climate was satisfactory as it existed, but some of the new managers considered the office the worst they had ever worked in from the standpoint of interpersonal relations. Many cross-currents of feelings had to be dealt with.

Other facets of the social situation at Basmanco needed to be worked out as well—the recognizable isolated ethnic groups among unionized employees and managers, and the fact that personnel managers had typically lasted only a short time and quit.

The plant was highly profitable and had been for several years. The plant manager was extremely capable, well respected, and clearly committed to top-leading the change effort and persevering with it—as solid and well-supported a commitment as an external change agent could expect.

The image of the bucket of smoke disbands in the face of the positive, ongoing team-building program that was instituted at Basmanco. It is scheduled to proceed into the future.

28

Stonewalling Plant Democracy

In the early 1970s, when everyone was talking about blue-collar blues and worker alienation, General Foods Corp. opened a dog-food plant in Topeka, Kan., designed to be run with a minimum of supervision. Many functions normally the prerogative of management would be performed by the workers themselves. Workers would make job assignments, schedule coffee breaks, interview prospective employees, and even decide pay raises.

The plant was widely heralded as a model for the future, and General Foods claims that it still is. "Very successful" is the way J. W. Bevans Jr., manager of organizational development for GF, describes the experiment. In fact, GF has applied a similar system at a second dog-food plant in Topeka and at a coffee plant in New Jersey. And it says it may eventually do the same at two plants in Mexico and among white-collar workers at its White Plains headquarters.

But management analysts and former employees tell a different story. And General Foods, which once encouraged publicity about the Topeka plant, now refuses to let reporters inside. Critics say that after the initial euphoria, the system, faced with indifference and outright hostility from some GF managers, has been eroding steadily.

"The system went to hell. It didn't work," says one former manager. Adds another ex-employee: "It was a mixed bag. Economically it was a success, but it became a power struggle. It was too threatening to too many people." He predicts that the plant will eventually switch to a traditional factory system. In fact, he says, the transition has already begun.

The problem has been not so much that the workers could not manage their own affairs as that some management and staff personnel saw their own positions threatened because the workers performed almost too well. One former employee says the system—built around a team concept—came squarely up against the company's bureaucracy. Lawyers, fearing reaction from the National Labor Relations Board, opposed the idea of allowing team members to vote on pay raises. Personnel managers objected because team members made hiring decisions. Engineers resented workers doing engineering work.

Balancing act

Of course, having workers take on such duties was the whole idea. The process was an attempt "to balance the needs of the people with the needs of the business," says Bevans. GF had had problems with negative attitudes and low productivity in its Kankakee (Ill.) pet-food plant in the late 1960s and wanted to offset them at Topeka. Specific goals, says Bevans, included maximum machine utilization, minimum waste, low distribution costs, low productivity costs, and low absenteeism and turnover.

The system, designed by a GF task force working with Richard E. Walton, professor of business administration at Harvard University, eliminates layers of management and supervisory personnel and assigns three areas of responsibility—processing, packaging and shipping, and office duties—to self-managing teams of workers. Each team on a shift has 7 to 14 members who share responsibility for a variety of tasks. The processing team, for instance, not only handles the actual pet-food manufacturing but also is responsible for unloading raw material and for equipment maintenance and quality control.

Working under the direction of a team leader, described as a "coach" rather than a foreman, team members rotate between dreary and meaningful jobs. Pay is geared to the number of tasks each individual masters. The teams make the necessary management decisions. GF even removed some of the status symbols of management that blue-collar workers resent. All employees use a common entrance, for instance, and there are no reserved parking spaces for management.

Instability

There is no question that the company has met many of its goals. Unit costs are 5% less than under a traditional factory system, Bevans estimates. This, says Walton, should amount to a saving of $1 million a year. Turnover is only 8%, and the plant went three years and eight months before its first lost-time accident. Even one who criticizes some aspects of the system, Lyman D. Ketchum, former manager of GF's pet-food operations and responsible for both the Kankakee and Topeka plants, says: "From the standpoint of humanistic working life and economic results, you can consider it a success."

But a former employee at the Topeka plant does not see it that way. "Creating a system is different from maintaining it," he says. "There were pressures almost from the inception, and not because the system didn't work. The basic reason was power. We flew in the face of corporate policy. People like stable states. This system has to be changing or it will die."

Change, of course, can be threatening in itself. "If you have a quality control manager who is successful, and along comes something very successful, he begins to wonder what's in it for him," says Ketchum. "Then there's the engineer who has been designing plants based on traditional principles. He gets anxious and perceives a threat. The controller wants someone from his fraternity in the system, and so on." As a result, Ketchum continues, "pressures come about. The system starts to be compartmentalized, and when you compartmentalize it, you degrade it." In other words, some management functions were again taken over by managers.

Weakened commitment?

Consequently, critics say, there has been a stiffening of the Topeka system, more job classifications, less participation, more supervision. GF has added seven management positions to the plant, including controller, plant engineering manager, and manufacturing services manager. GF says these were necessary because of a plant expansion. Last year, when GF geared up a plant adjacent to the first one to produce Cycle, a canned dog food, it introduced the Topeka process but deferred several elements of the system, including developmental training.

"This was interpreted by dry-plant members [at the first plant, which produces Gaines dog food] as evidence of a weakening of management commitment to the philosophy on which their own work system was based," writes Walton in a study of the plant prepared for a professional journal. He says the modifications contributed to the growing complacency and negative drift at Topeka. Walton and others have noticed a slight dip in quality, a buildup of minor problems because of fewer team meetings, and increased competition between shifts. Says one employee who left after two years: "There was too much competition because of jealousy between teams and team leaders."

Another problem area is pay. As the system was set up, team members voted on pay raises for fellow employees, which could be sticky. "You work with somebody for five years and get to be pretty good friends. It's a little tough to decide on a pay raise," says worker Rex Campbell. But that prerogative may be returning to management. A former manager claims that although workers still discuss one another's raises, the real decisions are made by management. GF declines comment.

More important, employees believe they ought to share financially in the system's success, an idea that has been backed by managers, though GF's headquarters is noncommital. A bonus at Topeka could cause complications at other GF plants that do not happen to pay bonuses. "The personnel people don't like that," says a former manager. "It threatens them."

Workers also perceive that Topeka managers have suffered because of their involvement in the system. Along with Ketchum, now a management consultant, Edward R. Dulworth has left General Foods. He was plant manager until November, 1975, and is now an executive with Tops Chewing Gum Inc. Two of three managers under him also left the company. Says one of them: "They saw we had created something the company couldn't handle, so they put their boys in. By being involved, I ruined my career at General Foods."

GF denies that anybody's career was hurt by the Topeka process. "They went to greener pastures," says a company spokesman. And Bevans defends the changes in the system when it was introduced outside the first Topeka plant. "You can't transplant the system whole," he says. "You take the important elements."

'The best place'

GF introduced the system in its Hoboken (N.J.) coffee plant two years ago to combat high production costs and the result was "significant," says Bevans. Pointing to plans to move the system into plants in Mexico and to headquarters in White Plains, he says: "We won't try to transplant it wholesale. We'll put it into the hands of local management so they can fashion it to meet their needs." But one critic scoffs: "The organization knows what happens to managers who innovate."

Such skepticism filters down to team members. "Every time you make a mistake, you wonder if White Plains thinks that maybe if we had a traditional system there wouldn't have been a mistake," says Campbell, the Topeka plant worker. Still, he adds: "It's the best place I ever worked."

That perhaps best sums up the Topeka experiment. While the system has not lived up to the goals of many of the managers involved, and while it seems to be deteriorating, it nevertheless has led to a productive working atmosphere and has met many of the goals set for it. The big question is whether it will renew itself or continue to erode, fulfilling the prediction of one manager that "the future of that plant is to conform to the company norm."

Professor Walton, summing up six years of the plant's operation, writes: "Never has the climate truly soured or even become neutral and indifferent." But he adds: "In my opinion, this will happen unless concerted effort is made to evolve the organization."

29

What's Good for the World Should Be Good for G.M.

Charles G. Burck

*T*he dealers in General Motors' salesrooms throughout the nation are armed with provocative sales jargon such as "autobiotic—a vehicle that relates to and is actually a part of an individual's mode of life." But when they tell prospective customers that there has never been another car quite like General Motors' new front-wheel-drive "X-car," that's not just hoopla. The X-car (the letter is G.M.'s code for its compacts) successfully combines traditional American-car qualities—comfort, roominess, and performance—with the European and Japanese virtues of efficiency and agility. G.M. might well have called the new car Proteus for its unprecedented diversity of characteristics. In the sixteen versions being marketed by four G.M. divisions, under such names as the Chevrolet Citation and Oldsmobile Omega, the X-car competes with everything from the Toyota Corolla to the Ford Fairmont to the Audi 5000. It even competes with G.M.'s own intermediates—e.g., the Chevrolet Malibu and Pontiac LeMans.

G.M. has spent an unprecedented amount of time and money bringing the X-car to market. Its development took more than four years, and cost almost $2.7 billion—$500 million for engineering, $880 million for new tooling, $500 million for a new plant in Oklahoma City, and $800 million for new assembly facilities in other plants. Though any other big automaker might have been able to develop something similar, none but G.M. could have done so at as low a cost per car. As John S. McGee, a University of Washington economist, observes, no automobile company in the world, G.M. included, has yet grown large enough to exhaust its potential economies of scale. "Other things being the same, that firm which sells the most cars can sell for less," he says. With the

SOURCE: Charles G. Burck, "What's Good for the World Should Be Good for G.M.," *Fortune* May 7, 1979, pp. 125–36. Reprinted with permission.

X-car, G.M. is positioning itself for a global challenge that might finally make even the Japanese feel the hot breath of a U.S. manufacturer in overseas markets.

Both Big and Well Managed

There are, of course, no automatic rewards for being a big, low-cost producer—as Henry Ford learned years ago when he clung too long to the Model T. During the last decade, Ford Motor Co. played the small-car market more skillfully than G.M., and gained relative market share in doing so. At the time of the Arab oil embargo of 1973, G.M. had the worst fleet mileage average of any U.S. manufacturer. In the aftermath of the embargo, its competitors gained at its expense. Back then, it was fashionable to argue that G.M. was an industrial dinosaur, too big to meet the challenge of a changing world, and that the future belonged to small, technologically innovative companies like Japan's Honda.

Today, it's clear that G.M. is both big *and* well managed. In the past few years, particularly, it has done a near-perfect job of anticipating the market. G.M. actually started planning for an energy-short world some two years before the 1973 oil embargo. It was able to come out in the 1977 model year with a "downsized" line of big cars, two full years ahead of Ford.

Few things irritate G.M. executives more than the complaint—made these days by some of their competitors—that the company's gains in the marketplace are the result simply of overwhelming financial and technical resources. "We didn't wait to get started" with resizing, says President E. M. (Pete) Estes with some heat. He adds: "And that two-year jump is going to give us time to make two changes instead of one" by 1985, when all manufacturers' fleets will have to average 27.5 miles per gallon. As a result, G.M. has an edge in developing new cars that are able to meet the demands of both the government and the marketplace.

Keeping Out of the "Econobox"

Equally important, G.M. began in the early 1970's to restructure its management to cope with accelerating change (see "How G.M. Turned Itself Around," *Fortune*, January 16, 1978). From the standpoint of new-car development, its most important innovation was the project-center concept. This involves forming an engineering group to shepherd each new car through its development, bringing together experts in design, manufacturing, assembly, customer service, and marketing. The basic job of a project center is to eliminate redundant work by the different divisions and ensure that nothing falls between stools. The center strives to keep manufacturing costs down and, at the same time, helps the divisions strengthen their separate identities.

Without the project center, it is doubtful that G.M. could have developed the kind of X-car it did. When G.M. first began planning a small front-wheel-drive car in 1973, what it had in mind was much more akin to, say, Ford's Fiesta. The company sent a group of twenty-six engineers to Germany to collaborate with Opel on a new subcompact design. It might have been the first "world car"—i.e., a basic design adaptable to all markets—but the oil-embargo crisis killed the project. G.M. decided it needed a new subcompact for the U.S. and needed it sooner than the new Opel could be developed. It turned to a crash effort to pull the Chevette together from existing components.

By the time G.M. picked up the front-wheel-drive thread again, in mid-1974, it had formed a new idea of what it wanted, shaped in part by what it had learned from consumers at product clinics—meetings at which the folks out there get a chance to tell the company what its cars should be. "We recognized the need to move people down, but not into econoboxes," says Robert J. Eaton, the engineer who headed the X-car project center; he is now assistant chief engineer at Oldsmobile. G.M. decided not to build simply another subcompact, but to create a completely new size category: the "Small Family Car"—a true five-passenger compact.

It was a considerable challenge. There is nothing new about the basic front-wheel-drive design of the X-car—it dates from the late 1950's, and is used in some twenty-five cars around the world, including Chrysler's Omni and Horizon. But most front-wheel-drive cars are either minuscule, like the Renault R-5 and the Honda Civic, or expensive, like the Lancia Beta or Audi 5000.

For years, American automakers were able to provide roomy comfort and high performance for the mass market, in good part because they could build big cars. A comfortable ride comes most naturally (and cheaply) with a long wheelbase, which minimizes the tendency of a car to jounce and pitch on bumpy roads. Big, slow-turning engines and tons of heavy metal, by the same token, make for a quieter car than a lightweight machine powered by a high-speed four-cylinder engine.

Moreover, the U.S. auto industry led the world in building cars whose major mechanical components gave long and faithful service even in the hands of neglectful owners. "Bigness gave us that reliability," says Robert C. Stempel, who was Chevrolet's chief engineer during the development of the X-car and is now general manager of Pontiac. "If you knew the safety factor, you doubled it, and the boss would then say you'd better go up another ten-thousandth, just in case."

Pay Now to Save Later

Building the treasured standards of comfort, performance, and reliability into a small car took endless, painstaking experimentation, and the redesign of many familiar pieces of hardware. Mounting a four-cylinder engine transversely, for example, both saves space and reduces its inherent tendency to vibrate. To get a minimum of vibration, engineers tried hundreds of different ways of isolating the drive train from the body. Among the critical bits of minutiae they incorporated into the car are vibration-absorbing couplings in the accelerator linkage, and a flexible ball joint in the exhaust system.

In its pursuit of reliability, G.M. subjected the X-car to the same kinds of tests and stresses that it previously imposed on its bigger cars, running test models until they literally fell apart. "At the end of the car's useful life, we would take it another couple of thousand miles," says Stempel. Torturing the test cars helped turn up instances in which G.M., by accepting some extra costs, could extend a part's life or reliability, or make it easier to repair. Says Stempel, "You might pay 50 cents more for the part when you buy the car, but it might later save you an hour's service time, and that's worth $20 or $30."

Fenders are bolted on, rather than welded—which is cheaper—so they can be more easily replaced. Engineers from the consumer-relations and service staffs insisted that the clutch in manual transmissions be designed for unusual longevity, because replacing the clutch in any front-wheel-drive car is complicated and time-consuming. For the X-car, they specified what they call a "B-10 clutch life"—a criterion for durability based on the wear and tear imposed during 50,000 miles of driving by the 10 percent of consumers who are most abusive of their cars.

Perhaps the project center's most important benefit for G.M. has been its success in maintaining—and indeed strengthening—the delicate balance between the autonomy and interdependence of the various divisions, such as Chevrolet or Oldsmobile. G.M. no longer considers them primarily manufacturing entities; the divisions, rather, are responsible for planning, designing, engineering, and marketing their products under their respective nameplates.

The changes in divisional roles have caused G.M. some embarrassment, as in the notorious "Chevymobile" flap of 1977, when some Oldsmobile buyers found Chevrolet engines under the hoods of their cars. The company had dropped its "Rocket" engine advertising theme for Oldsmobile before letting the division purchase the Chevrolet engines, but Olds buyers remembered the Rocket all too well. The irony is that G.M. actually builds more varieties of engines today than it did ten years ago—including diesels, there are forty-three, against twenty in 1970. However, the number of engines purchased from one another by the various car divisions has grown steadily, from three in 1970 to twenty-four today.

These days, the actual assembly of cars increasingly belongs to the General Motors Assembly Division. G.M.A.D. now assembles some 75 percent of the company's U.S. passenger cars. Chevrolet, in fact, builds no cars at all; it buys them from G.M.A.D., which in turn buys components from Chevrolet and other divisions.

Pontiac versus Chevrolet

Nonetheless, divisional distinctions are crucial to G.M.'s ability to blanket the marketplace with an array of cars tailored to different tastes. And fierce interdivisional competition is at least as important to the company's performance as competition with other automakers. With many models that overlap in price, the divisions often regard one another as their primary opponents. Thomas A. Staudt, Chevrolet's marketing director, underscored the intracompany rivalry when he observed recently that Buick, Oldsmobile, and Pontiac had been getting more and more smaller models "to compete with Chevrolet—and, of course, Ford."

During the years when cars were waxing fatter, divisional stylists enjoyed endless opportunities to offset growing mechanical similarities with their baroque treatment of sheet metal. But now that cars are shrinking, dramatic differences in appearance are harder to come by. In designing smaller cars, stylists have had to develop deft touches in making slight but strategic changes in body panels, grilles, front ends, and rear ends, all adding up to distinctive divisional "signatures." They are increasingly putting added emphasis on interior detailing, pointing out that customers, after all, spend most of their time inside their cars. Marketing surveys suggest that interior appointments are becoming more important in the consumer's decision about what model to buy. The stylists now enjoy greater latitude to play around with trim and fabric choices, seating positions, instrument-panel designs, and so on.

The project-center concept has succeeded in restoring some of the distinctions among G.M.'s various models. This outcome has surprised many divisional executives. "The project center used to be a dirty word," says Stempel, "but we got to know how to use it as a tool." The most important distinctions are mechanical, affecting steering, ride, and handling; these can be combined to produce a line of cars with a characteristic feel on the road.

Project-center engineers made extensive use of computer simulation to design both the X-car's basic suspension and the variations in it that distinguish the different cars. "With the computer, an engineer can put a wheel in a hundred different positions and see how it behaves over any road surface," says Stempel. The information is translated into design differences through "tuning"—using different kinds of shock-absorber valving, rubber mounts and bushings, and stabilizer bars to change handling characteristics. "The differences are subtle, but taken together, they become important," says Stempel.

X-car models have more parts in common than any earlier G.M. lines, but divisional variations are more substantial than they have been in years. "Five years ago these subtleties would have been lost," says Stempel. "But with the computer and the project center, tuning differences begin to play a big part in the personality of the car. We'll get even more of this precision in the future."

G.M.'s new-found ability to engineer both commonality and diversity into its cars reflects the careful attention it has given to trade-offs between volume manufacturing efficiency and the varying demands of the marketplace. The components that make the X-cars different for each division are those with relatively low tooling costs; they can be manufactured economically in shorter production runs. The major common parts—most notably, body panels—are the ones where volume production can bring costs down dramatically.

It Pays to Be Big

Trustbusters labor under the misapprehension that economies of size in auto-making are not great, and they base their case on the work of economists like Lawrence J. White of New York University. In his book

The Automobile Industry Since 1945, White asserts that body-panel dies—the biggest item in tooling costs—wear out after some 400,000 stampings.

Such short-lived dies are indeed used for producing parts in small volumes, but at G.M., dies routinely produce four million or more parts, and some are still in the presses after seven million stampings. G.M. is able to get such levels of utilization because most of the sheet metal for similar-sized cars in its five divisions comes from the same dies; inner body shells for similar-sized models in the various divisions are the same, and so are many of the outer panels. Differences among models are often achieved with relatively inexpensive die inserts.

Since a set of dies for a car the size of the X-car may cost some $75 million, savings from volume production can be significant. In a 1972 study entitled *Economies of Size in Auto Body Manufacture,* John McGee calculated that an automaker producing five essentially similar models with a total volume of four million units will pay only half as much per car for die tools as one making three models with a total volume of only 1.5 million. Using McGee's conservative formula, based on two-year production costs, and adjusting for inflation, the dies for the bigger producer might cost around $10 a car, against about $20 for the smaller producer—an important difference in an industry where pennies per car affect overall profit margins.

Those calculations only hint at the cost advantages of size. Today, for example, there are more common body parts in G.M. cars than there were when McGee did his research. His estimates, moreover, do not include a multitude of other economies, such as the utilization rates of the massive presses in which the dies are set. These rates increase dramatically with volume production. A couple of years ago, G.M. estimated that putting completely different doors on each of the four compact models it was then making might cost an additional $60 million, taking into account both tooling and sub-assembly facilities.

Savings in the volume manufacture of parts other than body panels vary widely and depend on factors other than machinery utilization. An engine-block assembly line approaches its optimum output at around 300,000 units. But in making wiring harnesses—that is, sets of electric wires—G.M. has found that it pays to use small plants with relatively low rates of output. When volume counts, the company over the years has increased its efficiency by integrating production. Parts for the various automobiles of the different divisions are made not only by component divisions, such as Delco Electronics and Hydra-matic, but also by the car divisions themselves, which can then supply one another with certain parts.

Spreading the Costs

The company has been astute across the board in making use of the advantages it gets from size. G.M. can, of course, realize economies of size by spreading the development costs of new models, such as the X-car, over its enormous volumes. The total cost of developing and tooling up for a single model to be produced in lower volumes would be less, but the costs per car would be relatively higher. It seems reasonable to estimate that four distinctly different X-cars would have cost at least twice as much to develop as four models of one X-car. If G.M. builds five million of the cars over the next six years, its engineering costs per car will amount to some $100. A manufacturer building an identical car at one-quarter the volume would have to charge another $100 or more per car to recover its development costs, or accept a lower profit margin.

Other carmakers around the world will be watching the X-car closely, and they will be concerned with more than how the U.S. consumer greets it. G.M. lags well behind Ford outside the U.S., but after years of what amounts to benign neglect of its overseas operations, the company is gearing up to become a truly global entity. The integration began back in 1974, when Pete Estes became president and was given command of overseas operations. Last year, foreign and domestic operating staffs were combined.

Tiltable Wheels Everywhere

The reorganization is already paying off. G.M.'s Detroit operations are absorbing engineering expertise from Opel, while the American branch provides sophisticated knowledge of component manufacture and merchandising to its various arms overseas. The X-car is an indication of G.M.'s ability to design cars roughly the size of those popular in other countries, but offering amenities and gadgetry—tiltable steering wheels, power windows and seats, air conditioning—at significantly lower costs than competitors in Europe. After driving preproduction models here last fall, a group of European dealers pleaded for larger allocations. G.M. has already shipped some 2,600 of the new X-cars abroad, instead of waiting, as it usually does, until a month or so after the U.S. introduction of a new model.

"The X could be a European car," says Estes. "We have no plans to build it there—at the moment, it may be a little on the large size. But we're going down in size over here, and they want a little larger car with tilt steering wheel and so on. It could all come together for us in Europe with the X-car or one a little smaller."

The X-car is not a true "world car," but the front-wheel-drive J-car will be. The J—G.M.'s designation for its European intermediate-size class, i.e., between the traditional U.S. subcompact and compact categories—seems to be that "little smaller" car Estes talks about. It is being put together on its own project center and will go on the world market in 1982.

G.M. is currently in the midst of planning the economic modules—i.e., determining the optimum volume for production of a given part—for setting up component production in many countries. Decisions about what to do where are complicated by local-content laws in many countries; these specify that, say, 40 percent of a vehicle sold in the country must be produced locally. To establish an economic module in a country where the market can't absorb its full output of a component, the automaker must persuade the government that it can reap the same benefits by offsetting imports of one component with exports of another.

Everybody Is Happy

So far, G.M. has announced only one such agreement, with Australia, where it will build the Opel-designed 1.6-liter overhead-cam engine. But "negotiations are going well" with other countries, says Alexander A. Cunningham, vice president and group director of overseas operations. "Everybody is happy because the consumer gets more value, the balance of trade is neutral, and the parts are cheaper because they will be produced in the most economical place." The effect on employment in any one country, he adds, is negligible.

World cars—those essentially similar models that can be built anywhere—present some difficulties. The nearest thing to a world car in production today is the Ford Fiesta, which is assembled in Spain, Belgium, and Germany from components made in England, Spain, and France. To be perfectly accurate, however, the Fiesta would have to be called a "hemisphere car," since it is imported into the U.S. G.M.'s Chevette is similar in Europe, the U.S., and Latin America, but relatively few components are interchangeable in the different regional versions.

The true world car will have to enjoy a high degree of commonality in its major components, and yet be adaptable to the demands of different markets. France is alone in the world in requiring yellow headlights; Japan demands a protective shield under the catalytic converter and a sensor in the dash to warn if the converter is overheating; Australia apparently intends to keep on using leaded gas, which will require a thermal reactor for emissions control rather than a catalytic converter. And different marketplaces demand different ride and handling qualities.

Some demands of the varying markets are easy to meet—or to ignore. "The French like a soft billowy seat, and the Germans like a firm one," says Cunningham. "But we don't make two different seats anymore. A lot of difference is in the mind, and if you have a well-designed seat, that's all you need." Other requirements, like those having to do with emissions controls, become complicated. Though most of the world is considerably less stringent than the U.S., each country has its own criteria and tests, and the varying rules must be observed precisely in each case. Moreover, pulling engineers together from around the world to work on the same car can present special problems of communications. "If you think it's difficult to coordinate between B-O-P [Buick-Oldsmobile-Pontiac] and Chevrolet, well, it's a new way of life to work with Opel and Isuzu," says Stempel.

In the project center, G.M. has a nearly ideal system for managing world-car development. A car suitable for France, Australia, and six or so other countries may have more permutations than one for four General Motors' divisions, but the process of designing the car for the best trade-off between commonality and distinction is pretty much the same. With the completion of the X-car, the project-center concept has weathered the test of producing an all-new design.

General Motors' sunny global horizon is marred by at least a couple of clouds. It has a long way to go to catch up with Ford overseas, not just in market share but in terms of practical experience with the complex task of building a world car. And up to now it has not been a leader in the sort of bold technological innovation that is a strength of the foreign automakers with whom it is competing.

G.M. has done a masterful job of nursing the conventional piston engine along, but even Estes thinks there is not much more that can be done with it. "We're on the part of the curve right now where there's not much improvement left," he admits. That leaves principally the diesel, whose prospects are troubled by possible future U.S. emissions standards. However, G.M. has a major diesel research program, and foresees significant improvements in the engine. "The diesel will get quieter and lighter in the Eighties," says Stempel.

A Test of Real Limits

G.M. is only monitoring the much-maligned Wankel engine, though Japan's Mazda has made phenomenal strides with it, achieving fuel economy and emissions comparable with conventional engines of the same power output. Toyota has an experimental stratified-charge rotary that gets between 15 and 20 percent better fuel economy than a conventional engine of comparable size and power, and has met 1981 emissions standards without using the expensive three-way catalyst system that U.S. automakers will have to incorporate in their 1981 cars. When and if a lighter, more compact, smoother-running rotary turns up in a rival's car, G.M. will have some tough decisions to make about its investment in conventional engines.

Nonetheless, G.M.'s global strength should grow to truly formidable proportions as it further integrates its domestic and overseas operations. The X-car has been a spectacular success in combining European performance with American amenities while keeping costs relatively low. It exemplifies what the U.S. auto industry—and G.M. in particular—has historically done best, which is not so much the pioneering of new technologies as it is adapting them to achieve the largest possible production volumes at the lowest cost. If the company's world cars come out as well as the X-car, G.M. may yet get to test the real limits of economic benefit from volume production in automaking.

30

One Firm's Family

Allan J. Mayer and Michael Ruby

A year ago, Christine O'Connor was in England, studying Greek and Latin at the University of Bristol and wondering what to do with her life, when a placement counselor mentioned that computer manufacturers often took on classicists to train as systems engineers. "I had never seen an entire computer before and I wasn't sure what a systems engineer did," she recalls. Intrigued, she talked to International Business Machines Corp., the world's largest computer maker. "The interview was amazing," said O'Connor, now an assistant systems engineer for IBM in New York. "They spent almost the whole time talking about the benefits they offer."

Well they might. More than any other major corporation in America, IBM smothers its employees with a dazzling array of womb-to-tomb benefits, ingenious motivational perks and sophisticated self-improvement programs. Not only does IBM pay its 300,000 employees generous salaries and cover their medical bills, it also counsels, trains and entertains them, supports their favorite charities and helps with their children's education. And uniquely among American corporations, it virtually guarantees its workers lifetime job security. The result: major corporate recruiting firms, as a recent poll shows, rate IBM the best company to work for—ahead of such corporate legends as Eastman Kodak, Procter & Gamble and Xerox.

Given its size, power and staggering wealth, IBM can afford to be generous. Its sales last year of $16.3 billion made it the nation's eighth biggest industrial corporation, and its after-tax income of $2.4 billion made it the third most profitable. There are many prosperous companies, of course, and many have expanded their benefits in recent years to meet what employee-benefits consultant Barnet N. Berin calls "the rising sense of entitlement among workers." But no major company goes quite as far as IBM.

SOURCE: Allan J. Mayer and Michael Ruby, "One Firm's Family," *Newsweek,* November 21, 1977, pp. 82–87. Reprinted with permission.

A Call for Loyalty

In the process, IBM has created a self-contained subculture whose beneficiaries are committed not so much to a job as to a way of life—a life that with all its comforts can also seem oppressive. Like any parent, Mother IBM demands obedience, and employees who step out of line face a formidable—if often subtle—wrath. On the one hand, IBM zealously guards the privacy of its employees; on the other, it inevitably intrudes into their personal lives—encouraging, if not exactly enforcing, what some IBM watchers describe as a numbing uniformity of attitude, appearance and action. "More than most companies, IBM has many of the attributes of a character-molding institution," says motivational-behavior expert Cyrus F. Gibson, an associate professor at the Harvard Business School and a sometime consultant to IBM. "It has a real impact on the way its employees think and on their outlook on life."

These contradictory impulses—some progressive and responsive, others autocratic and domineering—are deeply embedded in the IBM corporate personality. In large part, they reflect the legacy of Thomas J. Watson Sr., the motivational and marketing genius who reigned over the company, as a colleague once put it, as a "benevolent despot" for more than 40 years. "We are one great big family," Watson was fond of telling IBMers. But membership in the family, he was quick to add, was not without its price. "Joining a company," he wrote in one of the many IBM publications created to spread the word, "is an act that calls for absolute loyalty."

Beginning in 1914, when he left the National Cash Register Co. to take over the business-machines company that later became known as IBM, Watson practiced the carrot (money) and stick (punishment) method of motivation, converting it to a religion, with the order to THINK a corporate totem displayed in every office. He bombarded the faithful with inspirational sales talks, preached moral rectitude, demanded an IBM uniform (white shirt, dark suit) and brooked no deviation from his creed. The loyal, obedient and productive prospered. Even in its formative years, IBM made hundreds of salesmen rich and thousands of lower-paid workers comfortable, not only with commissions and salaries, but also with company-paid education, insurance, vacations and retirement plans long before they were widely accepted as an employee's due.

Watson lived only long enough to see the computer through its infancy, but he had made plans for the succession. Shortly before the patriarch died in 1956, Thomas J. Watson Jr. began a fifteen-year reign as chief executive. He modified his father's idiosyncratic approach to employee relations, institutionalized the more progressive elements and added countless touches of his own—leaving his successors an astonishing array of benefit programs to administer by the time he retired.

'Good Business'—

Today, a four-man corporate management committee runs IBM, and it devotes more time to personnel matters than to anything else. In all,

IBM spends an estimated $2.3 billion a year, about 14 per cent of its 1976 gross revenues, on various employee programs to keep its people happy. "It's good business," says chairman Frank T. Cary. "The more satisfied your employees are, the better they'll perform."

What do employees get for IBM's money? Practically everything. Like most large companies, IBM underwrites a generous pension plan, supplies group life insurance and covers most medical expenses. But its fringes far transcend traditional benefits packages. For employees who adopt children, for instance, IBM pays for up to 80 per cent of the related costs, and it rebates the tuitions of those who want to go back to school to prepare for a second career after retirement. IBMers can put their children in IBM day-care centers, stay at IBM hotels (called "homesteads"), jog on IBM tracks and play tennis on IBM courts. The company operates three dollar-a-year country clubs ("recreation areas") for workers and their families and runs a vast network of schools and training centers where employees can study everything from computer programing to international finance.

At the same time, IBM takes pains to cultivate a small-company atmosphere. In addition to an "open door" policy and a gripe-by-mail system called "Speak Up!", IBM's massive personnel department —itself a small army of 3,000—conducts regular opinion surveys to monitor employee moods on everything from the quality of food in company cafeterias to the fairness of pay scales. And early this year, Cary sat down with a dozen middle managers for a question-and-answer session that was videotaped and shown to IBMers around the world.

Officially, at least, top management's interest in learning about employees goes only so far; perhaps more than any other company in America, IBM protects its people from corporate invasions of privacy—and sets an example of how to deal with the snooping potential of its own products. IBM has simply stopped collecting much of the information other companies accumulate. To get a job at IBM today, a prospective employee fills out a form that asks little more than name, address and whether the applicant has been convicted—not simply arrested—for any crime in the last five years.

Security, Japanese Style

That doesn't mean IBM hires in the dark. "I interviewed at a number of top companies, and not one of them was nearly as thorough as IBM," says Steve Roehm, a 31-year-old marketing representative who's been with IBM for four years. "I must have seen a dozen people before they finally decided to hire me."

Such scrutiny is understandable, for IBM offers it workers the kind of security that characterizes large Japanese corporations. "You practically have to be caught fornicating with your secretary on the lawn outside your office to get fired at IBM," says editor E. Drake Lundell Jr. of Computerworld, an industry weekly. The more traditional reason for a pink slip—failure to produce—simply doesn't apply. "If a salesman doesn't meet the objectives we've set for him, he'll never be promoted to branch manager," says senior vice president Jacques G. Maisonrouge, who oversees IBM operations in Europe, the Mideast and Africa. "But he will stay with the company and we'll find out what he can do best."

Still, underperformers aren't apt to like what IBM finds for them—such as excommunication from the corporate power centers. "They'll shift someone to Boise, Idaho, and maybe he'll get the message and leave," says president Peter S. Redfield of Itel Corp., a financial-services and computer-leasing company. "But many IBMers have so much invested in the benefits program that they can't afford to leave, and they have to accept demotion. In effect, they're mentally retired by the company."

Keeping Them Busy

Even productive workers create problems, however. IBM hasn't laid off a single worker in nearly four decades for economic reasons, and its commitment to full employment means that its workers are, in effect, fixed assets. That creates difficulty now because IBM no longer seems impervious to the vagaries of the general business cycle: when the national economy slumps, the company has to scramble to find new ways to keep its workers busy.

When possible, it retrains and relocates employees if business conditions render their jobs redundant. Since 1970, about 18,000 IBMers have been moved into new positions as a result of such "manpower-balancing efforts." But sometimes the glut is too great even for IBM to absorb, and other measures must be taken. In 1971 and 1975, when the recession slowed its growth, the company offered nearly 15,000 workers a bonus equal to two years' salary if they would retire early. It was an awkward moment for Mother IBM: the "special-opportunity program," as it was euphemistically called, was supposed to be voluntary, but some managers hinted broadly to certain employees that they would be wise to take up the offer. As a result, says Walton E. Burdick, who at the time was personnel vice president, IBM was forced to take "aggressive action" to discipline the overzealous supervisors.

IBM still encourages the kind of selfless commitment and conformity of view that Watson Sr. saw as prerequisites for joining his company or any other. "There is an atmosphere of blind obedience," says physicist Herbert R. J. Grosch, one of the relatively few people ever to be fired outright by IBM. "The guys who don't salute don't climb." The result seems to be a distinctive IBM persona: a bright, sociable Jack Armstrong type who plays the game aggressively but doesn't question the rules. At that, the rules need not be explicit: IBM no longer has a formal dress code, but with the exception of scientists and programmers—oddballs in IBM's ordered world—its offices remain a sea of white shirts and dark suits.

Global Glue

Company executives acknowledge the existence of an IBM personality—though they consider it not so much forced as inevitable.

The IBM Way of Life

At the Jack Pascal household in Garden City, N.Y., IBM represents much more than the source of family income: it also serves as a kind of moral compass. "IBM embodies all the values we hold sacred—worth of the individual, pursuit of excellence, brotherhood, the work ethic," says Jack's wife, Diana. "And over the years, the children absorb this. I do feel that the company takes a personal interest in me and my children, that it provides us with security and cares about us."

Not all IBMers and their families feel quite so strongly about their employer, of course, but enough of them do that 46-year-old Jack Pascal—in attitude, career development and management technique—seems fairly typical of the breed. Now head of IBM's New York City financial branch, Pascal started work at IBM in 1956 after leaving the Army and has since held a succession of increasingly responsible posts. "I've had ten different jobs at IBM," he says, "every one an advancement or promotion, and every one exciting." Along the way, IBM has lavished not only salary increases on Pascal but also dozens of spot awards, ranging from sales-achievement pins and trophies to outright cash grants and company-paid trips. And he has been steeped in what IBM regards as corporate imperatives—"a positive approach, teamwork, a can-do attitude," he says.

Mirror image In many ways, his own branch operation of 100-plus employees is a small-scale mirror image of IBM itself. Like IBM's top brass in Armonk, N.Y., Pascal has an office that is comfortable but modest, and it's located just behind the reception area, not in a corner. Nearby, there's a massive floor-to-ceiling bulletin board of pinups: glossy photographs of all Pascal's subordinates under the headline, NEW YORK FINANCIAL ... THE DIFFERENCE IS PEOPLE. And like Mother IBM,

Pascal takes care of them, too. Two years ago, for instance, one of his marketing managers died suddenly of cancer, and for months afterward, Pascal spent at least one day a week at the widow's home. "She didn't understand many of the medical benefits, the life insurance and other things, so I helped her out," he says. "It's not just the benefits that count, it's also the personal involvement of IBM in the well-being of its people."

Pascal, in fact, downplays the importance of IBM's elaborate benefits, but he has used them liberally. "Our children all went to orthodontists," he says, "and IBM paid 80 per cent." And this year, his daughter contracted a sudden—and expensive—blood ailment; thus far, IBM has picked up $7,600 of the more than $8,000 in medical bills. Pascal has also built up a tidy nest egg of "several hundred shares" of IBM stock through the company's stock-purchase plan, which allows employees to buy shares at 85 per cent of market value. And every year, he spends two to four weeks at one of IBM's many educational facilities, at a cost to the company of $1,500-$2,000 per week.

Brooks Brothers Look What has IBM demanded from Pascal in return for its largesse? Very little, he insists. The Brooks Brothers look is his preferred style of dress—and the fact that it is IBM's as well is coincidental. He has even, on occasion, departed from the IBM norm—perhaps at a price. "IBM used to stand for 'I've Been Moved'," he says, "but we wanted to set down roots and raise a family in one area. I've been accommodated, but I may have limited my career a bit."

If he has, it never prompted him to seek work anywhere else. "I guess I always thought I'd be with IBM," Pascal says. "It's not the security that keeps me. I've had job offers and I could have made more money elsewhere in the short run, but when I added it up, it was always harder to see greener grass for the long term."

That is exactly how IBM wants its people to respond—and the remarkable thing is, most of them do.

"It's a self-selective process," says Dr. Alan A. McLean, IBM's eastern U.S. medical director and a prominent industrial psychiatrist.

"Like any organization, IBM draws the kind of people who think they'll be happy with the image they perceive this place as having. It's the glue that holds this loyalty together." Given IBM's global sprawl and its penchant for relocating employees at the drop of a computer contract, that glue may also be useful in promoting a peculiar kind of in-house togetherness. "As a transferred IBMer," says Computerworld's Lundell, "you know that wherever they're sending you, you'll be able to walk into a community of people who share your values and beliefs."

Under the Watsons, IBM nurtured its corporate value system by actively encouraging—and in some cases, requiring—its employees to mix socially as well as professionally. Today, most IBMers say, an employee's social obligations are fewer.

They pretty much leave you alone as long as you do your work," says one middle manager. "The whole IBM social whirl is still going strong, but you don't have to take part if you don't want to."

Even so, the company's *in loco parentis* traditions die hard. Managers in the field still throw periodic "family dinners" for subordinates and their spouses—and while attendance may not be mandatory, absences are noted and behavior is monitored. In such situations, says one ex-IBMer, "employees must be more careful about what they say and do than people at any company I've known. One wrong remark and you can find yourself in deep trouble."

But despite its sternly moral streak and corporate style, IBM still manages to maintain a remarkable dynamism that sets its people apart from those at other large companies. "I have a sense of IBM people as being different," says E. Raymond Corey, a Harvard Business School professor who has conducted advanced management seminars for senior IBM salespeople. "Compared to other 'corporate students,' they tend to be brighter, more articulate, able and ambitious. If there *is* a cradle-to-grave welfare system at IBM, it certainly hasn't produced a civil-service lethargy."

One key reason, of course, has to do with the nature of IBM's principal product. The company works at the cutting edge of technology, and its research labs are among the world's finest. "I've been with the company 33 years," says Hans R. Luethy, head of IBM operations in Switzerland, "and I still find it an intellectual challenge." But perhaps even more important, IBM has inoculated its people with a sense of higher purpose. "World Peace Through World Trade" remains the informal motto of IBM's giant foreign operations, and through its many internal publications, the company plays up the considerable scientific and social contributions its employees make.

"We're not in it just for the money," insists Ralph E. Gomory, the boyish-looking mathematician who heads IBM's huge research division. "We take real pride in the impact for good we have on the outside world."

The Price of Success

The outside world, however, has a slightly more jaundiced view of IBM. Right now, the company is fighting nine antitrust suits, including a massive case brought eight years ago by the Justice Department that seeks to break up the company into smaller pieces. It has also come under criticism from various church groups, which object to the sale of IBM computers to such repressive governments as those in South Africa and Chile. "Everything we do is endowed with Machiavellian, antisocial overtones by some people," complains financial vice president Dean P. Phypers. "I guess that's the price you pay for being big and successful."

It is, of course, a price IBM is willing to pay—and no one, in or out of the company, doubts that it will remain both big and successful. "This is a fantastic organization we have," says Cary. "I couldn't think of a better place to be." That the chairman of the board feels this way is not surprising. That most of the 300,000 people who work for him would probably echo those sentiments is something else again: in a time when large organizations—especially big business—are regarded with suspicion if not actual distrust, it is a sign that Mother IBM may indeed know best.